Region, Race, and Cities

Region
Race
and
Cities

INTERPRETING THE
URBAN SOUTH

David Goldfield

LOUISIANA STATE
UNIVERSITY PRESS

Baton Rouge and London

Designer: Amanda McDonald Key
Typeface: Bembo
Typesetter: Impressions Book and Journal Services, Inc.
Printer and binder: Thomson-Shore, Inc.

Some of the essays herein were first published, in somewhat different form, as follows: "A Regional Framework for the Urban South" (as "The Urban South: A Regional Framework"), *American Historical Review,* LXXXVI (1981), 1009–34, © 1981 by the American Historical Association; "Urban-Rural Relations in Old Virginia" (as "Urban-Rural Relations in the Old South: The Example of Virginia"), *Journal of Urban History,* II, No. 2, pp. 146–67, © 1976 by Sage Publications, Inc., reprinted by permission of Sage Publications; "Black Life in Old South Cities," in *Before Freedom Came: African-American Life in the Antebellum South,* ed. Edward D. C. Campbell, Jr., with Kym S. Rice (Charlottesville: University Press of Virginia, 1991), 123–53; "Black Political Power and Public Policy in the Urban South," in *Urban Policy in Twentieth-Century America,* ed. Arnold R. Hirsch and Raymond A. Mohl (New Brunswick, N.J.: Rutgers University Press, 1993), 159–81; "Cities in the Old South" (as "Pursuing the American Urban Dream: Cities in the Old South"), in *The City in Southern History: The Growth of Urban Civilization in the South,* ed. Blaine A. Brownell and David R. Goldfield (Port Washington, N.Y.: Kennikat Press, 1977), 52–91; "Education, Equity, and Quality of Life in the Sun Belt South" (as "Economic Development in the South: Education, Equity, and the Quality of Life"), in *Education, Environment and Culture: The Quality of Life in the South* (Research Triangle Park, N.C.: 1986 Commission on the Future of the South), 13–17; "The City as Southern History" (as "The City as Southern History: The Past and the Promise of Tomorrow"), in *The Future South: A Historical Perspective for the Twenty-First Century,* ed. Joe P. Dunn and Howard L. Preston (Urbana: University of Illinois Press, 1991), 11–48. "Jews, Blacks, and Southern Whites" was originally published as "A Sense of Place: Blacks, Jews, and White Gentiles in the American South" in *Southern Cultures* (March, 1997). Copyright © by the University of North Carolina Press. Used by permission of the publisher.

Library of Congress Cataloging-in-Publication Data

Goldfield, David R., 1944–
    Region, race, and cities : interpreting the urban South / David R.
Goldfield.
      p.   cm.
    Includes index.
    ISBN 0-8071-2189-4 (cloth : alk. paper).—ISBN 0-8071-2244-0 (pbk.:
alk. paper).
      1. Cities and towns—Southern States—History.   2. Southern
States—Race relations.   I. Title.
HT123.5.S6G65   1997
307.76'0975—dc21   97-18547
                                                                           CIP

for Blaine

Contents

Preface

Southern writer Willie Morris was in his twenties when he penned his auto-biography, *North Toward Home* (1967). Some critics wondered at the presumptive nature of such an endeavor at such a tender age. But Morris told a good story, and it is an effective book for learning about one articulate young man's experiences growing up in a South on the brink of a revolution.

A collection of essays is a presumptive work as well, although I am a bit older than Willie Morris was when he published *North Toward Home*. But as an unabashed promoter of southern urban history, I hope this collection underscores the importance of the field and how research in it may inform key issues in southern historiography. In addition to making eight previously published essays more accessible with this volume, I am sharing three unpublished pieces with a broader audience for the first time. In my case, it seems that "Present or Perish" is more appropriate than the old saw "Publish or Perish," and I have probably done as much talking as writing over the past two decades. I make no apologies for this, since one of my most important professional commitments is to bring history to the public.

This is the fourth book I have published with Louisiana State University Press. Someone said that the Press is going to keep publishing my books until I get it right. That's fine with me, as the staff has produced first-rate works that have contributed much to defining the field of southern history over the past quarter century.

My work with the Press is but one example of how no historian works in a vacuum. Throughout my career, mentors, colleagues, and, above all, my family have informed and supported my efforts. My wife, Marie-Louise, and my children, Erik and Eleanor, are the foundations of my life and work. I have been especially fortunate in having the close friendship of Blaine Brownell throughout the time I have been a historian. In fact, I consider Blaine not only a friend but also a mentor, colleague, and, yes, family. For that reason, and for all that we have shared together over the years, I dedicate this book to him.

INTRODUCTION: THE MAKING

OF A SOUTHERN URBAN HISTORIAN

When I first began to write about southern cities more than twenty-five years ago, a prominent southern historian told me he liked my work, but advised me not to fritter away my talents on such an obscure topic as the urban South. At the time, he had a point: as far as southern historiography was concerned, the urban South was an obscure topic indeed. Most southern historians, as David L. Smiley noted in his wry 1972 essay, "The Quest for a Central Theme in Southern History," wrote about "planter, plantation, staple crop, and the Negro, all set in a rural scene."[1] That scholars should emphasize such subjects was not surprising, given the predominantly rural nature of the South well into the twentieth century. But Smiley implied that perhaps the emphasis had become a fixation and that writers should look for other topics to illuminate the rich southern tapestry.

In that search, I was aided by a history faculty at the University of Maryland whose imagination and dedication to working with green graduate students like me were extraordinary. Through my mentor, George H. Callcott, and my teachers—Louis Harlan, Paul Conkin, Dan Carter, John Blassingame, John McCusker, and Herman Belz—I received a first-class education in the craft of history. And I needed it. I arrived at Maryland in 1966 with only the barest background in history. I had majored in political science

1. David L. Smiley, "The Quest for a Central Theme in Southern History," *South Atlantic Quarterly,* LXII (1972), 318.

at Brooklyn College and had taken just two history electives. But those two courses were taught by Hans Trefousse and John Hope Franklin. After graduation, I took my political science degree to law school. When I left law school, the memory I had of those instructors and their courses drew me to a career in history. The faculty at Maryland confirmed for me that I had made the right choice. All of them share complicity for bringing me to history.

When I entered the University of Maryland, I had no interest in the urban South. I had a great deal of interest in the South, however. People often ask me how someone raised in Brooklyn developed such a passion for the South. It is difficult to explain. My mother claims it was all the grits she ate while carrying me in Memphis. My uncle insists it was all those Civil War books he sent to me on birthdays and holidays. My father thinks that I used him as a role model for the South in that he embodied many of the characteristics of the region: he liked being different, an outsider, a Jew who was also a career navy man, who attended a cow college, who played with Roy Acuff in Memphis and Leonard Bernstein in New York, and who enjoyed thumbing his nose at middle-class neighbors who considered him too country for our middle-class urban life.

My maternal grandfather probably played a role as well. He was proud to be a Teamster at a time when our ethnic brethren ran from blue-collar status. Most of all, he was a genuine eccentric. He'd bring home monkeys, rabbits, and other assorted wildlife—sometimes, I think, merely to torment the neighbors rather than for any functional reason. He forever tinkered and usually with little talent, like painting our brick house red because the red brick looked dull, or using the wrong kind of paint for our sloping driveway so that when my father came home one night, the car slid right into and through the garage door.

Surrounded by individualists and proud-to-be-outsiders, I could not help but feel some affinity for the American South, a sometimes ornery region with a history of being apart from the American experience and often proud of that fact. Once the affinity took hold, there was no letting go. For the South I found—through my teachers and my reading, and later through my own research—was and is a fascinating place. The South is like waking up every morning and seeing the ocean out your window. The ocean is always there, but it's never the same: the color, the wave patterns, how the water washes the beach, how it blends into the horizon, and who or what is in it, change daily and sometimes hourly. One never tires of looking at the ocean, and I never tire of looking at the South. Maybe I have a short attention span, and that is the core of my attraction to the region. Southern writer Sharon McKern put it best when she noted, "Whatever else it may be, the South is multiple-choice. . . . There are numerous Dixies from which to choose, and the real one is the one *you* perceive."[2] For a congenital individualist, this type of roll-your-own history was tailor made.

I think part of the reason the South is "multiple choice" rests in the region's numerous contradictions and ironies. The South is a sensual place, especially in its climate, food, and speech, yet it is the most rigidly evangelical Protestant region in the nation. Tremendous store is put in rugged individualism here, yet the pressures for conformity can be stifling. Southerners have an innate suspicion of outsiders but seem to compete with each other to recruit, entice, entertain, and embrace them. As newcomers can attest, the Civil War still rages in these parts, with monuments, ceremonies, editorial debates, flag controversies, and reenactments all part of the contemporary scene. Seldom has a society made so much ado about failure.

But if the South was merely the habit of dour antiquarians, I doubt if I would be interested in studying the region. There is a sense of humor here, a tendency not to take things too seriously, that is engaging. Some of the South's outrageousness, for example, is a put-on. It's puttin' on Ole Massa or puttin' on the Yankee, a way of feeding the stereotypes of one's adversary while silently relishing the ruse. Flannery O'Connor found that "anything that comes out of the South is going to be called grotesque by the northern reader, unless it is grotesque, in which case it is going to be called realistic."[3] O'Connor liked to shock, and I appreciate this perverse glee.

Of course, living with numerous contradictions and playing different roles for different folks is likely to drive one crazy. And maybe those who have studied the South for a long time lose some mental balance. Certainly it affected Clarence Cason and W. J. Cash, to name two of the more prominent casualties of trying to understand a multiple-choice environment. Southern literature is littered with mental defectives, raging aunts, and tuned-out belles. Maybe that's why I feel I fit in. As Florence King explained, "Yankees always make the mistake of going home the moment they realize they are going mad, which is why they have never understood the South. They do not grasp the simple fact that losing one's mind is the most important prerequisite for fitting in with southerners."[4]

2. Sharon McKern, *Redneck Mothers, Good Ol' Girls and Other Southern Belles: A Celebration of the Women of Dixie* (New York, 1979), 262.

3. Quoted in Sally Fitzgerald and Robert Fitzgerald, eds., *Flannery O'Connor: Mystery and Manners* (New York, 1979), 40.

4. Florence King, *Southern Ladies and Gentlemen* (New York, 1976), 16.

My way of studying the South may be as unconventional as the reasons for my attraction to it. Although I cite the usual historical sources in many of the essays that follow, I also rely heavily on the work of other disciplines and especially on southern novels. The craft of history has difficulty with the South. Historians deal with facts, place them in a logical order, and interpret them. But it soon became apparent to me that southern history was not logical or orderly, and that scholarly interpretation often uncovered only part of the story. So I turned to fiction.

I always tell my beginning students or newcomers to the region that if they want to learn about the South, the best foundation is to read Faulkner, Wolfe, Welty, Warren *et al.* Why is this so? Again, O'Connor has the best answer. She writes that southern identity "lies very deep. In its entirety, it is known only to God, but of those who look for it, none gets so close as the artist." The South exists most definitively in the minds and spirits of southerners. As historian Charles Roland has noted, "It is not in economic, political, or racial affairs that the endurance of the South as a distinctive region is most pronounced. Rather, it is in the subtler areas of the mind and the spirit."[5] These are precisely the areas novelists capture best. Not that historians cannot; a few can, but most—myself included—flounder at this type of introspection. It is indeed an art.

But it is fun to try. And that, ultimately, is the South's great attraction: it is simply fun to study. I have said, along with Shreve McCannon in Faulkner's *Absalom, Absalom!,* "Jesus, the South is fine, isn't it? It's better than the theater, isn't it?"[6]

What drew me to the South, however, did not necessarily attract me to southern cities. That interest was piqued in a more prosaic fashion. My adviser, George Callcott, probably thinking it curious for an urban type like me to be poking around in the Old South, suggested that I look at U.S. census manuscripts to see what I might find about southern cities. He recommended cities in Virginia, since that was the southern state closest at hand. In its dry compilation, the census revealed a fascinating portrait of antebellum urban life. Subsequent research in more conventional sources rounded out the picture, and I was off and running.

My early investigations disclosed two general principles that have guided my research and writing ever since. First, southern cities are important, and they share a number of characteristics with cities elsewhere in the United

5. Quoted in Fitzgerald and Fitzgerald, eds., *Flannery O'Connor,* 58; Charles P. Roland, "The Ever-Vanishing South," *Journal of Southern History,* XLVIII (1982), 8.
6. William Faulkner, *Absalom, Absalom!* (1936; rpr. New York, 1972), 174.

States, if not the world. Second, southern cities are intimately connected with the South, and distinctions in development, institutions, and people derive in great part from their regional affiliation.

My work on cities in antebellum Virginia reflected the first of these two themes.[7] I uncovered an urban life in the largest slaveholding state in the nation that included functions, infrastructure, and institutions common to most American cities of the time. In other words, Virginia's cities were part of a vast urbanizing nation. I also found that despite their relatively small size, the Old Dominion's cities played a key role in the state's economic aspirations before the Civil War, and their commercial connections influenced the secession debates. This latter finding reinforced my hypothesis that the urban South was more important than its modest population would lead one to believe. It was also clear that the Old Dominion in the 1840s and 1850s was hardly a "pre-bourgeois" society, and the arguments of its leaders sounded very much like the proposals advanced by New South spokesmen after the war. But could one generalize from the experience of Virginia to the rest of the antebellum South?

The affirmative answer is in my essay "Cities in the Old South" in this collection, which initially appeared under a longer title in an anthology edited by Blaine A. Brownell and me. That volume emphasized the first of the two themes: the commonality of southern cities with urban America and their importance in southern history. Hence the self-conscious title *The City in Southern History,* which we borrowed from Arthur M. Schlesinger, Sr.'s pathbreaking essay "The City in American History."[8] Schlesinger wrote his article in part as an antidote to Frederick Jackson Turner's emphasis on the frontier in American history. Schlesinger argued that the city played an important role in shaping American ideals. Prior to Schlesinger's essay in 1940, there was scarcely anything that could be called "urban history." Although the essay did not immediately touch off a wave of research on American cities, it served as a basis for justifying pioneering urban research in the 1950s and 1960s. Young and immodest as we were, we hoped our collection of five essays spanning southern history from the colonial to the modern period would serve as a similar landmark and beacon for other historians to follow. As with Schlesinger's successors, the broad issue of importance soon gave way to a range of research topics, from race to infra-

---

7. David R. Goldfield, *Urban Growth in the Age of Sectionalism: Virginia, 1847–1861* (Baton Rouge, 1977).

8. Arthur M. Schlesinger, Sr., "The City in American History," *Mississippi Valley Historical Review,* 27 (1940), 43–66.

structure, that securely established southern urban history as a vibrant and legitimate field of southern history.

The collection marked the beginning of a long collaboration and friendship with Blaine Brownell. Blaine's work was very helpful in sharpening my view of southern urbanization. In 1970, I read his doctoral dissertation on the urban South of the 1920s, which was later published as *The Urban Ethos in the South, 1920–1930*.[9] In this era of the Ku Klux Klan and the boll weevil, not only did the South have cities worthy of the name, but these cities also shared a booster ethic and an urbanity—an ethos—with cities in other parts of the nation. His writing impressed me as much as the new sources and new interpretations. I sent Blaine probably his only fan letter (at least as far as his dissertation was concerned), and we resolved to meet at the Southern Historical Association convention in Louisville in November, 1970. I have found his insights and friendship valuable ever since.

My growing emphasis on the urban character of the South probably derived from my immersion in urban literature after I left Maryland in 1970. There was no urban historian at the University of Maryland, and much of my reading focused on American history in general and southern history in particular. As I continued to research the urban South and educate myself in urban historiography, I began to understand the importance of a more regional approach to the study of urbanization, one that connected the city to its rural and small-town surroundings in particular. Urban geographers and economists were especially helpful. Specifically, I noted that the boundaries between city and country were less rigid than I had thought.

I first explored this point in "Urban-Rural Relations in Old Virginia," which initially appeared in a special issue on the urban South in the *Journal of Urban History* in 1976. Although it focused on Virginia, the essay stressed the similarity of urban-rural interaction throughout antebellum America. I also noted that urban rivalry and geographic divisions within states were much more prominent issues than urban-rural conflicts in the Old South. This insight helped push my thinking toward a more inclusive view of the study of urbanization in the South that eventually led me to ask other questions and shift my emphasis on similarity to a focus on how and why the urban South was distinctive.

My visit to Sweden on a Fulbright senior lectureship in 1979 crystallized my perspective on the distinctiveness of the urban South. In Sweden, I encountered a different type of urban literature, especially that written by Gregor Paulsson, the dean of Swedish urban historians.[10] Swedish historians

9. Blaine R. Brownell, *The Urban Ethos in the South, 1920–1930* (Baton Rouge, 1975).
10. Gregor Paulsson, *Svensk stad* (Stockholm, 1950), I.

viewed urbanization as part of a continuum of rural-to-urban development, with each stage retaining aspects of the previous stage. Like southerners, Swedes expressed their preference for rural and small-town life in the design of their cities and in the customs they followed in their new surroundings. They "countrified" their cities as much as possible and escaped to *sommar stugor* (summer houses) in the countryside as soon as the weather turned warm. Sweden's great urban push occurred around the turn of the century—much later than in the rest of Europe—and the ties to the land were still strong among the urban descendants of the first generation of Swedish city dwellers. I also noticed patterns of rural cultural persistence, including certain idioms, child-bearing and child-rearing practices, and some foods. My experience in Sweden and my reading of Swedish urban literature led me to the work of other European urbanists and, eventually, to write an article for the *American Historical Review,* reproduced here as "A Regional Framework for the Urban South."

The basic premises of the article and of the book that followed were that the southern city derived its character from the South; that city and region were intertwined and inseparable; and that to understand the southern city, one must understand the South. I directly attacked the Wirthian idea— implicit in most of the work of American urban historians at that time— that the city was a distinctive environment, that the city destroyed or modified migrant cultures, and that the direction of culture flowed from the city to the countryside. None of this seemed to describe southern urbanization accurately. All of my subsequent work on the urban South has proceeded from this viewpoint. In retrospect, I think I might have been too rigid concerning the persistence of ruralism, race, and colonialism as major factors in southern history and southern urbanization. If anything is distinctive about southern race relations today, it is that blacks and whites seem to get along better in the urban South than in the urban North. As for colonialism, the South in the past fifteen years has solidified its position as the nation's most vigorous regional economy. I am more optimistic about the urban South today than I was fifteen years ago, looking back at a long regional history of prejudice and poverty. The burdens of history seem lighter today, but the southern city is still a different place from the urban North because the South remains a distinctive region.

Some of my colleagues have pointed out that the perspective of the *American Historical Review* article contradicted my earlier view of the urban South as a southern variant of the American urban experience. I would argue that the development of my thinking reflects more a change in emphasis than a change in viewpoint. Obviously, cities everywhere share problems of delivering services, paving streets, marketing products, and electing officials. There is not a southern way to lay a sewer pipe, although where that pipe runs and how it got there might reflect some regional, class, and racial distinctions. In other words, I do not see a contradiction in arguing that southern cities are similar in some respects to cities elsewhere yet are different in others, and that such differences derive from the South's distinctiveness.

Sweden altered my thinking on southern urbanization, and the Fulbright also gave me time to read a great deal of southern fiction. William Faulkner, as a Nobel Prize winner, is much admired in that country, and his works circulate widely in English. Faulkner's popularity carried over into an appreciation for southern fiction in general, and I readily obtained the works of other major southern writers. The novels helped me to understand the nuances of regional culture better (I am still learning), and their insights began to appear in my work as early as the article in the *American Historical Review*. I had particular fun with southern fiction, and its sometimes amusing fixation with the rural South and its antipathy to southern cities, in "From Boondock to Buckhead in Southern Literature," but I employed it with more seriousness in most of my published and presented work since 1980. In fairness to southern writers, I must say that most of the current fiction takes the suburban South to task, not the southern city. But still, it is unfortunate that the story of the Sun Belt South has yet to be told in fiction. The tension between modernity and tradition that permeates so much of southern fiction is as evident in the contemporary subdivision as it was in Yoknapatawpha or Asheville, North Carolina, in the 1920s.

After the *American Historical Review* article, most of my work on southern cities and the South has focused on the regional connection and influence. And except for the essay "Black Life in Old South Cities," my writing has focused more on topics related to the twentieth-century South.

"Black Life" derived from my work with the Museum of the Confederacy in Richmond, Virginia, as part of an interdisciplinary team charged to reorient and broaden the museum's interpretation of the Old South and the Confederacy. The resulting exhibit, "Before Freedom Came: African-American Life in the Antebellum South," offered a powerful rendering of a controversial topic. The museum presented the exhibit with great sensitivity—a tribute to curator Kym Rice and the museum staff.

In addition to the Museum of the Confederacy, in the late 1980s I became involved with other history museums, such as the Valentine, also in Richmond, the Memphis City Museum, the Museum of Science and History in Jacksonville, Florida, and the Octagon Museum in Washington, D.C.

There was no greater indication of the growth of the study of southern urban history in the 1980s than the fact that southern cities became the subjects of major exhibits at history museums across the South. The exhibits and their interpretation of southern urban history involved citizens, academic historians, and museum professionals in a productive collaboration. Museum consulting is especially rewarding because unlike dry monographs, exhibits reach the public. But my work with museums has also informed my research and writing. I have tried, as much as possible, to write for a broad audience and to treat the public's perception of the past with respect.

The essay that appeared as part of the Museum of the Confederacy collection underscored, once again, the interaction between city and countryside in the antebellum South and how the study of topics related to southern urbanization can inform a range of historiographical issues concerning the South in general—issues such as the flexibility of slavery, the antebellum origins of many New South systems of racial control, and the effect of class and ethnic conflicts among whites on the fortunes of blacks.

Although I enjoyed and learned a great deal through my work with the museum and from writing the essay, my interest by that point lay more with the twentieth-century urban South. But I have continued to think and read about the Old South. I have especially admired southern historians who have written on various periods and topics. To paraphrase W. J. Cash, although there are many Souths, there is only one South, and to appreciate its parts, one must study the whole.

My shift in focus to the twentieth century uncovered a range of topics related to my basic theme of southern urban distinctiveness. Especially interesting to me in the early 1980s was the study of regionalism, some of which interest I picked up from European writers but much also from the interwar works of Howard W. Odum and his colleagues at Chapel Hill. Their efforts became the core of my presentation "The Context and Legacy of Howard W. Odum's *Southern Regions*" (here retitled "The Origins of Southern Regionalism") at a Southern Historical Association convention session in 1986 to commemorate the fiftieth anniversary of that classic's publication. When I learned that regionalism had fallen out of favor with sociologists, I embraced it all the more.

I was especially intrigued by the European regionalists' devotion to translating research into policy—a connection that Odum promoted as well. Like the Europeans, Odum believed that education would solve many of the South's problems, that once its people knew why the region had fallen behind the rest of the nation, they would press for change. By the mid-1930s, Odum already had a model to show southerners—the Tennessee

Valley Authority. Unfortunately, both the promise of the TVA and Odum's faith in education fell short of fulfillment. But his regional perspective is a valuable framework for conducting southern and urban research and, not incidentally, for devising policy.

Conscious of the policy connection, I was delighted when George Tindall called that same year to ask me to prepare an essay for the Southern Growth Policies Board. Despite its booster name, the board was genuinely concerned about the impact of rapid economic development on the southern landscape and culture. My brief contribution, "Education, Equity, and the Quality of Life in the Sun Belt South," focused on how the South could sustain its prosperity amid growing national and international competition while at the same time preserving its quality of life. I wanted to show that development and quality-of-life issues were not mutually exclusive but were, in fact, complementary. I have used this argument numerous times subsequently in newspaper columns and in local government forums. I don't know if anyone has paid attention, but at least in my small region of the South, we are trying to accommodate the two issues.

The essay for the board reinforced my view that equity remained an important issue in contemporary southern life. As early as the 1981 article in the *American Historical Review,* the close connection between race relations and urbanization was apparent. I addressed that connection at some length in *Black, White, and Southern: Race Relations and Southern Culture, 1940 to the Present,* noting that the post–World War II migration of blacks to southern cities was a prerequisite for the civil rights movement of the 1950s and 1960s.[11] My research resulted in a series of essays, two of which are featured here: "The Urban South in World War II" and "Black Political Power and Public Policy in the Urban South."

I presented the World War II essay at one of the numerous symposia in the early 1990s on the fiftieth anniversary of the war. Despite the war's significant impact on the South, there is no monograph-length study on World War II in the South. Once I began my own investigation, it became clear that even though the war laid important foundations for the postwar era in the South, it was something less than a watershed event. As I mention in the essay, the war accelerated changes already underway in the urban South. These changes should not be underestimated. The civil rights movement took shape during and immediately after the war. And a new generation of urban leader emerged, dedicated more to economic development than to retaining white supremacy.

11. David R. Goldfield, *Black, White, and Southern: Race Relations and Southern Culture, 1940 to the Present* (Baton Rouge, 1990).

Whereas my essay on World War II anticipated the racial accommodation that followed, the article on black political power in the urban South looked at one of the results of that accommodation—voting rights. The piece is part of a broader interest in charting race relations in the South after 1965. The saga of the black ballot in southern cities provides an interesting study of the initial (and, in retrospect, unrealistic) enthusiasm for voting rights among southern blacks, and how and why basic political and economic structures beyond the manipulation of black elected officials seriously modified black political power. My interpretation supports the work of sociologists, such as William Julius Wilson, who blame the plight of black urban America much less on contemporary racism than on contextual economic and political institutions responding to factors that have little to do with race.[12] This is a fairly pessimistic essay because, short of major social policy commitments (an unlikely scenario), it is not clear what we can do to alleviate the condition of the black urban poor.

My interest in policy, reflected in both the board piece and the essay on black political power, is not only a scholarly concern. As a southerner, I care deeply about the region's future. I enjoy southern cities and am excited by their development, but I am also anxious about the social and environmental costs of such development. I want to believe that somehow the South will not be merely a late-blooming North and lose its beautiful landscape and relatively clean air and water. But there is a great deal of truth in George Tindall's reminder that "if experience is any guide, the South will blow it."[13]

My hope for the urban South is most clearly spelled out in "The City as Southern History," initially presented at a symposium on the South at Converse College in Spartanburg, South Carolina. I offer a broad overview of southern urban history, emphasizing the city's importance to the South, especially in the past quarter century. I argue that the southern city has become the repository for the region's memory, making the identity between city and region closer than ever before. As a popular 1995 country song claimed, "The city put the country back in me." The urban South is the place to find the essence of southern culture today.

Although this view updates an old theme of mine, I did come to a more positive conclusion in the essay than I did in *Cotton Fields and Skyscrapers*.[14]

12. See William Julius Wilson, *The Truly Disadvantaged: The Inner City, the Underclass, and Public Policy* (Chicago, 1987).

13. George B. Tindall, "Onward and Upward with the Rising South," in *The Rising South: Changes and Issues,* ed. Donald R. Nobel and Joab L. Thomas (Tuscaloosa, 1976), 24.

14. David R. Goldfield, *Cotton Fields and Skyscrapers: Southern City and Region, 1607–1980* (Baton Rouge, 1982).

I noted that the southern city's tradition, especially its scale, voluntarism, and concern about the past (even amid McCivilization), will provide not only a competitive economic advantage but also an opportunity to solve social problems.

My writing and my feelings have merged. I am vitally interested in seeing that the urban South, despite onslaughts from diverse quarters, remains southern. If, as I argue in "The City as Southern History," the city is now the South, then the region will rise or fall within its metropolitan boundaries. But I am also concerned that the goal of maintaining that identity does not override the need to sustain a civil and caring relationship among ourselves. We live in a prosperous region, but within it are places and people who do not share that prosperity. It is sometimes difficult to call attention to the shadows when the Sun Belt shines so brightly. And given the persistence of both the booster ethic and the tendency to emphasize the pleasant and the positive, the task can be daunting. But we ought to raise our voices and do it.

Sometimes I am concerned that my colleagues care too much about paradigms and subtexts and not enough about the communities in which they live. Historians who do not use their knowledge and writing skills to improve the place they call home are merely practicing antiquarians. Historians have the gift of perspective, and it would be a shame to reserve that gift for seldom-read monographs and journal articles.

Some of my concern for the contemporary South rubbed off in a recent interest—the relations between Jews and other southerners, black and white. I have not undertaken a major study of the topic, and much of what I have to say is probably unremarkable to experts in the field. But I wanted to connect my regional perspective to interactions between Jews and Gentiles in the South, much of which has occurred in the cities. If anyone doubts that the South is distinctive, then the place of Jews in the region and their relationship to their neighbors may serve as a corrective.

It is difficult to walk around most southern cities today without wondering what is distinctive about them. Skyscrapers gleam and shimmer as they do elsewhere, and shopping malls pop up in the places you would expect them to, with the same shops that populate malls in Minneapolis or Portland. New subdivisions arise out of distinctive red clay or black loam, but they bear the same English-sounding names and, sadly, the same porchless, generic architecture as elsewhere. Although all of this "beats the hell out of pellagra," as one Florida journalist noted, one has a sense of loss as the South moves ever closer to resembling the rest of homogenized America. What could be more depressing than to hear Montgomery, the

Cradle of the Confederacy, described as a "classic Southern Greek Mc-Nugget—a few doric temples surrounded by miles of motels and fast food joints"?[15]

But even in anesthetized Montgomery, there is plenty that is very southern. The city is a monument to southern history. Stand on the star where Jefferson Davis took the oath of office as the first and last president of the Confederacy and look across the street to Dexter Avenue Baptist Church, where Martin Luther King, Jr., came in 1954 to complete his doctoral dissertation in a quiet place, only to be thrust into the leadership of the greatest movement in southern history since the Civil War. The daily life of southern history may have occurred mostly on the farms and plantations, but the key stages for momentous change were the towns and cities that mobilized people and ideas.

Southern cities attracted me in the same way the South did: they were underappreciated, often denied, and dismissed as inconsequential by those inside and outside the region. Today, the wonderful contradictions of the Sun Belt South are played out lovingly, sometimes consciously, but mostly obliviously in the southern city. Atlanta, the quintessential New South city, incessantly promotes Tara and "Gone with the Wind" memorabilia, and at the New York Coffee Shop in Houston, grits appear on a kosher menu together with jalapeño bagels. The urban South has slid into multiculturalism without self-righteous fanfare, absorbing it as it has absorbed so much else. Shirley Abbott had it right when she admitted that "lately I go home in panic, for fear the South is gone. According to the news magazines, the solid block of eccentricity that lives within the boundaries of the old Confederate states has been gerrymandered into a rich, bland, hateful thing called the Sunbelt. . . . But when I go home, it always calms me to see that Southern cities, however slick and new, don't quite seem citified."[16]

In the end, that's what keeps me excited about the urban South. The southern city is at the center of great regional change yet somehow manages to retain a regional identity despite numerous epitaphs to the contrary. City and region have a resilience that defies homogenization and superficial analysis. If the essays in this collection have a coherence, it is in this interplay between southern city and region and how that interaction has shaped both.

15. Quoted in Joel Garreau, *The Nine Nations of North America* (Boston, 1981), 148; Michael Lewis, "Driving Miss Onnie," *New Republic,* August 16, 1993, p. 11.

16. Shirley Abbott, *Womenfolks: Growing Up Down South* (New Haven, 1983), 210.

I

REGION

THE ORIGINS OF SOUTHERN REGIONALISM

In July, 1904, Scots sociologist Patrick Geddes (1854–1932) presented a paper to the Sociological Society at the University of London entitled "Civics: As Applied Sociology."[1] It was a typical academic convocation of the era: a group of learned men gathering to hear a respected colleague expound on the evils of modern urban industrial life and propose solutions. Turn-of-the-century Britain was awash in reformist schemes of all sorts, many borrowed from the Continent, others homegrown, and all deriving from a keen sense of urgency that a civilization hung in the balance.

Their nostrums—housing reforms, poverty reforms, town-planning concepts derived from France and Germany, utopian social theories, and new design principles—tumbled like leaves and soon became as dead.[2] As a student thirty years earlier, Geddes had interspersed his studies in biology with nocturnal ramblings in London's squalid East End. For the slight Scotsman, but recently removed from provincial Edinburgh and the pristine Scottish countryside, the scenes he encountered raised questions concerning the implications of evolutionary theory he was ingesting under the tutelage of T. H. Huxley. Geddes' drift into sociology was a natural progression—an evolution, if you will. The discipline was part of a broader upsurge in the social sciences that accompanied the permeation of Darwinism into British academic circles after 1870.[3]

1. Patrick Geddes, "Civics: As Applied Sociology," in *Sociological Papers, 1904* (London, 1905), I, 103–38.
2. See Anthony Sutcliffe, *Towards the Planned City: Germany, Britain, the United States and France, 1780–1914* (Oxford, Eng., 1981).
3. For a thorough discussion of Geddes' formative years, see Philip Boardman, *The*

Herbert Spencer had emerged as the premier British sociologist, but for Geddes, his approach comprised too much science and not enough social. Spencer maintained that the role of the sociologist was to observe, not to act. No individual, he believed, could hope to counter the great evolutionary forces shaping man and his society. Geddes turned instead to the French human sociologists, especially to Frederic LePlay (1806–82), who argued that social scientists should not only elaborate theoretical models from the scientific collection of data but should also provide guidelines for practical work—to suggest, even advocate, social policy. To this end, LePlay devised a research framework that focused on three basic elements of social life: Place, Work, and Folk. The framework represented a synthesis of the emerging social sciences, especially geography, economics, and anthropology and history. Geddes hoped to apply this research methodology to the study of the modern city. He reasoned that the difficulty with current reforms was that they were too specialized: they looked at one aspect, say housing, in isolation from other variables. As a result, solutions were not only ineffective but mischievous as well. In addition, Geddes felt that the assumption by reformers—academics and policymakers alike—that the modern industrial city was a unique, almost pathological environment that sprang up with momentous technological and financial transformations was both limited and ahistorical. Borrowing both from LePlay and his own training as a biologist, Geddes insisted upon "the elemental rustic origins of industry, family types, and social organization."[4] In other words, study of the countryside and its history was essential to understanding the modern city. Armed with these dicta, Geddes sought to apprise his colleagues on how to develop an integrated, comprehensive policy apparatus to understand and manage the city in their midst.

Geddes proposed a tripartite reform model: research, education, and action. He organized his research around LePlay's elements, and from these he developed the regional survey—a comprehensive perspective on the city and its region derived from a copious collection of data. From the mass of detail he gathered, Geddes could then trace the evolutionary steps that led to a city's present condition. In his regional survey of Edinburgh, undertaken

---

Worlds of Patrick Geddes: Biologist, Town Planner, Re-Educator, Peace-Warrior (London, 1978), 27–79.

4. J. D. Y. Peel, *Herbert Spencer: The Evolution of a Sociologist* (London, 1971), 164; Patrick Geddes, "Civics: As Concrete and Applied Sociology," in *Sociological Papers, 1905* (London, 1906), Vol. I, Pt. 2, pp. 71–72; Patrick Geddes, *Cities in Evolution* (1915; rpr. New York, 1968), 150; Geddes, "Civics," in *Sociological Papers, 1905,* Vol. I, Pt. 2, pp. 60–61.

more than a decade before his Sociological Society presentation, Geddes had discerned two eras of urbanization—the *Paleotechnic* era, as he termed it, which was characterized by the rise of the factory system and dislocations in the countryside; and the *Neotechnic* era, the contemporary period, which had witnessed the maturation of industry and the rise of the great metropolis, with their attendant social evils. He believed, however, that with judicious planning and policy, a third era—the *Eutechnic* era—awaited the modern city and its residents. This new stage depended upon improving the relationship between organism and environment and the quality of the organism itself.[5] In nonbiological terminology, this meant enhancing the physical environment and providing opportunities for residents to better themselves educationally and economically.

Geddes was the first British social scientist to relate the physical environment to the social structure of the community, an integration possible only through his interdisciplinary research approach. Ebenezer Howard (1850–1928), Geddes' contemporary, who was also concerned about the physical and social blight of the modern city, emphasized physical solutions to the perceived urban crisis, even as he took a regional view. The father of the Garden City movement was an idealist, however, who disdained urban life and sought to develop completely new communities in the countryside. In addition, he ignored the historical context of urban development. Although Howard's Letchworth and Welwyn garden cities were successful as new towns, they had little impact on England's congested cities.[6]

Once Geddes completed his research and evolutionary analysis, the next two steps involved the derivation and implementation of policies to induce movement to the next evolutionary era. The first step was education. Geddes' generation held an inordinate faith in the value of education as a solution to a multitude of urban problems. Aside from the formal school system, which remained class-ridden, the popularity of public lectures, adult education, settlement houses, and public exhibitions indicated both the opportunity and the thirst for knowledge in late-Victorian Britain. Geddes proposed disseminating his research findings in several ways and at several levels. First, he held summer meetings of academics to discuss research findings. Next, he proposed to introduce the public to the research through the medium of exhibits. Accordingly, in 1895, Geddes opened the Outlook

5. Geddes, "Civics," in *Sociological Papers, 1904,* I, 105–12; Geddes, *Cities in Evolution,* 60–83.

6. See William Ashworth, *The Genesis of Modern British Town Planning* (London, 1954), 198.

Tower in Edinburgh. The regional evolution of the city was exhibited on the upper floors; as one descended the museum, the context grew larger to include Europe and, eventually, on the ground floor, Edinburgh's place in the world. This civic and regional museum not only attracted the public to its exhibits—exhibitions were great pastimes in turn-of-the-century Europe—but also sponsored community activities to encourage a more scientific interaction between citizen and city, a process that was expected to lead to a higher evolutionary stage.[7]

By thus engaging people in their own development, Geddes hoped to inaugurate the third phase of his program—action. He wanted the social survey to become social service. The political obstacles in implementing regional policy were not of particular concern to Geddes. With a steadfast faith in education, he believed that the path to evolutionary improvement would be so clear to citizen and policy maker that implementation would be irresistible.[8]

The members of the society received Geddes' paper politely but with indifference. The action-oriented program devised by the Scotsman, though grounded in thoroughgoing research, may have been too bold for the academics. The novelty of his regional perspective, his application of French sociological theory, and his insistence on the primacy of history for social analysis were likely jarring to a group that sought to establish its legitimacy by erecting and maintaining disciplinary boundaries. Nevertheless, the more policy-oriented town planners who included Geddes as the only social scientist in the newly formed Town Planning Institute were impressed with the regional survey as a way of understanding the modern city. The survey had the distinct advantage of not fragmenting the city as well as injecting a leavening of culture into an otherwise physically-oriented profession.[9]

Geddes' regional perspective and research methodology also found a receptive audience in the United States, especially after World War I, in the writings and plans of Benton MacKaye (1879–1975). As with Geddes, MacKaye came upon regionalism from a perception of urban crisis. MacKaye had grown up in a small New England community that, though still relatively unchanged in the automobile age, was threatened by the spreading metropolis extending from Boston to Washington, D.C.—what we call

7. Boardman, *Worlds of Geddes,* 136–46.
8. Geddes expresses the activist component of his research best in "Beginnings of a Survey of Edinburgh," *Scottish Geographic Magazine* (1919), 297.
9. Boardman, *Worlds of Geddes,* 215–18.

"megalopolis" today.[10] He and Geddes had taken long walks together, not in the urban netherworld but in the countryside. And the countryside remained MacKaye's preeminent focus.[11] He was not a wilderness romantic, however. He believed that the man who knew only wilderness was a savage; the man who knew only the rural was a country bumpkin; and the man who knew only the urban was an effete "civilizee." MacKaye preferred the composite man, and regionalism offered the method to promote an integrated approach to living in the twentieth century.[12]

Just as Geddes had devised an evolutionary scheme to explain regional development, MacKaye's studies led him to a regional typology revolving around what he called "folk flows." As applied to the American continent, the flows had evolved through three stages: farmer-settlers moving outward into the virgin lands after 1776; the impact of steam technology, which eventually reoriented the flow from waterways to the railroads; and this "reflow" giving way to an "inflow" in the late nineteenth century, when the frontier closed (at least in official terms) and the focus of settlement shifted to the cities. Urbanization was not necessarily a pathological process to MacKaye as long as the cities functioned in a harmonious relationship with the surrounding region. Such a connection would advance the culture of both city and countryside. MacKaye had also detected a fourth flow—a "backflow," or metropolitan invasion characterized by the advance of population and urban space out into the region, creating amorphous, inorganic, nonfunctional suburbs and "motor slums."[13]

In addition to tracing these folk flows, MacKaye analyzed the flow of waters via regional water systems and the flow of commodities over various natural and manmade commercial routes. Thus, his research plan resembled LePlay's Place, Work, and Folk design, also adopted by Geddes. But Mac-Kaye's analysis had a distinctive American bent to it: his interest was continental, and although he was concerned about the vicissitudes of life in the great American city, his greatest fear was that the spreading metropolitan civilization and increasing mobility of Americans would destroy regional balance and overwhelm the countryside. So his proposed solutions to the

10. Benton MacKaye, "Genesis and Jefferson," *Survey Graphic,* LXXXVI (December, 1950), 556–59.

11. MacKaye specifically acknowledged Geddes' influence in "From Homesteads to Valley Authorities," *Survey Graphic,* LXXXVI (November, 1950), 496–98.

12. Benton MacKaye, "Outdoor Culture: The Philosophy of Through Trails," *Landscape Architecture,* XVII (April, 1927), 168.

13. Benton MacKaye, "End or Peak of Civilization?" *Survey Graphic,* LXVIII (October, 1932), 443.

problem of backflow were designed less to restructure urban life than to protect the countryside.[14] And as with Geddes, MacKaye linked research to policy. For MacKaye, if sound research demanded an integrated regional framework, then the policies designed to restore balance required regional planning.

MacKaye's projects included the opening of the Appalachian Trail in 1927. The Appalachian region (for MacKaye, a precious wilderness area), was in the direct line of the eastern metropolitan invasion. The trail, extending from Maine to Georgia, would not only protect this sensitive area but would also introduce mobile urban dwellers to a nature fast disappearing from the East Coast. Thus chastened, urbanites would return to work for the development of the "true city"—an integrated, balanced urban environment that purportedly had existed in preindustrial America.[15] The educative function for MacKaye was less in urban-based exhibits than in rural projects designed both to protect sensitive environments from real-estate predation and to reintroduce urbanites to their country roots.

MacKaye was also a founder of the Wilderness Society and a staunch supporter of the Tennessee Valley Authority (TVA) in the early 1930s. He believed that the TVA would serve as the "seed of a national plan" that would establish regional authorities across the land to upgrade rural areas and thereby reverse their depopulation and the consequent overpopulation of cities. Located strategically along the Appalachian range, the TVA would act as another effective regional buffer against the intruding metropolis.[16]

MacKaye also joined a small circle of regional planners influenced by Geddes and Ebenezer Howard. Their organization—the Regional Planning Association of America (RPAA)—formed in 1923, included such prominent intellectual-practitioners as Henry Wright, Clarence Stein, Clarence Perry, and Lewis Mumford, as well as MacKaye. The basic assumption of the group was that regional imbalance caused by imperialistic central cities was threatening both city and countryside and, hence, American civilization. Primarily under their auspices and through their influence on prominent civic and commercial leaders, the 1920s became the heyday of regional planning and inspired federal efforts in the 1930s.[17]

14. Benton MacKaye, "Religion Building in River Valleys," *Survey Graphic,* XXIX (February, 1940), 106; MacKaye, "End or Peak of Civilization?" 444.

15. MacKaye, "Outdoor Culture," 171.

16. Benton MacKaye, "Tennessee: Seed of a National Plan," *Survey Graphic,* XXII (May, 1933), 251–54, 293–94.

17. For an excellent discussion of the origins, membership, and philosophy of the RPAA, see Daniel Schaffer, *Garden Cities for America: The Radburn Experience* (Philadelphia, 1982), 55–77.

The RPAA followed both the research framework and the regionalist philosophy devised by the French human geographers and applied by Geddes. The most explicit exposition of the association's views appeared in the *Report of the New York State Commission on Housing and Regional Planning* (1926), written by Henry Wright (though Clarence Stein's name appears as the principal author). The document recommended a state planning agency be established to "improve the conditions of life rather than promote opportunities for profit."[18] Accordingly, the authors called for a dispersal of people and work evenly throughout the state. Modern technology, especially the automobile and communications, had rendered such a settlement pattern possible. The result would be a revitalization of rural life that would thus restore a regional balance, removing the existing rigid distinction between city and country.

Wright and his colleagues sought to provide a concrete example of their regional philosophy by constructing a model community, Radburn, in the New Jersey countryside, only forty-five minutes from midtown Manhattan. The new town featured such concepts as street differentiation, curvilinear pathways, common grounds, siting and landscaping in harmony with nature, and the superblock, all to promote a sense of community and to conserve open spaces. Radburn was the antithesis of the amorphous suburb and strip development that MacKaye had condemned. Yet its relatively high densities and emphasis on interaction gave the settlement an urban component—a middle-landscape blend between rural and urban. RPAA leaders hoped Radburn would be the prototype for similar settlements that would at once save the rural portions of the region and decongest the city, making it more manageable and humane.[19]

By 1927, when Radburn opened, Lewis Mumford had emerged as the RPAA's (and the nation's) leading regional theorist. Mumford was adamant on the importance of a historical perspective both for identifying and resolving regional problems. He advocated that these historical studies be undertaken within a broad, interdisciplinary framework. Mumford employed Geddes' typologies of evolutionary development—the Paleotechnic and Neotechnic ages; but in addition, he foresaw a "biotechnic" age, when man would use technology for social ends.[20]

18. Henry Wright, *Report of the New York State Commission on Housing and Regional Planning* (New York, 1926), 2.

19. See Schaffer, *Garden Cities,* 147–209.

20. The most complete discussion of Mumford's evolutionary scheme occurs in his book *The Culture of Cities* (New York, 1938).

Among the numerous regionalist causes undertaken by Mumford during
the late 1920s and early 1930s, none was as vigorous as his attempt to
discredit the *Regional Plan of New York and Its Environs* (1929). The *Plan* was
a ten-volume magnum opus directed by British planner and Geddes disciple
Thomas Adams, funded by the Russell Sage Foundation, and supported by
leading businessmen concerned about New York City's future vitality as the
nation's premier metropolis. The great accomplishment of the *Plan* was its
regional survey, following Geddes' model, that provided the most comprehensive depiction of a metropolitan area we have had, before or since. The
Plan espoused some of the major regionalist principles of the time: "The
only cure lies in a more even growth, in a better balance between industry
and residence and between loosely-built up areas and open spaces."[21]

But the *Plan* departed in notable ways from several regionalist precepts,
and Mumford and other RPAA members quickly pointed out these shortcomings. The *Plan* assumed the continued expansion of New York City,
and its proposals sought to protect the city from loss of population and
economic base—objectives that were not surprising, considering the *Plan's*
sponsors. Despite professions of the need to secure a regional balance, the
Plan demonstrated little appreciation for the impact of continued urban
expansion on as-yet undeveloped areas of the region. The *Plan* proposed
superhighways and recreational areas for urban residents, but again, the perspective was urban rather than regional. The *Plan* also shortcircuited the
education function of the regional survey, omitting any formal structure for
community involvement. And finally, the 5,000-square-mile region, defined as a one-hour-or-less commute to the city, was too small, according
to Mumford and his colleagues. There would be fewer opportunities to
build satellite communities or new towns, a concept mentioned only briefly
in the *Plan*.[22]

The attack was especially strong because RPAA leadership believed that
the Plan and its extensive regional survey represented a lost golden opportunity to promote regionalism to a wide audience. But scarcely had the
furor subsided when the federal government entered the field of regional
planning in response to the dislocations generated by the Depression. In
1933, the National Resources Planning Board (NRPB) established eleven

21. Robert Duffus, *Mastering a Metropolis* (New York, 1930), 187. Duffus' book provided
a narrative summary of the Regional Plan.
22. For an extensive critique of the Regional Plan, see Lewis Mumford, "The Plan of
New York: I," *New Republic*, June 15, 1932, pp. 121–26, "The Plan of New York: II," *New
Republic*, June 22, 1932, pp. 146–53.

regional planning commissions across the country and, by 1938, had assisted in the creation of planning authorities in forty-one states. The board produced 370 major reports, many framed in a regionalist context, and its Urbanism Committee produced the first major study of American cities in their metropolitan, regional, and national contexts.

The federal government's major foray into regional planning was, of course, the TVA. At the time, it was the largest public-works project in the world, encompassing the 41,000-square-mile basin of the Tennessee River, including seven states. The authority represented the fulfillment of a major regionalist objective: the revitalization or upgrading of lagging rural areas, to help them compete better with the attractions of modern urban civilization. The concept of regional equilibrium was also apparent in Rexford Guy Tugwell's Resettlement Administration. As did MacKaye, Tugwell felt that a return to nature or rural resettlement was more nostalgia than nostrum, and that slum clearance was only a physical and, hence, partial solution to urban problems. Accordingly, Tugwell proposed a series of satellite cities or greenbelt towns outside major cities—not unlike the RPAA's new town of Radburn—that would represent the middle-landscape ideal.[23]

In this context Howard W. Odum (1884–1954) wrote *Southern Regions*. The era was alive to the possibilities of regional planning and certain of the connection between research and policy and of the scientific methodology behind that research. *Southern Regions* is both a state-of-the-art explication of regionalism and a brief for the efficacy of regional planning. Odum's bibliography for the book includes an extensive listing of international regionalist literature, including that of French human geographers, such as Lucien Brocard and Paul Vidal de la Blache; of American regionalists, such as Lewis Mumford and Benton MacKaye; and of policy makers, such as Tugwell and Thomas Adams. And the work reflects these influences.

Southern Regions is a survey conducted over a geographical area considerably larger than the boundaries of earlier surveys. To be sure, Geddes had acknowledged that regionalist methodology—the analysis of Place, Work, and Folk—could be expanded to include a country, even a continent. But for practical purposes, Geddes and his followers focused on the great cities and their hinterlands, defined broadly. The American South, of course, possessed no great cities, and those urban places characteristic of the region were hardly poised to devour their respective hinterlands. So Odum deter-

---

23. For an excellent discussion of regional planning in the New Deal era, see John L. Hancock, "The New Deal and American Planning: The 1930s," in *Principles and Policy: Urban Planning in the United States,* ed. Daniel Schaffer (London, 1986), 116–33.

mined the boundaries of his two regions (the Southeast and the Southwest) through an exhaustive screening of more than seven hundred variables. However idiosyncratic the extent of the regions, the methodology was standard. The survey included an analysis of natural resources and features (Place); general economy, technology, skill levels, and institutional supports (Work); and culture, including religion, politics, manners, and intellect (Folk). Odum placed these three elements within a specific area and studied them over time, thus synthesizing geography and history. Odum perceived the South as "the cumulative product of historical and geographic incidence." In an earlier work, *The Regional Approach to National Social Planning* (1935), Odum had argued, "The cultural equipment of the Southeast is not only powerfully conditioned by its geographic factors but can be understood only through a knowledge of historical backgrounds and regional incidence."[24]

Regionalist methodology did not end with the presentation of research findings; it posited two other objectives—education and action. Odum's regional survey led him to conclude that there existed a great "chasm between potentialities as indicated by resources and actualities as measured by facts."[25] Before devising policies to close the gap, it was necessary to educate the region's citizens. In fact, in cataloguing what the South must do, Odum placed "a more realistic facing of facts" at the top of his list.[26] And for more than a decade prior to the publication of *Southern Regions,* Odum had erected an institutional and research framework to collect and disseminate those facts. His Institute for Research in the Social Sciences (IRSS), established in 1924, had sponsored numerous studies on subjects rarely discussed publicly in the South, such as rural illegitimacy, lynching, welfare for black children, sharecropping, and corruption in county government. In 1922, Odum also launched a journal, *Social Forces,* that featured popular articles alongside academic essays on controversial topics. In addition, he convened numerous scholarly gatherings in the manner of Geddes' summer seminars, designed to analyze southern problems.[27] So by 1936, Odum had in place

24. Howard W. Odum, *Southern Regions of the United States* (Chapel Hill, 1936), 15; Howard W. Odum, *The Regional Approach to National Social Planning: With Special Reference to a More Abundant South and Its Continuing Reintegration in the National Economy* (Chapel Hill, 1935), 3.

25. Odum, *Southern Regions,* ix.

26. *Ibid.,* 191.

27. See Wayne D. Brazil, "Social Forces and Sectional Self-Scrutiny," in *Perspectives on the American South: An Annual Review of Society, Politics, and Culture,* ed. Merle Black and John Shelton Reed (New York, 1984), II, 73–104.

an institutional framework capable of conducting wide-ranging research and disseminating its results. To ensure a broader audience for the encyclopedic *Southern Regions,* Odum's colleague, Gerald W. Johnson, published *The Wasted Land* (1937), which summarized Odum's findings in little more than one hundred pages, as well as a manual-workbook prepared by another colleague, Lee M. Brooks, to be used by students and study groups.[28]

Odum's concern about erecting the proper institutional framework to provoke southerners to awareness emanated from his pessimistic view of the region's traditional educational structure. He lamented that the South lacked a "university of first rank" and a suitable number of libraries and books to encourage reading habits. The region's poverty, its inordinately high proportion of children in the total population, and the indifference, even hostility, of the leadership to intellectual pursuits rendered southerners incapable of taking the first steps toward their own improvement.[29] Odum hoped that the network he had developed in addition to an enlightened media would substitute for more formal educational institutions.

If Odum could attain a threshold of awareness, the next phase in the regionalist method was to prepare and execute a plan of action to translate research into policy. Odum's objective was to achieve a balance or equilibrium within the region and between the South and the nation. As he summarized in a later work, "We seek a balance and equilibrium between the people and wealth, between man and technology, between culture and civilization." The South was especially deficient in wealth, technology, and civilization, as the findings of *Southern Regions* demonstrated. As for a balance of wealth, Odum quoted Mumford approvingly: "The products of culture and civilization, instead of being confined to a prosperous minority . . . shall be available at every point in a region." Concerning the South's technological shortcomings, Odum hoped to alter agricultural patterns to serve an expanding industrial base. In this regard, he believed that the South held a potential advantage over much of the nation, where a "dangerous lack of equilibrium due to the preponderance of the urban-industrial over the natural agrarian elements" existed. The South's urban pattern, as colleague Rupert B. Vance has noted, "has much to commend it to the regionalist."[30] Cities were medium-sized at most, with few density or traffic

28. Gerald W. Johnson, *The Wasted Land* (Chapel Hill, 1937); Lee M. Brooks, *Manual for Southern Regions* (Chapel Hill, 1937).

29. Odum, *Southern Regions,* 19, 99–119.

30. Howard W. Odum, *The Way of the South: Toward the Regional Balance of America* (New York, 1947), 257; Odum, *Southern Regions,* 15; Lewis Mumford, quoted in Howard W.

problems, and industry was diffused evenly. But as long as agriculture failed to diversify, and capital failed to take advantage of farming-based industrial enterprise, the benefits of a balanced urban network would remain untapped.

Perhaps the region's greatest deficiency was the dichotomy between its natural potential and its human capabilities, especially as measured by the regional culture. Odum depicted regional culture as "immature" rather than "decadent," as still in a frontier stage of development, maintained in its primitive condition by a demagogic political system, a skewed view of history, and conspiring institutions, such as churches and schools. Odum quoted Mumford on the importance of a "soundly bottomed regionalism [which] can achieve cosmopolitan breadth without fear of losing its integrity or virtue." The South's fierce parochialism had shut out new ideas and influences, precluding the type of debate and feedback necessary to advance to the next evolutionary stage. In addition, the pervasive localism had not generated a community spirit but had reinforced individualism, a point William Faulkner was to make so well a few years later in his novel *The Hamlet* (1941).[31]

What policies, then, could draw southerners together for progressive ends and lend substance to their lagging institutions? *Southern Regions* presented a catalogue of suggestions to obtain a regional balance and, ultimately, the South's integration with the rest of the nation. Those recommendations hinged on the willingness and capability of southerners to engage in regional planning. Specifically, Odum urged the creation of a regional planning board that would transcend—though not usurp—state planning authority. Such a board, in Odum's view, could accomplish "agricultural reconstruction," engage "in land and other resources utilization," promote and establish "institutions of higher learning and research," and lobby for "social legislation" to improve working and living conditions. Regional planning would also head off the centralizing tendencies of the federal government and enable the South to control the pace and direction of evolution. Odum was especially pleased with the example of the TVA, which he termed "the perfect laboratory for the development of . . . dynamic regionalism." And

Odum and Harry Estill Moore, *American Regionalism: A Cultural-Historical Approach to National Integration* (New York, 1938), 23; Odum, *Southern Regions,* 430; Rupert B. Vance, *Human Geography of the South: A Study in Regional Resources and Human Adequacy* (Chapel Hill, 1932), 507.

31. Odum, *Southern Regions,* 15, 135, 153, 497–507; Mumford, quoted *ibid.,* 531; Daniel J. Singal, *The War Within: From Victorian to Modernist Thought in the South, 1919–1945* (Chapel Hill, 1982), 124.

he saw no reason why the southern states could not combine to effect the type of balanced growth that the TVA was promoting in its portion of the South.[32]

For Odum, the regional solution was an immediate—not a distant— objective. Like Geddes and MacKaye, he believed that evolutionary trends did not necessarily ensure higher and better civilization. Mumford often held up the medieval city as a model balanced environment, and MacKaye's "true city," if it had existed at all, was a phenomenon of preindustrial America. Moreover, Odum saw that both Old South or agrarian nostalgia and New South rhetoric were unequal to the task of generating a balanced region and, indeed, had obscured the South's real problems. He had complained in an earlier work that "not much is being done toward making clear the case" for regional planning. But *Southern Regions* demonstrated that political leaders and social scientists must make that case. The South was capable "either of superior achievements or of pathological developments," and the direction remained uncertain.[33]

Aside from providing a comprehensive regional survey of the South, a candid analysis of its problems, and suggestions for amelioration of its condition, *Southern Regions* also made a significant contribution to regionalist methodology. *Southern Regions* was the first major regional survey that lacked an urban focus or that was inspired by a perception of urban pathology. The work demonstrated the efficacy of the regionalist approach in a predominantly rural, backward area quite different from New York and its environs or from Edinburgh and London.

Southern Regions also represented a major milestone in southern history. Odum had pointed out with considerable candor (except with respect to race and class) the contradictions inherent in southern life, especially the abundance of human and natural resources and yet their heartbreaking waste. As Daniel Singal has noted, "To the generation raised on the certainties of the New South ideology, Odum's vision seemed strikingly new." And Odum's comprehensive perspective was an academic rebuttal to the creeping disciplinary specialization that became rampant after World War II. George Tindall remarked that Odum was "the most perceptive observer of the southern scene during the first half of the century. He saw it whole, the old and the new, the folk and the academic, the agrarian and the in-

32. Odum, *Southern Regions,* 189, 169.
33. Odum, *Regional Approach to National Social Planning,* 31; Odum, *Southern Regions,* ix.

dustrial, the spiteful and the generous—and saw it all with a profound sensitivity and respect."[34]

Yet rather than serving as a foundation for future regionalist studies, *Southern Regions* marked the end of an era for regionalism as both a research methodology and as a policy tool. Regional planning, which was the major vehicle for regional redemption, was in retreat by the time the book was published. The TVA had become little more than a supplier of electricity, its lofty aims of social planning undercut by administrative insensitivity and funding cutbacks. Tugwell's Resettlement Administration managed to complete only one new town—Greenbelt, Maryland, before Congress and World War II scuttled the program. And the NRPB was also a victim of budget trimming. Meanwhile, below the federal level, the New York regional plan had degenerated into a personal vehicle for Robert Moses to carry out his extensive land-grabbing and road-building schemes. Elsewhere, regional planning confronted jurisdictional conflicts. Even when regional planning experienced a brief revival in the 1960s and early 1970s, the powers of regional bodies were extremely limited, many existing only because of federal grant requirements.

Academics had abandoned regional planning as well, at least as far as promoting it in their research. The connection between research and policy in the social sciences, and especially in sociology, weakened. Advocacy was considered unprofessional. In addition, especially in the years after World War II, regional planning implied a type of centralized control that became confounded with the Cold War. Odum's advocacy of consecutive six-year plans for the South probably fed the implications. Finally, sociology and related disciplines encouraged more specialized studies. The skepticism that greeted Geddes' interdisciplinary regional vision persisted a half century later. As John Shelton Reed has noted, *Southern Regions* is "not the kind of sociology that gets assistant professors promoted today."[35] In fact, to some contemporary sociologists, the work may be an embarrassment for all its charts, maps, and tables. Odum was not above interspersing social science rhetoric with poetic narrative.

Here is an example from *Southern Regions:* "Deep, dark piney woods with their tall, graceful, and compact millions of swaying and sighing lumber trees, fragrant with the incense of woodland moisture and golden brown needles, rich in wealth of rosin and turpentine and lumber and timbers

34. Singal, *The War Within,* 140; George Tindall, quoted *ibid.,* 116.
35. John Shelton Reed, "Max Weber's Relatives and Other Distractions: Southerners and Sociology," in *Perspectives,* ed. Black and Reed, 116.

contrast with great swamps, forest-dark and mysterious, echoing with the cry of wild cat and panther, owl and hawk, tall gnarled cypress silhouetted against the sky or river bank."[36]

This is not sociology, perhaps, but it is the South. Odum fervently believed that "any adequate picture of the South must combine the poetic with the scientific." But "poetic sociology" was a hybrid few academics were willing or able to adopt.

There were other difficulties with the book. Most obviously, world war, the civil rights movement, and the accompanying prosperity rendered it obsolete. It quickly lost its relevance to sociology, a discipline with a strong focus on the present. In the turmoil of the 1950s, Odum's mild rebuke of biracialism in *Southern Regions,* his warning that racial change would not and could not occur for at least two generations or more, and his view that "stateways" could not overcome folkways made the work appear reactionary, though he had moved with the times. Finally, despite its faith in regional planning, the book offered no convincing ideas on how to remedy the South's political and educational systems and how to remove the awful burdens of history from the minds and hearts of southerners. Perhaps this was asking too much. But with education and action two important elements of the regional method, their application to the South and to southerners remained unclear.[37]

Odum hoped that eventually a revitalized South would be integrated into the nation. Regionalism was a methodology and a policy designed less to maintain southern identity than to prepare the way for the Americanization of Dixie. Accordingly, Odum's emphasis on the immaturity of southern culture implied a lag rather than a distinction. Once the region caught up, it could rejoin the American experience. But the book tells a different story, especially in the discussion of politics, religion, education, and the economy. The divergence from the American experience is significant, even in the midst of the Depression. Odum contrived six American regions to demonstrate that the Southeast shared a commonality of geography and culture with other parts of the country, but it was a forced effort. The events of the 1950s and 1960s merely underscored southern exceptionalism. Subsequent studies have indicated that underneath the skyscrapers and Blue Light Specials, the South remains the South.[38]

36. Odum, *Southern Regions,* 305.

37. Howard W. Odum, *An American Epoch: Southern Portraiture in the National Picture* (New York, 1930), x; Odum, *Southern Regions,* 483–87.

38. See John Shelton Reed, *Southerners: The Social Psychology of Sectionalism* (Chapel Hill, 1983).

This is not to say that our interest in *Southern Regions* today is antiquarian. The book was an extremely moving and inspirational force among a small group of southern liberals. Other writers, such as W. J. Cash and Gunnar Myrdal, profited from its contents. When Jonathan Daniels traveled throughout the South during the late 1930s, he came across a lawyer in rural Arkansas whose "library," so far as Daniels could tell, consisted of a Bible, a few law books, and *Southern Regions.*[39] How this reflects influence is difficult to say. Like the *Encyclopedia Britannica, Southern Regions* was a work that "advanced" Southerners equated with modern intellectual civilization. And like the *Britannica,* Odum's work would be cited and referred to but seldom read cover to cover.

Regionalism, at least in its southern rendition, soon joined *Southern Regions* on the shelf. Colleagues such as Rupert Vance continued to be productive after Odum's death in 1954, but two major institutional supports for regionalist research—the University of North Carolina Press and the IRSS—invested in other fields and in other locales. Elsewhere, regionalism languished as a research methodology except in France, where the *Annaliste* school led by Fernand Braudel's epic *La Mediterranée* (1949) carried on the tradition of the French human geographers. Braudel's work is a geohistorical survey of the Mediterranean region, focusing on the development of a regional urban system. As Braudel argued, "[The towns] knot everything together. . . . They animate everything, they explain everything."[40]

Braudel's research foreshadowed the regionalist revival in the United States during the 1960s and early 1970s among historical geographers such as Michael Conzen and Allan Pred.[41] The latter particularly focused on the evolution of urban regions as an explanatory model for the urban-economic development of antebellum America. Subsequent studies by Diane Lindstrom, Roberta Balstad Miller, and Pred again, among others, demonstrated the efficacy of studying urbanization from a regional perspective, incorporating the hinterland and other urban regions to explain development. But this was regionalism in truncated form—using the geographic area and

---

39. W. J. Cash, *The Mind of the South* (New York, 1941), viii; Gunnar Myrdal, *An American Dilemma* (New York, 1944), 1320–21; Jonathan Daniels, *A Southerner Discovers the South* (New York, 1938), 140.

40. Fernand Braudel, *The Mediterranean and the Mediterranean World in the Age of Philip II,* trans. Sian Reynolds (New York, 1972), 1093.

41. Michael Conzen, *Frontier Farming in an Urban Shadow: The Influence of Madison's Proximity on the Agricultural Development of Blooming Grove, Wisconsin* (Madison, 1971); Allan Pred, *Urban Growth and the Circulation of Information: The U.S. System of Cities, 1790–1840* (Cambridge, Mass., 1973).

historical perspective to discuss Work but little about Folk and Place. The perspective was urban, with the countryside playing a supporting role. In addition, much of this work was turgid, swollen with jargon, and lacked the literary grace of the early regionalists. Finally, these were distinctly academic works. Policy was not an objective except in the most general sense, a reflection of the continued alienation between so-called applied history and social science and academic work in those fields.[42]

More recent work by historians has expanded the narrow regionalism of the historical geographers to include Folk and Place. Not surprisingly, southern historians are leading the way. I say "not surprisingly" because the absence of great cities to rivet research attention enables southern historians to avoid the distracting and largely artificial dichotomies between "rural" and "urban" and concentrate on "place" as place. The definitional flexibility of "region," evident by the 1920s, is even more apparent today, a fact lending creativity rather than ambiguity to these studies.[43]

The research has focused on two regional areas—settled portions of Virginia and the Carolina Piedmont. The regional approach has produced innovative studies of both areas in different time periods. Rhys Isaac's brilliant study of mid- and late-eighteenth-century Virginia demonstrates the possibilities of the comprehensive, interdisciplinary framework offered by regionalism. Isaac's depiction of the physical, social, and cultural landscape of the colony around 1740 is poetic in places and insightful everywhere. His discussion of the evangelistic folk culture and its clash with the gentry culture reflects a political, economic, and cultural struggle. The Baptist victory meant an intensely localist polity, with the church serving as a magnet to draw individuals together into a community.[44] The atomized community and culture-bound religion of the South that Odum uncovered one hundred and fifty years later differed from Isaac's Virginia. Obviously, a second (or more) transformation occurred. How and why this happened would be a sequel central to understanding southern history.

Though less comprehensive than the *Transformation of Virginia,* county studies by Darrett and Anita Rutman (Middlesex County, Virginia) and

42. Diane Lindstrom, *Economic Development in the Philadelphia Region, 1810–1850* (New York, 1978); Roberta Balstad Miller, *City and Hinterland: A Case Study of Urban Growth and Regional Development* (Westport, Conn., 1979); Allan Pred, *Urban Growth and City-Systems in the U.S.* (Cambridge, Mass., 1980).

43. Odum identified five types of region: the natural region (*i.e.,* river valley); the metropolitan region; the provincial locality of folkways; administration of government regions; and the group-of-states region. Odum and Moore, *American Regionalism,* 29–30.

44. Rhys Isaac, *The Transformation of Virginia, 1740–90* (Chapel Hill, 1982).

Richard Beeman (Lunenburg County, Virginia) indicate that Work, Place, and Folk can lead to profitable results and a greater understanding of how societies change.[45]

The Piedmont studies have not yet produced the type of pathbreaking analysis presented by Isaacs. Both Odum and Vance understood the importance of this region in the scheme of a new South. Yet prior to the Civil War, it was peripheral to the South's fortunes. The transformation of the Piedmont from the periphery to the South's core area of development, especially after 1880, is a major episode of postbellum southern history. David Carlton has explored some of the manifestations of this transformation, focusing on upcountry South Carolina: the impact of millwork on erstwhile farmers—on their culture, politics, and status; the connections between town and countryside—rivalries, partnerships, and circular migration patterns; and ultimately, the development of a new society based on an aggressive urban middle class and a restless workforce. Research conducted by David Carlton, Paul Escott, and Lacy Ford is filling out this picture.[46]

Though these scholars do not explicitly link their work with Odum, the similarity is becoming apparent to others. Robert McMath's essay in an anthology of community studies edited by him and Vernon Burton cites Odum on the importance of region as a unit of study and proceeds to treat town and country as part of a larger regional entity. The essay includes discussions of religion, space, family, economy, and leadership—the type of comprehensive analysis that characterizes regionalist scholarship. Other social scientists are making a similar connection. Historical geographer Brian J. L. Berry and Chapel Hill sociologist John D. Kasarda have complained about the exclusion of cultural and motivational factors in their fields. They have suggested the following research framework for the study of what they call "ecology": population, organization, environment, and technology. These elements are another version of LePlay's trilogy. Berry and Kasarda stress the interdependence of these variables and their evolutionary or historical character.[47]

45. Darrett Rutman and Anita Rutman, *A Place in Time: Middlesex County, Virginia, 1650–1750* (New York, 1984); Richard Beeman, *The Evolution of the Southern Backcountry: Case Study of Lunenburg County, Virginia, 1746–1832* (Philadelphia, 1984).

46. David L. Carlton, *Mill and Town in South Carolina, 1880–1920* (Baton Rouge, 1982); Paul D. Escott, *"Many Excellent People": Power and Privilege in North Carolina, 1850–1900* (Chapel Hill, 1985); Lacy K. Ford, "Rednecks and Merchants: Economic Development and Social Tensions in the South Carolina Upcountry, 1865–1900," *Journal of American History* (September, 1984), 294–318.

47. Robert C. McMath, Jr., "Community, Region and Hegemony in the Nineteenth-

The studies of various regions in the South at different time periods underscore the South's distinctiveness. Isaacs' Virginia is a world apart from Revolutionary-era Massachusetts, and Vernon Burton's Edgefield is quite different from Michael Frisch's Springfield or Gunther Barth's San Francisco.[48] The interaction of race, class, gender, economy, polity, and geography evident in recent work continue the brief for southern distinction. And the studies add new twists to the continuity-discontinuity debate. The Virginia works imply that the South underwent significant transformations long before the Civil War; in contrast, the Piedmont research indicates that although the oppressive and hierarchical aspects of race and class have persisted from the antebellum era, the particulars of such phenomena, as well as the actors, have undergone significant alterations.

The regionalist legacy can not only assist with answering basic questions about southern history but can be of national significance as well. Though Odum focused on the South, his perspective was continental. As historical geographer D. W. Meinig has noted, "Regional formation leads logically and historically to national formation." Here may be a new synthesis for an American history.[49]

The policy element remains muted, if at all present, in the new regionalism. But if the findings of Isaacs and Carlton, among others, can filter down to southern schoolchildren, they would act as a valuable corrective to a number of regional myths. And understanding history is the first step in removing its burdens. Ironically, the policy element remains in place among Soviet regionalists. Geographer B. S. Khorev has written of the next evolutionary stage of regional development that his work seeks to promote—"[the] gradual erasing of differences between town and countryside, to yield a unified system of settlement, whose planned regulation may help to prevent haphazard and uncontrolled city growth."[50] This statement is within the Geddes-MacKaye tradition of regionalism.

But before we leave the policy phase of regionalism to the Soviets, it is well to note that Howard Odum's list of regional problems amenable to

Century South," in *Toward a New South? Studies in Post–Civil War Southern Communities,* ed. Orville Vernon Burton and Robert C. McMath (Westport, Conn., 1982), 281–300; Brian J. L. Berry and John D. Kasarda, *Contemporary Urban Ecology* (New York, 1977), 12–16.

48. Orville Vernon Burton, *In My Father's House Are Many Mansions: Family and Community in Edgefield, SC* (Chapel Hill, 1985). The existence of dispersed, quasi-urban settlement patterns as opposed to the denser, urban spatial character of northern regions plays a significant role in the works of Isaac and Burton.

49. D. W. Meinig, "The Continuous Shaping of America: A Prospectus for Geographers and Historians," *American Historical Review* (December, 1978), 1192.

50. B. S. Khorev, quoted in Berry and Kasarda, *Urban Ecology,* 406.

regional planning strikes a responsive chord a half century later: "Among the distinctive characterizations and problems basic to planning considerations would be included: problems of marginal and submarginal land and folks . . , special problems of low standards of living and housing in rural areas and the resulting conditions from rapid urbanization and migration from the farms . . . problems of cash-crop farming . . . [and] deficiencies in technological wealth and lack of capital."[51]

The South has changed considerably since Odum outlined regional shortcomings. But the Sun Belt hyperbole of the present-day South is uncomfortably reminiscent of the New South rhetoric during Odum's era, and it obscures a harsher reality in a similar way. The current bifurcation of the southern economy into prosperous metropolitan areas and declining rural districts, the devolution of textiles and the sharp growth of service employment, an educational system that still lags behind national standards, the continued importation of capital and technical skill, and the persistence of hunger—even malnutrition—in certain rural pockets indicate the persistence of a regional imbalance. If we could somehow devise a *Southern Regions* for the contemporary South, the details would be considerably brighter than the prospect offered by Odum, but such a work would also pinpoint the places of imbalance, the areas in which regional culture persists in its insular character, and the locations where the beauty that Odum depicted so often in his writings is threatened with the type of progress that has destroyed other parts of the country. And since educational institutions and awareness are considerably stronger in the region today, a contemporary *Southern Regions* could not only serve as a catalogue or a reference work but also as a primer for illuminating and preserving the South and its culture that Howard Odum loved so deeply.[52]

51. Odum, *Regional Approach to National Social Planning,* 22.

52. Regions outside the South continue to draw important scholarship. Among the best examples of recent works include Paul M. Hohenberg and Lynn Hollen Lees, *The Making of Urban Europe, 1000–1950* (Cambridge, Mass., 1985); T. J. A. LeGoff, *Vannes and Its Region: A Study of Town and Country in Eighteenth-Century France* (New York, 1981); Timothy R. Mahoney, "Urban History in a Regional Context: River Towns on the Upper Mississippi, 1840–1860," *Journal of American History* (September, 1985), 318–39. The European regional studies may be of particular value to southern historians because settlement patterns and dislocations of war and depression generated similar problems in both cultures.

A REGIONAL FRAMEWORK

FOR THE URBAN SOUTH

A short ten-minute drive from downtown Atlanta and you are no longer in the city; you are in the South. There it is still possible, journalist Pat Watters wrote, "of a late spring evening . . . to breathe the air of a small-town America (not suburbia) of the American past, suffused with the coolness and blossom fragrance of trees and bushes, roses, honeysuckle, and the wet smell of grass and weeds."[1] The aroma had barely subsided when historians began to draw a different portrait of the urban South, demonstrating that over the past two centuries, urban southerners were concerned about the same issues and problems as residents in cities elsewhere and were as aggressively capitalistic in pursuing growth and prosperity. If the urban South lagged behind the urban North in population and production, the lag was of time, not of quality. Southern cities, in short, were full-fledged members of the urban nation, distinguished only by latitude and pace.[2]

I am indebted to the suggestions of Leonard P. Curry, Don H. Doyle, and Howard N. Rabinowitz, who read earlier versions of this essay. The religious guidance provided by David E. Harrell and the sources recommended by my Stockholm University colleagues, Thomas Hall and Ingrid Hammarström, informed me and the article. David R. Godschalk graciously offered the resources of his Department of City and Regional Planning at the University of North Carolina, Chapel Hill, during the early stages of the article's preparation in 1979.

1. Pat Watters, *The South and the Nation* (New York, 1969), 138.
2. See, for example, Blaine A. Brownell, *The Urban Ethos in the South, 1920–1930* (Baton Rouge, 1975), and Blaine A. Brownell and David R. Goldfield, "Southern Urban His-

Such historical studies—and the complementary works of sociologists, geographers, and political scientists—had the beneficial effect of lifting the "Cotton Curtain" that had shrouded an important aspect of southern regional development. The South could no longer be thought of simply as "the plantation, the planter, the staple crop, and the Negro, all set in a rural scene."[3] The discovery of the southern city, moreover, had significance beyond the academy: it provided a new perspective on an old region and portended well for its future. As early as the 1930s, Howard W. Odum and the regionalists at Chapel Hill contended that urbanization would result in a cultural maturation that would alter the region's values. Southern political scientist V. O. Key asserted that "urbanization contained the seeds of political revolution in the South." Now cities were in a position to provide regional political leadership, which meant an end to the "tradition-bound" politics of the agrarian past.[4]

In the 1950s, urban analyst Robert Earl Garren predicted that urbanism as a "new way of life for the South" would solve "difficulties now present in human relationships"—that is, race relations. During the 1960s and 1970s, when the Sun Belt hoopla coincided with increased scholarly interest in the urban South, enthusiasm over the region's future abounded. In the mid-1960s, sociologist Edgar T. Thompson averred that "the city everywhere is the natural habitat of the liberal mind, and the southern liberal is increasing in number and making himself heard"; liberalism would bring racial peace and political harmony to the region. Another sociologist, Leonard Reissman, declared at the same time that urbanization was destroying the social homogeneity of the South. The solid South was not so any longer.

tory," in *The City in Southern History: The Growth of Urban Civilization in the South,* ed. Blaine A. Brownell and David R. Goldfield (Port Washington, N.Y., 1977), 5–22; Leonard P. Curry, "Urbanization and Urbanism in the Old South: A Comparative View," *Journal of Southern History,* XL (February, 1974), 43–60; Lyle W. Dorsett and Arthur H. Shaffer, "Was the Antebellum South Anti-Urban? A Suggestion," *Journal of Southern History,* XXXVIII (May, 1972), 93–100; and Richard J. Hopkins, "Are Southern Cities Unique? Persistence as a Clue," *Mississippi Quarterly,* XXVI (Spring, 1973), 121–41.

3. David L. Smiley, "The Quest for a Central Theme in Southern History," *South Atlantic Quarterly,* LXII (April, 1972), 318.

4. For this evaluation of Key's position, see James C. Cobb, "Urbanization and the Changing South: A Review of the Literature," *South Atlantic Urban Studies* (1977), 255. For an excellent discussion of the regionalists' perception of urbanization, see Don H. Doyle, "Urbanization and Southern Culture: Economic Elites in Four New South Cities, 1865–1910" (paper presented at the forty-fourth annual meeting of the Southern Historical Association, St. Louis, November, 1978).

A decade later, sociologists Thomas H. Naylor and James Clotfelter agreed that urban growth was "undermining the unity of the region."[5]

They had also miscalculated. These scholars assumed the existence of a community of cities—that is, American cities sharing certain characteristics that made them more like each other than like their nonurban surroundings.[6] The assumption is based upon an urban model designed by Chicago sociologist Louis Wirth in the 1930s. In his seminal essay "Urbanism as a Way of Life," Wirth contended that the city is a distinctive environment, set apart from the countryside and capable of altering human behavior by the very fact that it is a city.[7] For an increasing number of social scientists, however, it is becoming evident that this model is "both time- and culture-bound to the immigrant city of North America at the turn of the twentieth century."[8] Although the divergence of pluralistic Chicago from the homogeneous Illinois cornfields provided an empirical justification for Wirth and his followers, the dissociation of city and region has been less apparent to later scholars studying other urban settings.

Accordingly, the growing propensity in the social sciences has been to study cities in the context of regions, under the assumption that regional and urban characteristics interact, influencing the development of both.[9] The flexibility of the regional model is one of its major advantages. It does not attribute a specific set of characteristics to either city or region but instead views the city as one environment among many in a given region.

5. Robert Earl Garren, "Urbanism: A New Way of Life for the South," *Mississippi Quarterly,* X (Spring, 1957), 68; Edgar T. Thompson, "The South in Old and New Contexts," in *The South in Continuity and Change,* ed. John C. McKinney and Edgar T. Thompson (Durham, 1965), 478; Leonard Reissman, "Urbanization in the South," in *The South in Continuity and Change,* ed. McKinney and Thompson, 87; and Thomas H. Naylor and James Clotfelter, *Strategies for Change in the South* (Chapel Hill, 1975), 222.

6. For two different expressions of the view that urbanization mutes regional distinctions, see David Harvey, *Social Justice and the City* (Baltimore, 1973), 309, and Richard C. Wade, "An Agenda for Urban History," in *American History: Retrospect and Prospect,* ed. George A. Billias and Gerald N. Grob, (New York, 1971), 393.

7. Louis Wirth, "Urbanism as a Way of Life," *American Journal of Sociology,* XLIV (July, 1938), 1–24. Actually, Wirth began to formulate and articulate these ideas at least a decade earlier; see, for example, his book *The Ghetto* (Chicago, 1928).

8. Brian J. L. Berry and John D. Kasarda, *Contemporary Urban Ecology* (New York, 1977), 376.

9. For some examples of regional studies in a historical context, see Michael P. Conzen, *Frontier Farming in an Urban Shadow: The Influence of Madison's Proximity on the Agricultural Development of Blooming Grove, Wisconsin* (Madison, 1971); Robert Dykstra, Jr., *Cattle Towns* (New York, 1968); and Diane Lindstrom, *Economic Development in the Philadelphia Region, 1810–1850* (New York, 1978).

The concept of region itself is flexible, in that a region may consist of the immediate hinterland, a nation, or even several nations. Canadian urban historian Gilbert A. Stelter has argued, for example, that fully to "appreciate any differences that might exist between Canadian and American cities" requires scholars to "go beyond urban development and examine the extent to which the Canadian experience differs from that of the United States." Context is the key to urban analysis under the regional model. As geographer Brian J. L. Berry has asserted, "one cannot study the ecology of an urban area in isolation." [10]

This essay proposes a regional framework for the study of the urban South. Applying Stelter's suggestion to the South, elements of regional distinction provide insights on how southern cities differ from their counterparts elsewhere. Assuming that the South qualifies as a region, isolating factors of regional distinction is a necessary first step to analyzing their impact on regional and, especially for the purposes of this analysis, urban growth. [11] At least three general factors have characterized the South's historical development: ruralism, race, and colonialism. These elements have appeared in other American regions, but in terms of their combination and continuity, they are distinctive to the southern region and, therefore, to the southern city.

The Wirthian model of urbanization established "urban" and "rural" as dichotomous environments. Contemporary scholars, however, are less cer-

---

10. Bruce M. Stave, "A Conversation with Gilbert A. Stelter: Urban History in Canada," *Journal of Urban History,* VI (February, 1980), 181; Berry and Kasarda, *Contemporary Urban Ecology,* 85.

11. I make two assumptions here: first, that the South qualifies as a region, and second, that the southern region is distinctive. There is a problem in treating the South as a geographic entity. I agree with David L. Smiley that the "South defies . . . location"; see Smiley, "Quest for a Central Theme." Terms like *Piedmont, Tidewater, valley, coastal plain, piney woods, Delta, black belt, low country, upcountry,* and *mountain* describe the various geographic divisions of the South and the peculiarities of life within them; thus, there is no single geographic South. My own imprecise geographic definition of the South includes the eleven Confederate states plus Kentucky. Within this area, regional characteristics had their greatest impact. The search for southern distinctiveness, wherever its "location," has become a major regional theme in itself. All American regions originated as agricultural areas: biracialism is a national phenomenon, and other regions have submitted to the northeastern economic juggernaut. Thus, cities throughout the nation most likely share certain characteristics because their regions have shared aspects common to American life in general. I argue, however, that the continuity and combination of these characteristics were unique to the South. Consequently, according to the regional framework of urban analysis, southern cities were distinctive as well.

tain of the differences, and a few have asserted that what distinctions exist are, in Berry's phrase, "meaningless." Patterns of American postwar urbanization support this view. According to Oscar Handlin, "The differences between city and country have been attenuated almost to the vanishing point."[12] But even in the industrial era at the turn of the century, when urban-rural distinctions were perhaps more obvious, social scientists groped for definitional demarcations. Pioneer urbanist Adna F. Weber complained that in the United States, the "town" is a rural concept but that in Europe it is considered urban, and that the numerical thresholds assigned to each concept were inadequate. Weber was most satisfied with the German subdivision of *Landstadt* (literally, "country town") as a definitional middle ground between rural and urban places that combines elements of both.[13]

12. Berry and Kasarda, *Contemporary Urban Ecology,* 174; and Oscar Handlin, "The Modern City as a Field of Study," in *The Historian and the City,* ed. Oscar Handlin and John Burchard (Cambridge, Mass., 1963), 24, as quoted in Berry and Kasarda, *Contemporary Urban Ecology,* 254. The rapidly disappearing distinctions between urban and rural increase the definitional problems surrounding the question of what is—and what is not—a city. Scholars typically use size or function indicators to measure "urbanism," but they do not agree on the particular thresholds that constitute the designation "urban." See Gilbert Rozman, "Urban Networks and Historical Stages," *Journal of Interdisciplinary History,* IX (Spring, 1978), 65–91; and Ronald C. Tobey, "How Urbane is the Urbanite? An Historical Model of the Urban Hierarchy and the Social Motivation of Service Classes," *Historical Methods Newsletter,* VII (Winter, 1974), 259–75. The population thresholds devised by the U.S. Census Bureau are inadequate because they reveal little about a particular environment's function and influence. In addition, the relative population, function, and influence thresholds that distinguish towns and cities must change over time. To compound the definitional problems, an urban place can be a city in terms of possessing a relatively large number of inhabitants but a "town" in its functional characteristics—that is, performing basic agricultural marketing activities. It is important, nevertheless, to note some distinctions among various urban environments. My solution has been to assign definitional priority to population levels and secondary emphasis to function and influence. Thus, I consider an urban place a "town" if it possessed fewer than 1,000 inhabitants in 1820; 1,500 in 1850; 2,500 in 1880; 5,000 in 1910; 7,500 in 1940; and 10,000 in 1970. "Town" functions are basically agricultural marketing, and "town" influence rarely extends beyond the immediate hinterland. When I use the adjective "small" to describe a city, I am referring to those urban places with populations of 1,000 to 2,500 in 1820; 1,500 to 4,000 in 1850; 2,500 to 10,000 in 1880; 5,000 to 15,000 in 1910; 7,500 to 25,000 in 1940; and 10,000 to 40,000 in 1970. Their functions typically include some wholesaling and, perhaps, basic processing industries; their market influence extends beyond the adjacent hinterland but not throughout the region. These definitions are merely guidelines and are not meant to be descriptive beyond the rudimentary characteristics presented here. I appreciate the assistance of University of North Carolina geographers Clyde E. Browning and Richard Garrity in developing these definitions.

13. Adna F. Weber, *The Growth of Cities in the Nineteenth Century* (New York, 1899), 14–16.

Indeed, Europeans in general have perceived the interchange between city and country characteristics. In the 1950s, Swedish urban historian Gregor Paulsson wrote that "*alla städer ligger på landet*" ("all cities are in the countryside"), referring to the rural manifestations evident in Swedish urban life. Similarly, French urbanist Henri Lefebvre contended that "urbanization of the countryside involves a subsidiary ruralization of the city." [14] European urban history is replete with examples to support the views of both Paulsson and Lefebvre.

The medieval European city included farms and orchards. As late as 1200, Paris' Left Bank was "semiurban," with sprawling vineyards. Seventeenth-century London was a "pleasant country town with many gardens and broad green fields." And even after the Industrial Revolution, agriculture remained a part of urban life. English urban historians H. J. Dyos and Michael Wolff described the Victorian city as still tied to its "rural connections. The largest of them still conducted extensive backyard agriculture . . . cowstalls, sheep-folds, pig-sties above and below ground, in and out of dwellings, on and off the streets, wherever this rudimentary factory-farming could be made to work." [15] Cities that have lost their rural connections are of relatively recent origin and confined only to a highly industrialized segment of the United States and Western Europe. As late as the 1920s in China, market-garden farms and duck ponds were typical features of the larger cities.

Life in southern cities in the nineteenth century remained tied to agricultural cycles. There was, as Lewis Mumford noted of Greek cities, "a tidal drifting in and out of the city with the seasons." Towns slept from late spring to early fall and awoke with the arrival of the first cotton or tobacco shipments. Even a metropolis such as New Orleans did not have a life of its own apart from the dictates of the cotton fields. "About the first of June," journalist J. D. B. De Bow wrote with some dismay, New Orleans "begins to show evidences of waste. People inquire of steam and rail routes and are buying trunks." [16] Many were also escaping a potential outbreak of yellow

---

14. Gregor Paulsson, *Svensk stad* (Stockholm, 1950), I, 6; and for this statement of Lefebvre's views of urbanization in *La Revolution urbaine* (1970) and *La Pensée Marxiste et la ville* (1972), see Harvey, *Social Justice and the City,* 308.

15. Yi-Fu Tuan, "The City: Its Distance from Nature," *Geographical Review,* LXVIII (January, 1978), 3; and H. J. Dyos and Michael Wolff, "The Way We Live Now," in *The Victorian City: Images and Reality,* ed. H. J. Dyos and Michael Wolff, (London, 1973), 899, as quoted in Tuan, "The City," 3–4. Tuan presents an excellent discussion of agricultural activities in Western and Oriental cities throughout history.

16. Lewis Mumford, *The City in History* (New York, 1961), 128; and J. D. B. De Bow, "Editorial Miscellany," *De Bow's Review,* XXVII (January, 1859), 117.

fever; but had the city been healthy, there was simply little to do while cotton was in the fields. The tempo picked up in the fall and especially in the early winter. Cities arranged their yearly social and cultural calendars around staple marketing time.

Southern urban architecture and landscape further reflected agrarian connections. Antebellum planters moved readily between country and city residences in larger cities like Charleston and established themselves more or less permanently in smaller places like Natchez and Demopolis; their presence contributed to the southern city's hybrid appearance. Their homes, turned sideways to show narrow frontage on the street, had verandahs along the side and verdant gardens in the back to lend a country atmosphere. Travelers commenting on the distinctions between northern and southern cities frequently lapsed into rural metaphors. Palmettos and magnolias graced the streets of Charleston, while a walk on the Battery "to inhale the pure and cool breezes . . . and to enjoy the view" was an essential part of the itinerary of any visitor. Savannah, one visitor wrote to his northern friends, "is a city of trees and gardens." Away from the wharf, this traveler noted an "almost rural quiet." Even on the Texas frontier, Galveston was "one of the most charming places—in appearance—that I have ever seen," one traveler exclaimed; the landscaping and the elegance of the residences along the Strand bespoke the same pastoral quietude of more civilized Natchez and Savannah.[17]

Southern cities continued to attract notice as middle landscapes into the twentieth century. Novelist Sherwood Anderson, absorbing the exotic culture of New Orleans during the 1920s, was most impressed not by the city's urbanity but by its close relationship to nature. In a letter to his publisher concerning the impending appearance of *Dark Laughter,* a novel he wrote in New Orleans, Anderson related, "The Negro, the earth, and the river—that suggests the title." The narrator in Anderson's "A Meeting South" stated, "All good New Orleanians go to look at the Mississippi, at least once a day." This urban commune with nature, which struck Anderson as so unusual, had been the southern urban condition for two centuries. Edd W. Parks summarized the relationship in 1934 by stating that the urban South

17. Jane M. Turnbull and Marion T. Turnbull, *American Photographs* (London, 1860), 92, as quoted in Ivan D. Steen, "Charleston in the 1850s: As Described by British Travelers," *South Carolina Historical Magazine,* LXXI (1970), 38; and Curtis B. Pyle, "Letters from the South," *Masonic Mirrors and American Keystone,* II (1853), 115, 125–26, and [Samuel Adams Hammett], "Drafts at Sight in the Southwest," *Literary World,* V (1849), 21–22, 217–18, both as quoted in Eugene L. Schwab, ed., *Travels in the Old South* (Lexington, Ky., 1973), 527, 430.

was "governed and given character by the country immediately surrounding it."[18]

The relatively low density of population in southern cities complemented the rural physical appearance. Because many southern cities experienced their most rapid growth during the twentieth century—the age of annexation and the automobile—most of them remain uncluttered and sprawling. But the horizontal structure of southern urban space was evident in the nineteenth century, long before technology affected land use. Single-family dwellings, no matter how modest, characterized residential areas. Blacks and poor whites on the urban periphery merely re-created their small wooden rural shacks. The ample gardens of the larger homes lent an air of spaciousness to more affluent residential districts closer to the city center.[19] The low-rise aspect of residences persisted after local boosters began building commercial towers in refurbished downtowns at the turn of the century.

Rural elements not only permeated the physical environment of southern cities but determined the very existence of those cities as well. Agriculture, especially staple agriculture, molded the region's economy and directed the size and nature of urban growth. Geographer Carville Earle and historian Ronald Hoffman have demonstrated how particular staple crops induced a specific pattern of southern urbanization in the colonial era. Geography and the marketing practices of tobacco farmers limited urban development in the Chesapeake colonies, and shipping was the primary role towns performed. Though numerous, they were consequently small. When wheat cultivation engaged part of the area in the 1740s, larger settlements like Baltimore evolved. The processing and subsequent storage requirements of the crop stimulated the growth of larger urban places. Rice, like wheat, required extensive marketing, storage, and processing facilities. Charleston became the thriving center of rice cultivation in the eighteenth century. The Carolina port also grew as a result of the slave trade, but that, too, was staple-inspired. Ira Berlin has demonstrated that profits from staples en-

18. Sherwood Anderson, *Letters of Sherwood Anderson,* ed. Howard Mumford Jones and Walter B. Rideout (Boston, 1953), 142, and "A Meeting South," in *The Portable Sherwood Anderson,* ed. Horace Gregory (New York, 1956), 522, as quoted in Michael Fanning, "New Orleans and Sherwood Anderson," *Southern Studies* (1978), 206; Edd W. Parks, "Southern Towns and Cities," in *Culture in the South,* ed. William T. Couch, (Chapel Hill, 1934), 512, as quoted in Brownell, *The Urban Ethos,* 6.

19. See Constance M. Green, *American Cities in the Growth of the Nation* (New York, 1965), 24; and Mary Fulton Green, "A Profile of Columbia in 1850," *South Carolina Historical Magazine,* LXX (April, 1969), 106.

couraged consolidation of landholdings, which in turn created huge labor demands.[20]

Urban growth, or the lack thereof during the colonial era, is indicative of the influence of staple agriculture. But not until the antebellum period did a distinctive southern urban system take root. With the emergence of cotton as the region's leading staple, New Orleans developed into the South's and, for a time in the 1830s, the nation's leading export center. In the Cotton Belt in general, however, urban civilization barely existed. The rural quietude of Natchez was matched by dozens of other Delta towns. Except for Mobile, New Orleans seemed to enjoy an urban monopoly. Of the ten leading southern cities in 1850, only Memphis, Mobile, and New Orleans were in the Cotton Belt.

Cotton, like tobacco, required relatively few concentrated services. Processing occurred elsewhere, in New England or Great Britain, so the only requisite for the crop's commercial success was an outlet to both of these locations. New Orleans merchants organized the trade by sending agents into upriver towns to collect the crop and, in turn, supply the planters with wares. The volume of cotton production and the need for quality control and price stability militated against the kind of diffuse trade that marked tobacco commerce in the early colonial era. The functions of upriver towns were limited to collection points for the staple. New Orleans' early regional dominance of cotton commerce, moreover, inhibited urban growth by restricting capital accumulation. Crescent City merchants came to control local banks as well. Finally, as the regional center for the slave trade, New Orleans had another economic monopoly to drain capital from the hinterland. So cotton and capital flowed to the Delta port.

Soil exhaustion and the limited marketing procedures surrounding tobacco cultivation restricted the development of cities similar in size to those in the North. The Chesapeake (not including Baltimore, which was tied to wheat-cultivating areas) and the North Carolina Tobacco Belt provided little sustenance for Richmond, Lynchburg, and Petersburg. Only in the 1850s, when these cities added processing industries, did growth occur, though on a modest scale. Thus, New Orleans was the dominant metropolis of the antebellum South; it had no rivals. Charleston, its nearest competitor in population, was one-quarter its size in 1860 and had slipped from sixth to fifteenth in national rank according to size in less than a generation.

20. Carville Earle and Ronald Hoffman, "The Urban South: The First Two Centuries," in *The City in Southern History,* ed. Brownell and Goldfield, 23–51; Ira Berlin, "Time, Space, and the Evolution of Afro-American Society on British Mainland North America," *American Historical Review,* LXXXV (February, 1980), 58–61.

Urbanization did indeed occur in the antebellum South. What did not, however, was the development of large cities. An urban place inhabited by fewer than four thousand persons (by 1860) was more characteristic of the antebellum South than of any other region. The urban population of the region was, therefore, more diffuse—a condition consistent with the relatively few economic functions such cities performed in support of a staple crop economy. It was urbanization without cities.[21]

The pattern persisted for nearly another century. The development of the southern urban system following the Civil War reflected the South's increased dependence on staple agriculture. During the period of agricultural recovery, 1865–80, urbanization came to a virtual halt. The percentage of the South's population residing in cities increased from 9.6 percent in 1860 to only 12.2 percent by 1880. In the highly urbanized Northeast, by contrast, city dwellers increased from 35.7 to 50.8 percent of the population during the same period. The ground lost by the laggard pace of southern urbanization immediately before the Civil War was never recovered. In 1830, five southern cities were among the nation's twenty leading cities; in 1900, only one—New Orleans—remained, and only six southern cities were among the fifty major cities in the United States.

Changes in both marketing and processing cotton led to the even greater prevalence of smaller urban places in the southern urban system than had existed in the antebellum period. The appearance of country stores, storehouses, and taverns around rural railroad stations signified a localization of cotton marketing. Normally, this system should have benefited southern port cities, which could be expected to supply these merchant-crossroad settlements. The extent of the national railroad network, however, enabled these storekeepers to bypass southern cities in favor of connections with northern cities. In this way, the country merchants could market the local cotton crop in exchange for goods without requiring contact with southern ports.

The precipitous decline of New Orleans reflected the new marketing arrangements. New Orleans remained the major southern cotton port, but only because the lower Mississippi provided easier transportation for some

21. On the antebellum southern urban system, see Clement Eaton, *The Growth of Southern Civilization, 1790–1860* (New York, 1961), 248–50; Curry, "Urbanization and Urbanism in the Old South," 43–55; David R. Goldfield, "Pursuing the American Urban Dream: Cities in the Old South," in *The City in Southern History,* ed. Brownell and Goldfield, 56–57; and Rupert B. Vance and Sara Smith, "Metropolitan Dominance and Integration," in *The Urban South,* ed. Rupert B. Vance and Nicholas J. Demerath (Chapel Hill, 1954), 120.

planters than did the railroads running eastward and westward; not until 1883 did cotton receipts at the port attain prewar levels. Population growth, moreover, declined with commerce: in 1860, New Orleans was the sixth largest city in the nation; by 1900, it had slipped to fifteenth and was continuing to move downward.

In addition to marketing changes, the improvement of staple processing techniques in the late-nineteenth-century South induced further decline in the region's major ports. Technological innovations that enabled cotton gins to process more cotton encouraged the removal of ginning from individual plantations to nearby towns along rail routes, where cotton could be cleaned more cheaply in greater volume. By the 1880s, two new processing techniques had appeared—cotton compressing, which reduced the size of the bales, and cottonseed oil mills, which extracted oil from crushed cottonseeds. Both of these techniques required relatively sophisticated machinery that could handle the product of roughly thirty cotton gins at one time. Such industries, therefore, commanded a wider market area than the ginning enterprises and, consequently, produced urban growth. Until 1930, communities that were able to secure all three processing services were the fastest-growing cities in the Cotton Belt. These additional services left the planter even less reason to patronize the once-flourishing seaports.

Although the processing communities were major beneficiaries of Cotton Belt urban growth, they attained the limits of their expansion relatively quickly. By 1900, these towns, which were scattered remarkably evenly throughout the area of cotton cultivation from Texas to southern Georgia, had reached a population of five to ten thousand inhabitants and rarely grew beyond that. The market area required by the new procedures remained relatively stationary, and since the processed cotton was immediately transshipped by rail to major rail centers in the South, like Dallas and Atlanta, or to northern cities, the towns had little need to develop higher economic functions. Actually, cities that were outside the Cotton Belt or had very little contact with the staple were the most successful in generating large-scale urban growth. As in the antebellum era, cotton cultivation, produced a significant number of urban places, but their size was severely restricted by the limits of the marketing and processing activities imposed by the crop.

As staple cultivation came to characterize the postwar South to an even greater extent than it did in the antebellum era, the small city became even more typical of Southern urban settlement. In 1850, 68.7 percent of the South's urban population lived in cities of more than twenty-five thousand inhabitants; by 1900, only 48.1 percent did, even though more southerners lived in cities by the later date. Cities that served as major transshipment points for cotton or had little direct contact with the staple became the region's new growth centers. Among the South's five most populous cities in 1920, Atlanta possessed only a few hundred citizens in 1850, and Birmingham did not exist at that date. But Atlanta and Birmingham were only the most prominent examples of urbanization beyond simple marketing and processing. The appearance of cities like Durham, Winston-Salem, and Greenville in the Carolina Piedmont reflected a more complex industrial base than simple processing. The rise of Florida cities such as Jacksonville and Tampa, which grew from a mixture of commerce and industry, and the growth of Chattanooga, Knoxville, and Nashville, which became prominent as a result of various railroad, industrial, and educational and cultural enterprises—all within the last two decades of the nineteenth century—indicate that urban economies served other masters besides or excluding King Cotton.

These new urban centers together with the proliferating cotton marketing and processing towns represent a shift from the antebellum pattern of one primary city—New Orleans—with a few secondary seaports and a host of small urban communities. The shift did not, however, signify a change in the nature of southern urbanization but merely a change in geography. The South remained overwhelmingly a region of the small urban settlement.[22]

As long as staple crop cultivation, especially cotton, characterized southern agriculture, this pattern remained. In the 1930s and 1940s, federal policy, mass migration, and mechanization diminished the significance of staple cultivation. In 1940, cities of less than ten thousand still typified the region's urban growth. In that year, one-third of the nation's population lived in cities of more than one hundred thousand inhabitants; only one out of eight southerners did. During the 1940s, small-city urbanization began to decline in importance. That this decline occurred simultaneously with the transformation of southern agriculture indicates that staple mar-

22. On the postbellum southern urban system through the 1920s, see Curry, "Urbanization and Urbanism in the Old South," 55–60; L. Tuffly Ellis, "The New Orleans Cotton Exchange: The Formative Years, 1871–1880," *Journal of Southern History*, XXXIX (November, 1973), 545–47; T. Lynn Smith, "The Emergence of Cities," in *The Urban South,* ed. Vance and Demerath, 25–27; Kenneth Weiher, "The Cotton Industry and Southern Urbanization, 1880–1930," *Explorations in Economic History,* XIV (April, 1977), 122–24; Clyde E. Browning and Richard Garrity, "Southern Urban Evolution: A Cartographic Portrayal" (paper presented at Conference on the Urban South, Norfolk, Va., February, 1977); and James M. Russell, "Atlanta: Gate City of the South, 1847–1885" (Ph.D. dissertation, Princeton University, 1971), Chap. 5.

keting no longer sustained urban development. Industry and service activities became greater determinants of urbanization in the post–World War II South. For the first time in its history, the growth of cities of more than ten thousand inhabitants exceeded the rate for cities and towns of less than ten thousand. Two genuine metropolises now anchored the southern urban system—Atlanta in the east and Dallas in the west. Both owed their early prosperity to cotton; but finance, diversified commerce, and industry built them into regional pacesetters. Finally, the most rapid urban growth in the region occurred in Florida, where agriculture had only an indirect impact on urbanization. Miami and Tampa–St. Petersburg counted almost one million persons between them in 1950. From the Florida panhandle to eastern Texas, however, the small city remained the characteristic urban settlement. Low in density, these communities continued to grow horizontally in the 1950s.[23] C. Vann Woodward has called this semiurban sprawl "rurbanization," a term that captures well the hybrid form of southern urban settlement.[24]

A more subtle and pervasive rural quality than size and concomitant marketing functions lingered as well: the rural values of the millions of migrants who, since the eighteenth century, moved from the countryside to the city. The Wirthian concept of urbanization advanced two assumptions about urbanization and culture: the urban environment modified or destroyed migrant cultures, and cities functioned as disseminators of culture to the hinterland. Recent studies on ethnicity demonstrate, however, that immigrants' premigration cultures persisted in cities, despite the adverse impact of the city on immigrant life. As Kathleen Neils Conzen has pointed out, "Considerable residues of ethnic culture can remain among socially assimilated individuals,"[25] so that the strength of these cultural values can be maintained over time. More pertinent to the southern urban situation are studies of value persistence among native rural migrants. In 1941, anthropologist

23. On the southern urban system since the 1920s, see Naylor and Clotfelter, *Strategies for Change in the South,* 223; George B. Tindall, *The Emergence of the New South, 1913–1945* (Baton Rouge, 1967), 95; Reissman, "Urbanization in the South," in *The South in Continuity and Change,* ed. McKinney and Thompson, 79–100; Smith, "The Emergence of Cities," in *The Urban South,* ed. Vance and Demerath, 29–37; Jonathan Weiner, "Class Structure and Economic Development in the American South, 1865–1955," *American Historical Review,* LXXXIV (October, 1979), 990; and Browning and Garrity, "Southern Urban Evolution."

24. C. Vann Woodward, *The Burden of Southern History* (New York, 1961), as quoted in Watters, *The South and the Nation,* 236.

25. Kathleen Neils Conzen, "Immigrants, Immigrant Neighborhoods, and Ethnic Identity: Historical Issues," *Journal of American History,* LXVI (December, 1979), 613.

Robert Redfield discovered a broad range of values and institutions that remained intact or were only slightly modified among the rural migrants of urban Mexico; voluntary associations and kinship patterns persisted in the urban environment. More recently, African scholars have demonstrated not merely the maintenance of but also the increase in tribal consciousness among transplanted rural Africans, especially in cities where intergroup conflict is strong.[26] This finding may have particular relevance for the persistence of rural black folk culture amid the hostile white environment of the southern city. Not only in the Third World but in Western societies as well, the resilience of rural values in an urban setting is a prevalent phenomenon.[27]

In view of these findings on rural cultural persistence, anthropologists have questioned the city's role as a disseminator of culture. Robert Redfield and Milton B. Singer have distinguished between primary and secondary urbanization. In the primary phase, cities carry the region's culture forward "into systematic and reflective dimensions." The city organizes and refines this core culture but does not alter it. During the secondary phase of urbanization—a phase induced through vast technological changes and the influx of diverse peoples—the cultural flow approaches the direction assumed by the Wirthian model. Even here, however, "The processes of cultural innovation . . . are far too complex to be handled by simple mechanical laws concerning the direction, rate, and 'flow' of cultural diffusion between 'city' and 'country.' " Redfield and Singer termed primary cities *orthogenetic* and secondary cities *heterogenetic*.[28]

Southern cities have evinced orthogenetic cultural patterns for most of the past two centuries—that is, rural folkways have persisted in southern cities. In the nineteenth century, the roots of the southern urban population were sunk deep in rural soil, especially in the postbellum era. As early as 1868, one-half of Atlanta's population had arrived from the countryside in

26. For a summary of some of the recent work on African urbanization, most notably that in Kenneth L. Little, *West African Urbanization* (Cambridge, Eng., 1965), and H. Miner, ed., *The City in Modern Africa* (New York, 1967), see Berry and Kasarda, *Contemporary Urban Ecology*, 377.

27. The question of rural cultural impact on urbanization is currently attracting considerable research interest in Sweden. For a recent effort that supports the view of rural cultural retention in an urban setting, see Sven B. Ek, *Stadens fodelse* (Eslov, 1978).

28. Robert Redfield and Milton B. Singer, "The Cultural Role of Cities," *Economic Development and Cultural Change*, III (March, 1954), 59, 71. Southern sociologist Edgar T. Thompson has employed the concept of "orthogenetic city" to define such antebellum southern cities as Charleston, Savannah, Mobile, and New Orleans; see Edgar T. Thompson, "God and the Southern Plantation System," in *Religion and the Solid South*, ed. Samuel S. Hill, Jr. (Nashville, 1972), 57–91.

the three years following the end of the war. Rural migration receded in the 1870s, but a steady stream flowed into southern cities for the remainder of the century. Memphis, one of the region's few prosperous larger cities, was also its most rural. By 1900, 80 percent of the city's residents were from the adjacent Mississippi or Tennessee countryside. Percentages of recent rural migrants were almost as high in Jacksonville, Birmingham, and Atlanta. Whereas rural proportions increased, the immigrant population usually declined. In Memphis, for example, 37 percent of the population was foreign born in 1860; by 1900, only 15 percent was.[29] Southern cities at the turn of the century were becoming both more rural and less diverse.

With the agricultural transformation during and after the Depression, migration from the farms quickened. As author Lillian Smith noted succinctly in the 1940s, "People have moved to town." Although the region's farm population declined by 20 percent between 1940 and 1945, southern cities increased by nearly 30 percent, exceeding the rate of urban growth in other regions. The acceleration of rural migration and agricultural diversification continued into the next decade. In 1950, South Carolina still produced more than seven hundred thousand bales of cotton. By 1960, cotton cultivation had virtually disappeared, as the white fields receded before a green wave of pasture, soybeans, and corn. The croppers and tenants—more than one hundred and fifty thousand of them—who worked those cotton fields were mostly gone, to small cities like Columbia, Spartanburg, and Greenville.[30]

In addition to their demographic impact, the rural migrants brought their distinctive cultural baggage to the city. Although the effect of rural values on southern urban development is not clear, several suggestions can be ventured. Family and religion were southern rural bulwarks. "The family," southern historian Francis Butler Simkins wrote, "was the core of Southern society; within its bounds everything worthwhile took place." The strength of family ties possibly meant the weakness of the community or collective ethic in southern cities; kinship patterns determined social standing, and tradition counted more than novelty. Honor, vengeance, and pride, especially when women were involved, were above all family values, and they

29. William D. Miller, *Memphis During the Progressive Era, 1900–1917* (Memphis, 1957), 7–9, and "Myth and New South Murder Rates," *Mississippi Quarterly* (1973), 146; and Eugene J. Watts, *The Social Bases of City Politics: Atlanta, 1865–1903* (Westport, Conn., 1978), 90.

30. Lillian Smith, *Killers of the Dream* (New York, 1949), 41; Ernest M. Lander, Jr., introduction to *Two Decades of Change: The South Since the Supreme Court Desegregation Decision,* ed. Ernest M. Lander and Richard J. Calhoun (Columbia, S.C., 1975), 2–3.

governed behavior outside the home as well. Southerners believed and practiced, as historian Gerald M. Capers has noted, "the right of private vengeance." [31] New South urban murder rates, for example, were typically higher than for cities in other regions. During the early 1900s, the national homicide rate per one hundred thousand inhabitants was 7.2; every southern city with more than twenty-five thousand exceeded that rate. Memphis, the most rural (in terms of its population) of major southern cities, was also the nation's murder capital, with a rate of 47.1; Charleston was a distant second at 27.7.[32]

The violence contrasted with, yet was curiously connected to, the deep religiosity of the rural migrants. The southern church, historian George B. Tindall wrote, "is something unique in all Christendom in its single-minded focus on salvation, its sense of assurance, and its rejection . . . of other versions of Christian experience. It serves as one of the chief instruments of ethnic solidarity." [33] As Tindall's description implies, it was not the deep religiosity of southerners that was unique but rather the philosophical structure of their religious devotion. Evangelical Protestantism, which first swept over the frontier South in the 1830s, came increasingly after the Civil War to define southern religious practices and principles and to mark religion as one of the distinctive features of southern identity.

Specifically, this southern religious tradition was pessimistic, emphasizing man's basic depravity, with individual salvation possible only through a conversion experience. The evangelical sects (primarily Baptists, Methodists, and Presbyterians) and their ministers were well established by 1860, but not until after the Civil War, when southern religion became entwined with the Lost Cause, did evangelical Protestantism pervade every cultural pore of the region. The pain and the martyrdom evoked by the Lost Cause blended well with a religion obsessed with suffering and salvation. For a region wrapped in grief and defeat, where dull poverty was commonplace,

31. Francis Butler Simkins, *A History of the South* (3rd ed.; New York, 1968), 388, as quoted in George B. Tindall, "Beyond the Mainstream: The Ethnic Southerners," *Journal of Southern History*, XL (1974), 15; and Gerald M. Capers, "The Rural Lag on Southern Cities," *Mississippi Quarterly*, XX (Fall, 1967), 261. Also see Smith, *Killers of the Dream*, 141.

32. Miller, "Myth and New South Murder Rates," 143–50. John Shelton Reed discovered the persistence of such rural regional characteristics as localism, violence, and religiosity in southern cities into the 1960s. The persistence and pervasiveness of these factors, Reed argued, set the region apart from the rest of the nation. See John Shelton Reed, *The Enduring South* (Rev. ed.; Chapel Hill, 1975), esp. 89–90.

33. Tindall, "Beyond the Mainstream," 16.

evangelical ritual, liturgy, and promise filled a deep spiritual need. By 1900, a distinctive civil religion was evident, distinguishing southern culture from the optimistic, scientific, social gospel sweeping northern ecclesiastics and society. What began as a fervent rural pastime in the early nineteenth century became a regional hallmark by the beginning of the twentieth.[34]

Evangelical Protestantism affected southern culture by standing as a regional bulwark against change. The focus on individual sin and salvation and on otherworldly rewards regardless of earthly deprivations shifted attention from society to the individual and his compact with God. "Christ-centeredness," southern theologian Samuel S. Hill, Jr., averred, "easily shades off into fearful self-centeredness." Individual suffering, poverty, and pain "have to be endured," since "the Christian is merely a sojourner in this world" and must await reward in the next. These precepts readily shunted attention from the very real-world injustice of a biracial society, for example. The great upsurge in revivalism between 1890 and 1906 coincided with the nadir of black fortunes in the South. Finally, whatever ministerial interest in social reform prevailed was diffused by the emphasis upon individual salvation and, especially in an urban setting, upon the number of individuals brought into the flock. "Being a Christian," southern theologian Langdon Gilkey observed, "thus becomes merely the operation of expanding itself."[35]

Evangelical Protestantism was and is replete with certainties: the certainty of sin, the certainty of salvation through conversion, and the infallibility of

34. For the rise of evangelical Protestantism in the antebellum era, see Anne C. Loveland, *Southern Evangelicals and the Social Order, 1800–1860* (Baton Rouge, 1980); and for the late nineteenth and twentieth centuries, see Kenneth K. Bailey, *Southern White Protestantism in the Twentieth Century* (New York, 1964); Samuel S. Hill, Jr., "The South's Two Cultures," in *Religion and the Solid South,* ed. Hill, 39; Anne Firor Scott, "Women, Religion, and Social Change in the South, 1830–1930," in *Religion and the Solid South,* ed. Hill, 92–116; and Charles Reagan Wilson, "The Religion of the Lost Cause: Ritual and Organization of the Southern Civil Religion, 1865–1920," *Journal of Southern History,* XLVI (May, 1980), 219–38. The authors concur that sectional denominationalism and the philosophical bases of evangelical Protestantism pervaded southern identity by the late nineteenth century and set the region apart from the rest of the country. Even today, as Bailey has pointed out, "Perhaps in the sphere of religion . . . Southern identity is best delineated"; see Bailey, *Southern White Protestantism,* ix.

35. Samuel S. Hill, Jr., "Toward a Charter for a Southern Theology," in *Religion and the Solid South,* ed. Hill, 192, and Hill, "The South's Two Cultures," *ibid.,* 41; Langdon Gilkey, *How the Church Can Minister to the World Without Losing Itself* (New York, 1929), n. 64, as quoted in Hill, "Toward a Charter for a Southern Theology," 198.

the Bible. Since change means uncertainty, to allow any change would undermine faith and, eventually, southern society. Indeed, southern religion
was virtually indistinguishable from southern society in the late nineteenth
century. As Hill observed, "Southern mores are accorded a certain divine
quality. They are not only the way things are, they are the way things should
be." Novelist Thomas Wolfe stated it in more secular terms when he decried
the "hostile and murderous entrenchment against all new life" that permeated the region in the 1920s.[36]

As a part—perhaps the most dominant part—of southern culture, evangelical Protestantism invariably affected southern urbanization, and vice
versa. Although the evangelical sects first prospered on the southern frontier,
the spirit of revivalism soon penetrated the cities and towns of the antebellum South. The antebellum evangelists appealed to the "middling ranks
of southern society" and thus found numerous adherents in the urban
South. Then, too, the evangelists' efforts to reach the greatest numbers for
conversion and salvation meant that cities became logical centers for evangelical activity. The sheer size of the urban populations and the frequent
opportunities to speak outside the church afforded the evangelist a "wider
influence than he could ever hope for in the country."[37]

After the Civil War, religion as a southern cultural mainstay flourished
in southern cities and became inseparable from urban life. "Church was our
town," author Lillian Smith recalled of her childhood during the early decades of the twentieth century. Wood planks or carpeting may have replaced
the dirt floor of the forest, but the old enthusiasm and demonstrative preaching of guilt, sin, fear, and salvation persisted in the urban milieu. The evangelical church's "general spirit and outlook were transplanted to the nearby
town center," Edgar T. Thompson reminisced. "Southern town and even
city churches generally might almost be described as transplanted rural institutions," he concluded.[38] Church and urban society remain closely connected. Religious affiliation is as important as lineage in describing a person
today. The southern urban church is the best place in the city to attain and
maintain social and business contacts. And even though framed by expensive
architecture, the basic principles of evangelical Protestantism continue to

36. Hill, "The South's Two Cultures," in *Religion and the Solid South,* ed. Hill, 45; and
Thomas Wolfe, *Look Homeward, Angel* (New York, 1929), 155, as quoted in C. Hugh Hol-
man, " 'The Dark, Ruined Helen of His Blood': Thomas Wolfe and the South," in *Thomas
Wolfe: Three Decades of Criticism,* ed. Leslie A. Field, (New York, 1968), 17.
37. Loveland, *Southern Evangelicals,* 32, 50.
38. Smith, *Killers of the Dream,* 85; and Thompson, "God and the Southern Plantation
System," in *Religion and the Solid South,* ed. Hill, 57–58.

issue forth from urban pulpits, especially in the numerous Baptist and Christian congregations.[39]

Evangelical Protestantism and the values associated with it have maintained the orthogenetic character of southern cities perhaps more than staple agriculture has. By blocking out ideological competitors and by supporting traditional beliefs, southern urban religion helped make southern cities bastions of conservatism—if not reaction—rather than of change, as in cities elsewhere in the United States. Evangelical churchmen, concerned with individual salvation or fearful of disrupting their flocks, generally either ignored or supported the biracial society—slavery in the antebellum period and segregation after the Civil War. Even so-called liberal churchmen in the twentieth century "condemned forces which they felt encouraged religious and social diversity within the city." Since evangelical precepts also divided society into absolutes of good and evil, laymen rarely questioned the status quo of urban society that the church had sanctified as the holy order. "Our first lesson about God made the deepest impression on us," Lillian Smith related. "We were told that He loved us, and then we were told that He would burn us in everlasting flames of hell if we displeased Him." Naturally, every child hoped to avoid that fate. "The best way," Smith concluded, "was never to question anything but always accept what you were told." [40]

The evangelical faiths facilitated the perpetuation of myths—about slavery, the Lost Cause, and the New South. The role of the church complemented that of the ubiquitous boosters who, in their exaggerated rhetoric, revealed the same defensiveness, insecurity, and self-righteousness that the evangelical ecclesiastics exhibited.[41] The "commercial-civic elite," as Blaine A. Brownell called such boosters, flourished in both the Old and the New South but rarely as virulently as in the decades after World War I; their rhetoric adopted religious metaphors (indeed, Paul M. Gaston's New South "Creed" implies a religious connotation), and they proclaimed the ecumenicism of their policies, which generally opposed change.[42] In the early twentieth century, for example, urban leaders converted new methodologies

39. See Erskine Caldwell, *In the Shadow of the Steeple* (London, 1967), 84–85, 129–34; and Bailey, *Southern White Protestantism,* 152–54.

40. Wayne Flynt, "Religion in the Urban South: The Divided Religious Mind of Birmingham, 1900–1930," *Alabama Review,* XXX (April, 1977), 125; Smith, *Killers of the Dream,* 85, 86, 99.

41. See Hill, "The South's Two Cultures," in *Religion and the Solid South,* ed. Hill, 50.

42. See Brownell, *The Urban Ethos,* 47–48; and Paul M. Gaston, *The New South Creed: A Study in Southern Mythmaking* (New York, 1970).

like planning to conservative objectives designed to preserve the existing social and political structure.[43] They dissembled to avoid pursuing policies that could threaten their hegemony. When the Memphis Chamber of Commerce boasted in early 1941 that "there is no housing shortage in Memphis . . . Memphis is well-housed," the city had one of the worst housing shortages in the nation, and nearly four out of every five blacks and one out of three whites were living in substandard housing. Above all, like the ministers, they claimed to be the keepers of the community's welfare, creating an identity between community welfare and the leaders' policies. In this manner, as Richard Sennett has noted, "the image of community is purified of all that might convey a feeling of difference, let alone conflict, on who 'we' are."[44] This was precisely the thrust of evangelical Protestantism, of course: purification, antipathy to change, and a sharp distinction between "we" and "them."

Although boosters and ministers occasionally clashed in the early decades of the twentieth century on, for instance, blue laws, their objectives frequently coincided. It was not unusual to see Bishop Warren A. Candler and the *Manufacturers' Record* agreeing that the Scopes trial was "one of the South's supremest advertisements." The *Record* also noted with approval that the "agnosticism and atheism so prevalent throughout the North and West" was relatively unknown in the South. In smaller urban settlements, like Lubbock, Texas, the interface between preacher and politician was, perhaps, more complete: "They [the ranchers and merchants] and the preachers joined in the enterprise of creating an orderly community safe for churches and secure for business enterprises."[45] Whereas the urban boosters borrowed freely from the church preachings, the ministers, especially after the 1930s,

---

43. See Howard L. Preston, *Automobile Age Atlanta: The Making of a Southern Metropolis, 1900–1935* (Athens, 1979), 102; Blaine A. Brownell, "The Commercial-Civic Elite and City Planning in Atlanta, Memphis, and New Orleans in the 1920s," *Journal of Southern History,* XLI (August, 1975), 339–68; and Christopher Silver, "Urban Planning and Urban Development in the New South: Richmond, 1900–1960" (paper presented at conference on the New South, Norfolk, Va., February, 1978).

44. Memphis Chamber of Commerce, *A Brief Survey of Industrial Opportunities* (Rev. ed.; Memphis, 1941), as quoted in Robert A. Sigafoos, *Cotton Row to Beale Street: A Business History of Memphis* (Memphis, 1979), 208; and Richard Sennett, *The Uses of Disorder: Personal Identity and City Life* (New York, 1970), 33, as quoted in Brownell, *The Urban Ethos,* 219.

45. Warren A. Candler, "Liberalism Proposing to Liberate the South," Nashville (Tenn.) *Christian Advocate,* September 18, 1925, as quoted in Bailey, *Southern White Protestantism,* 91; and Merton L. Dillon, "Religion in Lubbock," in *A History of Lubbock,* ed. Lawrence L. Graves (Lubbock, Tex., 1961), Pt. 3, p. 457, as quoted in Hill, "The South's Two Cultures," in *Religion and the Solid South,* ed. Hill, 30.

used booster promotion tactics in revivals and membership campaigns. Revivals were a most successful business enterprise that required sophisticated organizing and advertising strategies. Although Atlanta novelist Ward Greene despaired of "howling god-hoppers running the town for purity and pep" during the 1930s, revivals were one of the few exciting and lucrative activities in the Depression-ridden South.[46] After World War II, when membership drives occupied an increasing amount of ecclesiastic attention, booster tactics proved especially availing. The Georgia *Christian Index* observed with approval that "many tricks of the advertising trade can be adapted to the promotion of the church and its program."[47]

The close attention urban clerics and boosters paid to citizens' civic and spiritual ideals seems to have exhausted their communitarian spirit. Churchmen and businessmen generally neglected the social needs of their constituents. With a religious philosophy that emphasized individual sin and salvation and a booster creed that stressed public unity for economic development and racial stability, social policies were superfluous, diversionary, and potentially disruptive.[48] Not surprisingly, from the mid-nineteenth century to the present day, per capita expenditures in southern cities, especially for social services, have lagged far behind similar expenditures in other cities. In 1902, for example, at a time of high spiritual and civic revival, no southern city spent the national per capita average for education ($4.37), and most educational spending was one-third to one-half less than that average. From libraries to street paving to public-health services, southern cities traditionally lagged behind cities elsewhere. As late as 1970, no southern city matched or exceeded the national average per capita urban expenditure for public welfare ($11.98).[49]

46. Ward Greene, *Ride the Nightmare* (New York, 1930), 72, as quoted in Blaine A. Brownell, "The Urban South Comes of Age," in *The City in Southern History,* ed. Brownell and Goldfield, 144. Of course, revivalists engaged in promotional activities at least a century earlier, and it may be argued that the economic snake oil peddled by southern urban boosters owed its success to minds already trained and "organized" by effective preachers of the gospel.

47. Macon (Ga.) *Christian Index,* December 10, 1942, as quoted in Bailey, *Southern White Protestantism,* 132.

48. On the poor social record of the southern "civic-religious" leadership, especially in the twentieth century, see Caldwell, *In the Shadow,* 84–85; Brownell, "The Urban South Comes of Age," in *The City in Southern History,* ed. Brownell and Goldfield, 153; and Hill, "The South's Two Cultures," in *Religion and the Solid South,* ed. Hill, 36, 41, 48–49. On the nineteenth century, see Loveland, *Southern Evangelicals,* 119, 161–62, and Scott, "Women, Religion, and Social Change," in *Religion and the Solid South,* ed. Hill, 116.

49. On inadequate social services in the antebellum period, see Goldfield, "American Urban Dream," in *The City in Southern History,* ed. Brownell and Goldfield, 68–83; in the

The urban South's dismal performance on social services restricted urban development. Nobel laureate economist Theodore W. Schultz devised the concept of human capital as an essential programming element for developing areas.[50] "The decisive factor," Schultz declared, "is the improvement in population quality."[51] Education, health, and housing of the poor are the most important improvements and investments in human capital. The paucity of southern investments in these areas has reduced the quality of the regional population and, hence, its ability to contribute to the region's development.

The aversion of the civic and religious elite to such investments in human capital resulted not only from the philosophical bases of booster and evangelical ideology but also from the immense presence of a biracial society. Too much improvement in population quality implied the threat of population equality—a situation that would have eroded "civic-religious" hegemony and, therefore, the foundation of regional society. Accordingly, the region's economic and religious institutions sought to regulate, separate, isolate, and subjugate the black race. Since urban life created greater opportunities for racial interaction, urban whites were as vigilant as, if not more vigilant than, their rural counterparts in maintaining the biracial society.[52]

The biracial society in an urban setting restricted blacks to certain low-level occupations. Agriculture and its institutions—slavery in the antebellum era and sharecropping, tenancy, crop lien, and peonage following the Civil War—restricted the free flow of black labor to the cities. This restriction provides yet another example of how agriculture controlled the economic life of the city. Having migrated to the city, blacks found that their primarily

---

late nineteenth century, see Howard N. Rabinowitz, "Continuity and Change: Southern Urban Development, 1860–1900," *ibid.,* 110–12; and for the contemporary southern city, see Peter A. Lupsha and William J. Siembieda, "The Poverty of Public Services in the Land of Plenty: An Analogy and Interpretation," in *The Rise of the Sunbelt Cities,* ed. David C. Perry and Alfred J. Watkins (Beverly Hills, 1977), 173.

50. The clearest statement of this concept appears in Theodore W. Schultz, "The Economics of Being Poor," Nobel Lecture, December 8, 1979, Stockholm, Sweden.

51. *Ibid.,* 2. Demographic shifts to the Sun Belt have not upset the regional value of structure but have tended to reinforce it instead. The predominantly suburban and white-collar migrants have sought low taxes and racial homogeneity as much as employment opportunities and a temperate climate.

52. See Brownell, "The Urban South Comes of Age," in *The City in Southern History,* ed. Brownell and Goldfield, 146; and Rabinowitz, "Continuity and Change," *ibid.,* 122.

agrarian skills were ill suited to urban jobs and ensured them employment only in low-status occupations.[53] The biracial system almost guaranteed that blacks stayed there. Although such cities as Charleston and New Orleans had a small black elite in the antebellum period, blacks' occupational status suffered drastically with emancipation and increased migration to the cities.[54] The existence of such a relatively large body of marginal consumers further lowered demand and capital accumulation in the urban South and provided an economic excuse for the poor, selective quality of public services.

The Civil War also produced changes in blacks' residential status in ways that solidified the biracial society. The change from exclusion to segregation, which Howard N. Rabinowitz has advanced as the regional biracial pattern after 1865,[55] allowed blacks access to some features of urban life that they had not enjoyed prior to the Civil War but did not, however, signify an urban departure from traditional regional racial mores. As orthogenetic entities, southern cities "carried forward," rather than transformed, regional racial patterns. Segregation was such an adjustment, much as crop lien and peonage were racial accommodations in the rural districts. Segregation may have allowed blacks greater participation, but they could participate only on white terms. Moreover, segregation generalized blacks, ruthlessly isolating them from the mainstream of urban life; residential patterns show most clearly the impact of segregation.

Black residential patterns in southern cities were distinctive, resembling more the spatial characteristics of lower-caste groups in developing societies than the neighborhood arrangements of northern cities. Some residential dispersion existed in the antebellum era due to the necessities of slavery. Rather than the single large ghetto found in northern cities, concentrations of blacks that reflected the scattered nature of undesirable housing sites

53. On the limits that agricultural labor systems placed upon both blacks and urbanization, see Claudia D. Goldin, *Urban Slavery in the American South, 1820–1860: A Quantitative History* (Chicago, 1976); Jay R. Mandle, *The Roots of Black Poverty: The Southern Plantation Economy After the Civil War* (Durham, 1978); Roger L. Ransom and Richard Sutch, *One Kind of Freedom: The Economic Consequences of Emancipation* (Cambridge, Eng., 1977); Gavin Wright, *The Political Economy of the Cotton South: Households, Markets, and Wealth in the Nineteenth Century* (New York, 1978); and Ralph V. Anderson and Robert E. Gallman, "Slaves as Fixed Capital: Slave Labor and Southern Economic Development," *Journal of Southern History,* XLIV (February, 1977), 24–46.

54. For a superb account of blacks and southern cities, see Howard N. Rabinowitz, *Race Relations in the Urban South, 1865–1890* (New York, 1978).

55. Rabinowitz, *ibid.,* esp. 125–254.

emerged in the postbellum South. In 1877, the Nashville Board of Health reported that the city's blacks "reside mainly in old stables, situated upon alleys in the midst of privy vaults, or in wooden shanties, a remnant of war times, or in huts closely crowded together on the outskirts."[56] These "neighborhoods," especially those on the periphery, presented a primitive, rural appearance: the dirt roads, outdoor facilities, poor drainage, and frame "double-pen" houses or "shotgun shacks" differed little from sharecroppers' dwellings. And by the 1890s, the lines dividing black and white residential communities had hardened.[57]

Housing clusters continued to characterize black residential patterns in the urban South during the twentieth century—typically, one large cluster in the most decrepit area near the center, surrounded by smaller clusters moving outward toward the periphery. The peripheral neighborhoods were frequently either the "temporary" communities that sprouted to house freedmen immediately following the Civil War or erstwhile rural areas annexed by the southern cities' voracious appetite for land. In some of the older cities like Savannah and Charleston, reminders of the antebellum past persisted in the 1920s and 1930s, as long fingers of blacks' residences intruded into white neighborhoods on the narrow lanes behind the major residential thoroughfares. But these vestiges disappeared after World War II as whites began to abandon the centers, and residential patterns similar to those in newer southern cities replaced such antebellum holdovers. Birmingham, for example, had a primary black neighborhood adjacent to the downtown area and several smaller clusters scattered wherever poor urban land existed.[58]

The isolation of blacks from white areas has increased during this century. By 1960, only 5.5 percent of the southern urban population resided in

56. *Report of the Board of Health, 1876–1877* (Nashville, 1877), 108, as quoted *ibid.*, 118.

57. On black residential patterns during the late nineteenth and early twentieth centuries, see John Kellogg, "Negro Urban Clusters in the Postbellum South," *Geographical Review,* LXVIII (July, 1978), 311–21; and Zane L. Miller, "Urban Blacks in the South, 1865–1920: The Richmond, Savannah, New Orleans, Louisville, and Birmingham Experience," in *The New Urban History: Quantitative Explorations by American Historians,* ed. Leo F. Schnore (Princeton, 1975), 199–200.

58. On black residential patterns since the 1920s, see Brownell, *The Urban Ethos in the South,* 26–28; Ronald H. Bayor, "Ethnic Residential Patterns in Atlanta, 1880–1940," *Georgia Historical Quarterly,* XLIV (Fall, 1979), 435–47; Nicholas J. Demerath and Harlan W. Gilmore, "The Ecology of Southern Cities," in *The Urban South,* ed. Vance and Demerath, 135–64; and Dana F. White and Timothy J. Crimmins, "Urban Structure: Atlanta," *Journal of Urban History,* II (February, 1976), 231–52.

integrated neighborhoods, compared with 31.8 percent in the Northeast. Although black neighborhoods in the South were more dispersed than they were in northern cities, they were usually more segregated. In addition, southern urban blacks are still more likely to be peripheral and suburban residents than their northern counterparts are—a legacy from Reconstruction and annexation. In 1970, 14 percent of the South's metropolitan black population resided on the metropolitan periphery, compared with only 3 percent in the Northeast.[59]

Black ecological patterns in southern cities in the past one hundred years have resembled those found in preindustrial societies of the Third World. Peripheral settlement in poor housing is a common spatial phenomenon. Analysis of social areas—that is, census tracts and neighborhoods—in cities indicates that southern cities conform to non-Western patterns primarily because of the presence and the character of the black population: a separate and unequal society within the region and its cities. The virtual identity between ethnicity and socioeconomic status—a characteristic of social areas in underdeveloped societies—describes the separate black communities in southern cities.[60] Sociologist Allison Davis' description of this convergence in 1941 could be applied to Indian or Middle Eastern outcast groups: "Life in the communities in the Deep South follows an orderly pattern. The inhabitants live in a social world clearly divided into two ranks, the white caste and the Negro caste. These colored castes share disproportionately in the privileges and obligations of labor, school, and government."[61] Regional biracialism has given the southern city a non-Western character, perhaps more than any other regional characteristic has.

In 1941, researchers undoubtedly believed that biracialism had created a unique urban social environment that would persist as long as color remained a decisive factor in regional life. But biracialism possessed within it, ironically, the potential for regional and urban change. Blacks themselves, first alone and then with outside support, produced alterations in southern urban society, especially following World War II. The vestiges of biracialism remain, however, and race continues to play its distinctive role in the region and its cities. Black political power, for example, is more shadow than sub-

59. Carl Abbott, "Colonial Place, Norfolk: Residential Integration in a Southern Urban Neighborhood" (typescript kindly provided by the author).

60. For a discussion of Third World urban ecological patterns, see Berry and Kasarda, *Contemporary Urban Ecology*, 154–55.

61. Davis *et al., Deep South: A Social Anthropological Study of Caste and Class* (Chicago, 1941), 539, as quoted in Berry and Kasarda, *Contemporary Urban Ecology*, 155.

stance. Blacks have secured only a minimum of white political support. In 1979, when Birmingham elected its first black mayor, Richard Arrington, only 10 percent of the white voters supported him. Black political strength and security depend on sheer numbers, not on changing attitudes in the white community. Several southern cities have already attempted to push through reapportionment, at-large elections, annexation, and consolidation schemes under the guise of political reform, when actually these policies have been aimed at diluting black political strength.[62]

The stakes of urban political power, however, are becoming less important. When blacks finally ascend to the highest offices in urban politics, they soon discover that they have inherited, as historian James C. Cobb has noted, "more of a problem than a prize."[63] As the pace of annexation slows and as white residents and commerce continue to abandon the southern city, economic problems mount. Black political power is circumscribed by the absence of black economic power.

Blacks' economic deficiency is shared, in a relative sense, by the region and its cities. Rural agricultural patterns and values (especially evangelical Protestantism) and biracialism have limited capital accumulation and have skewed investment patterns to labor and land, rather than to specifically city-building enterprises. A persistent colonialism has reinforced these indigenous factors—ruralism and biracialism—to form the third major element in the region's eternal triangle.

Colonialism denotes a colonial power. In the eighteenth century, it was the British, but in the nineteenth and twentieth centuries, it has been—and is—the North. The development of a national economy, centered in New York beginning in the 1840s, fastened a type of regional specialization upon the South that remains with it to the present day. The South as the producer and occasionally the basic processor of raw materials has been in continuous economic servitude to the North not only for manufactured products but also for all of the financial, credit, legal, accounting, and factoring services that attend a national economy. Cities are the "instruments" of regional articulation in a national economy and set the economic tone for the region.

62. For discussions concerning the limits of black political power in the urban south, see Numan V. Bartley, "Atlanta Elections and Georgia Political Trends," *New South*, XXV (Fall, 1970), 22–30; Cobb, "Urbanization and the Changing South," 253–66; Samuel Dubois Cook, "Southern Politics Since 1954: A Note on Change and Continuity," in *Two Decades of Change*, ed. Lander and Calhoun, 5–19; and Virginia H. Hein, "The Image of 'A City too Busy to Hate': Atlanta in the 1960s," *Phylon*, XXXIII (Fall, 1972), 205–21.

63. Cobb, "Urbanization and the Changing South," 262.

Thus, cities were regional colonial headquarters as the South sank deeper into economic dependence. Southern cities served as collection points for and funnels to northern centers and as distribution points for the return flow. This system limited capital accumulation in the region, which reduced the opportunities for the region to develop beyond its colonial economy. And everything limited urbanization. In fact, as the national economy grew after the Civil War, southern cities shrunk relative to their northern (national) counterparts.[64]

Northern investors encouraged the economic development of the region only insofar as it enhanced their dominance in the national economy. After the Civil War, northern control of southern railroads, for example, ensured profitable and speedy transfers to and from the colonial region. In the antebellum era, however, local investors dominated southern railroad directorships. The Panic of 1873 dealt struggling southern-owned companies a financial death blow, and northern capital willingly revived the corpse. In 1870, northerners constituted only 19 percent of the South's railroad directors; by 1880, that percentage had reached 37. By 1900, when financial capitalists like J. P. Morgan consolidated and reorganized the nation's railroad systems, northern financiers controlled the South's five major rail lines, and 60 percent of the directors were northerners.[65]

The patterns of northern investment in the South were selective, but even so, they restricted southern industrial development and hence urbanization. The potential of Birmingham's steel production frightened rather than attracted northern investors in the late 1870s. Whatever advances the city made during the next decade occurred because of local capital. Eventually, during the early years of the twentieth century, the Pittsburgh Plus system and financial control by U.S. Steel effectively limited Birmingham competition and assured northern industrial superiority. Textile milling became a northern investment beneficiary in the twentieth century. But as an industrial activity that occurred in a predominantly rural setting, it generated relatively little capital for the region or its cities. Low wages coincided with

---

64. For a discussion of the formation of the national economy and its impact upon the antebellum southern city and region, see David R. Goldfield, *Urban Growth in the Age of Sectionalism: Virginia, 1847–1861* (Baton Rouge, 1977), 235–46; Allan R. Pred, *The Spatial Dynamics of U.S. Urban-Industrial Growth, 1800–1914* (Cambridge, Mass., 1966); and Louis B. Schmidt, "Internal Commerce and the Development of the National Economy Before 1860," *Journal of Political Economy,* XLII (August, 1939), 798–822.

65. Rabinowitz, "Continuity and Change," in *The City in Southern History,* ed. Brownell and Goldfield, 102, 105–106.

low investments in human capital. The textile mill was an industrial plantation with all of the same human debilities as its agricultural counterpart.[66]

The Great Depression revealed the shallowness of the South's economy. The region's cities were the nation's "basket cases" during the 1930s. The Depression also resulted in a modification of the national economy as the federal government became a major force for economic redistribution. Federal grants accelerated the regionalization of the national economy. Southern cities were the direct beneficiaries of this process as the federal government paid for capital facilities that northern cities had bought for themselves in earlier decades and on which they were still paying off the debt. The almost-free modernization that southern cities received proved to be an important economic advantage in subsequent decades.[67]

During World War II, the redistribution of national economic advantages continued as military bases and, more significantly, industry both demonstrated the increased federal presence. Indeed, federal assistance to southern urban industry effectively primed the pump of the regional and urban economies. The government helped stimulate new industries as, for example, in Houston and released old ones from colonial restrictions, as in Birmingham. Military spending in southern cities encouraged the development of electronics research and manufacturing firms, scientific equipment companies, and aeronautics machinery plants. The growth of high-technology industry has had a positive impact on a region traditionally burdened with low-technology, low-wage industries. Between 1940 and 1960, the high-wage industrial sector increased by 180 percent in the South (the national rate was 92 percent for the same two decades), and the industrial labor force in the region grew by more than one and a half million, with almost 90 percent of these jobs in high-wage industries. Moreover, these industries were primarily urban-based. By 1960, therefore, low-wage industries accounted for only two out of every five manufacturing jobs in the region.[68]

The multiplier effect of federal economic policy did not ensure regional deliverance from the inequities and unbalanced development of the old

66. On the patterns of late-nineteenth-century northern investment in the South, see Miller, *Memphis During the Progressive Era,* 43; Jonathan Weiner, *Social Origins of the New South; Alabama, 1860–1885* (Baton Rouge, 1978), 162–84; and Weiher, "The Cotton Industry and Southern Urbanization," 124.

67. See Tindall, *Emergence of the New South,* 476–77.

68. See Lorin A. Thompson, "Urbanization, Occupational Shift, and Economic Progress," in *The Urban South,* ed. Vance and Demerath, 38–53; and Alfred J. Watkins and David C. Perry, "Regional Change and the Impact of Uneven Urban Development," in *The Rise of the Sunbelt Cities,* ed. Perry and Watkins, 19–54.

ante- and postbellum industrial regime. Just as vestiges of the biracial society cling like Spanish moss to the urban South, traditional industrial patterns based on a rural, colonial economy linger on. The textile mill culture persists. In South Carolina, West German flags fly in Spartanburg, Kuwaiti money flows on Kiawah, and boosters prattle innocently yet revealingly, saying, "What we've done here ought to be done in the underdeveloped countries. We established a good political atmosphere and showed we had a real commitment to economic growth." And indeed, the industrialization that came in a wave during the 1960s and 1970s has transformed South Carolina from a poor agricultural state to a poor industrial state. The state ranks forty-sixth in per capita income. The average mill worker earns 20 percent less per hour than the national average. South Carolina continues to lead the nation in illiteracy and infant mortality. Manufacturing remains primarily a nonmetropolitan—that is, small-town—activity.[69]

Colonialism persists in other areas of the southern economy as well. Although the growth of air and truck transport after World War II reduced the railroad's dominance over southern cities, other aspects of the national economy have a distinctly northern flow. The region's cities depend upon northern banks to finance large-scale operations. Most of Houston's corporations list a New York institution as their principal bank. Any firm in the urban South with international business connections invariably goes through New York banks. Corporations in southern cities patronize New York and Washington law offices. They also use New York accounting firms. All of this means that northern interests continue to control large-scale investment in southern cities. With major banking, accounting, and legal services for the South still based in the North, capital accumulation remains a regional problem. Economist Charles F. Haywood asserted in 1978 that "the South has long been a region of capital shortage. It remains so today and will be so for some years to come." Haywood suggested that the connection of the major southern urban corporations with the national banking network need not impede their growth. But activities "that are heavily dependent on local sources of funds—housing, local businesses, and . . . local government"—may experience some difficulty.[70] The emergence of interstate banking in the 1980s and especially the rise of Charlotte-based NationsBank in the 1990s have altered this colonial pattern to a great degree.

69. Washington *Post,* April 30, 1978. Also see Dale Newman, "Work and Community Life in a Southern Textile Town," *Labor History,* XXXVIII (Spring, 1978), 204–205.

70. Robert B. Cohen, "Multinational Corporations, International Finance, and the Sunbelt," in *The Rise of the Sunbelt Cities,* ed. Perry and Watkins, 211–26; Charles F. Haywood, "The South's Future Capital Needs," *Southern Living,* January 1978, pp. 30–32.

The comparison advanced above between South Carolina and under-developed countries is apt because the South's subsidiary role in the national economy also corresponds in some degree to the role of underdeveloped nations in the world economy. Historian John H. Coatsworth, for example, identified two major obstacles to economic development in nineteenth-century Mexico—"inadequate transport and inefficient economic organi-zation." The South has been afflicted by both, and its cities have been similarly victimized. An over-reliance on rivers and the late development of a railroad system retarded regional economic development. The unor-ganized nature of a southern economy based on the individual decisions of staple entrepreneurs, the restrictions on the mobility of capital and labor, and the low priority of innovation or of any new ideas contributed to what Coatsworth termed for Mexico "inefficient economic organization."[71] Thus, the rural value system helped bring about the North's colonial control of the South. As historian David Bertelson has maintained, "The South was an individualistic, chaotic economy in an America whose other inhabitants held some idea of community purpose."[72]

Mexico ultimately extricated itself from its backwardness by capitalizing on its own economic vulnerability, which provided "vast comparative ad-vantages for foreign technology and resources." In the South, especially after the Civil War, northern capital and expertise produced a transportation system and organized the production and processing systems to suit north-ern commercial and industrial requirements. This relieved southern back-wardness to some degree—but not regional dependence. Coatsworth con-cluded that, although Mexico was not likely to create its own viable, self-sufficient economy, the decision to turn to foreign entrepreneurs and capital produced "a long-term dependence on foreign technology, re-sources, and markets."[73] By 1865, it was obviously too late for the South to secure regional economic independence or even parity; the result was "long-term" dependence on the North. The role of southern cities and the limits this economic system placed on their development reflected the re-gional situation of economic subservience.[74]

71. John H. Coatsworth, "Obstacles to Economic Growth in Nineteenth-Century Mexico," *American Historical Review,* LXXXIII (February, 1978), 91, 92.
72. For this statement of Bertelson's views in *The Lazy South* (New York, 1967), 82–83, see Smiley, "Quest for a Central Theme," 317.
73. Coatsworth, "Obstacles to Economic Growth," 100.
74. The interaction between colonialism and urbanization in the South is evident from the inability of geographers successfully to apply central place theory to the southern urban system, which evinces a colonial, rather than a modern, industrial pattern; see Browning and

Southerners were aware of their economic inferiority and wrestled with its consequences for more than a century. Antebellum southerners like Virginian George Fitzhugh and New Orleans journalist J. D. B. De Bow sought to remove from the South its "indelible brand of degradation" by developing the region's cities, industries, and commercial facilities and connections.[75] The Civil War dashed dreams of economic equality, and urban-based boosters like Henry W. Grady and Richard H. Edmonds were more accommodationist in their approach to colonialism. Their extravagant claims and grandiose programs produced few results, but their rhetoric enabled local leaders to wrap themselves in the mantle of southern patriotism and maintain a biracial society to secure elusive and illusory economic objectives.

It was cruel irony that the urban boosters' very striving for economic success only deepened their region's economic inferiority. They auctioned their labor to the lowest industrial bidder, sacrificed services to maintain tax advantages for prospective investors, and allowed polluters and exploiters to carve up and destroy urban space and environment—from the railroad tracks dominating the central business districts to the once-beautiful rivers.[76] The economic accomplishments of the New South and its Sun Belt offspring have barely changed—or have sometimes altered for the worse—region and city. Progress and tradition, like region and city, are bound together. The battle with colonialism has been, as Pat Watters noted, a "misguided effort of the South to catch up to something that was essentially sorry and shabby in the rest of America."[77]

The promising future that social scientists predicted for the South as a result of urbanization remains elusive. The prophecies have foundered because they assumed that southern cities were distinct from their region. They

---

Garrity, "Southern Urban Evolution"; and Berry and Kasarda, *Contemporary Urban Ecology,* 391. On the confusion resulting from the application of ahistorical geographic models to the southern urban system, also see Rudolf Heberle, "The Mainsprings of Southern Urbanization," in *The Urban South,* ed. Vance and Demerath, 6–23.

75. Alexandria *Gazette,* February 7, 1854. Also see George Fitzhugh, *Cannibals All! or Slaves without Masters* (New York, 1857), 59, and *Sociology for the South: or, The Failure of Free Society* (New York, 1854), 136, 141–42; and Buckner H. Payne, "Contests for the Trade of the Mississippi Valley," *De Bow's Review,* III (February, 1847), 98.

76. On the continued exploitation of labor and land, see Watters, *The South and the Nation,* 94–97; Lupsha and Siembieda, "The Poverty of Public Services," in *The Rise of the Sunbelt Cities,* ed. Perry and Watkins, 176–77; David C. Perry and Alfred J. Watkins, "People, Profit, and the Rise of the Sunbelt Cities," in *The Rise of the Sunbelt Cities,* ed. Perry and Watkins, 277–305; and the New York *Times,* May 12, 1978.

77. Watters, *The South and the Nation,* 530.

were—and are—not. Since the eighteenth century, southern cities were inextricably tied to and in some aspects indistinguishable from the southern countryside. What southern cities did not do for the region in the twentieth century is a measure of the continued strength of this connection. Rural values dominated southern cities because rural people inhabited southern cities. Evangelical Protestantism fired the souls of frontiersmen and townsmen alike. Cities adopted biracialism wholeheartedly. Were it not for the persistence of the primary victims of the biracial society—blacks—and the timely, if somewhat halting, assistance of the federal government, urban society per se would not have removed many of the obstacles that biracialism signified for blacks. Resistance to integration was perhaps more sophisticated in southern cities than in the countryside, but it was equally if not more effective. Finally, there were hopes that southern cities would lead the region to economic parity. But the cities, rather than becoming regional leaders, are lagging behind regional growth.[78] In addition, the southern city still performs a secondary role in the national economy, especially in the area of capital investment and financial services.

Ruralism, race, and colonialism have always characterized a distinctive region and its cities, although these factors and their impact upon urbanization have not been immutable over time. The shift to mechanized agriculture, the growth of modernism in religion, the evolution of biracialism from slavery to exclusion to segregation to integration, and the altered balance in the national economy since the Depression and World War II have affected migration patterns, ways of thought, racial interaction, and capital accumulation in the region—and, hence, urbanization. Nevertheless, these regional elements persist and have collectively produced a particular and limited urbanization that exists in the region to this day. The regional model of urbanization advanced in this essay could provide a helpful framework for further study of the linkages between these elements and urbanization over time. In addition, the model should prove useful in relating the distinctive characteristics of southern urbanization to urban growth in cities and regions outside of North America. Moving from a world view back to Atlanta, the regional model eliminates the incongruity of Pat Watters' bucolic neighborhood set peacefully in the shadows of those imposing downtown skyscrapers. The southern city and the South sprang from the same soil, sheltered the same people, and suffered the same burdens—both self-inflicted and superimposed.

---

78. See Gurney Breckenfeld, "Refilling the Metropolitan Doughnut," in *The Rise of the Sunbelt Cities,* ed. Perry and Watkins, 238–39.

URBAN-RURAL RELATIONS IN OLD VIRGINIA

In the early decades of English settlement in North America, settlers appreciated the efficacy of harmony between urban and rural environments. Planners of colonial cities were careful to preserve the country aspects of city life. From colonial New England to Savannah, Georgia, city-builders incorporated agricultural patches, greenery, and airy corridors in their urban plans. Population pressures combined with profit-hungry speculators and declining zeal, however, to subvert the intention of the early planners.[1] It seems as if town and country have been drifting apart ever since—physically and intellectually. Americans have juxtaposed urban and rural as polar opposites to a point where the division is fixed in the American consciousness.

Until recently, historians have accepted the urban-rural polarity, regardless of whether they followed the tradition of Frederick Jackson Turner or Arthur Schlesinger, Sr.[2] Since the 1960s, scholars have attempted to study town and country in connection with each other rather than in isolation from or opposition to each other. The results of this scholarship cast new light on both environments and provided a perspective on regional and national economic relationships.[3]

1. John W. Reps, *Town Planning in Frontier America* (Princeton, 1969).
2. Richard C. Wade, "An Agenda for Urban History," in *American History: Retrospect and Prospect,* ed. George Athan Billias and Gerald N. Grob (New York, 1971), 367–98.
3. See, for example, Michael P. Conzen, *Frontier Farming in an Urban Shadow: The Influence of Madison's Proximity on the Agricultural Development of Blooming Grove, Wisconsin* (Madison, 1971); Robert R. Dykstra, *The Cattle Towns* (New York, 1968); Richard C. Wade, *The Urban Frontier: Pioneer Life in Early Pittsburgh, Cincinnati, Lexington, and St. Louis* (Cambridge, Mass.,

Scholars have conducted much of the work on urban–rural relations within the framework of the frontier. The necessity of an urban reinterpretation of the frontier and the obvious interdependence of metropolis and hinterland in a frontier context have made the frontier an ideal laboratory for the study of urban–rural interaction. Richard C. Wade's *The Urban Frontier,* Robert R. Dykstra's *The Cattle Towns,* and Kenneth W. Wheeler's *To Wear a City's Crown* have been particularly helpful in illuminating the complexities of town-country interdependence. We now know, for example, that urban rivalry on the frontier was a considerably more powerful force than urban–rural animosity; that cities influenced the nature of the frontier economy to a greater extent than their rural neighbors; and that only rarely could urban and rural residents, respectively, muster unanimity on any issue. Finally, we can better understand the role of urban–rural cooperation on a regional level in facilitating the development of a national economy in the nineteenth century.

Considering the valuable return obtained from frontier studies, it would seem appropriate to inquire whether other sections of nineteenth-century America exhibited similar urban–rural cooperation and conflict. Such studies could demonstrate that urban–rural interdependence was a national phenomenon of which the frontier was only its most patent setting. The antebellum South seems an especially fruitful and untouched area of inquiry. Scholars have observed urban–rural relations on the borders of the Old South but have not delved into the more traditional southern states.[4] The reasons for the dearth of scholarship on urban–rural relations in the antebellum South emphasize the necessity of such studies.

Students of the Old South have depicted that region as dominated by the plantation—both as an agricultural unit and as a political force—or at the very least, by rural society. Agricultural slavery, the handmaiden of the plantation, has similarly been the focus of scholarly treatment of the Old South. Writers have mentioned the antebellum southern city as an afterthought or as an example of the debilitating effects of plantation slavery on urban development. Urban–rural relations were addressed only in terms of the planters' sumptuous urban residences and the hostility or indifference of rural leaders toward the city.[5]

1959); Kenneth W. Wheeler, *To Wear a City's Crown: The Beginnings of Urban Growth in Texas* (Cambridge, Mass., 1968); Robert R. Dykstra, "Town-Country Conflict: A Hidden Dimension in American Social History," *Agricultural History,* XXXVIII (July, 1964), 195–204.

4. Wade, *Urban Frontier;* Wheeler, *To Wear a City's Crown.*

5. See, for example, Wilbur J. Cash, *The Mind of the South* (New York, 1941), 99;

Virginia in the late antebellum period presents an opportunity to study urban-rural interdependence in an area removed from the frontier, as well as to explore urban activities in an allegedly rural-dominated society. Virginia was the largest slaveholding state in the Union and the most urbanized state in the South. During the decade prior to the Civil War, when the fires of sectionalism presumably consumed whatever progressive southern spirit existed, Virginians in town and country advanced a multitude of schemes to regain their lost preeminence and to establish a defense against northern verbal and physical aggression. Urban-rural cooperation formed a major theme of Virginia's economic renaissance that outweighed areas of conflict between the two environments. By the time of the Civil War, a consensus of opinion had formed between town and country in the Old Dominion as a result of growing interdependence among commerce, finance, labor, the press, and personal life.

Commerce was the foundation and sectionalism the stimulus of the urban-rural entente in late antebellum Virginia. Since ancient times, access to market has formed bonds of mutual interest between town and country. In nineteenth-century America, this traditional relationship took on a new importance as cities sought to rationalize and expand their trade network; agriculturists, spurred by technology and education, produced increasingly for urban market centers.[6] Urban and rural Virginia arrived at this point during the decade before the Civil War.

That the wedding of town and country took place in the context of sectionalism placed added urgency on the attempts of urban and rural Virginia to effect a mutually beneficial union. "Agriculture is commerce, and commerce is agriculture. . . . Possessed of this fundamental truth the days of our commercial vassalage are numbered," Virginia's oracle, the Richmond *Enquirer,* proclaimed in 1859. Economic prosperity and commercial independence would accrue from a town-country union. "True independence," observed Francis Mallory, a Tidewater political leader, "must be

---

Charles N. Glaab and A. Theodore Brown, *A History of Urban America* (New York, 1967), 36; Eugene Genovese, *The Political Economy of Slavery* (New York, 1965), and *The World the Slaveholders Made: Two Essays in Interpretation* (New York, 1969); Julius Rubin, "Growth and Expansion of Urban Centers," in *The Growth of the Seaport Cities, 1790–1825,* ed. David R. Gilchrist (Charlottesville, 1967), 3–21. For a recent exception to the general trend, see Blaine A. Brownell, "Urbanization in the South: A Unique Experience?" *Mississippi Quarterly,* XXVI (Spring, 1973), 105–20.

6. See Douglass C. North, *The Economic Growth of the United States, 1790–1860* (Englewood Cliffs, N.J., 1961); George Rogers Taylor, *The Transportation Revolution, 1815–1860* (New York, 1951).

based on power, and no State living in commercial vassalage to others can long preserve the property and liberty of its citizens." The first step toward alleviating this unfavorable position was to "let the merchants and the farmers of the South but *unite,* and they have it in their power completely to coerce both the North and grasping Britain."[7]

Iron forged the initial unity between farmer and merchant. The railroad was the avenue of commercial prosperity in mid-nineteenth-century America, and both farmer and merchant viewed the Iron Horse with a respect that approached reverence. Virginians found they could agree with Charles Sumner, a Massachusetts senator, when he declared, "Under God, the [rail] road and the schoolmaster are the two chief agents of human improvements."[8] Americans believed that railroads would transform the countryside and build cities. C. S. Tarpley, a Mississippi agriculturist, presumed that a railroad connection with New Orleans would transform central Mississippi from an area of plantation monoculture to a region of small, diversified farms.[9] The *Enquirer* was equally sanguine about the benefits of railroads: "We must have commerce and manufactures. We need no longer depend on abolitionists for everything we use. . . . Railroads will do this for us, and will kill abolition in Congress."[10] Little wonder that Americans greeted completion of rail lines with a singular enthusiasm that underscored the urban-rural union.[11]

Whatever else their supporters may have claimed for them, railroads greatly facilitated communication between rural and urban residents. As Henry Varnum Poor, the nation's leading railroad expert, put it: "Railroads . . . are necessary to farming communities in creating a value for their products, in opening a market for them. They explain the rapid growth of cities that are the *termini* of a large number of railroads." Easier access to market generally meant increased agricultural production, greater inventory for merchants, increased value of real estate, and cheaper transportation costs. Urban and rural Virginians appreciated these benefits and noted the effects of closer town-country commercial ties. Richard Irby, a Tidewater farmer

7. Richmond *Enquirer,* October 21, 1859; Norfolk *American Beacon,* March 15, 1854; Richmond *Enquirer,* October 17, 1851.

8. Charles Sumner, "Influence of Railroads," *Hunt's Merchants' Magazine and Commercial Review,* XXVI (July, 1852), 506–507, hereinafter cited as *Hunt's.*

9. Merl E. Reed, *New Orleans and the Railroads: The Struggle for Commercial Empire, 1830–1860* (Baton Rouge, 1966), 88–89.

10. Richmond *Enquirer,* August 28, 1855.

11. *Ibid.,* December 20, 1850; see also David G. McComb, *Houston: The Bayou City* (Austin, 1969), 41.

and merchant, averred that the Southside Railroad, from Petersburg to Lynchburg, was "a great boon to farmers who were prior to this cut off from market for half the year, but now could ship their crops at any time at a cost less than half what it was before the railroad was built." Charles W. Dabney, a Piedmont planter, was equally laudatory about improved communication with Virginia's cities since the late 1840s: "We had such a necessity for improved modes of transit, as you will hardly realize now. . . . It was then bad enough for the farmers to take their little crops of wheat and tobacco through the summer heat and dust to the market town, the vehicles returning empty. Now we are part and parcel of the great commercial-agricultural world—fetching and carrying at all seasons."[12]

Rural manufacturers and miners in Virginia also looked forward to improved communications with Alexandria, Lynchburg, Norfolk, and Richmond. Operators of coal fields in the upper Valley, lead mines in southwest Virginia, and rural furnaces throughout Piedmont Virginia hoped to supply urban Virginians with fuel and raw materials for nascent heavy industry. Without a ready market, rural mineral resources would be underexploited.[13]

The benefits emanating from improved access to market reverberated throughout the state to such a degree that lack of such facilities seemed a local disaster. Railroad schemes proliferated as farmers and country merchants pressured their representatives to secure an avenue to the metropolis. In turn, rural politicians succeeded in exploiting the issue of access to market before their constituents.[14]

Just as rural Virginians eagerly sought urban markets, so urban Virginians sought rural markets. The Old Dominion's cities looked forward to ex-

12. Henry Varnum Poor, "Effect of Railroads on Commercial Cities," *Hunt's*, XXVII (November, 1852), 249. Richmond *Enquirer*, April 4, 1854; B. M. Jones, *Railroads: Considered in Regard to Their Effects upon the Value of Land in Increasing Production, Cheapening Transportation, Preventing Emigration and Investments for Capital* (Richmond, 1860); Richard Irby, "Recollection of Men, Places, and Events, 1845–1900" (MS in Richard Irby Papers, Alderman Library, University of Virginia); Charles W. Dabney to Robert L. Dabney, March 29, 1853, in Charles W. Dabney Papers, Southern Historical Collection, University of North Carolina Library.

13. "Statement Relating to Certain Lead Interests in Virginia, 1853" (MS in Campbell-Preston Papers, Library of Congress); Leesburg *Democratic Mirror*, January 5, 1859; Richmond *Daily Dispatch*, January 18, 1860; Charles B. Dew, "Disciplining Slave Iron Workers in the Antebellum South: Coercion, Conciliation, and Accommodation" (paper delivered at the annual convention of the Organization of American Historians, 1973).

14. Alexandria *Gazette*, June 4, 1857; Fincastle *Democrat*, February 23, 1848; Charles W. Dabney to Robert L. Dabney, March 14, 1851, in Dabney Papers; Robert A. Banks to James L. Kemper, January 13, 1854 (James L. Kemper Collection, Alderman Library, University of Virginia); Richmond *Daily Dispatch*, April 6, 1860, May 19, 1860; quoted in Lynchburg *Virginian*, August 25, 1851; Richmond *Daily Dispatch*, October 1, 1855.

panded investment in manufactures, growth of hinterland trade, increased property values, and a prosperous mercantile community as a result of reciprocal trade. The guano trade provides an example of the multiplier effect of reciprocal trade. The farmer's demand for the organic fertilizer resulted in increased direct importation into the ports of Norfolk, Richmond, and Alexandria, where railroad cars waited to speed the product to country merchants or to farmers. The fruits of guano fertilization—increased crop yields on heretofore undernourished soils—found their way back to the urban markets, and as one urban merchant noted, "where a farmer sells, he will buy." Country residents bought more, and more often, as rail communications cut three days' travel in some cases to six hours. In 1859, a Richmond editor stated a widely accepted axiom of the day when he concluded that "the increase of Richmond has been owing to a very simple cause—namely, the increase of facilities for getting to market." [15]

As the flow of commerce created mutual interests and increased personal intercourse, the financial bonds between town and country tightened in direct proportion. Railroad construction necessitated liberal stock subscriptions from cities and rural counties, and their respective residents. Virginia's system of mixed enterprise required that private and local sources subscribe to two-fifths of a company's stock before the state could purchase the remainder. [16] The financing of the Alexandria, Loudoun, and Hampshire Railroad was typical of the period. Individuals in Alexandria and in the rural counties to be traversed by the road subscribed $450,000; the city of Alexandria subscribed $250,000; Clarke, Hampshire, and Loudoun Counties, $100,000 apiece; and the town of Winchester pledged $30,000. [17] Ownership of railroads was widespread in the Old Dominion and offered another example of town-country cooperation. The rural stockholders attended conventions regularly, and the proceedings indicate that they were vocal and

15. Lynchburg *Virginian,* October 2, 1852; Norfolk *Southern Argus,* June 16, 1854; Richmond *Enquirer,* October 15, 1852; "Mr. John W. Gilliam in a/c with Thomas Branch, 1851–1852" (Gilliam Family Papers, Alderman Library, University of Virginia); "Woods–Belmont Farm Journal, 1854–1861," 10–24 (Woods–Belmont Farm Journals, Alderman Library, University of Virginia); Alexandria *Gazette,* August 22, 1854, September 24, 1851; Charles W. Dabney to Robert L. Dabney, August 12, 1853, in Dabney Papers; Richmond *Daily Dispatch,* August 17, 1859.

16. See Carter Goodrich, "The Virginia System of Mixed Enterprise: A Study of State Planning of Internal Improvements," *Political Science Quarterly,* LXIV (September, 1949), 355–87.

17. "Report of the President of the Alexandria, Loudoun, and Hampshire Railroad Company," Alexandria *Gazette,* October 22, 1856.

effective in shaping company policy.[18] Further, the rural stockholders were typically men of wealth and power in their locales. A survey of twenty-six of the largest country stockholders in several railroad companies reveals that twenty-one were farmers, four were lawyers, and one was a physician. Their average real property holding was $24,000, placing them in the top 3 percent of real estate wealth in Virginia, and their average slaveholding was of plantation size—twenty-eight. Finally, they were mature men who were settled in life. Their average age was fifty-two at the census date closest to their stock purchases.[19] Few planters failed to have at least several shares of an internal improvement company in their stock portfolios.[20]

In addition to common ownership of internal improvements, real estate investments formed another area of urban-rural financial interdependence. Urban entrepreneurs owned country property and affluent rural residents purchased town lots. The reasons for such investments varied. Some city residents like William H. Macfarland, a Richmond banker, and Henry L. Brooke, a prominent Richmond attorney, owned vast tracts of land in western Virginia for speculative purposes and secondarily to develop their mineral potential.[21] Other urban dwellers procured small country residences to escape the increasing rigors of city life.[22] Finally, some townsmen acquired farms in the area and began farming careers.[23] Country residents purchased town property similarly, for a variety of reasons—for speculation, for seasonal residence, and for business. John Rutherfoord, for example, a Piedmont tobacco farmer and a powerful figure in the Virginia legislature,

18. Jeremiah C. Harris Diary, November 1, 1851 (Jeremiah C. Harris Diaries, Alderman Library, University of Virginia); Virginia Board of Public Works, *Thirty-Eighth Annual Report, 1853–1854; Report of the President of the Manassa Gap Railroad Company,* (Richmond, 1854), 291–313.

19. U.S. Bureau of the Census, Seventh Census of Virginia, 1850: Free Inhabitants, I, XVI, XXI, Slave Schedule, I, X; Eighth Census of Virginia, 1860: Free Inhabitants, XIII, XV, XVIII, Slave Schedule, VI, VII; Alexandria *Gazette,* October 23, 1857, September 28, 1858; Richmond *Enquirer,* October 25, 1850, November 28, 1851.

20. See, for example, Harris Diary, November 28, 1859 (Harris Diaries); "Inventory and Appraisement of the Estate of William Massie, 1862" (William Massie Notebooks, Duke University Library); "Meeting of Stockholders of the Alexandria, Loudoun, and Hampshire Railroad Company," Alexandria *Gazette,* September 8, 1858; "Annual Meeting of the Stockholders of the Orange and Alexandria Railroad," Alexandria *Gazette,* October 23, 1857.

21. Richard K. Cralle to William H. Macfarland, April 12, 1857 in Richard K. Cralle Papers, Alderman Library, University of Virginia); Samuel S. Thompson, "Farms in Western Virginia," *American Agriculturist,* XIV (March, 1854), 330.

22. Campbell County Land Books, 1848–1861, and Norfolk City Land Books, 1851–1855 (Virginia State Library).

23. *Ibid.;* Alexandria *Gazette,* August 2, 1855; see also Dykstra, *Cattle Towns,* 180.

owned a row of tobacco warehouses in Richmond.[24] Not coincidentally
perhaps, Rutherfoord championed Richmond internal improvement projects throughout the 1850s.[25]

The increasing and mutually beneficial relations between urban and rural
Virginia, grounded in a desire for commercial prosperity and independence,
would not have been secure without the existence of a consensus on slavery
in the supercharged atmosphere of the 1850s. Here again, mutual interest
formed the necessary bond between town and country. Slaveholding was
widespread among Virginia's urban leadership. Leaders in Norfolk and
Richmond—those individuals who appeared often at public meetings, were
active members of business and political organizations, and who took a
continuing interest in community affairs—were typically slaveholders. In
Richmond, fifty-three of sixty-five leaders owned slaves during the 1850s.
In Norfolk, forty-nine out of fifty-five entrepreneurs owned bondsmen.[26]
If slaveholding was a major criterion for orthodoxy on the slavery issue,
then rural slaveholders need have had no qualms about the soundness of
their urban business partners.

Slaveholding, though, is at best an indirect example of mutual interest in
slavery between town and country. Urban and rural Virginia intertwined
on slavery in deeper ways. Richmond and Alexandria were important slave
markets, much like New Orleans and Natchez in the cotton South.[27] Extensive slave traders such as Pulliam and Slade and the Omohundro brothers
made Richmond the hub of the domestic slave trade.[28] As urban and rural
Virginia moved closer to each other, rural buyers and sellers from as far
away as southwest Virginia sent agents or went themselves to Richmond to
buy and to sell slaves.[29] The domestic slave trade provided another bond
between town and country.

24. John B. Danforth to John C. Rutherfoord, September 4, 1857 (John B. Danforth
Letter Press Copy Book, Duke University Library).

25. Thomas Taylor to John C. Rutherfoord, December 12, 1853 (John C. Rutherfoord
Papers, Duke University Library); Richmond *Enquirer,* June 1, 1858.

26. Seventh Census of Virginia, 1850: Slave Schedule, IV, IX; Eighth Census of Virginia,
1860: Slave Schedule, III, V; see also D. Clayton James, *Antebellum Natchez* (Baton Rouge,
1968), 163.

27. See Frederic Bancroft, *Slave-Trading in the Old South* (Baltimore, 1931); James, *Antebellum Natchez,* 97.

28. Bancroft, *Slave Trading,* 96.

29. Pulliam and Slade, "Bill of Sale," February 7, 1850 (Harris-Brady Papers, Alderman
Library, University of Virginia); Silas and R. F. Omohundro, "Accounts, 1857–1863," January 3–April 27, 1860 (Omohundro Papers, Alderman Library, University of Virginia).

In addition to functioning as rural Virginia's slave market, the cities also served as clearinghouses in the growing slave hiring business. Slave hiring had existed in Virginia since the colonial period, but in the 1850s, new and greater labor requirements on farms, in factories, and for internal improvements caused slave hiring to blossom into a business that created another common interest between town and country with regard to slavery.[30] As slaves from farms flooded the cities seeking employment in the late 1840s, agents appeared for the purpose of either seeing to it that a country client's slaves secured proper employment or that urban clients received their necessary complement of hirelings.[31] These middlemen became important liaisons between town and country. By 1860, 52 percent of the hired slaves in Richmond were hired through agencies.[32] Rent-a-slave services existed in Lynchburg and in Norfolk as well.[33] N. B. Hill, a prominent Richmond merchant who not only marketed his customers' wheat and tobacco but their slaves as well, illustrates the value of the agents. A Mr. Atkinson of a neighboring county entrusted Hill with nine slaves to hire out. Hill secured employment for all, and the variety of employers is some indication of the range of the slave hiring system: three women hired out as domestics; one man to a lumber merchant, another to a commission merchant; two men to the Manchester Cotton Factory just outside Richmond; one man to the city of Richmond for use on public works projects; and finally, one elderly male slave as a servant. The total return for Atkinson was $880.[34]

At the supply end of the system, farmers, individually and collectively, provided city agents with a pool of slaves. The Turpin family of Piedmont, Bedford County, included a father, two sons, and an uncle. They rented more than forty slaves to Lynchburg clients. All the Turpins were farmers.[35]

30. "Forge Wages to Negro a/c," 1850–1852 (Tredegar Journal, Virginia State Library); Virginia Board of Public Works, *Report of the Virginia Central Railroad, 1859–60* (Richmond, 1860), 144; Richmond *Daily Dispatch,* September 14, 1859; Richmond *Enquirer,* October 28, 1851.

31. R. Lewis to Dr. A. G. Grinnan, December 29, 1860, in Grinnan Family Papers, Alderman Library, University of Virginia; advertisements in Richmond *Daily Dispatch,* January 1, 1853. Edward N. Dabney proudly advertised in the *Dispatch* of January 1, 1858, that he had been an "agent of negro hires" for twelve years, one of the oldest slave-hiring agencies in Richmond.

32. Eighth Census of Virginia, 1860: Slave Schedule, IV.

33. *Ibid.,* II, V.

34. N. B. Hill to Mr. Atkinson, February 7, 1855, in James Southgate Papers, Duke University Library.

35. Eighth Census of Virginia, 1860: Free Inhabitants, III, 396, 416, 424, 426, Slave Schedule, I, 322, 326, 327, 328.

The Langhorne family of nearby Campbell County and the Moorman family of Bedford County also initiated slave hiring enterprises.[36] Individual slaveholders offered as many as ten slaves each to the hiring pools of Lynchburg and Richmond.[37]

The cooperation between urban and rural Virginia to rationalize the expanding slave hiring system carried over to the implementation of solutions to problems besetting the system. Historians have disagreed as to whether slave hiring represented a step toward freedom for the slave or a move backward to a more severe form of servitude.[38] Nevertheless, urban and rural leaders both viewed slave hiring as an unnatural form of the peculiar institution. The Norfolk *Southern Argus* asserted, "We do not think it wise or expedient that a man should invest his property in slaves for the purpose of living upon their wages. This is an abuse of the institution of slavery."[39] Charles W. Dabney agreed: "I have always considered it [slave hiring] a most absurd, abnormal condition."[40] Yet both the *Argus* and Dabney realized the efficacy of the labor system and both sought to reform it rather than to kill it. Joint efforts to hold the hirer to greater accountability, to encourage masters to keep tighter control of their charges before hiring, and to forbid a slave from hiring his own time and finding his own lodging generally failed, however.[41] The profitability of the system and the need for labor persuaded farmers, agents, and urban employers to live with the system's drawbacks.

The burgeoning of the slave hiring system in the 1850s and the reluctance of participants to tamper with it emphasized the growing need for labor in both urban and rural Virginia. With a return of agricultural prosperity, farmers as well as urbanites found it necessary to resort to slave hiring to fill out their labor requirements.[42] Thus, both urban and rural Virginians had a stake in stabilizing the labor pool threatened by the rapid exodus of

36. Eighth Census of Virginia, 1860: Slave Schedule, II.

37. See, for example, Eighth Census of Virginia, 1860: Free Inhabitants, XXII, 374, 385, IX, 754, II, 495, Slave Schedule, V, 68, 77, III, 186–87, I, 244.

38. See Dew, "Slave Iron Workers."

39. Norfolk *Southern Argus,* November 23, 1858.

40. Charles W. Dabney to Robert L. Dabney, August 22, 1851, in Dabney Papers.

41. Alexandria *Gazette,* February 29, 1856; Richmond *Daily Dispatch,* April 15, 1859; "Hiring Negroes," *Southern Planter,* XII (March, 1852), 376–77.

42. See Solon Robinson, "Farm of Mr. Bolling in Virginia," *American Agriculturist,* VIII (February, 1849), 261; A. A. Campbell, "Capital and Enterprise: The Bases of Agricultural Progress," *Southern Planter,* XX (January, 1860), 36–39.

slaves south in the domestic slave trade. City and farm journals urged their readers to conserve labor and use it wisely. Edmund Ruffin, Virginia's leading agriculturist, warned that continuing participation in the domestic slave trade would "remove so many of our slaves as necessarily to destroy the institution of negro slavery within the limits of Virginia."[43] The *Argus* complained in a similar vein, "Every slave that is sold to go out of the State diminishes the amount of production in the State. We need all the labor we now have and more."[44]

The heavy emigration of slaves—about ten thousand yearly in the 1850s—resulted in high labor costs that adversely affected urban and rural residents. A. A. Campbell of the Farmer's Club of Nottoway County complained that with "the high price of labor . . . the farmer cannot judiciously increase his labor as his necessities demand." The Richmond *Daily Dispatch* presented a phase of the urban side of the problem: "If the negro exodus continues . . . the mass of householders in our cities will find the price of black labor rising steadily and hopelessly above their means."[45] The domestic slave trade, however, continued apace. Although the traffic's participants neglected the consensus of labor supply and demand attained by some urban and rural residents, they too moved within the framework of town-country interdependence as they reaped the profits of sale of their plantation slaves by experienced slave traders in Alexandria, Norfolk, and Richmond. The urban-rural alliance was so varied that even Virginians working at odds with each other fell under its umbrella.

With a mutuality of interest in commercial prosperity, financial relations, and slave labor, urban and rural Virginians found cooperation in other phases of economic life relatively facile. The alliance between farmers and merchants, for example, blossomed into a union between country and city journalists as they passed the gospel of cooperation along to their respective readerships. From Philadelphia to Abilene, editors were in the vanguard of promoting growth and cooperation of city and hinterland.[46] The Alexandria *Gazette* typified the invitations of the urban press: "Let our friends from the country try this market and they will be satisfied that they can purchase

43. Edmund Ruffin, "The Effects of High Prices of Slaves," *Southern Planter,* XIX (August, 1859), 472–77.

44. Norfolk *Southern Argus,* April 27, 1857.

45. Campbell, "Capital and Enterprise," 37; Richmond *Daily Dispatch,* May 26, 1857.

46. See, for example, Dykstra, *Cattle Towns,* 149; Wade, *Urban Frontier,* 130–32; Carl Abbott, "Civic Pride in Chicago, 1844–1860," *Journal of the Illinois State Historical Society,* LXIII (Winter, 1970), 421.

their supplies in their own state as advantageously as they can by going abroad." [47]

The country press similarly courted their rural subscribers for neighboring urban markets. The Rockingham *Register* echoed the *Gazette* when it urged, "There is no need of any of our Valley merchants going beyond Alexandria to purchase supplies." The Staunton *Messenger,* a prominent paper in the Valley, advised its readers with typical sectional overtones, "Pride of state interest—everything, in fact, should prompt us of the Valley, to trade with Richmond, and Richmond to trade with us. Come let us try it; and endeavor to make ourselves truly independent of the North." [48]

In addition to the medium of the press, urban and rural Virginians sought more personal means of strengthening the commonality of interest between town and country. Common membership in agricultural societies and attendance at fairs allowed farmer, country merchant, manufacturer, and city merchant to mingle with benefit to all. The Virginia State Agricultural Society, formed in 1850 to promote scientific, market-oriented cultivation, secured healthy memberships from Alexandria, Lynchburg, Norfolk, and Richmond. By 1856, Richmond had at least three times as many members in the society as any other county or city in the state. Thirteen of Richmond's sixty-five business leaders were members of the State Society, including merchant William H. Richardson, vice-president of the society. [49]

Not surprisingly, the State Society usually held its major event, the annual fair, in Richmond. Richmond was Virginia's most extensive urban market and farmers looked forward to showing off their stock and produce there. For example, Micajah Woods, a farmer near Charlottesville, sold four pigs and a beef cow at the fair in Richmond in 1856. In addition, Woods won $81 in premiums. His total income from the fair amounted to $199. The fair also proved a boon to Richmond entrepreneurs. Not only could they display their manufactured products from cigars to ploughs, but visitors attracted by the fair, spurred by the holiday mood and encouraged by persuasive advertisements, divested themselves of a considerable amount of currency for omnibus rides, canes, concerts, dry goods, jewelry, and the like. Understandably, when the State Society chose a rival city as the site for its

47. Alexandria *Gazette,* September 8, 1852; see also Lynchburg *Virginian,* June 12, 1856; Richmond *Enquirer,* April 10, 1855.

48. Rockingham *Register,* n.d., quoted in Alexandria *Gazette,* March 21, 1857; Staunton *Messenger,* n.d., quoted in Richmond *Enquirer,* September 21, 1853.

49. Alexandria *Gazette,* November 29, 1856; Lynchburg *Virginian,* October 20, 1858; Norfolk *Southern Argus,* September 15, 1854; Richmond *Enquirer,* April 11, 1856; *ibid.,* February 28, 1850, February 20, 1852.

1858 fair, the incensed Richmond members seceded to form the Virginia Central Agricultural Society and staged a fair of their own despite the financial difficulties of that year. The rebel organization proved short-lived, however, as the State Society returned the fair to Richmond in 1860.[50] The fair was thus another example of the rewards gained from urban-rural intercourse.

As city and country in Virginia became friends and neighbors through mutual ties in commerce, finance, slavery, the press, and through events like the annual fair, proximity generated conflict. These conflicts, although not severe enough to undermine the basic mutuality of interest, illuminated the problems of a growing commercial economy. Much of rural discontent centered around the marketing of farm produce by urban businessmen— the point where town and country acted most closely and most frequently. Farmers from the Great Plains to the bayous of Louisiana suspected urban merchants of devious practices, and Virginia's agriculturists voiced similar complaints.[51] At the root of these charges lay the necessity of businessmen in a modern commercial economy to unite in order to better compete with other cities. In 1857, for example, Alexandria merchants organized to bring their credit system in line with New York and Baltimore merchants by offering country merchants short-term credit of four to six months instead of long terms of eight to twelve months. Country merchants expressed dissatisfaction about the alteration in credit accommodations, but a city merchant defended the action by noting, "In Philadelphia, New York, and Baltimore, the short credit system is most rigidly adhered to, and its beneficial effects evidenced in the prosperity of trade and the wealth of the merchants. We do not think it can be reasonably expected that Alexandria should be excluded from the benefits of the short credit system, when her merchants buy on the same plan and sell as low as those of Baltimore."[52] The situation was typical of market conditions of the 1850s, which found

50. Nathaniel F. Cabell, "Some Fragments of an Intended Report on the Post-Revolutionary History of Agriculture in Virginia," *ca.* 1860 (MS in Nathaniel F. Cabell Papers, Virginia State Library); Richmond *Enquirer*, April 30, 1858; "Woods-Belmont Farm Journal, 1854–1861," 3–10, 30 (Woods-Belmont Farm Journals, University of Virginia); Norfolk *Southern Argus*, October 14, 1858; Kathleen Bruce, *Virginia Iron Manufacture in the Slave Era, 1800–1860* (New York, 1931); Richmond *Enquirer*, May 11, 1858; *Southern Planter*, XX (November, 1860), 756.

51. See Dykstra, *Cattle Towns*, 182–206; Wheeler, *To Wear a City's Crown*, 131, 143; Reed, *New Orleans*, 65.

52. Alexandria *Gazette*, September 10, 1857; see also *ibid.*, May 9, 1856; Richmond *Enquirer*, June 11, 1858.

Virginia's cities attempting to play "catch-up" against larger cities beyond their borders after decades of somnolence, while at the same time accommodating their much-needed rural customers.

Urban residents also discovered that the increased frequency of contact with rural Virginians created problems that grated on the town-country alliance. The rural-dominated legislature received much urban invective for failure to appreciate the changing financial needs of urban society in the 1850s. Specifically, city merchants desired repeal of a merchant's sales tax law to enable local merchants to compete with out-of-state rivals; the repeal of usury laws to facilitate borrowing; and the approval of real estate mortgages so that city dwellers could borrow money on real estate. Urban businessmen failed to realize any of these legislative goals, but this was probably due more to the short biennial sessions of the legislature than to an antiurban or anticommercial prejudice among lawmakers. Agricultural societies, too, petitioned their representatives in vain for tighter inspection laws, an agricultural commissioner, and encouragement of popular education.[53] Features of commercial life that could be modified by local boards of trade were so changed. Aspects of commerce that required state legislation had to wait in line.

Urban-rural conflict was relatively innocuous when compared with other divisions in Virginia society, such as urban rivalry, sectional antagonism, and intraurban conflict. Urban rivalry was a dominant theme of city development in the nineteenth century. Galveston versus Houston, the Kansas cattle towns, St. Louis and Chicago, Baltimore and Philadelphia— these were only a few of the bitter conflicts that historians have chronicled.[54] In the Old Dominion, four cities—Alexandria, Lynchburg, Norfolk, and Richmond—vied for commercial supremacy, and their rivalry surpassed the animosity engendered by urban-rural divisions. The very lines of internal improvement that drew town and country together separated Virginia's cities as competition for the trade of the hinterland increased.

A brief examination of the rhetoric of the conflict is an indication of its virulence. The completion of a Tidewater canal connection from Rich-

---

53. Lynchburg *Virginian,* March 23, 1857; Norfolk *Southern Argus,* March 21, 1860; Richmond *Enquirer,* September 18, 1857; Richmond Board of Trade, *Address to the Merchants of Virginia* (Richmond, 1857); Alexandria *Gazette,* December 31, 1856; "The Inspection Laws," *Southern Planter,* XVI (January, 1856), 86–88.

54. Wyatt W. Belcher, *The Economic Rivalry Between St. Louis and Chicago, 1850–1880* (New York, 1947); Dykstra, *Cattle Towns;* Julius Rubin, *Canal or Railroad: Immitation and Innovation in Response to the Erie Canal in Philadelphia, Baltimore, and Boston* (Philadelphia, 1961); Wheeler, *To Wear a City's Crown.*

mond to Norfolk allowing Lynchburgers to free themselves from dependence on the Richmond market caused the Lynchburg *Virginian* to view the event as a "commercial Jail Delivery." The Richmond *Enquirer* said of the attempt of Norfolk and Alexandria to draw the Valley trade toward their respective cities: "They are sapping our life's blood." After the Virginia Senate defeated a railroad proposal, the Norfolk *Southern Argus* threatened secession and raged: "Are [the] Senators insane? Have they determined that a 'Mason and Dixon's line' shall be drawn through the State of Virginia, South of Richmond, and North of Norfolk—that Norfolk shall be kept in perpetual bondage below this line, while the privileges of tapping the improvements South of it, shall be cordially extended to Richmond and Alexandria?"[55]

Sectional rivalry—equally as bitter and stemming from the same commercial improvements as urban rivalry—was also more devastating than urban–rural conflict. The dissension between eastern and western Virginia has received ample historical attention.[56] A more virulent strain of sectional rivalry appeared in the 1850s, however, as rural Virginia lined up behind favorite market centers, creating new sectional divisions and exacerbating interurban conflicts.[57] At one point in a heated debate over a railroad bill, a western delegate whose county marketed at Lynchburg and another westerner whose constituents preferred Richmond engaged in fisticuffs over rival railroad schemes.[58] Well could the Richmond *Daily Dispatch* lament, "We don't know a country on the face of the earth more divided against itself than Virginia has been on the subject of internal improvements."[59] Urban and sectional rivalries tied up the legislature and committed the state to wasteful logrolling expenditures.[60]

Finally, each Virginia city contained internal elements of discord. Divisions in Virginia's cities were not as clear cut as, say, oldtimers versus new-

55. Lynchburg *Virginian,* August 2, 1854; Richmond *Enquirer,* August 11, 1854; Norfolk *Southern Argus,* March 13, 1856.

56. See Charles H. Ambler, *Sectionalism in Virginia, 1776–1861* (Glendale, Calif., 1910); James C. McGregor, *The Disruption of Virginia* (New York, 1922); Henry T. Shanks, *The Secession Movement in Virginia, 1847–1861* (Richmond, 1934).

57. See Charles W. Russell to John D. Imboden, September 16, 1852, in John D. Imboden Papers, Alderman Library, University of Virginia; Colin Bass to John McCauley, February 4, 1854, in John McCauley Papers, Alderman Library, University of Virginia; Richmond *Daily Dispatch,* February 10, 1860.

58. Richmond *Whig,* February 4, 1851; see also Richmond *Enquirer,* February 4, 1851.

59. Richmond *Daily Dispatch,* October 29, 1860.

60. Lynchburg *Virginian,* June 17, 1854; Norfolk *Southern Argus,* March 2, 1854; Richmond *Examiner,* March 12, 1861.

comers on the frontier, Americans versus Germans in Texas, or Americans versus French in New Orleans. Intraurban conflict in the Old Dominion involved a range of groups and a variety of issues: rivalries between fringes of the city and the central business district over urban services; and between conservatives who feared further taxation and debt would ruin city finances, and progressives who viewed taxation and debt as means to greater ends of economic supremacy.[61]

Urban-rural conflict, then, was only a small portion of the divisions that beset Virginia society. Often, urban and sectional rivalries were manifestations of increasing cooperation between town and country. When major economic programs came up before the legislature, votes typically went along sectional lines drawn by market access patterns.

By 1861, urban and rural Virginia had at least a decade of contact and cooperation behind them, resulting from a common desire to facilitate the flow of commerce, from financial interests that intimately involved urban and rural residents with the economic fate of each other's environment, from the mutuality of interest in slavery, and from the common ties in the press and in agricultural societies. The most tangible fruit of this relationship was the most extensive rail network in the South, which urban and rural allies pieced together through numerous legislative battles.[62] The influence of urban-rural cooperation in other phases of Virginia's economic improvement is more difficult to assess. What portion of increased agricultural production, for example, owed itself to closer ties with the city, and what portion resulted from higher prices, organic fertilizers, new agricultural implements, or more draft animals? We can only infer this and other answers indirectly through statistical information and from the urban and rural residents themselves.

One of the most dramatic increases in Virginia agriculture occurred in the production of market garden crops, which increased more than 400 percent—more than any other agricultural crop during the 1850s.[63] Market gardening is primarily a creature of a growing urban market and of rapid, inexpensive communication with that market.[64] Urban journals, farmers,

61. Dykstra, *Cattle Towns,* 212, 237; Reed, *New Orleans,* 31; Wheeler, *To Wear a City's Crown,* Chap. 6; Alexandria *Gazette,* April 12, 1853, July 16, 1853.

62. *Compendium of the Eighth Census, 1860: Mortality and Miscellaneous,* 331.

63. *Compendium of the Seventh Census, 1850,* 274–82; *Compendium of the Eighth Census, 1860: Agriculture,* 154–64.

64. Alexandria *Gazette,* March 16, 1853; "Garden Farms in Virginia," *American Agriculturist,* XIV (February, 1854), 166; John T. Schlebecker, "The World Metropolis and the History of American Agriculture," *Journal of Economic History,* XLI (March, 1968), 187–208.

and railroad promoters wrote about the efficacy of market gardening, and by 1860, market products were the single most profitable business in lower Tidewater near Norfolk.[65] Rapid transit to urban markets also stimulated wheat production, according to contemporary observers, particularly in those areas heretofore remote from cities.[66] Virginia agriculture began to evince a pattern of cultivation consistent with access to urban centers. Farm size tended to decrease as land became more valuable and specialized near urban areas; beyond the immediate vicinity of cities, grain cultivation increased as Virginia became the largest wheat-producing state in the East; and beyond the Wheat Belt, grazing became the primary activity.[67] Alterations toward a market-oriented agriculture did not occur in one decade, of course, but the trends were evident.

The effect of closer ties with the countryside on Virginia's cities could be seen in the increased volume of trade, in the rapid development of agricultural processing industries as Richmond became the most productive tobacco manufacturing city in the world, and in urban Virginia's incorporation into a national economy as commercial ties with northern ports increased. The physical bonds of union with the hinterland enabled cities like Richmond and Lynchburg to monopolize the staple trade as smaller interior towns like Farmville and Clarksville suffered. Further, increased specialization by urban merchants as well as improved inventory resulting from greater proximity to northern markets hurt country merchants.[68] Finally, the rail network, which stretched out to the countryside, allowed farmers and country merchants to take advantage of the higher prices for crops and lower prices for wares offered by Baltimore, Philadelphia, and New York by allowing them to bypass Virginia's cities. Although Virginians talked and wrote voluminously on sectional independence, the lures of a modern com-

65. Peter C. Stewart, "The Commercial History of Hampton Roads, Virginia, 1815–1860" (Ph.D. dissertation, University of Virginia, 1967), 43–45.

66. Richmond *Whig*, November 6, 1855; see also *Compendium of the Eighth Census, 1860: Agriculture*, xxix.

67. Richard Irby, "Notes for the Sub-Commissioner's Report on Nottoway County, 1854" (Richard Irby MS, Alderman Library, University of Virginia); Alexandria *Gazette*, March 20, 1858; Jones, *Railroads*, 45; Lewis C. Gray, *History of Agriculture in the Southern United States* (2 vols.; Washington, D.C., 1933), II, 920–22.

68. Richmond *Enquirer*, October 20, 1857; "Tobacco Trade of Virginia," *Hunt's*, XL (March, 1859), 343; Richmond *Enquirer*, April 9, 1858; "Virginia Tobacco and Flour Trade," *Hunt's*, XXXI (September, 1854), 600; "Flour Inspections in Virginia," *Hunt's* XLI (December, 1859), 356; "Tobacco in Virginia," *Hunt's* (1860), 734; "Accounts," 1846–1860 (MS in Thomas Garland Papers, Alderman Library, University of Virginia); Alexandria *Gazette*, September 19, 1851.

mercial economy proved irresistible. The irony of southern history, at least for Virginians, was that as they approached the Civil War, their contacts with the North increased.

While Virginians were moving closer to the North, they were also moving toward greater intimacy with each other. The "great commercial-agricultural world" was indeed a small one. City and country met every day on the streets, in warehouses, at slave blocks, in country homes, urban hotels and theaters, at fairs, and in the legislature. Generally, these encounters were amiable and productive. Out of them came railroads, marketing arrangements, and labor agreements. Whatever private misgivings urban and rural Virginians may have had about country gulls or city slickers, personal interest led to mutual interest and in turn generated a progressive, market-oriented society quite remote from the feudal and backward environment alleged by some. As the *Argus* observed, "The city is benefitted with the country; their interests are often one in the same."[69] When the Civil War came, urban and rural Virginia stood together, and in view of a decade of close intercourse and cooperation, this should not be surprising. When the Old Dominion dissolved, it broke along sectional, not urban-rural lines.

The mutuality of interest and cooperation between urban and rural Virginia has an implication for the continuing search for southern identity. Historians engaged in this quest have been so impressed with the uniqueness of southern civilization that few have stopped to consider the similarities with the rest of the nation.[70] The experience of urban and rural Virginians in the decade before the Civil War was the experience of urban and rural Americans: the desire and reality of better access to urban and rural markets; the development of market-oriented agriculture; the countryside as the repository of a labor pool; the common memberships in agricultural societies; the vigorous role of the press, urban rivalry, intraurban animosities, and sectional disputes. These were part of a national pattern in the mid-nineteenth century that witnessed rapid urban growth, development of large-scale commercial agriculture, and the beginnings of a national economy. Aside from geography, the striking feature of urban-rural cooperation in Virginia was its similarity to rather than difference from the rest of nineteenth-century America.

69. Norfolk *Southern Argus,* June 16, 1854.
70. See Michael O'Brien, "C. Vann Woodward and the Burden of Southern Liberalism," *American Historical Review,* LXXVIII (June, 1973), 589–604; David L. Smiley, "The Quest for a Central Theme in Southern History," *South Atlantic Quarterly,* LXII (Summer, 1972), 307–25.

FROM BOONDOCK TO BUCKHEAD IN

SOUTHERN LITERATURE

Novelist Pat Conroy is fond of quoting his mother's distillation of contemporary southern fiction: "On the night the hogs ate Willie, Mama died when she heard what Papa did with sister."[1] These slack-jawed, gap-toothed, in-bred, hard-drinking, tobacco-spitting, trigger-happy, Bible-thumping, pellagra-ridden specimens for whom *Deliverance* is a love story and the toothbrush is a rumor are more caricatures than characters. Southern reality, however, has left southern fiction far behind. Southerners have gone to the city. Peachtree Street has replaced Tobacco Road as the instantly recognizable southern thoroughfare, and hanging ferns are crowding out the kudzu.

The story of this newest South has yet to be told. Southern writers have excelled at telling the story of their country at the crossroads, when a new world is poised to overcome the old and its residents are in various stages of resisting or resigning themselves to the inevitable new order. The metropolitan South lacks this tension, at least from the perspective of southern writers. When they talk about regional landscapes, they inevitably mean rural or small-town landscapes. In a 1981 interview, Alice Walker told a reporter that "the first thing" that occurs to her in framing a story is "landscape." For Walker, landscape is synonymous with the countryside. "I think that if I had been brought up in New York City," she told the reporter, "I

1. Quoted in Susan Ketchin, "Short Stories and Tall Tales," *Southern Exposure,* XIX (Spring, 1991), 13.

would not write stories with the land so much a part of them—trees being so big, and silence being so necessary, and birds being so present."[2] Southern writers have not ignored the urban landscape, but they typically have not written about southern cities on their own terms. Instead, they have shrouded the urban South in rural metaphors and mourned the rise of southern cities as marking the passing of regional traditions.

Southerners, perhaps more than other Americans, have felt uncomfortable with urban life. Soil, climate, and rural traditions have softened the southern city, and writers have dwelled on the blend between "man-places and nature-places" in framing their urban environments. Flannery O'Connor writes of a Georgia urban landscape marked by a "profusion of azaleas [that] wash[ed] in tides of color across the lawns" and inspired citizens to boast that "beauty is our Money Crop." The rural atmosphere abroad in larger places, such as New Orleans and Atlanta, has captured writers' attention. In *Mosquitoes* (1927), set in New Orleans, William Faulkner sees Jackson Square framed by "silver mimosa and pomegranate and hibiscus beneath which lantana and cannas bled and bled." More than sixty years and several dozen bolldozers later, Anne Rivers Siddons, in her novel *Peachtree Road* (1988), still finds it is possible "to drive into residential North Atlanta in the springtime, or in the bronze and blue of a good October . . . leave the world and move into pure enchantment."[3]

For Siddons, these neighborhoods are sanctuaries from the city in the city. They serve as security in an unfamiliar environment and connect residents to a rural past. Lillian Hellman wrote that a large fig tree in New Orleans became her "first and most beloved home," an escape from the city and a place to dream and imagine. Tom Wingo and his family in Pat Conroy's *Prince of Tides* (1986) find refuge and connection in Atlanta amid the spacious grounds of the Candler estate. "We resumed our interrupted life as country children in the middle of the South's largest city," Wingo recalls. "We would come to the forest to remember who we were, what we had come from, and where we would be returning." The soul-caressing quality of a rural landscape, even modest renderings of nature, is evident in Robert Coles's conversation with a poor young black boy who braved mobs to

2. Krista Brewer, "Writing to Survive: An Interview with Alice Walker," *Southern Exposure,* IX (Summer, 1981), 14.

3. Nicholas Davis, "Beulah Land," *Southern Quarterly,* XIX (Fall, 1980), 196; Flannery O'Connor, "The Partridge Festival," *The Critic,* XIX (March, 1961), 426; William Faulkner, *Mosquitoes* (New York, 1927), 14; Anne Rivers Siddons, *Peachtree Road* (New York, 1988), 525.

attend a desegregated school in New Orleans. "Every time I get discouraged," the boy explained, "I go look at the azaleas and I sit in [my grandmother's] chair under our little palm tree and catch the sun and then move to the shade. My daddy says that we haven't got much, but we have a good backyard, with soil that will grow anything and with weather to match." [4]

Urban residents without natural sanctuaries live empty and rootless lives, according to some writers. The displaced rural residents of a mill town in Olive Ann Burns's *Cold Sassy Tree* (1984) subsist in such a sterile landscape. "There weren't any trees," she writes. "No shrubbery. Families sat crowded on the hot little porches, cotton lint from twelve hours in the mill still clinging to their hair and overalls and dresses." [5]

Like a modern-day Antaeus, the southerner loses his or her identity if contact with the earth is lost. To assure themselves and outsiders, southerners are often given to framing their community in rural terms. When the Memphis *Commerical Appeal* asked a venerable resident of De Soto Point, Arkansas, in Willie Morris' *The Last of the Southern Girls* (1973), to describe the Mississippi River town for its readers, the gentleman obliges and writes, "We are bosomed by the earth that conditions us, touched by the river that has never threatened and liberated us. We think as our land thinks. . . . Our faith is in God, the river, next year's crops, the strange benevolence of nature, and the Democratic party." [6]

Recently, some southern writers have challenged these testimonials to the rural identity of urban places but few with more venom than the gifted chronicler of modern New Orleans, John Kennedy Toole. His leading character, Ignatius Reilly, in *The Confederacy of Dunces* (1980), disavows the city's connection with nature, especially the river: "Actually, the Mississippi River is a treacherous and sinister body of water whose eddies and currents yearly claim many lives. I have never known anyone who would even venture to stick his toe in its polluted brown waters, which seethe with sewage, industrial waste, and deadly insecticides." As for the other purported rural connections of New Orleans, Toole writes, "I have never seen cotton growing and have no desire to do so." [7]

---

4. Quoted in Ruth A. Banes, "Southerners Up North: Autobiographical Indications of Southern Ethnicity," in *Perspectives on the American South,* ed. James C. Cobb and Charles R. Wilson (New York, 1985), III, 14; Pat Conroy, *The Prince of Tides* (Boston, 1986), 2; quoted in Robert Coles, *Farewell to the South* (Boston, 1972), 11–12.

5. Olive Ann Burns, *Cold Sassy Tree* (New York, 1984), 70.

6. Willie Morris, *The Last of the Southern Girls* (New York, 1973), 84–85.

7. John Kennedy Toole, *A Confederacy of Dunces* (Baton Rouge, 1980), 103.

Even though few southern writers abjure the rural character of the southern urban landscape as thoroughly as Toole, some admit that the relationship between townscape and countryscape is tenuous and often hostile. The city can transform natural beauty into something unsightly. In *The Wild Palms* (1939), written more than a decade after *Mosquitoes,* Faulkner returns to New Orleans and sees "quietly rotting brick," a "stagnant pool" in a courtyard, and a "mass of lantana" in the French Quarter. The landscape of Clinton, Mississippi, as Barry Hannah depicted it in "Testimony of Pilot," includes an "overgrown garden, a vine-swallowed fence . . . and much overgrowth of honeysuckle vine."[8] In these renderings, nature is no longer the soft, meliorative agent of urban life or the refuge from it, but has overrun "man-places" and has lost its beauty in the process.

More typical, however, is the representation of the city overtaking the natural landscape. How the process of urbanization has ruined nature is a stock theme among southern writers. They recount not only the physical desecration of the landscape but also the passing of values and traditions the natural environment embodies.

The urban South has experienced three great building booms during the twentieth century. The first occurred during the 1920s, a decade in which urban prosperity contrasted with rural poverty in the South. In the two decades after World War II, a second building frenzy transformed the South into the Sun Belt. After catching its breath during the 1970s, the southern urban economy surged again during the 1980s. During each cycle, southern writers have measured less the extent of gain than the degree of loss the region suffered from untrammeled progress.

What happened to Thomas Wolfe's native Asheville, North Carolina, in the 1920s nearly broke his heart, and in his novels he conveyed the rage and helplessness he felt in witnessing the summary destruction of his once-peaceful urban-rural landscape. In *You Can't Go Home Again* (1934), the protagonist, George Webber, returns to a fictional replica of Asheville for his aunt's funeral, only to plunge into deeper mourning at the death of his hometown. "A spirit of drunken waste and wild destructiveness was everywhere apparent," he observed. "The fairest places in the town were being mutilated at untold cost. In the center of town there had been a beautiful green hill, opulent with rich lawns and lordly trees, with beds of flowers and banks of honeysuckle, and on top of it there had been an im-

8. William Faulkner, *The Wild Palms* (New York, 1936), 36; Barry Hannah, "Testimony of Pilot," in *Stories of the Modern South,* ed. Ben Forkner and Patrick Samway (New York, 1977), 155.

mense, rambling, old wooden hotel. From its windows one could look out upon the vast panorama of mountain ranges in the smoky distance. It had been one of the pleasantest places in the town, but now it was gone. An army of men and shovels had advanced upon this beautiful green hill and had leveled it down to an ugly flat of clay, and had paved it with a desolate horror of white concrete." Parts of the town "looked like a battlefield, cratered and shell-torn with savage explosions of brick, cement, and harsh new stucco."[9]

In the heady atmosphere after World War II, southern towns became cities, and southern cities grew to gobble up rural neighborhoods and farms. In *Set This House on Fire* (1968), William Styron uses Peter Leverett to express his sadness over the postwar transformation of Newport News, Virginia. Although hardly a small, isolated hamlet, prewar Newport News abounded in natural landscape. "As a boy," Peter remembers, "I had known its gentle seaside charm, and had smelled the ocean wind, and had lolled underneath giant magnolias." But now "the magnolias had been hacked down to make room for a highway along the shore; there were noisy shopping plazas everywhere, blue with exhaust and rimmed with supermarkets."[10]

Buckhead, an affluent, sylvan suburb adjacent to Atlanta, also underwent a disconcerting transformation after the war. After Atlanta annexed the community in 1952, Buckhead's leaders helped to formulate a strategic plan for the city's economic development. They were too successful. Within a decade, the city's booming prosperity had overwhelmed the once-forested community. Anne Rivers Siddons chronicled this ironic turn of events in *Peachtree Road*. Like George Webber and Peter Leverett, Sheppard Gibbs "Gibby" Bondurant has returned to his native soil—in this case Buckhead—after a brief absence in New Jersey. As he travels up Peachtree Road, a relatively quiet, almost rural thoroughfare as he recalls it, he notes that a "river of automobile lights and the glare of neon . . . limned the landscape as clearly as at sunset." This artificial light heralded the demise of his neighborhood. "Now many of the small forests were gone," he comments with amazement. "Raw, square new two and three-story commerical buildings shouldered in among the offended houses, and many of these houses themselves wore the discreet signage of business: insurance companies, law and dentist's offices, regional or branch or sales offices of national concerns. . . . While I was not looking, the city had beaten Buckhead."[11]

9. Thomas Wolfe, *You Can't Go Home Again* (New York, 1934), 111–12, 145.
10. William Styron, *Set This House on Fire* (New York, 1968), 223.
11. Siddons, *Peachtree Road,* 524–25.

If any urban landscape in the South typified the excessive 1980s, it was urban Texas. Peter La Salle captures the dynamic transformation of Austin in his novel *Strange Sunlight* (1984). At first, the main character, Jack Willington, a refugee from Rhode Island, is fascinated and exhilarated by the pace of change. Coming from economically disabled New England, he has found both love and a job in Austin. The Texas capital seems vital and alive, a bulldozer its most appropriate symbol. "In the city you sensed that nothing would ever be finished," he exults. "Out here on the south side of town, the low cinnamon dirt hills, peppered with scrub mesquite and prickly pear cactus, were constantly being gouged out for more apartment complexes— more mazes of redwood sides, tinted glass, stick-thin little trees, chlorinated aqua pools, exercise rooms, and patiodecks cluttered with hibachis." But after a few years in this charged environment, Willington sees behind the façades, the empty values they represent, and the decay they obscure. "Finally," La Salle writes, "just like his noticing the litter and the bad side of Austin, he started to become acutely aware of the pistol-peddling pawnshops and the dozens of gun slayings in the city. It was madness." Willington, who was once very much at home in Austin, discovers he has no home there and resolves to leave.[12]

What writers like Wolfe, Styron, and Siddons regret is the loss of youth and the memories associated with that special time of life. In the towns and cities of their childhood, the landscape assumed human dimensions, with trees, houses, streets, cemeteries, schools, and stores identified with particular people, their lives and deaths. You can't go home again because home as you remembered it no longer exists, and therefore a part of yourself is lost as well.

The sense of belongingness and the connection with the past are vitally important to southerners. The physical transformation of the urban South rent the ties that bound urban southerners to place. Whether Thomas Wolfe's Asheville in the 1920s, William Styron's Newport News after World War II, or Barry Hannah's Clinton, Mississippi, at the end of the Vietnam era, the native returns and is lost. To George Webber, "The town of his childhood . . . was changed past recognition." As Peter Leverett digested the evidence of destruction around him, he "was touched . . . by whatever it was within me . . . that I knew to be irretrievably lost . . . estranged from myself and from my time, dwelling neither in the destroyed past nor in the fantastic and incomprehensible present." And finally, as Arden Quadberry

12. Peter La Salle, *Strange Sunlight* (Austin, 1984), 49, 140.

returns from Vietnam, his friend William lists the changes to his native Clinton and sighs, "It's not our town anymore, Ard. It's going to hurt to drive back into it. Hurts me every day." [13]

The evidence of personal loss imbued in the changed urban landscape includes a broader lesson as well. The South has also lost much to the process of urbanization. According to southern writers, towns and cities have either created an ersatz South or have not bothered to retain anything southern at all. Whether phony or indifferent, the southern city simply is not southern. Amid contemporary Atlanta's sprawling metropolitan domain, the magic name of "Tara" affixes itself to dry cleaners, car washes, and a shopping center. That cotton once grew where parking lots, highways, and office towers now expose their New Southness to the endless parade of automobiles may be the only genuine historical connection between the nouveaux Taras and the memorable plantation in *Gone With The Wind*. The Corinthian-columned homes that march along tony Paces Ferry Road offer the same out-of-place attempt to trade on Old South traditions. The neighborhood movie house is called, naturally, the Loew's Tara.

In a more subtle but nonetheless powerful way, Flannery O'Connor's story "The Artificial Nigger," about an elderly man and his grandson visiting Atlanta for the first time and their encounter with a lawn ornament popular in the 1950s, captures the artificiality of Atlanta's Old South re-creations. As the grandfather marvels, "They ain't got enough real ones here. They got to have an artificial one." [14] Had O'Connor's characters stayed around a decade or so, they would have seen an equally incomprehensible site as John Portman attempted to re-create the great outdoors with his prototype Hyatt Regency Hotel in the 1960s.

Southern cities scrambled time. Rural and small-town southerners abided by two time clocks. One related to the seasonal cycles on the farm, the other was simply the past. The past encompassed present and future, or at least informed and dictated their shape. Cities in the contemporary South are impervious to seasonal clocks. Air conditioning and modern medicine have removed the debilities associated with southern summers. August is no longer "lay-by" time. Although urban southerners frequently use gardening as a surrogate for farm life and time, the landscape that surrounds their homes and workplaces typically either denies or caricatures the past.

13. Wolfe, *You Can't Go Home Again,* 145; Styron, *Set This House On Fire,* 223; Hannah, "Testimony of Pilot," in *Stories,* ed. Forkner and Samway, 178.

14. Flannery O'Connor, "The Artificial Nigger," in Flannery O'Connor, *The Complete Stories* (New York, 1971), 269.

Even small towns can move ouside southern time. In *Sanctuary* (1931), William Faulkner captures the difference through the eyes of country people as they visit Jefferson. "Slow as sheep they [the country people] moved, tranquil, impassable, filling the passages, contemplating the fretful hurrying of those in urban shirts and collars with the large, mild inscrutability of cattle or of gods, functioning outside of time, having left time lying upon the slow and imponderable land green with corn and cotton in the yellow afternoon."[15]

The current fascination with historic preservation and re-creation in southern urban downtowns reflects a recognition that neither visitors or residents appreciate coming to a city center that reminds them of Indianapolis or Minneapolis, however attractive those city centers might be. History, especially southern history, is good business. Charleston learned this many years ago and had the good sense to remain impoverished through the early building booms and construct a reputation for priceless Old South artifacts that progress would not dare to threaten. Sometimes the attempt to make the urban article genuine, as in Richmond or Columbia, results both in good history and good business. On other occasions, it is a financial disaster, as with many urban pedestrian malls and so-called festival marketplaces. In Dallas, a city that desperately seeks tradition and approval but whose actions deny both, city fathers have declared an abandoned cabin miraculously discovered in downtown as the residence of the city's founder, John Neely Bryan. Although reputable historians have thoroughly debunked this theory, the city persists in promoting the tale.

Whereas cities are trying, the suburbs are hopeless, and southern writers have attacked these communities with a vengeance. The suburb represents more than merely a new scar on the rural landscape. If reflects an imported culture, a denial of traditions, and a rootlessness in a land deeply devoted to place. The suburban cancer is not a new topic for southern writers. William Faulkner and Thomas Wolfe discovered its insidious presence decades ago. In the 1920s, in *Look Homeward, Angel* (1929), Wolfe beheld a vista of Altamont, the fictional surrogate for Asheville, and saw the "little bright raw ulcers of suburbia" on the otherwise verdant landscape. Already in the 1930s, Faulkner's fictional Jefferson had sprouted these alien growths. In *Light in August* (1932), the road from Jefferson was suddenly cluttered on its borders by "small, random, new, terrible little houses in which people who came yesterday from nowhere and tomorrow will be gone wherenot,

15. William Faulkner, *Sanctuary* (1931; rpr. London, 1952), 88.

dwell on the edges of towns."[16] For the rooted South, where the urban landscape assumed anthropomorphic qualities, and where placing people was a vital part of social intercourse, such impermanent residents and dwellings were out of time and out of place.

More than fifteen years later, Jefferson's proto-suburb had grown substantially, as depicted in *Intruder in the Dust* (1948). Faulkner offered a searing portrait of the mature development: "Neat small new one-storey houses designed in Florida and California set with matching garages in their neat plots of clipped grass and tedious flowerbeds, three and four of them now, a subdivision now in what twenty-five years ago had been considered a little small for one decent front lawn, where the prosperous young married couples lived with two children each and (as soon as they could afford it) an automobile each and the memberships in the country and bridge clubs and the junior rotary and chamber of commerce and the patented electric gadgets for cooking and freezing and cleaning . . . while the wives in sandals and pants and painted toenails puffed lipstick-stained cigarettes over shopping bags in the chain groceries and drugstores."[17] And there you have the modern South: generic housing, clubs, activities, and fashion, living out of bags instead of from the soil, and patronizing stores not owned by neighbors.

But if these residents of anonymous suburbia felt a twinge of guilt about their new environment, they did not show it. After a century of poverty and the third-rate, they could at last share the American Dream and enjoy the good life while they relaxed on the deck (not the front porch). Reminiscent of Henry Grady's famous funeral oration a century earlier, the scene evokes scarcely anything southern, save the soil.

Southern writers have composed numerous epitaphs for Dixie. There is splendid tragedy in writing about something soon to be irretrievable, except in memory. They may be right in portraying how the urban landscape reflects the mangling of nature and southern traditions, both personal and regional. But in another view, the urban South, precisely because it is not the rural South, has also liberated southerners from the constraints of a country environment.

The southern city represented a measure of freedom for southern women. The freedom of Edith Pelletier in New Orleans to choose to live apart from her husband and children and pursue her own desires, even to the point of

16. Thomas Wolfe, *Look Homeward, Angel* (New York, 1929), 450; William Faulkner, *Light in August* (1933; rpr. London, 1952), 198.

17. William Faulkner, *Intruder in the Dust* (New York, 1948), 119–20.

suicide, in Kate Chopin's *The Awakening* (1899). And the freedom of Scarlett O'Hara in Margaret Mitchell's *Gone With The Wind* (1936) to shed the restraints of plantation society on her gender and become a prosperous businesswomen in post–Civil War Atlanta. As Mitchell writes, "Scarlett had always liked Atlanta. . . . Like herself, the town was a mixture of the old and new in Georgia, in which the old often came off second best in its conflicts with the self-willed and vigorous new." Scarlett drew strength and determination from the city's rise from the ashes of defeat. Surrounded by the clamor of rebuilding on Peachtree Street, Scarlett silently roared encouragement to her adopted city and to herself as well: "They burned you and they laid you flat. But they didn't lick you. They couldn't lick you. You'll grow back just as big and sassy as you used to be!"[18]

Deriving inspiration from the transforming urban landscape of the city, Lee Ann Deehart, like Scarlett O'Hara, achieves liberation in Peter Taylor's story "The Old Forest" (1979). Set in Memphis in the 1930s, the story turns on a minor automobile accident in Overton Park. Nat Ramsay, son of a prominent Memphis family, is driving his car on an icy day with Lee Ann seated next to him. Ramsay is betrothed to the equally well-connected Caroline Braxley. Unlike Lee Ann, both Nat and Caroline are bound by southern traditions of gender. Lee Ann and her single girlfriends have all come to Memphis from someplace else, from small towns and farms in Arkansas, Mississippi, and Tennessee. But in Memphis they have found jobs and a freedom from the restraints of traditional southern society, especially from place and status. As Taylor writes, the girls "did not care who each other's families were or where they had gone to school. . . . They were all freed from old restraints put upon them by family and community."[19] Taylor celebrates the rootlessness of southern urban life that disturbed Faulkner and Wolfe.

Ironically, however, Lee Ann cannot totally free herself from southern expectations. She flees the scene of the accident through the old forest, itself a metaphor for freedom. The city that has helped Lee Ann become a more natural person enables her to survive the old forest and seclude herself with friends. It is Caroline who insists on finding Lee Ann. Caroline's reputation as a southern woman is at stake: a broken engagement and the potential rumor of her fiancée in the arms of another on the eve of their wedding would stain her reputation. She is also disturbed by Lee Ann's freedom, her

18. Margaret Mitchell, *Gone With The Wind* (New York, 1936), 142, 555.
19. Peter Taylor, "The Old Forest," in *Growing Up in the South: An Anthology of Modern Southern Literature,* ed. Suzanne W. Jones (New York, 1991), 289, 295.

freedom to pick up and leave, and especially her freedom from men. "It isn't only Lee Ann that disturbs me," she explains to Nat. "It began not with what she might be to you but with her freedom to jump out of your car, her freedom *from* you. . . . [G]irls like Lee Ann treat men just as they please."[20] But freedom to a point. Caroline eventually finds Lee Ann living with her grandmother, the owner of a disreputable roadhouse across the river in Arkansas. Saving Nat from scandal had not, after all, compelled Lee Ann into flight; rather, the public discovery of her connection to this woman could damage her reputation, even in liberated Memphis. Although the city provided a cover for unconventional behavior, in a crisis like Lee Ann's, or twenty years later in the civil rights movement, southern conventions would resurface in force. Scarlett O'Hara's bittersweet career in Atlanta underscores this point as well. The urban landscape may defy regional traditions, but its residents, well schooled in those traditions, understand the limits of their freedom.

Black southerners learned a similar lesson about the urban landscape. On the one hand, blacks found cities liberating. In *Black Boy* (1937), Richard Wright recounts his move from Mississippi to Memphis and how he devoured the city's diversity and educational opportunities. "The people of Memphis," he writes, "had an air of relative urbanity that took some of the sharpness off the attitude of whites toward Negroes." After some time in the city, he returns to rural Mississippi, and the contrast startles him. "I had all but forgotten that I had been born on the plantation and I was astonished at the ignorance of the children I met. . . . I saw a bare, bleak pool of black life and I hated it; the people were alike, their homes were alike and their farms were alike."[21]

But the southern urban landscape also underscored a harsher reality for blacks: racial segregation. Although the words "white" and "colored" circumscribed the lives of urban southerners, the most telling and hurtful were signs without words, as Lillian Smith noted in *Killers of the Dream* (1949): "Big white church on Main Street, little unpainted colored church on the rim of town; big white school, little ramshackly colored school; big white house, little unpainted cabins; white graveyard with marble shafts, colored graveyard with mounds of dirt."[22] This landscape provided blacks with daily reminders of their inferior status.

Once the barriers of segregation fell, some inequalities in the black and white urban landscape disappeared. Schools, infrastructure, and facilities in

20. *Ibid.,* 318.
21. Richard Wright, *Black Boy* (1937; rpr. New York, 1951), 245, 150–51.
22. Lillian Smith, *Killers of the Dream* (New York, 1949), 95.

public buildings became color blind in their design and placement. Although inequalities prevail, the urban South is today the best hope for the economic and educational advance of black men and women.

And that really is the key to understanding the contemporary southern urban landscape: it is the center of regional opportunity. No longer a region primarily of small towns and farms, the South is urban, suburban, and metropolitan. If the excitement of the Greenville schoolgirl taking her annual trip to Memphis to shop for new school clothes and dine on chicken salad and iced tea in Lowenstein's tea room is mostly gone, it is because there are fewer of us who live in small towns and more of us who reside in larger metropolitan areas. We have become urbane sophisticates with major-league sports franchises, Starbucks coffee houses, and symphony orchestras. If before World War II, Houston was merely a bigger version of Tioga, and if Atlanta was merely La Grange writ large, this is no longer the case. The big southern city is a breed apart from other southern urban places that share more in common with the rural South than with the larger cities. The question is if the major city is much less southern.

I don't think so. The scale is different, to be sure, but the intention is mainly southern. Erskine Caldwell, who contributed as much as anyone to the country Gothic version of the South, believed that in religion at least, the difference between urban and rural is primarily one of degree: "Rural camp-meetings have been replaced by suburban brick-walled auditoriums and revival tents by rainproof sheds. . . . [B]aptismal tanks have been installed in churches, dressingrooms provided for the baptistery, and the immersion heated to a comfortable swimming-pool temperature."[23] In other words, technology has modified southern design but not southern culture. The message of southern religion remains much the same. And so does the food, the speech, the way of doing business, and the music, even if genericism crowds these venerable regional institutions. The landscape may resemble Indianapolis, but the southern soil lies beneath the concrete and steel.

Sociologist John Shelton Reed has argued that the metropolitan southerner is probably the most consciously southern of all southerners. This resident of the modern South travels and reads widely, maintains contact with people outside the region, and therefore understands the differences, values those differences, and strives to conserve the best of them. The metropolitan southerner will seek to accommodate regional traditions to a modern, post-industrial region without sacrificing either, following writer Stark Young's dictum of sixty years ago: "We can accept the machine, but

---

23. Erskine Caldwell, *In the Shadow of the Steeple* (London, 1967), 40.

create our own attitude toward it."[24] It is this struggle that is worthy of novelistic treatment, for it is the most common and most southern battle we face today.

When southern writers have attempted to explain this new phenomenon, they have usually ignored the complexity of the city in a southern setting. They have dwelled on loss, emphasizing how the southern urban landscape has overwhelmed the region's natural heritage and traditions. The small town still abounds in regional fiction; the tension between "was" and "is" allegedly no longer exists in the spreading suburbs of the Sun Belt. Walker Percy posed the problem two decades ago: "What to do with a big urban sprawl like Baton Rouge. How're you gonna write that? How're you gonna write about New Orleans—not the French Quarter, but Gentilly?"[25]

The question remains unanswered, and it is an important one. Twentieth-century southern writers have provided us with the best view of a region and a people in conflict with themselves, their past, and outsiders. They have helped us to understand the rural South, the small-town South, and even a bit about the big cities. But there is something going on in the loose egg yolk that is the metropolitan South. Historians can cite statistics, quote anecdotes, and chronicle change. But we have a difficult time discerning what these findings mean for the people and what it means for the South. The novels that will help us understand this newest South remain unwritten.

24. Stark Young, "Not in Memoriam, But in Defense," in *I'll Take My Stand,* ed. Twelve Southerners (New York, 1930), 355.

25. Walker Percy, quoted in Jack Temple Kirby, *Media-Made Dixie: The South in the American Imagination* (Baton Rouge, 1978), 160.

II

RACE

BLACK LIFE IN OLD SOUTH CITIES

T he clock struck four. It was still dark when Emmanuel Quivers rose from bed. Wagons already rumbled in the street, voices called, a whistle shrieked in the distance. The workday in the city had begun. Soon, Quivers left behind his wife and children and took the short walk across the James River and Kanawha Canal to the Tredegar Iron Works, just beside the James River. Quivers' step was more purposeful that day. By nightfall, he and his family were to leave Richmond, accompanied by the blessings of Tredegar's owner, Joseph Reid Anderson, and clutching documents declaring the Quivers family free. Quivers recalled when he came to work for Anderson a decade earlier as a hired slave among dozens of other hired slaves in Tredegar's hot furnace room. By the early 1850s, Quivers had established himself as a hard and reliable worker, earning as much as one hundred and twenty dollars as a year through bonuses and overtime. As a reward, Anderson negotiated a loan for Quivers, enabling the slave to purchase his freedom. Anderson then promoted Quivers to facilitate the repayment of the loan. By 1857, Quivers was earning as much as eight to twelve dollars a week and had secured a second loan from Anderson to purchase his family and migrate to the West. The ironworker soon paid off the loan and planned to move his family to California.[1]

Andrew Marshall drove a dray through the streets of Savannah, but his thoughts were on serving the Lord. Marshall had purchased his freedom with a two-hundred-dollar advance from his owner, Savannah merchant

---

1. Kathleen Bruce, *Virginia Iron Manufacture in the Slave Era* (1930; rpr. New York, 1968), 239–42.

Richard Richardson. Using the contacts he had made while serving Richardson as a coachman, Marshall began a dray business and, by 1824, was
probably the wealthiest free black in Savannah. He owned several parcels of
real estate, a slave, and a coach. By this time, however, Marshall, then in his
sixties, felt another calling. Financially secure, he began to minister to the
slaves and free blacks who attended the First African Baptist Church in the
city. Marshall organized the one-thousand-member congregation into an
institutional church, establishing a benevolent society, a missionary group,
and a Sunday school. By the time he died in 1856 at the age of one hundred,
Marshall had established a legendary reputation among both Savannah's
white and black populace.[2]

William Wells Brown played an important role in the New Orleans slave
trade. The Crescent City was the most active slave market in the South,
with slaves and accompanying speculators converging on the city, coming
down the Mississippi, up from the Gulf of Mexico, or overland from the
Southeast. On any winter weekday, planters seeking hands for the sugar or
cotton plantations along the lower Mississippi, or local residents hoping to
find domestic workers or laborers, visited the auction blocks at the foot of
Canal Street or tried the more opulent atmosphere of the St. Charles Hotel.
Slave trading was a big business in the urban South, rivaling staple crops in
profitability. Brown's role in the business was to prepare slaves for sale. A
slave himself, Brown empathized with the unfortunate men and women,
many of whom had already been separated from their families, and most of
whom had doubtless heard stories of the rigors of plantation labor in the
Deep South. It was a task Brown loathed but nevertheless performed well.
As he recalled several years later from the vantage point of freedom in the
North, "Before the slaves were exhibited for sale, they were dressed and
drawn out into the yard. Some were set to dancing, some to jumping, some
to singing, and some to playing cards. This was done to make them appear
cheerful and happy. My business was to see that they were placed in those
situations before the arrival of the purchasers, and I have often set them to
dancing when their cheeks were wet with tears."[3]

These were extraordinary men. Blacks in the cities of the Old South
were typically not as successful as these three, nor did they leave much trace

---

2. Fredrika Bremer, *The Homes of the New World: Impressions of America,* trans. Mary
Howitt (1853; rpr. New York, 1868), I, 354.

3. Quoted in Michael Tadman, *Speculators and Slaves: Masters, Traders, and Slaves in the
Old South* (Madison, 1989), 102.

of their existence. Their lives, slave or free, were typically mundane: they scratched out an existence from work and fellowship, all the while aware that their status and their lives could be changed dramatically by the actions of individual whites or the larger society. Despite their unique positions in antebellum southern urban society, the lives of Quivers, Marshall, and Brown highlight a number of features common to the lives of all blacks then living and working in southern cities.

Although slaves and free blacks invariably occupied the lowest rungs of the urban occupational ladder, there were considerably more opportunities to learn skills and to apply business acumen in the city than in the countryside. Moreover, most successful slaves and free blacks owed a great deal to white benefactors or supporters. This client relationship filtered through all levels of urban black society. Masters and employers offered some protection for slaves, and influential customers or neighbors vouched for free blacks. From getting work to getting out of legal difficulties, blacks understood the value of white support. Third, black life in the urban South belied basic white southern beliefs about blacks. Urban slaves were not content with slavery, as their masters assumed; given a sliver of hope, they would invariably choose freedom. Blacks also had allegedly limited intellectual abilities. Yet the presence of respected black preachers, the thirst for knowledge represented by the scattering of clandestine schools in the city, and the good business sense evidenced by the black elite all challenged claims of inferiority.

Finally, whatever the possibilities inherent in urban life for antebellum black southerners, reminders of their subservient and precarious position were frequent. The presence of the slave trade was only the harshest of many reminders that blacks, particularly slaves, had limited control over their own lives. Every southern city had ordinances supported by custom that restricted movement, employment, education, worship, and recreation. Though enforcement of these provisions was notoriously lax, on occasion white authorities swept down on blacks, capriciously and cruelly. A constant tug-of-war raged in the cities of the Old South. Slaves sought to expand their freedoms, whereas whites wanted to limit them; free blacks strove to protect their anomalous position in a society that identified blacks with slavery, whereas whites sought to reduce their position to virtual bondage. Yet even in this tense and often hostile environment, black southerners carved out lives within the community. Only in the 1850s did these lives seem threatened by forces within and beyond the urban South.

The history of black life in the antebellum urban South may be interesting, but is it important? After all, only one out of ten slaves lived in cities, and even though free black urban residents constituted one-third to one-half of all free black southerners, less than 5 percent of the South's black inhabitants were free. Not many white southerners lived in cities, either—less than one in eight. And except for New Orleans, antebellum southern cities were modest affairs, typically with fewer than thirty thousand inhabitants by 1850. New York, Philadelphia, St. Louis, Chicago, Boston, Baltimore, and Cincinnati each had well over a hundred thousand residents by that date. New Orleans was the only southern city among the ten most populous urban centers in the United States in 1850.

But numbers are not necessarily reflective of importance and impact. Antebellum southern cities were the South's outlet to the wider commercial world, conduits for information, manufactured goods, staple crops, and labor resources. Planters maintained close connections with urban merchants, slave traders, family members, and, in capital cities, legislators. Plantation slaves also visited cities as often as possible to market their garden crops, sell some cotton or tobacco, visit friends and relatives, and attend church. The boundary between city and country was permeable. What occurred in the city invariably had an impact on the countryside and, therefore, on the South as a whole. The flexibility that slavery demonstrated in an urban setting and the economic assertiveness of free blacks affected the slavery debate, race relations, and perhaps most important, life in the postwar South. Urban slaves and free blacks often assumed leadership positions after the Civil War. The institutions they formed in the antebellum era, especially the black churches, served as community focal points in the years after emancipation. Moreover, the class, color, and status divisions that marked urban black communities before the war persisted to some degree after the war. Finally, the mechanisms whites employed to maintain order in the Old South cities—segregation, the leasing of convict labor, and black codes—became the foundation for white supremacy in the postwar era. The story of black life in the antebellum urban South, in other words, not only helps us to understand more fully the history of the Old South but the origins of the New South as well.

Many visitors to Old South cities came away with at least one misimpression, judging by their written travel accounts. An English visitor to New Orleans in the early 1850s wrote, "The vast proportion of blacks in the street soon struck me. I should think they were five to one of the white population." Swedish traveler Fredrika Bremer recorded a similar impression of Charleston in 1850, where "Negroes swarm the streets. Two-thirds of the people one sees in town are negroes." And a visitor to Richmond a few years later observed that the city was "literally swarming with negroes."[4]

Such observations were, for the most part, wildly inaccurate. New Orleans' alleged five-to-one ratio of blacks to whites was almost directly the opposite. Bremer's perception of Charleston was closer to reality but still considerably off the mark, since less than half of the city's population was black. Though Richmond's chronicler offered no figures, the impression he left was that of a heavily black city. Yet less than 40 percent of Richmond's residents were black. What accounts for these discrepancies?

A simple answer is that compared with the northern cities these travelers had visited, the urban South was by comparison essentially dark-complexioned. New Haven, Connecticut, had the highest percentage of blacks— 4.9 percent—of any northern city in 1850. Every southern city easily exceeded that figure. But even without the shock of comparison, it was understandable how newcomers misinterpreted the black population of the urban South. Blacks were prominent in the urban work force, on the streets, in the shops, along the wharves, and in the factories. The early-morning city, the city of Emmanuel Quivers, was a black city, with workers trudging off to factories, docks, and terminals, domestic servants marketing for their masters and mistresses, black-driven drays clamoring over the streets, and black laborers digging culverts or repairing streets. "Now go down to the markets," the Richmond *Daily Dispatch* invited its readers in 1853, "and you will hear the voices of hundreds, wrangling, chaffering, buying and selling, till you would imagine yourself in Babel, but for the reason that the tongues are almost all of one kind, those of colored people."[5]

The contributions of black labor to the urban antebellum South were indeed significant. Slaves, for example, accounted for more than 70 percent of the unskilled labor in Richmond and Charleston, 50 percent in Mobile, and more than 40 percent in Nashville. But these figures barely indicate the versatility and importance of slave labor in the urban South. In cities such as Louisville and Richmond in the Upper South, slave labor provided most of the industrial work force. The tobacco factories used slaves almost exclusively. In Richmond, more than one-half of all male slaves living in the

---

4. J. Benwell, *An Englishman's Travels in America: His Observations of Life and Manners in the Free and Slave States* (London, 1853), 113; Adolph B. Benson, ed., *America of the Fifties: Letters of Fredrika Bremer* (New York, 1924), 96; Robert Russell, *North America, Its Agriculture and Climate: Containing Observations on the Agriculture and Climate of Canada, the United States, and the Island of Cuba* (Edinburgh, 1857), 151.

5. Richmond *Daily Dispatch,* August 18, 1853.

city in 1860 worked in tobacco factories. These were typically unskilled operatives whom factory owners had either purchased or leased from agents. Visitors often commented on the spectacle of tobacco-factory slaves "stripped to the waist" on summer days, "tugging and heaving at long iron arms, which turned screws, accompanying each push and pull by deep-drawn groans."[6] Hours were long—fourteen a day in summer, as high as sixteen in the winter—and working conditions were difficult. But the slaves often set their own pace, occasionally pacing their work to songs, much as field hands often set the cadence of their picking or sowing. Iron foundries also employed slave labor. The Tredegar Iron Works in Richmond, soon to be the arsenal of the Confederacy, employed a large slave force on the eve of the Civil War.

Industries were scarcer in the Lower South, reflecting the predominance of women among urban slaves in such cities as Charleston, Augusta, Savannah, Mobile, and New Orleans. Yet when entrepreneurs promoted industrial enterprise in these places, they often touted the benefits of slave labor in the bargain. "The South can manufacture cheaper than any part of the world," a writer in the New Orleans *Times-Picayune* boasted in 1859, a feat made possible, he added, "with slave labor that, under all circumstances and at all times, is absolutely reliable." In 1827, the Macon *Telegraph,* promoting the establishment of textile factories, observed that "slaves are most profitable of all operatives. . . . They are more docile, more constant, and cheaper than free men."[7] By the 1840s, several textile mills in Macon employed slave labor, a fact of great concern to some white laboring men who sought to block such competition. But a resolution of cotton planters in 1851 and a strong editorial that same year defended the use of slave labor in much the same terms as had the editorial nearly twenty-five years earlier.

Southern railroad companies headquartered in cities held large numbers of bondsmen for railway repair and construction work. The South Carolina Railway in Charleston owned 103 slaves in 1860. Three railroads in Richmond owned nearly 600 bondsmen among them. Although many of these slaves worked in the countryside, they lived in and contributed to the life of the city.

Although slave labor was important to the South's nascent industrial and corporate activities, most urban slaves toiled as domestic servants. The vast

6. Charles Weld, *A Vacation Tour in the United States and Canada* (London, 1853), 313–14.

7. Quoted in Richard C. Wade, *Slavery in the Cities: The South, 1820–1860* (New York, 1964), 37; quoted in Donnie D. Bellamy, "Macon, Georgia, 1823–1860: A Study in Urban Slavery," *Phylon,* XLV (December, 1984), 302.

majority of urban slaveholdings were small (two or fewer slaves), reflecting the dominance of domestic labor. These slaves, primarily women, performed the usual tasks associated with domestic service in the plantation big house: cleaning, cooking, and assisting with child rearing. In cities, domestic slaves took on additional responsibilities, such as marketing. As a New Orleans resident noted, "Almost the whole of the purchasing and selling of edible articles for domestic consumption [is] transacted by colored persons."[8] The smaller proportion of male domestic servants often assisted their masters' businesses as general laborers or as assistants to butchers, carpenters, wagon makers, and shoemakers.

The working conditions of domestic slaves were scarcely better than those encountered by workers in tobacco factories. They, too, rose before dawn and went to bed as late as ten o'clock at night. Unlike the tobacco operatives, domestic servants were on call twenty-four hours a day, seven days a week. They often lived in cramped quarters attached to the main house, so they enjoyed less privacy than did the factory workers, who generally lived off the premises. The saving element in domestic slaves' work lives was that their duties frequently required them to be out and about the city, driving a dray for a master (as Andrew Marshall had done), delivering packages or messages, or shopping at the food market. It was here, in the moil of the city, that domestic slaves could take their respite, linger awhile over the array of goods at the market, or (if a male slave) step into one of the numerous groceries or grog shops for something to eat or drink.

Skill levels among urban slaves were generally low. If an economic ladder existed for urban slaves, it was one with very few rungs. In the late eighteenth century, urban slaves possessed artisanal skills. By the late 1840s, however, immigrants, native-born whites, and free blacks dominated the skilled trades—competitors who, with the exception of native-born whites, were much less evident a half century earlier. Also, manumission laws were generally lenient in the post-Revolutionary era, which meant that skilled slaves were able to purchase their freedom and remain in their communities. The result was that the pool of skilled slave labor was reduced. Subsequent legislation limiting the ability of urban slaves to learn a trade further eroded slave skills. This is not to say that some southern cities did not depend on some skilled slave labor. An 1848 census in Charleston revealed that nearly one out of five male slaves had artisanal skills, concentrated primarily in the building and shipping trades. But Charleston was an exception. In most

8. Quoted in Wade, *Slavery in the Cities,* 29.

southern cities either a majority or a substantial minority of urban slaves possessed few skills.

Although urban slaves possessed few more skills than a plantation field hand, the nature of urban work often required different types of work arrangements than those of plantations. The cultivation of cotton, rice, tobacco, and sugar was a year-round activity. Plantation slaves were also required to fill numerous odd jobs, from fence mending to hauling logs. Urban businesses, on the other hand, often had seasonal variations; merchants, for example, were busiest from October to April, and textile mills frequently shut down during the summer months. Moreover, urban enterprises required significant capital investments in machinery and physical plants, so that additional outlays for a labor force were not possible. Also, most businesses in the urban South were small in scale, rarely requiring more than one or two additional workers besides family members. Purchasing a slave or two could be difficult for a struggling new enterprise, and the money could be better spent on equipment, rent, or shipping.

A system of slave hiring evolved to meet such particular urban requirements. Actually, urban slave hiring probably appeared simultaneously with the growth of southern colonial towns. In 1712, the South Carolina legislature made disapproving note of slaves who hired out their own time in Charleston. During the nineteenth century, especially during the last two antebellum decades when urban economies expanded across the South, slave hiring became a prominent method of utilizing slave labor in cities. For large enterprises, such as manufacturing establishments, slave hiring replaced outright ownership by the 1850s. Virginia cities such as Danville, Lynchburg, and Richmond, where manufacturing played a significant role in the urban economy, resorted extensively to slave hiring. More than one-third of the slaves working during the 1850s in Lynchburg and Richmond, for example, were hired. The percentage of slaves working under hiring contracts was considerably less in cities of the Lower South, usually under 15 percent, because most of those cities lacked the large-scale enterprises that most favored hiring over ownership. Throughout the South, roughly 5 percent of slaves worked in a hiring relationship, indicating that the system was primarily an urban labor form.

Typically, slaves worked with a fixed term of hire—six months or one year—with the employer providing appropriate clothing, food, lodging, and medical care in addition to a hiring fee paid to the owner. Slaves and employers got together in several ways. Sometimes an urban slave owner heard that a neighbor or local businessman was looking for a slave to perform domestic or other labor and thus concluded an agreement; on other occasions, slaveholders, either in the city or on farms in adjacent counties, sent slaves to brokers, who then found suitable employment; and slaves, usually with the consent of their masters, sometimes took the initiative and found an employer. By the 1840s, slave hiring had become so commonplace in the urban South that hiring brokers proliferated to handle the volume. Every December their advertisements crowded newspapers. A typical notice, this one appearing in a Louisville newspaper, read: "An experience of many years business with the citizens of Louisville and vicinity renders us competent of judging and picking good homes and masters for your negroes."[9] Slave owners generally paid a commission of from 5 to 8 percent to the brokerages.

Not all slave hiring was so formalized. The nature of the urban economy required short-term weekly, daily, or even hourly work. For these purposes, slave owners and potential employers usually dealt directly with each other or were brought together by an enterprising slave. Cities hired slaves for short-term work on roads, trash collection, sewer construction, and bridge building. Owners typically received up to fifty cents a day. New Orleans authorities, for example, expended about thirty thousand dollars annually in slave-hiring fees. By the 1850s, nearly one-third of the slaves hired in Richmond and Savannah were hired for a period of less than one year. The work undertaken by most hired slaves indicated that males dominated the hiring system. Urban slave owners generally did not release their female domestic slaves for hired work.

The essence of slave hiring was its flexibility, its ability to adjust to an expanding and seasonal urban economy. For some white southerners, slave hiring was too flexible, particularly the practice of slaves' hiring their own time. The idea of slaves negotiating with employers for the best "arrangements"—housing, bonuses, treatment, and food—irked some who believed that such behavior created an independence and an attitude that might prove ultimately subversive to the institution of slavery. As early as 1712, the South Carolina legislature attacked self-hire in Charleston as allowing slaves "to maintain themselves, and other slaves their companions, in drunkenness and other evil courses." Cities sought to regulate self-hiring by outlawing it entirely (though unsuccessfully) or by requiring slaves who wished to work in a hire arrangement to purchase badges at stiff prices, ranging up to seven dollars annually in Charleston—although slave owners often purchased the badges for their slaves, thus nullifying the intent of the law. Frustrated editors and petitioners surfaced periodically to decry the practice. Hired slaves,

9. *Ibid.*, 42.

some complained, were without benefit of the master-slave relationship and "its controlling and ameliorating influences." Essentially, some alleged, the system allowed the slave to "choose his master," one, the slave hoped, who "will grant him the largest license." The upshot was to render the slave "insubordinate and vicious," resulting in a general "deterioration in morals, in habits, and in health."[10]

Slaves who hired their own time had a different perspective. Former slave Frederick Douglass recalled the exhilaration he felt the first time he hired out on his own: "After learning to caulk, I sought my own employment, made my own contracts, and collected my own earnings; giving Master Hugh no trouble in any part of the transactions to which I was a party." Douglass added that "some slaves have made enough, in this way, to purchase their freedom."[11] A few slaves became entrepreneurs in their own right, employing other slaves and hiring out as teams for construction work.

Despite the pique of some whites, self-hire persisted and probably grew in the late antebellum decades. As Douglass indicated, a master could merely set a specified fee with his slave and leave it to the bondsman to secure a hiring contract to fulfill that agreement. In the meantime, the slave could obtain a hire that not only paid his master but in the bargain also left some money for himself. The latitude allowed the slave also reflected the urban labor market that, during periods of prosperity, was chronically short of labor. At these times, especially during the prosperous 1850s, calls to reopen the African slave trade or to import workers from Europe were heard most often. Usually, flush times in the city coincided with a prosperous farm economy, and both city and farm competed for available labor. Purchase prices increased, putting slave ownership out of the reach of some city residents; unskilled slaves from the countryside went back to the farms; and some urban slaveholders took advantage of the higher prices and sold their slaves to farmers. The result was a smaller, more skilled urban slave-labor pool, too expensive to purchase but reasonable enough to hire. Merchants, city administrators, factory owners, and just plain householders were not likely to be finicky about whether they received their help via a broker, slave owner, or through inquiries from the slaves themselves.

The limited success of employment restrictions and the eagerness with which blacks took advantage of the exigencies of the urban labor market is

10. Quoted in Ulrich Bonnell Phillips, "The Slave Labor Problem in the Charleston District," *Political Science Quarterly*, XXII (September, 1907), 422; Richmond *Daily Dispatch*, April 15, 1859; "Hiring Negroes," *Southern Planter*, XII (1852); Richmond *Whig*, August 27, 1852; Norfolk *Southern Argus*, September 26, 1849, November 23, 1858.
11. Frederick Douglass, *My Bondage and My Freedom* (New York, 1855), 318, 328.

even clearer with respect to urban free blacks. Free blacks were the most urbanized group in the Old South, with roughly one-third residing in antebellum southern cities. The attractions of the city were obvious. Unless free blacks owned property, their status in the countryside as farm laborers was only slightly better than the slaves'. Other economic opportunities were limited or nonexistent in rural areas. Also, a free black out and about in the countryside risked confrontation with patrols or individual whites who presumed he was a slave. Anonymity was easier in the city. It was not startling that fugitive slaves sometimes did not go north but went to the nearest city. Most important, perhaps, there was the possibility of making a living in the urban South.

The character of the free-black population differed markedly between cities in the Upper and Lower South. Free blacks in Upper South cities had usually gained their freedom in the period immediately after the American Revolution, when manumissions were easier. In fewer cases, some (such as Emmanuel Quivers and Andrew Marshall) had purchased their freedom. Although there were free blacks in Lower South cities who attained their freedom in these ways, many were mixed-blood offspring of black slave women and prominent white men who had set the woman (and, therefore, her child) free, often teaching the child a trade or providing some financial support. This was especially the case in the former French ports of New Orleans and Mobile, but it was also evident in such southeastern cities as Savannah and Charleston. The free blacks of the Lower South, therefore, tended to be lighter-skinned, more affluent, higher-skilled, and perceived themselves as being more distinct from slaves than their counterparts in the cities of the Upper South. These distinctions were reflected in the respective urban labor markets.

Generally, the skill levels and occupational status of free blacks tended to increase the farther south one traveled; free black occupational status was lowest in New England cities, for example, and highest in New Orleans. In New Orleans, free people of color (as they were called) even occupied some white-collar positions in professional, managerial, and scientific occupations. They accounted for 5 percent of the total work force in these activities, easily outdistancing their counterparts in every other city in the nation. The affluence of the Crescent City's free people of color also exceeded other cities', with nearly one-third of free-black household heads in the city owning property in the 1830s. The percentage of free-black property holders in Upper South cities at that time was typically under 10 percent.

But New Orleans was not the only Lower South city where free blacks lived in relative prosperity. In Charleston, three out of four free black men worked at skilled trades. They accounted for 25 percent of the city's carpenters, 40 percent of its tailors, and 75 percent of the millwrights, even though they comprised only 15 percent of the work force. Occasionally, free blacks were among the wealthiest citizens in southern communities. William Johnson, of Natchez, Mississippi, a free-black barber, owned several properties in town, a plantation, and numerous slaves. Andrew Marshall, mentioned earlier, was among Savannah's leading landholders in the 1820s.[12] Solomon Humphries, a free black in Macon, owned a grocery store and a textile mill.

Free blacks clustered in certain occupations that whites perceived as "nigger work." Despite the prejudicial nature of such perceptions, they enabled free blacks to carve out a narrow but significant niche in the skilled labor market of southern cities. Barbering, for example, was the quintessential "nigger work." Though few free-black barbers amassed the fortunes of William Johnson, barbering provided a comfortable living and good connections to prominent whites. Free blacks also monopolized catering, carting, and stable services in some cities. The definition of "nigger work" varied from city to city. Tailoring was a prominent free-black occupation in Charleston but not in Richmond, for instance. In the former city, 45 percent of skilled free blacks were clustered in either tailoring or carpentry work. In Richmond, the building trades, shoemaking, and barbering accounted for 80 percent of skilled free-black labor.

The typical free black, however, whether in New Orleans or Richmond, worked in menial occupations. Their wages were generally lower than those of comparable white laborers, and their willingness to work for less and their perceived tractability (especially when compared with Irish workers) generally guaranteed them some employment. They often worked alongside hired slaves in factories, on city work crews, or along the wharves. Skilled free-black women were rare. The vast majority worked in domestic service as cooks, laundresses, and housekeepers. Occasionally, a few might peddle some handicrafts or garden produce at the market.

Demographics eventually conspired to challenge slave and free-black labor in the urban South by the 1830s. Except in a few industrial cities,

---

12. William Ransom Hogan and Edwin Adams Davis, eds., *William Johnson's Natchez: The Ante-Bellum Diary of a Free Negro* (1951; rpr. Baton Rouge, 1993); Edwin Adams Davis and William Ransom Hogan, *The Barber of Natchez* (1954; rpr. Baton Rouge, 1973); Whittington B. Johnson, "Andrew C. Marshall: A Black Religious Leader of Antebellum Savannah," *Georgia Historical Quarterly,* LXIX (Summer, 1985), 173–92.

females predominated among the urban black population. The skewed sex ratios limited natural increase. At the same time, immigrants from Europe began to filter into southern cities, frequently by way of northern urban centers. Also, the white farm population, attracted by opportunities in the city and the lack of the same chance in the countryside, continued their steady migration to the urban South. As a result, southern cities became whiter, and the work force whiter still, since many of the white newcomers were of prime working age.

By 1850, immigrants constituted more than 20 percent of Charleston's population, 25 percent of Savannah's, and more than 33 percent of Mobile's. But their representation in the workforce was much greater: two-thirds of free workingmen in Mobile and half in Charleston. In Richmond and Nashville, foreign-born workers counted for more than 40 percent of the free workforce. Although immigrants soon picked up the racial customs of the South, their ambivalence was reflected in their frequent fraternization with urban blacks and, at the same time, their willingness to engage in fierce and occasionally violent labor competition with them.

The success of immigrants in challenging urban black labor varied from city to city. In Charleston, for example, hired slaves and free blacks dominated the drayage business until the 1840s; by 1860, Irish workingmen accounted for two-thirds of the city's teamsters. Slaves were the primary victims of the displacement, indicating that the demand for slaves in the countryside, rather than preference for white teamsters, accounted for most of the shift. In other cities, the rising cost of hiring slaves, even for the most menial work, actually made immigrant labor cheaper. On the other hand, immigrants were less successful in Charleston in dislodging slaves and free blacks from artisanal work. Blacks had built up a loyal white clientele who did not switch, regardless of racial preferences. In Richmond, slaves and free blacks continued to dominate the tobacco and iron industries. The general wisdom among Richmond businessmen was that slave labor was more efficient than comparable immigrant labor.

Immigrants were sometimes more successful in driving out free blacks. They were less concerned than native-born whites about the stigma of "nigger work," and they began to intrude on such venerable free-black occupations as barbering and drayage. In Norfolk, prior to 1850, free blacks dominated shipping-related artisanal trades. By 1860, these trades were shifting to immigrant labor. In New Orleans, however, free blacks persisted in the dock trades but lost ground to immigrants in drayage and hotel service. Whether or not free blacks remained in traditional black occupations varied widely from place to place, depending on local customs, the skills of immigrants, and the degree of prosperity and hence labor demand in a particular city. Generally, though, free blacks' occupational status tended to decline after 1840. Immigrant workers were willing to underbid free-black labor, accounting for the anomaly in the 1850s of an expanding economy and declining wages in unskilled and semi-skilled occupations.

Charleston was an exception to free-black occupational erosion, if for no other reason than that the locals resisted economic and social changes more than residents of most other cities. During the 1830s, the city experienced a significant influx of Irish immigrants from the glutted labor market of New York. Although they were successful in challenging hired slaves for some of the drayage business, they were unable to dislodge free blacks from artisanal work. By 1860, free blacks still dominated the tailoring, butchering, bricklaying, shoemaking, and painting trades.

Immigrants were not the only competitors whom blacks, slave and free, confronted in the urban labor market. Native-born whites also threatened the occupational status of slaves and free blacks, especially in skilled positions.[13] Although they generally disdained to compete for "nigger work," native-born whites guarded the traditionally white artisanal crafts fiercely, even resorting to violence on occasion. Frederick Douglass recalled the severe beating he received when he hired out as a caulker in Baltimore in 1836. Yet he understood the animosity he encountered: "The white laboring man was robbed by the slave system of the just results of his labor, because he was flung into competition with a class of laborers who worked without wages."[14] Employers often used slaves as strikebreakers, a tactic not likely to reduce tensions between black and white workers. Although such individual encounters may have been numerous in the urban South, none of the mass racial rioting that plagued Boston, Philadelphia, and Cincinnati from the 1820s through the 1840s occurred in southern cities.

White workers in the urban South sought rather to eliminate or control the presence of blacks in the work force through legislative prohibitions. As early as 1783, white carpenters and bricklayers in Charleston demanded protection from black artisans who undercut their wages. The authorities declined to act. In 1822, white butchers in Savannah petitioned the city

13. For a sampling of the skilled trades available to nineteenth-century African Americans, see "Directory of Occupations Held by Black Artisans and Craftsmen Prior to 1865," in *The Other Slaves: Mechanics, Artisans, and Craftsmen,* ed. James E. Newton and Ronald L. Lewis (Boston, 1978), 243–45.

14. Frederick Douglass, *Life and Times of Frederick Douglass* (1892; rpr. New York, 1962), 180.

council "to prevent slaves from butchering and selling meats in the Market on their own account and for their individual benefit," allegedly because these meats were "unfairly acquired." Evidently the council tabled the petition, since a similar request from the same group appeared before it twenty years later. In 1847, a group of skilled iron puddlers at Richmond's Tredegar Iron Works went out on strike to protest the presence of slaves alongside them. Tredegar's owner, Joseph Reid Anderson, promptly fired the white workers and replaced them with blacks. The Richmond newspapers backed Anderson completely, asserting that the protesters' action "strikes at the root of all the rights and privileges of the master, and if acknowledged, or permitted to gain foothold, will soon wholly destroy the value of slave property." [15]

Not all white workers' efforts to limit or eliminate black competition failed. Occasionally, under the guise of security or enforcement of existing legislation, white workers sought to eliminate black competition. White workers in Natchez initiated an "inquisition" against free blacks in 1841, ostensibly to investigate their conduct. According to an 1831 law in Mississippi, any free black convicted of even a minor violation was to be removed from the state. The workers succeeded in frightening a good number of free blacks into leaving Natchez, though more prominent individuals, such as William Johnson, rode out the storm. Elsewhere, white workers persuaded city administrations in the 1830s and 1840s to pass minimum-wage laws under the theory that if wages were set high enough, slaves or free blacks could not undercut white workers. The impact was marginal, however. City administrations, again responding to pressure from white workers, barred blacks from certain skilled trades as early as the 1780s. Cities also experimented with legislation restricting or prohibiting self-hire and requiring slaves to purchase badges if they were to be hired out. As noted earlier, these constraints failed to reduce black labor competition.

Why were white workers so unsuccessful (at least prior to 1850) in limiting job competition from urban free blacks and slaves? Visitors noted that the occupational status of blacks in the urban South was often higher than that of blacks in northern cities. As one student of the subject concluded, "Certainly there was no lack of racial prejudice in the South, but it does appear that this prejudice did not make itself felt in the form of discrimi-

15. Quoted in Claudia Dale Goldin, *Urban Slavery in the American South, 1820–1860: A Quantitative History* (Chicago, 1976), 29; Richmond *Times and Compiler,* May 28, 1847, quoted in Charles B. Dew, *Ironmaker to the Confederacy: Joseph R. Anderson and the Tredegar Iron Works* (New Haven, 1966), 25.

nation in employment to the degree that was common in northern cities." There are several reasons for this seeming anomaly. First when white workers attacked slave labor, they indirectly attacked slave owners, a powerful group in southern society. To limit slave hiring or reduce the presence of slaves in certain occupations affected the masters' profits. When Joseph Reid Anderson dismissed the striking white workers the Richmond *Enquirer* defended the action by noting that had Anderson not acted accordingly it would "render slave property utterly valueless and place employers in the power of their employed." [16]

From the perspective of the white employer or customer, blacks performed valuable services in cities where labor, especially skilled labor, was often in short supply. When Richmond acceded to a demand to ban blacks from the drayage business in 1810, merchants besieged officials, complaining that "there is at present a great want of waggons, drays and carts for transporting articles from one quarter of the City to another (a sufficient number of white drivers not having yet engaged in the business)." The city temporarily lifted the ban but, even then, only extended it until forty white drivers could be found. A South Carolina legislative committee in the 1840s, investigating the lax enforcement of self-hire restrictions in Charleston, acknowledged the evils of the system but added that without it, it "would be impossible to have [the] sort of labor" in cities necessary to advance the urban economy. "Until you can change the direction of the public prejudice, presuppositions & habit, you can never enforce a law which conflicts with them." [17]

Finally, when immigrants constituted the protest group, white authorities had even less sympathy with their demands. The loyalty of immigrants to the institution of slavery was open to question. As a delegate to Kentucky's 1849 constitutional convention observed, Louisville's immigrants were "hostile to slavery and its continuance." A writer in the *Southern Quarterly Review* that same year was equally pessimistic about the growing numbers of immigrants in Charleston and other cities: "Every city is destined to be the seat of free-soilism. It is unconsciously making its appearance in Charleston, and it is destined to increase with every fresh arrival of European immigrants. Whites are driving our slaves from their old employments all

16. Leonard P. Curry, *The Free Black in Urban America, 1800–1850: The Shadow of the Dream* (Chicago, 1981), 34. Richmond *Enquirer,* May 29, 1847.

17. Quoted in Marianne Buroff Sheldon, "Black-White Relations in Richmond, Virginia, 1782–1820," *Journal of Southern History,* XLV (February, 1979), 40; quoted in Wade, *Slavery in the Cities,* 52–53.

fostered by the cities." There was also concern that, despite competition, immigrants and blacks might eventually recognize a common cause—a prospect not only threatening to peaceful labor relations but also to the institution of slavery itself. As Fanny Kemble wrote in the late 1830s about the influx of Irish workers to Georgia, "There is no saying but what they might actually take to sympathy with the slaves, and I leave you to judge of the possible consequences."[18] And whatever racial solidarity existed, immigrants probably forfeited it by competing directly with slaves and free blacks for work and wages.

So slaves and free blacks clung precariously to their niche in the urban labor market. Slaves sought to advance their autonomy within the context of urban work, and free blacks hoped to maintain their economic and hence personal freedom despite their anomalous position in southern society. The relative success of both slaves and free blacks in fulfilling these objectives enabled each group not only to draw a modicum of satisfaction and identity from work but also to enhance their lives away from work.

Just as did work in the city, black family life reflected both the constraints and the promise of urban life. The slave family was a significant yet often unstable institution on the plantation. The sale of family members, whites' sexual and labor demands, escapes, and death all tore at the fabric of plantation family life. Similar pressures existed in the city for both slave and free-black families, yet both privacy and opportunities were greater in the urban areas.

Fathers and husbands on the plantation and in the city, for example, had limited authority in the family. The master controlled the work, discipline, and eventual sale of family members. On the other hand, the urban male slave might have command over his own work—an opportunity not available on the plantation. The self-hire system and the chance to earn money placed male slaves closer to the role of family breadwinner.

Urban slaves also might have the opportunity of living elsewhere, or living out, as it was called. Despite restrictions against this practice, hired slaves could, with the master's permission (and sometimes without), establish a household away from the owner's domicile. It is difficult to know the percentage of urban slaves who did so, but based on newspaper accounts

18. Randall M. Miller, "Aliens in the WASP Nest: Ethnocultural Diversity in the Antebellum Urban South" (paper in the author's possession), 42 (first quotation), 45–46 (second quotation); Frances Anne Kemble, *Journal of a Residence on a Georgian Plantation in 1838–1839,* ed. John A. Scott (1961; rpr. Athens, Ga., 1984), 125.

and local census records, one out of six slave households was living out by the late 1840s. Many masters preferred the system because it meant that they did not have to provide housing for their slaves or worry about feeding them. Some large slaveholders, such as manufacturers, provided their hired slaves with a housing allowance. A few cities, such as Athens and Mobile, required slave owners to remit a fee to enable their slaves to live elsewhere (although such was contrary to both Georgia and Alabama law).

Most accommodations were spartan at best and wretched at worst. A mid-nineteenth-century traveler, Charles G. Parsons, noted of Savannah that although "many of the dwelling houses are spacious and elegant" and the stores both "large and well filled," there were other areas filled with "low, dingy, dirty, squalid, cheerless negro huts." Slaves who lived out resided on the margins of the law, and their residences were often even worse than what Parsons described. Slaves lived in jerry-built shacks, warehouses, and even the hallways of hotels. A visitor to a Charleston hotel found "the male servants of the house . . . already laid down for the night in the passages with their clothes on. They had neither beds nor bedding, and you may kick them or tread upon them (as you come in) with impunity." In New Orleans, the traveler added, "they had no beds . . . to sleep on,—all lying, like dogs, in the passages of the house." [19]

Some slaves were able to rent out houses, however modest, for themselves and their family. Henry Box Brown, who hired out in a Richmond tobacco factory, paid seventy-two dollars a year for a house; at that, his family had never "been so pleasantly situated before." A British traveler to Richmond noted that "the dwellings occupied by the lower classes of coloured people are of a miserable kind, resembling the worst brick-houses in the back-lanes of English manufacturing towns." Such houses were often located on the urban periphery, outside of areas controlled by fire codes that prohibited the erection of flimsy wooden structures. As early as 1838, for example, the Neck area north of Charleston "rapidly filled with small cheap wooden houses" erected by slaves working in the city. [20] This residential concentration by race was unusual in the antebellum urban South, since blacks, slave and free, typically resided in all parts of the city. In any case, the ability to

19. Charles G. Parsons, *An Inside View of Slavery: A Tour Among the Planters* (1855; rpr. Savannah, 1974), 9; James Stuart, *Three Years in North America* (3 vols.; New York, 1833), II, 68, 132.

20. Henry Box Brown, *Narrative of Henry Box Brown, Who Escaped from Slavery Enclosed in a Box Three Feet Long and Two Wide* (1849; rpr. Philadelphia, 1969), 50; William Chambers, *Things as They Are in America* (Philadelphia, 1854), 271–72; quoted in Wade, *Slavery in the Cities,* 70.

live out, regardless of the quality of dwelling, allowed slave husbands and wives to remain together even if they were owned by separate masters—a practice almost impossible in the countryside.

The majority, though, lived with their masters, since most urban slaves worked in domestic service and in one- or two-slave households. Sometimes husband and wife worked and lived together with the same master; more often, they visited each other in their separate domiciles. When slaves did reside with their masters, they occupied a room that was either in the house or part of a modest slave quarters attached to the main house. The slave quarters that characterized life on large plantations were obviously not possible in cities, given the cost of urban land and the generally small slaveholdings. Occasionally, modest slave quarters emerged near factories, but since these dwellings were more similar to male dormitories than permanent living quarters (factory work forces were overwhelmingly male), there was little opportunity for family life to flourish. A typical arrangement of slave quarters in Charleston for slaveholdings of more than four was a two-story building attached to the owner's house. The first floor was reserved for a kitchen, storage, and a stable. Above were two or more rooms, usually measuring no more than ten by fifteen feet. These rooms were more often than not crowded, certainly poorly ventilated, and considering their proximity to the main house, offered little privacy. The casual coming and going, the entertaining of friends (and even of fugitive slaves), or the rearing of children apart from a master's dominion were all considerably more difficult under these living conditions than in living-out arrangements.

Although living out was conducive to a more private life for a slave family, the ability of individual slaves to form families in cities was more limited than on the plantation. Female slaves generally outnumbered male slaves in most southern cities, reflecting the dominance of domestic work. In Mobile, for example, slave women outnumbered men by a two-to-one ratio. Industrial cities of the Upper South, however, relied more heavily on male labor. In these cities, men dominated the slave population. Both Louisville and Richmond had more than one and a half times as many male as female slaves in the 1840s and 1850s.

Even if the gender ratios were relatively close, the precarious nature of the male slave's residence in the city rendered stable family life difficult. Unskilled slaves were vulnerable to sale to the countryside, especially during periods of agricultural prosperity. Urban slave populations tended to decline or stabilize during the early 1830s and through most of the 1850s, primarily due to high demand in the plantation South. The rapid expansion of the Cotton Kingdom through the lower Mississippi Valley accounted for the first wave of urban sales, and continued expansion into Texas as well as relatively high prices for cotton contributed to the boom in the 1850s. It is difficult, though, to tell how many slaves who were sold in southern cities were actually urban-based rather than brought in from the countryside. Historians have calculated that a southern slave was likely sold at least once in his or her lifetime. The chances for urban slaves were much greater. One historian has estimated that one in five urban slaves was sold annually in New Orleans. Since the majority of those sold were probably adult males, the threat if not the reality of sale to the countryside was always present for male slaves. One such individual, Peter Randolph, later wrote that "the city slave (whose lot is thought to be so easy) suddenly finds himself upon the auction-block, knocked down to the highest bidder, and carried far and forever from those dearer to him than life . . . by a fate worse than death."[21] Sometimes a mother and her child or children were sold together, but rarely was an entire family placed on the block in one unit. In other words, in the event of sale, it was unlikely that urban slave families remained intact.

The urban slave trade was extensive even during the winter months, especially in such cities as Richmond, Charleston, and New Orleans. Newspapers were filled with advertisements from slave traders; auction blocks and slave pens were often within or on the edge of the major business streets; and coffles (gangs of slaves chained together) paraded into town—each offering the urban slaves a grisly spectacle of what might become their fate. Aside from the visual reinforcement, the thought of fieldwork generated considerable anxiety. William Wells Brown recalled the time he was sold from the city: "As I had been some time out of the field, and not accustomed to work in the burning sun, it was very hard."[22] Not surprisingly, masters and employers found the threat of sale an effective disciplinary tool.

Family life for urban free blacks was relatively more stable than slave family life, though free blacks suffered from similar obstacles. Females predominated among the urban free-black population, especially in such Deep South cities as Mobile and New Orleans, where manumission patterns favored women. Still, even in such Upper South cities as Petersburg, free-black women outnumbered men by a three-to-two ratio. And in an era when female heads of household were relatively rare, free-black women in Petersburg accounted for more than half of the free-black household heads.

21. Peter Randolph, *Sketches of Slave Life; or, Illustrations of the Peculiar Institution* (2nd ed.; 1855; rpr. Philadelphia, 1969), 59.

22. William Wells Brown, *Narrative of William W. Brown, An American Slave* (London, 1849), 34.

In other cities, free-black women constituted a majority or at least a strong minority of household heads.

The prevalence of free-black women as household heads does not, however, imply that the free-black family structure was weak. In a society that attributed both slavery and freedom to race, free blacks were always in a precarious position, none more so than free-black males, who conjured up all sorts of fears among whites. Given the presence of fugitive slaves (mostly male) in the city, as well as the chance that restrictive laws could be applied arbitrarily, urban free-black males sought to maintain low profiles. Announcing their presence to the census taker, frequently a local white resident, may not have been the wisest course. In some instances, the male in the household may have posed as a slave. Urban free blacks held slaves, of course, but many if not most held those slaves for reasons other than labor exploitation. Slaves held relatives in bondage for the purpose of freeing them or because ever-tightening manumission laws required such arrangements. In other words, assessing the extent and stability of free-black families is a difficult task.

Unlike slaves, urban free blacks had the opportunity to establish households in relative freedom, though they generally followed similar residential patterns. Urban free blacks, because of limited income, restrictions on movement, and the desire to remain as anonymous as possible, also sought out alley dwellings, shacks outside of town, or stables and warehouses in various parts of the city. Since free blacks had attained a higher occupational status and greater relative acceptance in Deep South cities, residential patterns tended to be more exclusive, though nothing approaching the growing black ghettos of northern cities such as "Nigger Hill" in Boston or "Hayti" in Pittsburgh. In Charleston, for example, Coming Street was the residential heart of the free-black community. In Savannah, little more than half of the free-black population by the 1850s lived in the Oglethorpe ward. Workshops, warehouses, and a railroad depot dominated that neighborhood, making its location least desirable for residential dwellings but most affordable for free blacks. The ward had few brick dwellings and, unlike the city's other wards, contained no public square. These and other free-black districts, though lacking in aesthetics and service amenities, provided the opportunity for fellowship in recreation, religion, and mutual support. It was from these small and tenuous communities that post–Civil War black leadership emerged.

It is more proper to speak of a black community rather than of separate slave and free-black communities in the antebellum urban South. Free blacks and slaves came together in family situations, leisure activities, and in churches. They shared race, a most significant standard of Old South life; they shared living accommodations, work, resistance against and experiences of oppressions real and potential, and the capriciousness of a society unsure of, yet dependent upon, its black population. The interaction was greatest in the cities of the Upper South, where skin color, their own recent life as slaves, small numbers, and a harsh prejudice against free blacks combined to push the free into close association with the enslaved. It was precisely these relationships (many of which, ironically, were occasioned by the hostility and exclusion of white society) that raised alarms among some whites concerned that fraternization would plant destructive thoughts in the mind of slaves.

These concerns were often well founded. Whites often mentioned the Denmark Vesey conspiracy in Charleston in 1822 as an example of the adverse influence free blacks might exercise over slaves. Vesey was a blacksmith who had purchased his freedom in 1800. According to the testimony of other free blacks and slaves, Vesey had planned to rally blacks inside and around the city to gather at strategic points on the night of June 16, seize the guardhouse and arsenal, and proceed to murder the whites, plunder the city, and escape to the Caribbean. The conspirators never had an opportunity to carry out their plot due to the timely intervention of a slave, Peter Devany Prioleau, who, on the advice of his friend, William Pencil, a free black, informed his master, who in turn notified white authorities. Once the hysteria had subsided by the late summer and thirty-five blacks had been executed for their alleged role in the plot, the Vesey conspiracy became a symbol of the dangers posed by free blacks and especially by free black–slave associations (ignoring the fact that just such a relationship uncovered the plot).[23]

Whites did not require proof of murderous conspiracies to doubt the wisdom of free black–slave connections. In 1858, the New Orleans *Times-Picayune* claimed the existence of an organization of slaves and free blacks that transferred freedom papers from ex-slaves living in the North to slaves in New Orleans. There were also periodic complaints in port cities that free-black pilots or seamen passed information and literature on to slaves or, worse, helped to hide fugitives. Some cities passed ordinances prohibiting free blacks from entering the water-transport trades for these reasons, but as with most legislation restraining occupations or work relationships, they were of limited effectiveness.

23. Lionel H. Kennedy and Thomas Parker, *The Trial Record of Denmark Vesey* (1822; rpr. Boston, 1970); see also Robert S. Starobin, ed., *Denmark Vesey: The Slave Conspiracy of 1822* (Englewood Cliffs, N.J., 1970).

Despite the perceived dangers of such relationships, free blacks and slaves consorted often and even openly in antebellum southern society. After work especially, there were numerous opportunities for camaraderie between the two. All southern cities possessed taverns, grog shops, and grocery stores that served food and drink to patrons at reasonable prices. Many of these establishments were concentrated in the least desirable parts of town typically inhabited by blacks and working-class whites. They were the poor men's social clubs of the era. Although it was illegal to serve liquor to slaves throughout the urban South, the shops' proprietors (who were typically white) rarely bothered to distinguish between slave and free customers and only occasionally were they hauled before the authorities to answer for their conduct. The problem was less the sale of alcohol to slaves than the alleged plots that might be hatched in such a convivial and heady atmosphere. As one New Orleans journalist observed, the shops were "places of temptation to the lower classes, where intoxication can be cheaply purchased, where mobs and caucuses of our Slaves nightly assemble at their orgies, to inflame the brains with copious libations, and preach rebellions against their white masters."[24]

Still, it was nearly impossible for city authorities to stop the illicit traffic or the assemblages of free blacks and slaves on these premises. The frustrated mayor of Mobile, who had vowed to clean up such dens, complained that "for the convenience of [black] guests side and back doors are provided sufficiently numerous to assist a spiriting of the 'spirits' out of sight when *necessary.*" Even when caught, proprietors often escaped punishment. To the charge that they were serving brandy to blacks, "The keeper of the cabaret and his employees . . . swore positively that it was sasparilla and water." Case dismissed. A South Carolina legislative committee, investigating the situation in Charleston grog shops, blamed "the combinations which are formed by the Army of Retailers for defeating and eluding the vigilance of the strictest police."[25] The ineffectiveness of the legal constraints against the liquor trade not only underscores the sovereignty of free enterprise in the urban South but also indirectly demonstrates the extent to which slaves and free blacks were allowed to consort with each other during leisure hours.

A more sedate but equally common means of getting together was visiting. Since free blacks and slaves who lived out often resided in proximity to each other, if not in the same household, visiting must have occurred

24. Quoted in Wade, *Slavery in the Cities,* 158.
25. *Ibid.,* 152, 153.

regularly. Given the inherent instability of black family life in the city and the constraints on black life in general, visiting enabled blacks to develop an informal support network as well as to fulfill social needs. In each other's dwellings, they could discuss such taboo subjects as the sectional crisis, emancipation, and escape; they could vent frustration and anger at whites; they could pass down stories of family and past generations; and they could share neighborhood gossip. Similar interactions occurred in the evenings on the plantation, but urban blacks had more mobility and less direct white surveillance. There were no overseers and few masters in black urban districts.

Perhaps the most open and extensive fellowship between urban free blacks and slaves occurred on Sundays. Sunday provided the chance to break from the world of work and regimentation. They expressed this limited freedom by frequenting the grog shops (which were open on Sundays), visiting, dressing up, and going to church. The first two were also weekday activities; dressing up, however, was usually reserved for Sundays and provided an opportunity for self-expression in a society that frowned on black individuality.

Visitors frequently commented on such Sabbath finery, a sharp contrast to the drab costumes of the workweek. Marianne Finch, an English visitor to Richmond, noted that a black person "only appears in full-bloom on a Sunday, and then he is a very striking object; whether male, or female, whether in silks and muslins; or beaver and broadcloth."[26] Frederick Law Olmsted admired the black women he saw in Richmond: "Many of the coloured ladies were dressed not only expensively, but with good taste and effect, after the latest Parisian mode. Some of them were very attractive in appearance, and would have produced a decided sensation in any European drawing-room."[27]

Others were more shocked than impressed by such displays. Antebellum southern society placed considerable emphasis on show: a fine house, expensive appointments, and fashionable clothes helped to define the status of a lady or gentleman. Clothing, in other words, was a reflection of an individual's place in society. It was inconceivable and irritating to some that those with the least status—African Americans—should presume to be

26. Marianne Finch, *An Englishwoman's Experience in America* (London, 1853), 295; see also John T. O'Brien, "Factory, Church, and Community: Blacks in Antebellum Richmond," *Journal of Southern History,* XLIV (November, 1978), 520.

27. Frederick Law Olmsted, *The Cotton Kingdom: A Traveler's Observations on Cotton and Slavery in the American Slave States,* ed. Arthur M. Schlesinger, Sr. (New York, 1953), 37.

something they were not—full and equal citizens of southern urban society. A writer to a Charleston newspaper in 1832 expressed this view, relating that he saw a man walking in front of him whose manner and dress reminded him of a friend. "I therefore quickened my pace, came up, and slapt him on the shoulders, but, to my no small surprize . . . a sable Dandy stared me in the face." The chagrined writer complained, "How shall I distinguish our coloured Dandies and Dandresses from a Gentleman or Lady?" Coming in the wake of the Vesey conspiracy, such violations of etiquette were difficult to swallow. Soon, a Charleston grand jury proposed requiring blacks to dress "only in coarse stuffs" because "every distinction should be created between the whites and the negroes, calculated to make the latter feel the superiority of the former."[28] The proposal went nowhere, although dress codes for blacks continued to be a contentious issue among some white southerners. In 1859, a Charleston free black was mobbed by whites, ostensibly because of his flashy attire.

Sunday was a day not just for drinking, visiting, or dressing up; in fact, for many, these activities were extraneous to the day's major function as the Sabbath. If clothing represented a rare public expression of individuality, the black urban church was the ultimate private expression of the African American spirit.

Black urban churches owed their origins to the wave of black religious conversions that occurred during and after the Great Awakening in the 1740s. The evangelical sects—Baptist, Methodist, and Presbyterian—were especially eager for slave conversions. At the same time, the antislavery stance of some of these groups and their emphasis on God's rather than man's law were attractive to blacks. Some whites also found the egalitarian message of the new religious enthusiasm alluring. Though the vast majority of southern blacks and whites remained outside any church whatsoever, the Baptists and Methodists were gaining adherents. The evangelicals impressed on the masters the importance of religious training for their slaves, even while denouncing the institution of slavery. In 1785, the General Committee of the Virginia Baptist Church stated succinctly that "hereditary slavery [is] contrary to the Word of God."[29] By 1800, however, economic realities as well as the desire for increased membership and respectability muted or silenced the evangelicals' antislavery rhetoric.

Their basic tenets, however, remained attractive to southern blacks. Their presence in interracial evangelical congregations was less often an example

28. Quoted in Wade, *Slavery in the Cities,* 126, 130.
29. Quoted in Ira Berlin, *Slaves Without Masters: The Free Negro in the Antebellum South* (New York, 1974), 25.

of coercion by white masters eager to impart lessons of obedience (though
such occurred, of course) than because black southerners were eager to hear
the Gospel and express their joy at God's work. Frederick Douglass' conversion to evangelical Christianity in the 1820s was doubtless repeated many
times. As he recalled it:

I was not more than thirteen years old, when, in my loneliness and destitution, I
longed for some one to whom I could go, as to a father and protector. The preaching of a white Methodist minister . . . was the means of causing me to feel that in
God I had such a friend. He thought that all men, great and small, bond and free,
were sinners in the sight of God; that they were by nature rebels against [H]is
government; and that they must repent of their sins, and be reconciled to God
through Christ. . . . Though for weeks I was a poor, broken-hearted mourner
traveling through doubts and fears, I finally found my burden lightened, and my
heart relieved. I loved all mankind, slaveholders not excepted. . . . I saw the world
in a new light, and my great concern was to have everybody converted.[30]

Whereas most southern blacks, Douglass included, typically worshipped
in interracial churches (though they were segregated by seating), they
increasingly founded their own churches, especially in cities where there
was a sufficient number of blacks close enough to one another and at least
some black capital to support a church building and its activities. Independent black churches began to emerge in southern cities as early as the 1770s.
Black Baptists established churches in Williamsburg, in Augusta, and in
Savannah during the revolutionary era. Savannah's First African Baptist
Church grew so quickly that by 1803, two new black Baptist churches
appeared in the city. All three had free-black ministers.

Whites were of two minds on the creation of separate black churches.
On the one hand, worship services were preferable to the more secular and
raucous diversions possible in southern cities. Also, some whites took seriously the evangelical clergy's admonition that masters had a duty to con-
vert slaves to Christianity. The growth of black churches was gratifying proof
that genuine conversion was occurring. There was also the simple matter
of logistics. The popularity of evangelical theology among blacks filled interracial churches to more than capacity—the alternative was to build new
and bigger churches or let blacks organize their own. Considering the price
of urban lots and construction, the latter was easier. Sometimes the black

30. Douglass, *Life and Times of Frederick Douglass,* 90; see also Clarence L. Mohr, "Slaves
and White Churches in Confederate Georgia," in *Masters and Slaves in the House of the Lord:
Race and Religion in the American South, 1740–1870,* ed. John B. Boles (Lexington, Ky.,
1988), 154.

congregation existed as an adjunct of a white church, with a white minister overseeing the services, though usually in a perfunctory manner. More often, blacks went off with the white congregation's blessing; the whites were relieved to be spared any additional expense as well as the spectacle of the emotional and demonstrative worship patterns of black congregants.

Whites were concerned, though, about unsupervised assemblages, especially under the leadership of free-black preachers. They were well aware that the gospel was open to varying interpretations and that religion might not be the only topic at services. The leadership opportunities that churches provided, the possibility that Sunday schools were employed for teaching reading and writing, and the independence blacks might feel with their own building, minister, and worship style all ran counter to prevailing notions of the black's place in southern society. As a group of white Charlestonians noted in 1847, independent black churches gave blacks such a "plentitude of freedom of thought, word and action" that they might get "excited by the privileges they enjoy, as a separate and to some extent independent society."[31]

Charleston whites may have been especially sensitive to this issue, since they believed that the black churches had fomented the Vesey conspiracy. After authorities uncovered the plot, a mob destroyed the city's black Methodist church and officials began an harassment of black congregations that lasted the remainder of the antebellum period. Yet, despite these views, there were an estimated six thousand black Methodists in Charleston during the 1850s, and even as tolerance plummeted late in the decade, the Presbyterians erected a new, twenty-five-thousand-dollar church exclusively for a thousand-member slave and free-black congregation.

White ambivalence notwithstanding, urban blacks continued to establish churches, especially after the early 1840s, when another evangelical wave swept the South. Also, black urban populations had by then increased to a point that many congregations had outgrown their buildings or been split by theological or personal disagreements. Equally important was the splitting of national evangelical church organizations. Baptists, Methodists, and Presbyterians purged their ranks of antislavery remnants while redoubling their efforts to bring the gospel to slaves. Blacks thus took the opportunity to found new churches, even in smaller communities. In Macon, Georgia, for example, blacks between 1845 and 1860 formed separate Baptist, Methodist, and Presbyterian churches.

31. Quoted in Wade, *Slavery in the Cities,* 83.

Urban blacks were active in other religious denominations as well. An Episcopal church in Charleston, occupied by free blacks and slaves, was the target of mob wrath in 1849, though police dispersed the crowd before any damage occurred. Worshipping in interracial churches, black Catholics existed throughout the South, with a heavy concentration in New Orleans. But the predominantly Irish clergy had little understanding or appreciation of black Catholics. In New Orleans, white Catholics forced the Holy Family nuns to abandon their mission to the city's blacks. Affluent free people of color, however, were able to isolate themselves from the Irish clergy, preferring to maintain ties to their French heritage. They were also active in establishing charities directed at needy black families, though they never attempted to establish a separate black Catholic church. In fact, there were no black Catholic churches anywhere in antebellum America. It is not surprising, then, that after the Civil War, black Catholics often converted to one of the evangelical denominations or to the African Methodist Episcopal (A.M.E.) or African Methodist Episcopal Zion (A.M.E. Zion) churches.

Formed from interracial Methodist churches, the A.M.E. church was born of the 1816 merger of a black church in Baltimore and another in Philadelphia; in 1822, another Philadelphia congregation joined with a New York congregation to form the A.M.E. Zion church. Both churches recruited actively in the South, but with difficulty and little success—though in Charleston as many as fourteen hundred blacks (mostly slaves) were members of the A.M.E. church in the early 1820s, only to be routed in the wake of the Vesey conspiracy. Whites closed down a New Orleans congregation a decade later, enforcing an ordinance banning any black organization not under the control of whites. The fact that blacks typically included the word *African* in the name of their church underscores the close connection between religion and ethnic identity. There were an estimated twenty-two black churches, headed by black ministers, in the eleven largest southern cities by 1860. And there were countless other congregations that met secretly or as adjuncts to white churches.

White visitors often noticed the contrast between the blacks' services and their own—a difference born of the African Americans' distinctive experience and cultural heritage. Some visitors were shocked. Frederick Law Olmsted saw the service as "a delusive clothing of Christian forms and phrases" added to "the original vague superstition of the African savage." Clapping, singing, shouting, and even dancing punctuated the minister's sermon. Yet Olmsted was not unmoved by the scene. He described an old black man responding to the preacher: "Oh, yes! That's it, that's it! Yes,

yes—glory—yes!" Soon the congregation erupted into "shouts, and groans, terrific shrieks, and indescribable expressions of ecstasy—of pleasure or agony—and even stamping, jumping, and clapping of hands." Olmsted found "my own muscles all stretched, as if ready for a struggle—my face glowing, and my feet stamping." A more sympathetic white observer from New England left this account of a black service in antebellum Louisville: "The meeting commences with singing, through the congregation. Loud and louder still, were their devotions—and oh! what music, what devotion, what streaming eyes, and throbbing hearts; my blood runs quick in my veins, and quicker still, as they proceed and warm up in this part of the exercises. It seems as though the roof would rise from the walls, and some of them go up, soul and body both." [32]

Though some southern whites disapproved, they did not interfere. They believed that the service offered a release of energy and emotion otherwise prohibited in antebellum southern society. They also believed the sermons could reinforce prevailing notions of race. When white ministers officiated over black churches that was sometimes the case, but when blacks assumed the pulpits, the opposite often occurred. Some black ministers avoided contemporary and racial issues entirely, preferring to sway their congregations with lurid sermons of sin and damnation. Others, however, succeeded in weaving more worldly themes into their remarks, even if indirectly. Visiting a Baptist church in Savannah, Fredrika Bremer described such a minister recollecting the visit of the president of the United States to a local wealthy resident. Blacks and other poor residents had been cordoned off, while members of the local elite entered the house to pay their respects. "Now, did Christ come in this way? No! Blessed be the Lord! He came to the poor! He came to us, and for our sakes," the preacher cried. Bremer recalled that cries of " 'Amen! Hallelujah!' resounded through the chapel for a good minute or two; and the people stamped with their feet, and laughed and cried, with countenances beaming with joy." [33]

An important member of his community, the black preacher alone could openly, if indirectly, express the conditions and aspirations of slave and free black alike. Since most professions were closed to free blacks, talented black men went into the ministry. They often held other positions during the week, however, as congregations composed primarily of slaves could offer

32. Frederick Law Olmsted, *A Journey in the Black Country* (1860; rpr. Williamstown, Mass., 1972), 189; Philo Tower, *Slavery Unmasked: Being a Truthful Narrative of a Three Years' Residence and Journeying in Eleven Southern States* (Rochester, 1856), 252.

33. Bremer, *Homes of the New World,* I, 353.

only a pittance of a salary. Once in the pulpit, ministers had to satisfy both their congregation and those whites who might visit occasionally. Successful ministers learned to be circumspect without being obsequious and exercised their leadership outside the pulpit in educational and social matters quietly but effectively.

Andrew Marshall, noted earlier, was one such minister. He served as pastor of the First African Baptist Church in Savannah for more than thirty years, organizing benevolent societies to aid elderly free blacks and providing pensions to widows and children of deceased members. Free-black women in his congregation performed missionary work among the city's black poor. In 1826, Marshall initiated a Sunday school for two hundred members, mostly slaves. The school at first operated under the guidance of a white Presbyterian church but in 1835 passed to his parish's control. Marshall's caution served him and his congregation well; white Baptist churches invited him to preach, whites worshipped in his church, and he became the first black minister to address the Georgia legislature. When he began in the early 1820s, First African had a thousand members; by the mid-1830s, the church had grown to nearly twenty-five hundred slaves and free blacks.[34]

Like Marshall, black ministers led their congregations in matters transcending religion. But whereas a good deal of associational life in the black urban community emanated from the black church, formal educational institutions for blacks were rare. And if they existed at all, they periodically met with strong opposition, even violence. Francis Pinckney Holloway, a prominent free black in Charleston, opened a private school solely for free blacks but eventually had to flee the city in the face of threats against his school and person. Free blacks in Richmond opened a night school for freedmen and slaves in 1811, only to see it soon destroyed by angry whites. Henry Morehead, a slave craftsman, attended a clandestine night school in Louisville. "My owners used to object to my going to school," he later recalled, "saying that I could learn rascality enough without it." Their response "dampened my feeling for getting learning, somewhat, but I went to a night school, at my own expense of course, to learn to spell and to read. My owners found it out, and set policemen to break the school up." Such "put an end to my schooling—that was all the schooling I ever had."[35]

There was no legitimate, institutionalized way that urban blacks, espe-

34. Johnson, "Andrew C. Marshall," 173–92.

35. Benjamin Drew, *The Refugee; or, The Narratives of Fugitive Slaves in Canada* (Boston, 1856), 180.

cially slaves, could obtain an education in the Old South. When southern cities established rudimentary public education during the 1850s, only Mobile provided for black education at public expense. (In fact, Mobile merely subsidized an already existing program for free-black Creoles.) Some blacks learned by picking up newspapers or pamphlets, or through the benevolence of a master or mistress, or a white colleague at work. But many learned to read and write from ministers in Sunday school classes or in secret sessions in the church basement on weeknights. Although it is not possible to venture a guess at the degree of black literacy in the antebellum urban South, visitors who were aware of the laws against learning were astonished by what they saw. As James Stirling, who traveled to several southern cities observed, "Many slaves have learned to read in spite of all prohibitions." In Richmond, for example, "I am informed [that] almost every slave-child is learning to read."[36] Though obviously an exaggeration, the black church played an important role in eliciting that impression.

Church membership also provided the basis for mutual aid and benevolent societies that pooled the resources of one or several congregations. Aside from promoting black fellowship and welfare, these associations underscored the very real differences between black life on a plantation and in the city. Seldom did plantation blacks have a chance to form their own churches; even rarer were the instances of black rural organizations. Although not as extensive as similar black groups in the North, the southern versions offered a modest amount of support, especially for free blacks.

The extent of black benevolent societies is unknown because few African Americans applied for state charters as did their white counterparts, who were in any case uncomfortable with any assemblage of blacks. Benevolent societies dispensed donations from affluent blacks to the black poor, while mutual aid societies collected funds to support any members who were unemployed, ill, or unable to afford a decent burial. As early as 1783, free blacks in New Orleans organized the Perseverance Benevolence and Mutual Aid Association; in 1790, elite free blacks in Charleston founded the Brown Fellowship Society as a mutual-aid association. The Minors Moralist Society, of Charleston, composed of affluent free blacks, funded the education of poor and orphaned free-black children. Free-black women also organized societies such as the New Orleans Colored Female Benevolent Society, founded in 1846, dedicated to the "suppression of vice and inculcation of virtue among the colored class," and formed "to relieve the sick and bury

36. James Stirling, *Letters from the Slave States* (London, 1857), 295.

the dead." [37] Free blacks also joined national fraternal organizations such as the Masons.

A common feature of these groups was the insistence on proper burial for blacks. In a society that afforded African Americans little dignity, funerals took on significance as distinctive cultural expressions. They were also another way to escape white surveillance, which accounts in great part for why blacks lingered so long at funeral services and embellished them with music and song. As one historian noted, "The funeral became one of the most important occasions in the social life of many black communities." It was a high social occasion, a time to dress in the uniform of the mutual-aid or fraternal organization, an opportunity for eloquence, and a good excuse for socializing. Whites, though, complained about these events. According to one Charleston resident, "Three or Four, sometimes every evening in the week, there are Funerals of Negroes, accompanied by processions of 3, 4, and 5 hundred Negroes and a tumultuous crowd of other slaves who disturb all the inhabitants around the burying Ground." [38] Although whites complained as they did about any gathering of blacks, they nevertheless generally respected the black way of death, since funerals were sacred to them as well.

Some of these organizations were separate from churches, but nearly all were infused with religious principles and drew their members from the various congregations. And although they helped create both the sense and the reality of an African American urban community, the blacks' associational life also reflected the fissures within that society. Whites often feared that free blacks and slaves would make common purpose, but commonality was often difficult, especially in Lower South cities with lengthy traditions of affluent free-black populations. It is not surprising that whites in these cities were less frequently concerned about the free blacks' machinations against institutions or white society in general. But even in other parts of the South, divisions in black communities made concerted action within the constraints of a biracial society less probable.

Legal status provided the obvious basis of distinction within the antebellum urban-black community. Despite or perhaps because of the efforts of white society to compress the two groups into a caste of color, free blacks

37. See, for example, James B. Browning, "The Beginnings of Insurance Enterprise Among Negroes," *Journal of Negro History,* XXII (July, 1937), 417–32; E. Horace Fitchett, "The Traditions of the Free Negro in Charleston, South Carolina," *Journal of Negro History,* XXV (October, 1940), 144–45, 150.

38. Berlin, *Slaves Without Masters,* 307–308, 307.

not only sought to protect their legal differences from slaves but also maintain their distance as well. These efforts were especially evident in Deep South cities, where color, status, and ethnic differences between free blacks and slaves were most apparent. In these cities, light skin was a badge of freedom, though dark-skinned free blacks existed. Among the Deep South's heavily urbanized free-black population, more than 75 percent was mulatto, compared with a region-wide figure of 10 percent. Free blacks were also likely to be relatively well off, have ties to the white community (Louisiana law, for example, required every free black to have a white guardian), and, in New Orleans and Mobile at least, have French ancestry.

The divisions between free blacks and slaves in the Deep South's cities were more complex than skin color, however. The ethnic dimension was especially important in the Gulf Coast cities, even transcending legal status. The key distinction in New Orleans was between "Latin Negroes" and "American Negroes." The former resided in the French quarter, the latter in the American district. Theaters in the Crescent City provided separate seating for the "free people of color," apart from both white and black patrons. In Mobile, Creole free blacks (those with French or Spanish ancestry) were distinguished by law from other free blacks and from slaves. There were religious differences as well, with Creole blacks (slave and free) more often belonging to the Catholic church. In both cities, Creole blacks sent their children to French- and Spanish-language schools.

Class divisions also separated free blacks from each other and from slaves, too. Elite free blacks (never more than 10 percent of the free-black population in a given city) such as Natchez barber William Johnson identified with white society, held slaves, and looked with condescension toward their less-well-off brethren, both slave and free. They were likely to have white protectors or benefactors and generally escaped the periodic crackdowns on free-black privileges.

Ironically, the black church—perhaps the single most unifying element in the antebellum black community—also reflected the divisions within that same community. In the early 1800s, an interracial Methodist church in Norfolk had integrated seating for blacks and whites, but free blacks seated themselves separately from slaves. Free-black elites typically attended interracial churches rather than independent African ones. The interracial churches were likely to be Episcopalian or Presbyterian, where the service was more sedate than in the African Methodist or African Baptist churches, with their poorer free blacks and slaves. In Gulf Coast cities, it was not unusual for Creole free blacks to purchase pews in the cathedral.

Divisions within black urban communities paled in the 1850s as white society, for a variety of reasons, sought to compress black society. The heightening sectional controversy, the changing nature of southern cities, the increasing political and economic power of the urban white working class, and the white elite's anxieties about all these trends created a decade of uncertainty and turmoil for southern urban blacks. In many respects, the 1850s presaged the post–Civil War years in terms of white attempts to limit black freedoms and in terms of blacks—especially free blacks—seeking to counter those threats.

Southern cities in the 1850s were generally whiter than they had been at any other time in the nineteenth century. A combination of increased white migration, both from abroad and from the countryside, the selling or return of slaves to the booming agricultural economy, and growing restrictions on the presence, livelihoods, and mobility of free blacks together accounted for the trend. Although urban slave populations demonstrated a cyclical pattern throughout the antebellum period, the relative decline was especially significant during the 1850s. Slave populations declined absolutely in Charleston, Louisville, New Orleans, and Norfolk, whereas they increased at a slower rate than in previous decades in Mobile, Richmond, and Savannah. Smaller cities, where white migration was less significant, were less sensitive to the attractions of a prosperous agricultural economy. Baton Rouge, Little Rock, Macon, and Natchez experienced strong increases in their respective slave populations during the 1850s. On the other hand, during the same period, the free-black population increased (though at lower rates than before) in all the major southern cities except Charleston. The great boom occurred in the foreign-born population, continuing a trend begun in the 1840s. By 1860, 44.5 percent of the white inhabitants in New Orleans were foreign born, while Savannah, Mobile, Louisville, and Memphis registered one-third of the population as foreign born. As noted earlier, the percentage of these newcomers in the work force was even higher, since the vast majority were young adults.

Although southern cities were becoming more pluralistic, they were also becoming more complex. The urban South experienced its greatest decade of growth in the 1850s, sharing a national trend. New areas of the cities opened to accommodate their populations. City services, previously perfunctory, now became more routinized as local government expanded its responsibilities. Police and fire services, street numbering, public health measures, street paving and repair, and welfare services were initiated or measurably expanded. There were also additional pressures on local officials as several states expanded their suffrage rights to include all adult white males. The Democratic party in particular sought to integrate the newcomers into the political process—a tactic that both heightened government accountability and raised nativist concerns. The southern city became more fragmented, more separated into different racial, ethnic, and status groups. As southern society pulled together to counter a common enemy—the North, and more particularly, the Republican party—the demography of the urban South posed a potential threat to southern unity. The dilemma for local leaders was how to order the increasingly disparate urban environment and yet retain both its economic vitality and political orthodoxy.

Local leaders faced other pressures as well. As the sectional crisis worsened, white southerners feared that the growing economic dominance of the Northeast would eventually result in the political subjugation of their region. The concern increased as an avowedly sectional party—the Republican party—emerged in the mid-1850s. In an attempt to compete with northeastern cities and reduce financial dependence on northern merchants and brokers, leaders of the urban South launched programs to build railroads, extend international trade, and develop indigenous industry. The attempt, which fell short of its objectives, served further to heighten anxieties and sectional tensions, especially when it appeared that the Republican party would gain control of both the White House and the Congress in 1860. These three factors—changes in the South's urban population, the role of its cities in the national economy, and increasing sectionalism—formed the context within which the racial policies of the 1850s were formulated and implemented.

Southern cities and states legislated new restrictions against slaves and free blacks and renewed enforcement of old legislation that had temporarily lapsed. Given the context of the 1850s, the reasons for these measures included a desire to maximize the efficiency of a limited supply of labor, a response to pressures from increasingly influential white workingmen, anxieties over internal security, and concern about the future of slavery. Policies bore most heavily on free blacks. Slaves had "built-in" protectors in their masters; free blacks also had white supporters, but the financial link was much weaker. Free blacks, in other words, were more vulnerable to the shifting trends.

The general direction of legislation and reenforcement during the 1850s was to reduce the distinction between free black and slave. Especially late in the decade, after the Panic of 1857, after John Brown's raid on Harpers Ferry in 1859, and after the rise to prominence of the Republican party, white southerners—particularly working-class whites—sought to eliminate or reduce drastically this anomalous class. Many agreed with the Mobile *Register*'s statement in 1859 that "We can have a healthy State of society with but two classes—white and slave."[39] This was not a new crusade. Limits on manumission and free-black civil rights had existed since the late eighteenth century. Also, after the Gabriel conspiracy in Richmond in 1800, the Denmark Vesey conspiracy in Charleston in 1822, and the Nat Turner rebellion in southside Virginia in 1831, southern states and cities levied harsh new laws against free blacks, though their enforcement was deferred.

The changes in manumission legislation reflected both these trends and the worsening racial climate of the 1850s. After chipping away at individuals' ability to manumit slaves, southern states finally closed the door to freedom during the 1830s, permitting manumission only by judicial or legislative decree. By the late 1850s, most southern states had locked the door, prohibiting manumission altogether. These were statewide measures, but they affected southern cities most directly since after 1830, even though manumissions had declined in the countryside, they increased in the city despite the need to obtain outside permission.

Urban masters were also more resourceful in getting around restrictions on liberation. Unable directly to manumit a slave, they executed a deed of trust, that is, they "sold" a slave to a friend or even to a free-black relative for a nominal sum (usually one dollar), stipulating, as a Charleston mistress did, that "Kitty and Mary shall enjoy free and undisturbed liberty as if they had been regularly emancipated."[40] These "slaves," then, had virtual freedom. The practice of evading state law was so common in Mobile, for example, that city census takers established the category of "quasi-free people of color." Free blacks, after the 1830s, secured the freedom of many of their kin in this way, designating a white guardian in a deed of trust.

In the eyes of the law, however, they were still slaves, and their offspring were slaves as well. During the 1850s, authorities in South Carolina decided to enforce the 1822 state law prohibiting manumissions. Therefore, any black unable to prove manumission prior to that date was a slave, regardless of any deed of trust or other arrangement. The crackdown was especially hard on Charleston's free blacks, since as one white observed in 1848, there were "evasions [of the 1822 law] without number."[41] In connection with

39. Quoted in Harriet E. Amos, *Cotton City: Urban Development in Antebellum Mobile* (University, Ala., 1985), 99.

40. Quoted in Berlin, *Slaves Without Masters,* 144.

41. Quoted in Michael P. Johnson and James L. Roark, eds., *No Chariot Let Down: Charleston's Free People of Color on the Eve of the Civil War* (Chapel Hill, 1984), 88.

the renewed enforcement of an 1820s law requiring slaves to wear badges in order to obtain work, the strictures posed a dilemma for the city's blacks. To work without a badge one had to prove freedom—either the black or his mother or grandmother (since freedom descended from the mother's line) had to have been manumitted prior to 1822 and possess the papers to prove it. If the authorities arrested a black without a badge and the individual could not prove his or her freedom, the penalty was typically appropriation of the black and the black's property by the city. But to buy a badge was an admission that one was not, in fact, a free black but a slave. Charleston's officials swooped into action during the spring of 1860, a time of heightened sectional tension and growing political power among white workingmen (1860 was the first time in the city's history that census takers had recorded a white majority). Arrests of "slaves" working without badges went from zero in March to twenty-seven in April, and to ninety-three in August. In a sense, the sweep was an attempt to re-enslave free blacks.

The implications of the new restrictions and re-enforcements were perhaps the most tragic but not the only example of increased racial tensions during the 1850s. The cities also fashioned extensive black codes that prescribed slave and free-black behavior and served as prototypes for the codes used during Reconstruction. The regulations were usually more restrictive in the cities of the Upper South, where free blacks and slaves mingled more often, than in some of the Gulf Coast cities, where free blacks often stood apart from slaves and where whites were content to stress the differences between the two black groups. Richmond authorities, for example, passed a new code in 1857 that proved typical. The regulation banned self-hiring by slaves; it drastically reduced the ability of blacks to assemble without white supervision; it required a slave or free black to obtain a pass from his master or employer designating "the particular place or places" where he could go; it excluded blacks altogether from certain parts of the city unless to "attend to a white person." The code also specified street etiquette, prohibiting smoking, carrying a cane, standing on the sidewalk, or using "provoking language."[42] The law also assigned fines for whites who helped blacks to evade any of these provisions. Such provisions had been discussed and some even implemented in numerous southern cities prior to the 1850s. But only in that decade were all of these measures codified into a comprehensive code.

Other city ordinances reflected both the changing nature of the southern city and the growing racial tensions. Segregation, evident in churches and

42. Quoted in Wade, *Slavery in the Cities,* 107–108.

theaters since the late eighteenth century, spread as southern cities developed new institutions and technologies. Cities began to segregate jails, hospitals, and public burial grounds as they became local responsibilities after the 1830s. When horse-drawn railways appeared in the 1850s, some cities, such as New Orleans and Richmond, kept separate cars for blacks. Segregation went further in New Orleans—given the three-caste system of slaves, free blacks, and whites—as authorities provided for three separate graveyards. The city also insisted on segregated brothels, though in this instance the categories were reduced to two—black and white. Segregated seating prevailed in interracial churches, though both whites and blacks continued to prefer separate churches for each race. This preference clashed, however, with the new restraints on black gatherings. A "solution" was for black churches, increasingly harassed, to affiliate formally with a white church. In 1859, for instance, all four black congregations in New Orleans placed themselves under a white Baptist church. Their slave ministers then worked with the direction of a white minister.

In some cases, blacks were not only segregated, they were also excluded. The rise of the public school in southern cities during the 1850s is a case in point. Exclusion from certain employment is another. Charleston, for example, prohibited teaching slaves artisanal crafts. Blacks were also excluded (except as staff or as assistants to white masters) from hotels and restaurants.

Many of these new restrictions (and their enforcement) limited the role of blacks in the urban economy. The limitation was not coincidental; white workingmen supported and, in numerous instances, initiated such legislation or clamored for enforcement of existing measures. They had protested before, of course, but their growing political power, increasing economic importance (as unskilled slaves left for the countryside), and the anxieties generated by the free-black population helped white workers win new adherents among local leaders.

Ethnic politics also emerged during the 1850s. Charleston's white elite added Irish and German candidates to their citywide tickets; in Savannah, police harassment of immigrant shopkeepers became an important municipal issue. Native-born politicians, especially Democrats, courted immigrant votes. Thomas Avery, a successful congressional candidate whose district included an Irish neighborhood in Memphis, felt concerned about taking his three daughters to a labor-union party at which the young Irish men would expect them to dance. Avery expressed his appreciation to the girls for what had been distasteful both to himself and to them: "You have done splendidly. I know how you feel, but luckily I don't think those fellows know. You made them think you were having the time of your life. It will make them feel kindly toward me."[43]

Workingmen's clubs and unions grew in the 1850s along both ethnic and craft lines—such as, for example, the Irish union that Avery visited or the New Orleans Typographical Society, made up of native-born craftsmen. Under these new circumstances, it is not surprising that the measures white workers had been advocating so unsuccessfully for decades became law in the 1850s. Since the 1820s, for instance, white butchers in Savannah had tried to eliminate competition from black butchers. In 1854 they succeeded in getting an ordinance passed to that effect. Perhaps the most concerted efforts occurred in Charleston, where the new majority-white population clashed with free-black artisans. A new political coalition of upcountry law-makers and Charleston's white workingmen caused slaveholders and the free blacks' white allies to pause before actively opposing new racial restraints.

The assaults of Charleston's white workers accelerated in the 1850s and climaxed in 1859 and 1860. They elected their champion, Charles Macbeth, as mayor, and although the city council refused to give in to their demands to prohibit all slave hiring, it did agree to enforce existing laws to the letter. The re-enforcement of the badge and manumission laws was a direct result. And from the perspective of a white workingman, the pressure had effect. As James M. Johnson, a prominent Charleston free black, wrote to his brother-in-law in August, 1860, "It [the crackdown] must prove the Death of many & the loss of earthly goods, the hard earnings of a life time, to others." He reported at least one beneficiary to this policy: "Col. Seymour stood in front of our House speaking to an Irish carter on the subject & pointed to No 7 & 9 as being for sale."[44]

Encouraged, white workingmen pressed their case further with the state legislature. They elected two of their own in 1859—James M. Eason and Henry T. Peake. In 1860, they introduced a bill to prevent free blacks from engaging in any artisanal occupations, a measure sure to deal a severe blow to Charleston's free-black population. The bill failed, but the two mechanics were undeterred and introduced an even more damaging bill to enslave all free blacks living within the state by January 1, 1862. The objective was to

43. Elizabeth Avery Meriwether, *Recollections of Ninety-Two Years, 1824–1916* (Nashville, 1958), 41; see also Randall M. Miller, "The Enemy Within: Some Effects of Foreign Immigrants on Antebellum Southern Cities," *Southern Studies,* XXIV (Spring, 1985), 50.

44. James M. Johnson to Henry Ellison, August 28, 1860, quoted in Johnson and Roark, eds., *No Chariot Let Down,* 101.

induce free blacks to leave the state—thereby eliminating a workforce competitor. That bill also failed. Soon thereafter, the firing on Fort Sumter and
the war overcame efforts to remove blacks from the labor force.

Not all whites had united against blacks in the 1850s. As in the past, the
harshest measures failed because white elites, motivated by both economic
self-interest, conscience, and class prerogatives (especially strong in the class-
conscious Carolina low country) refused to support them. Frustrated white
workers thus soon recognized that blacks were not their only enemies. In
1858, the South Carolina Mechanics Association, of Charleston, unsuccessfully petitioned the legislature for a law to subject "to indictment both
the hirer as well as the owner of any slave hiring out time."[45] Besides elites,
other whites were put off by the immigrants' competing with slaves for
"nigger work." And finally, as the South's urban economy became increasingly complex, skilled slave labor performed an essential role that whites
could hardly ignore.

Free blacks also received support—though belated in the case of Charleston—from white benefactors. The ownership of property, personal probity,
and hard work were all concepts that mid-nineteenth-century Americans
valued; defenders of free blacks stressed these very traits. Implicit in the
defense was the absence of such characteristics among white workingmen.
When a group of Richmonders attacked free blacks as a criminal element,
an editor replied, "On the contrary, they number among them men of the
highest character and respectability—men of piety—men of substance—
men of considerable intelligence."[46] The argument is interesting not only
for its defense of free blacks but also because it contradicted an increasingly
prevalent assumption of the late antebellum era that blacks were inherently
inferior and incapable of making their own way in the world. After the
Civil War, when white supremacy became even more the guiding tenet of
southern society, such defenses grew yet fewer. Before the war, some whites
were less conscious of the contradiction. Others did not especially subscribe
to the conventional racial wisdom but dared not challenge it directly.

Consider the arguments advanced by John Harleston Read, Jr., a low-
country legislator who led the fight against the enslavement bill in 1860.
He testified that free blacks were "good citizens, and [exhibited] patterns
of industry, sobriety and irreproachable conduct." "They are the owners,"
he added, "of a vast amount of property, both real and personal." Read also
reminded his colleagues that, aside from the economic consequences of such

45. Quoted in Goldin, *Urban Slavery,* 29.
46. Richmond *Daily Dispatch,* February 15, 1853.

a law, its moral foundation was extremely weak: "Whilst we are battling for our rights, liberties, and institutions, can we expect the smiles and countenance [sic] of the Arbiter of all events when we make war upon the impotent and unprotected, enslave them against all justice?"[47]

Although direct protest by urban blacks was obviously limited during the 1850s, they did not entirely leave their defense to wavering white protectors or owners. When Richmond authorities passed the comprehensive black code of 1857, the city's free blacks hired a white lawyer to contest (unsuccessfully) the statutes. As the Charleston debacle unfolded in 1859 and 1860, free blacks there resorted to several tactics. They challenged police sent to enforce regulations (and from at least one account, the police retreated), and they lobbied influential whites, particularly their customers who depended upon their labor. After these strategies proved of limited effectiveness, many chose another option—migration, even though for some that meant the forced sale of property. They left for the North—Philadelphia, or Boston, for example, some for Haiti, and some to other cities in the South where they had friends or relatives. A few stayed. Between August and November, 1860, more than seven hundred free blacks left Charleston. The Philadelphia correspondent of the New York *Tribune* filed the following report: "All have been driven suddenly out of employments by which they gained a living, and are now seeking, under great disadvantages, to begin life anew. Many had acquired real estate and other property, but in the haste to get away were compelled to sell at great loss, while of what they leave behind unsold, they fully expect to be cheated. Some leave relations behind them—an old mother, a decrepid [sic] father—whom they are unable to bring away. Some have brought with them their copper badges, which read thus: Charleston, 1860, Servant, 1243."[48]

This was obviously the most unsatisfactory option of all: leaving one's home, where one had lived and worked and had shared fellowship for generations. The new destination was not likely to afford better opportunities. To be black in America, regardless of latitude, meant to be less than free. This was only slightly more of an option than slaves faced during the 1850s, many of whom found themselves back on the farm or in a different part of the South entirely.

Yet the southern city had provided slave and free black alike with a life different from and, in many respects, better than life in the country. Work was more varied, and the opportunity for making a living and earning cash

47. Quoted in Johnson and Roark, eds., *No Chariot Let Down,* 136.
48. *Ibid.,* 145.

wages was greater. So was the ability to form a black community with fellowship and institutions. Although these advantages were precarious, they served as crucial foundations for building a black life after the Civil War. It was not surprising that the core of black leadership, protest, and intellect emerged from the urban South after 1865; nor was it surprising that the southern city would become the wellspring of the civil rights movement nearly a century later. This is the ultimate legacy of black life in the cities of the Old South.

Jews, Blacks, and Southern Whites

Jews, as quintessential outsiders, have developed a sixth sense to take cues on public behavior from the host society. Survival has often depended on their relative invisibility to the Gentile population. They have had to balance the pursuit of their culture and religion with the necessity of maintaining a low profile. This tension between preservation and invisibility has lessened in recent decades in the United States, but it still forms a theme of Jewish life in the South. For the South remains the most evangelical Protestant region of the country, the most conservative part of the United States, and the place most imbued with rural culture. Jewish religious, social, and settlement traditions do not match the southern regional profile. Their success in the South, up to and even beyond the civil rights movement, depended on minimizing these differences.

The Jewish "place" in southern life—how they are perceived by white and black Gentiles—plays a key role in determining Jewish-Gentile relations in the South. As the historically dominant group in southern society, white Gentiles became accustomed to "placing" individuals as a way of ordering a chaotic and often violent region. Placing factored a long list of characteristics, including family name, birthplace, religion, occupation, and education. Placing also depended on conformity to the customs of a given rural area, town, or city, at a particular point in time. To know one's place and to act accordingly was important for getting along in the South, especially before the civil rights era.

Race remained a peripheral element in placing individuals. Although white southerners distinguished blacks by color, status, gender, and adherence to racial etiquette, African Americans occupied the lowest place in southern society, regardless of other variables. Jews usually escaped the mark of race but initially failed most of the other criteria. Once they established themselves, however, and proved their fealty to local customs, Jews qualified on several counts and moved up on the place list, though rarely if ever to the topmost rung. Mobility for Jews was possible, even probable; for blacks, rarely, if ever.

A caveat here. Jewish southerners were and are a diverse lot, despite their relatively small numbers. Sephardim in the colonial era, German Jews in the nineteenth century, and Eastern European (mainly Russian) Jews thereafter, brought distinctive traditions that did not always blend into one happy community. And denominational preferences—Orthodox, Conservative, and Reform—further divided southern Jewry. Southern white and black gentiles also included distinct social, denominational, and ethnic groups. These variations qualify some of the generalizations in this essay. But as journalists and historians have noted, although there are many Souths, there is also One South—a common set of assumptions revolving around race, religion, and most important, history. An individual's place within southern society originates from those common assumptions.

At first glance, few groups seem more out of place in the South than Jews. Centuries of restrictions in Europe made them an urban and mercantile people. Southerners have exalted rural life and looked with suspicion on cities and mercantile pursuits, which they have associated with modernism, exploitation, and alien ideas. The South also has been the nation's most dominant evangelical Protestant region for the past century. Jews are either prime targets for conversion or permanent outsiders. Finally, in a region where roots counted a great deal, Jews were from nowhere. They were a people without a country, wandering the earth to find a home anywhere, yet at home nowhere, seemingly loyal only to themselves.

Despite these major differences, the South has been hospitable to Jewish aspirations and security. Jewish southerners have attained economic and political influence far beyond their meager numbers. Their own cultural attributes account for some of this success as well as their relatively small numbers. Never comprising more than one percent of the region's population, even in cities, Jews have rarely been perceived as threatening the prevailing culture. Also, several countervailing factors in southern culture— foremost racism toward blacks—ameliorated some of the obvious differences between Jew and white Gentile in the South.

None of these moderating elements, however, have enabled Jewish southerners to overcome the distinctions between themselves and white Gentiles. Indeed, the South has always been ambivalent about Jews, sometimes embracing those in their midst but railing against "foreign" or Yankee

Hebrews, at once exuding an almost embarrassing philo-Semitism while at the same time propagating the crudest stereotypes about Jews. The South is a land of great irony, and the place of Jews in that land reflects that characteristic very well.

Few elements of southern culture demonstrate this ambivalence, even contradiction, better than evangelical Protestantism. Take the recent resolution passed by the Southern Baptist Convention to reconstitute the mission to the Jews. On the one hand, the resolution acknowledges the Jews' importance to evangelical prophecy; on the other, the thrust of the proposal is to obliterate the Jewish religion. Or take Sunday school lessons. Children learn to respect and adhere to the lessons of the Old Testament. But while numerous qualifiers frame the story of the crucifixion, many southern Gentiles learn in their lives that Jews are "Christ killers."

Evangelical Protestantism shares a number of tenets with Judaism; yet as a folk religion of the South, it also diverges from Jewish theology in several important aspects. Civic and religious leaders in the South have periodically acknowledged the Judaic roots of evangelical Protestantism. For two decades after the Civil War, three-term North Carolina governor Zebulon Vance toured the country giving a speech about Jews entitled "The Scattered Nation." He noted that "all Christian churches are but off-shoots from or grafts upon the old Jewish stock. Strike out all of Judaism from the Christian church and there remains nothing but an unmeaning superstition."[1]

Both evangelical southerners and Jews have considered themselves "Chosen People," special groups anointed by God to carry His work forward and reap the benefits in the afterlife despite setbacks on earth. As W. J. Cash observed in *The Mind of the South,* the relationship is more than parallel; it is an acknowledged bond between the two religions. On southerners' belief that they will prevail, he wrote, "Did He not suffer the first Chosen People to languish in captivity, to bleed under the heel of Marduk and Ashur and Amon and Baal?"[2] Evangelical southerners are well versed in the Old Testament, perhaps more so than other Protestant denominations. They have interpreted the Jewish State of Israel as the fulfillment of biblical prophecy on the ingathering of Jews in the Holy Land. Also, southern Protestantism, like Judaism, is inextricably bound to the culture of the people.

There are numerous incidents throughout southern history that demonstrate the philosemitism of evangelicals: the close cooperation and prox-

1. Quoted in Maurice A. Weinstein, ed., *Zebulon B. Vance and "The Scattered Nation"* (Charlotte, N.C., 1995), 23.

2. W. J. Cash, *The Mind of the South* (New York, 1941), 132.

imity of Jewish and evangelical religious institutions in many southern towns and cities; how Gentile store owners closed on Saturday morning in early-twentieth-century Woodville, Mississippi, to hear the preaching of an itinerant rabbi; and as historian Eli Evans has related, how eastern North Carolina farmers came to his grandfather's store to be blessed in the "original Hebrew." Or how a Methodist in Port Gibson, Mississippi, purchased and restored an old synagogue in 1988 simply because, as he explained, "The Jewish heritage is deep rooted here, and that's where we all come from, after all, back to Abraham." [3]

Finally, both southern evangelical Protestantism and Judaism have been relatively immune to theological fads. In 1909, Harvard's Charles W. Eliot, in his speech "The Religion of the Future," anticipated some of the religious trends of the late twentieth century, but not as practiced by Jews or southern evangelicals today. He predicted that the new religion would have "no worship, express or implied, of dead ancestors, teachers, or rulers," and that, above all, it would not "perpetuate the Hebrew anthropomorphic representations of God." [4]

Southerners and Jews have also shared a similar historical perspective. That perspective is different from the American view of history as the story of inevitable progress. Both groups conflate time zones: the past, present, and future blend into one, with the past most important of all. Traditions, especially family traditions, are very important, and in the literature and music of both cultures, the tension between traditions and the modern world forms a prominent theme. For this reason, literary critic Lewis Simpson noted, "Southern fiction and Jewish fiction have been the most complex and vital expressions of American fiction in this century. Both expressions derive from visions in which faith in the American's ability to make his own world has had an entangled confrontation with an experience of memory and history that tells him he cannot do it." [5]

Perhaps this is one reason for southern writers' fascination with Jewish themes and people, both professionally and personally. Will Percy's relationship with Caroline Stern and Thomas Wolfe's stormy affair with Aline Bernstein are two personal examples. The works of Walker Percy, Robert

---

3. Eli Evans, *The Lonely Days Were Sundays: Reflections of a Jewish Southerner* (Jackson, Miss., 1993), 59, 341; Peter Applebome, "Small-Town South Clings to Jewish History," Charlotte *Observer*, September 29, 1991.

4. Quoted in Marion Montgomery, "Solzhenitsyn as Southerner," in *Why the South Will Survive*, ed. Fifteen Southerners (Athens, Ga., 1981), 184.

5. Lewis P. Simpson, "The Southern Recovery of Memory and History," *Sewanee Review*, XLV (Winter, 1974), 14.

Penn Warren, Willie Morris, William Styron, and Pat Conroy indicate the literary attraction. On southerners and Jews, Willie Morris has written, "Despite the most manifest disparities they have emerged from two similar cultures, buttressed by old traditions of anguish and the promise of justice." Both groups, Morris notes, have "an affinity in the historical disasters of our ancestral pasts."[6]

Collective memory is also a key element in both cultures to maintain group solidarity and distinguish the group from others. Journalist Ben Robertson's comment about his upbringing in rural upstate South Carolina pertains to Jews just as much as to his kin: "All about me, on every side, was age, and history was continuous. . . . I was Southern, I was old."[7]

Jews and southerners, especially southern writers, share a sense of loneliness. The feeling of enforced detachment or exile derives from their common view of history as apart from the American experience. In *Flood,* a novel about the impending inundation of a small Tennessee town by a dam, Robert Penn Warren uses Izzie Goldfarb, a long-deceased resident of Fiddlersburg, as a metaphor for southern loneliness. We first meet Izzie as he is sitting in front of his shop on a summer evening, alternately reading and gazing out at the river, thinking we do not know what, but enveloped in a centuries-old loneliness, a weariness of flight and exile. Later in the book, as lead character Brad Tolliver and his friend search for Izzie's grave before the river obliterates it and the town, he delcares, "Hell, the whole South is lonesome. The shared experience . . . that makes the word South is lonesomeness."[8]

To be a child of history is to be set apart, especially in America, where the past is irrelevant. History has exiled both the southerner and the Jew. As Walker Percy wrote in *The Moviegoer,* "I am Jewish by instinct. We share the same exile." In an almost identical vein, journalist Jonathan Daniels asserted, "For good or for ill, being a southerner is like being a Jew. . . . There is, of course, the sense of exile."[9]

Exile implies homelessness, and Jews have been among the world's most mobile people, just as southerners have been America's most migratory group. Perhaps because of this mutual itinerancy, the attachment to place

6. Willie Morris, *The Last of the Southern Girls* (New York, 1973), 41–42; *North Toward Home* (Boston, 1967), 410.

7. Ben Robertson, *Red Hills and Cotton: An Upcountry Memory* (Columbia, S.C., 1942), 245.

8. Robert Penn Warren, *Flood* (New York, 1964), 171.

9. Walker Percy, *The Moviegoer* (New York, 1961), 89; Jonathan Daniels, *A Southerner Discovers the South* (New York, 1938), 8.

has attained almost mythic proportions for both. When Eli Evans, a writer and businessman, took a vial of North Carolina dirt into a New York City delivery room as his son was born, every southerner understood the meaning. It was a gesture that no northerner, Jew or otherwise, would likely make. Thomas Wolfe's rootless character, George Webber, ironically finds his "place" among the world's most placeless people in the most placeless city, in the most transient neighborhood. *"Place!"* Webber exclaims. "The East Side was a Place—and that was the thing that made it wonderful." Such furtive mutual recognition can sometimes drive both parties to distraction, as Wolfe discovered. As Barbra Streisand complains at the end of the movie *Prince of Tides,* "I've got to find me a nice Jewish boy; you guys are killing me." [10]

Considering the intersection of God and history in the cultures of both groups, it is not surprising that Jews found a welcome home in the South. The lure of the regional culture, so like their own in many ways, facilitated their acculturation and distinguished them from their coreligionists in the North. As Eli Evans has flatly stated, "I believe that no one born and raised in the South, even if one moves away physically, can escape its hold on the imagination." Such affinity does not imply a loss of cultural identity. In fact, being southern reinforces Judaism, as Jews have assumed the regional churchgoing habit, attending synagogues in much greater frequency and proportion than do their coreligionists in the North. [11]

The appreciation and involvement in the regional culture occasionally results in some unusual combinations for southern Jews. Food has a strong ritual element for both southerners and Jews. Some Jewish families ring in the New Year with hoppin' john, a mixture of black-eyed peas and hog jowls that brings good luck throughout the year. Children participate in public pageants that often have Christian overtones. Alfred Uhry, Atlanta-born author of *Driving Miss Daisy,* recalled that as a boy he enjoyed going on Easter-egg hunts and receiving Christmas gifts. As a member of the Atlanta Boys Choir, he participated in the annual Easter recital, belting out, "Lord, I want to be a Christian in my heart." In smaller communities, the integration has been more complete. Alfred O. Hero noted in his survey of southern Jewry more than a generation ago that small-town Jews "played poker with the sheriff, fished with the county judge, hunted with the plant-

10. Evans, *Lonely Days,* dedication page; Thomas Wolfe, *The Web and the Rock* (New York, 1937), 323, quoted in Evans, *Lonely Days,* 286.

11. Evans, *Lonely Days,* xxiii. John Shelton Reed makes this point in *One South: An Ethnic Approach to Regional Culture* (Baton Rouge, 1982), 111.

ers, and became leaders of the local Chamber of Commerce, Rotary, and other service groups."[12]

So thoroughly acclimated have Jews become that some Gentiles have regretted the assimilation. In the 1930s, Will Percy complained to David Cohn, his Jewish neighbor in Greenville, Mississippi, "I have a great grievance against southern Jews. It is that they have fallen to the level of Gentiles." He recalled discussing music and literature with local Jews twenty years earlier, "but now [they] are just like everybody else—nice people and rooters for the home team. I never did expect to be able to talk to many Gentiles, and now that I can't talk to the Jews, I sit here a lonely man."[13]

Part of the Jewish success in the South results from the place occupied by blacks, the third side of the triangular relationship between Jews and black and white Gentiles. The Jewish place in the South relates to their distance from blacks. As Jonathan Daniels noted, "The direction of racial prejudice at the Negro frees the Jew from prejudice altogether—or nearly altogether." In the 1950s, the Little Rock White Citizens' Council expelled one of its leaders for anti-Semitism. A council spokesman explained, "You see, we had to throw him out, because we can't afford to be seen as an anti-Jewish organization. Why, we are having trouble enough just being anti-Negro." Which confirms Hodding Carter's comment that "it takes perseverance to hate Jews and Negroes and Catholics all at the same time." The South, in short, has been the land of the ethnic meltdown. As historian George B. Tindall observed, "Over the years, all those southerners with names like Kruttschnitt, Kolb, De Bardeleben . . . Toledano, Moise . . . or Cheros got melted down and poured back out in the mold of good old boys and girls, if not of the gentry."[14]

The meltdown, however, has not been complete for Jewish southerners. The very factors that drew Jews and southerners together also pulled them

12. Quoted in Jim Auchmutey, "Daisy: The Long Drive to Hollywood," *Southpoint,* I (December, 1989): 43; Alfred O. Hero, Jr., *The Southerner and World Affairs* (Baton Rouge, 1965), 482.

13. Quoted in James C. Cobb, ed., *The Mississippi Delta and the World: The Memoirs of David L. Cohn* (Baton Rouge, 1995), 171.

14. Daniels, *A Southerner Doscovers the South,* 259; quoted in Thomas F. Pettigrew, "Parallel and Distinctive Changes in Anti-Semitic and Anti-Negro Attitudes," in *Jews in the Mind of America,* ed. Charles H. Stember *et al.* (New York, 1966), 377; quoted in Howard N. Rabinowitz, "Nativism, Bigotry, and Anti-Semitism in the South and Nation (paper presented at Temple Beth Ahabah, Richmond, Virginia, November 13, 1986); George B. Tindall, "Beyond the Mainstream: The Ethnic Southerners," *Journal of Southern History,* XL (February, 1974), 8.

apart and created ambivalent if not downright contradictory Jewish–Gentile relations. Evangelical Protestants may trace their theology to the ancient Hebrews, but they have also viewed Jews as "Christ-killers." They have clashed with Jews over such issues as Sunday-closing laws and school prayer. Also, Talmudic traditions are based on doubt: that is, Judaism is rife with interpretive differences and constant questioning of biblical meaning; debate, analysis, and reinterpretation are expected. Evangelical Protestantism, as often practiced in the South, abjures doubt and is uncomfortable with skeptical inquiry.

The tempering factors in national religious life, such as religious diversity and the strict separation of church and state, have been less evident in the South. The religious monopoly of evangelical Protestantism and the historical resistance of Jews to conversion lead to mutual distrust and suspicion. During the PTL scandals of the late 1980s, when Jim Bakker and Jerry Falwell struggled for control of the ministry, the most telling canard that the Bakker forces used against Falwell was that he might have Jewish blood.[15]

Some white southerners perceived Jews as sufficiently alien to place them on a par with blacks, or even worse. The lynching of Leo Frank in 1915 jolted Jewish southerners, and its memory hovered over Jewish life in the South through much of this century. More than any other event, the Frank lynching demonstrated that acceptance, however widespread, and success, however attainable, were qualified. The lynching reinforced the importance of vigilance and circumspection as the cost for maintaining a comfortable life in the region, and it also affected Jewish relations with African Americans.

Leo Frank, a New York Jew, managed a pencil factory in Atlanta. The plant employed many young white girls from surrounding farms and towns. The girls worked at low wages amid filthy conditions with little privacy. Rumors circulated that supervisors traded promotions and better pay for sexual favors. The rapid urban and industrial growth of the South during the early twentieth century, coupled with declining farm income, uprooted families, removed children from the supervision of parents, and placed employers in positions of power over youngsters. Many working-class white families both feared and resented the new urban industrial order and its implications for family life.

Thirteen-year-old Mary Phagan typified many of the workers in the pencil factory. Her family had lost their farm and worked as tenants. She

15. See Hunter James, *Smile Pretty and Say Jesus: The Last Great Days of PTL* (Athens, Ga., 1993), 151.

moved to Atlanta to help support her family. On Confederate Memorial Day, someone robbed and murdered Mary as she left the factory to attend the parade downtown. Frank, a northern urban Jew who employed poor white Gentile southern girls, became the convenient focus of the investigation. He was arrested, charged, tried, and sentenced to death for the murder, largely on the testimony of a black janitor with a criminal record. Much of the evidence pointed to the janitor, and not to Frank, as the killer.

That a prosperous manager would rob and then kill a poor young employee made little sense. But rumors surfaced that Mary had been raped, a charge unsubstantiated by the medical examiner's report. The rumor, taken as fact, fueled a torrent of anti-Semitic rhetoric about lustful Jews ravishing young white Christian girls. Georgia politician Tom Watson described the pencil factory as "a Jewish convent as lascivious as a Catholic monastery."[16] What made the case more bizarre was that white public opinion ignored the mounting evidence against the black janitor at a time when the image of black fiends raping white women had spurred a frenzy of lynching in the South.

The whole affair embarrassed Atlanta's leading white citizens, and they supported a movement to convince the governor to at least commute Frank's death sentence. At great personal and political peril, Governor John Slaton did just that. But a group of twenty-five men calling themselves the "Knights of Mary Phagan" pulled Frank from his cell in August, 1915, drove to Marietta, Mary's hometown, and lynched their prisoner.

The Leo Frank lynching reverberated throughout southern Jewry, particularly in Atlanta. Josephine Joel, a Jewish high school student in Atlanta in 1915, recalled that so great was the fear of anti-Semitic terrorism when Governor Slaton commuted Frank's sentence, that many Jewish families packed children and women off to relatives in other parts of the country. Josephine's father sent his entire family to live with relatives in Birmingham. When Josephine returned to Atlanta, she noted in her diary that her French teacher took special care to make her welcome. The teacher was Mattie Slaton, the governor's sister.[17]

---

16. Quoted in Nancy MacLean, "The Leo Frank Case Reconsidered: Gender and Sexual Politics in the Making of Reactionary Populism," *Journal of American History,* LXXVIII (December, 1991), 942. Although there are numerous accounts of the Frank lynching, MacLean's is the best among the more recent studies in placing the event in a broader regional context.

17. Mark K. Bauman, "The Youthful Musings of a Jewish Community Activist: Josephine Joel Heyman," *Atlanta History,* XXXIX (Summer, 1995), 46–59.

Although Josephine's life returned to normal, and Atlanta's Jews weathered the crisis without any diminution in their status or influence, the Frank lynching served as a lesson that skin color did not give Jewish southerners immunity from the fury of white supremacy. The Frank lynching also reminded Jews that although they were not black, many southerners did not consider them white. Almost like William Faulkner's mulatto, Joe Christmas in *Light in August,* Jewish southerners sometimes wandered in a half life between the legitimacy of being white and the outcast state of being black. Being neither, they were suspect by both. Invisibility proved the best defense; and in the context of southern society prior to the 1960s, invisibility meant the public acceptance of racial segregation, even if silence tortured the Jewish soul privately.

The association of Jewish southerners with blacks in Gentile perceptions heightened Jewish vigilance during periods of racial tension. "It was always an axiom of Jewish life in the South," Eli Evans explained, "that racial trouble meant heated passions and a dangerous atmosphere that was 'bad for the Jews.' "[18]

White Gentile southerners used more subtle ways than violence or its threat to exclude Jews or, more properly, to remind Jews that they were not completely citizens of the South. As in the North, certain clubs, resorts, and neighborhoods refused them entry. Some universities, such as Emory in Atlanta and the University of North Carolina in Chapel Hill, restricted Jewish admissions in a few graduate programs.[19]

More than specific instances, however, an atmosphere prevailed that excluded Jews from full membership in the southern brotherhood. Louis D. Rubin, Jr., whose southern credentials none would deny, told of a recurring dream he had had as a child in Charleston. In his recollection, Confederate soldiers are patrolling the gateway to Hampton Park. "The soldiers who patrolled the gateway did not bar my passage through the gate," he recalled, "but they were present, going about their business, unconcerned with who I was or what I might want. To get into the garden I should have to go through the Confederate soldiers." Rubin never made the attempt in his dreams, but it symbolized the Rubins' place in Charleston. As Rubin noted, "We were part of [Charleston's] community life. But we were Jewish."[20]

18. *Ibid.,* 110.
19. See Edward C. Halperin, "Frank Porter Graham, Isaac Hall Manning, and the Jewish Quota at the University of North Carolina Medical School," *North Carolina Historical Review,* LXVII (October, 1990), 385–410.
20. Louis D. Rubin, Jr., "The Southern Martial Tradition: A Memory," *Southern Cultures,* I (Winter, 1995), 289.

An objective of Jewish existence in the South has been to minimize this "but" factor. White southerners have welcomed Jews warmly but conditionally. The Jewish adjustment to their place in southern life involved accepting southern traditions, especially racial customs, so as not to arouse suspicion or confirm prejudices while, at the same time, maintaining Jewish identity. Jewish life in the South proceeded in a particular cadence, a delicate dance between assimilation and distinctiveness.

Relations between Jewish southerners and blacks fit within the context of this dance. Blacks understood the dance because they had internalized many of the steps. They balanced humiliation with self-respect, adopting the appropriate subservient etiquette as their public selves, while privately building a race-conscious community. Even partial assimilation was never a realistic objective for them as it was for Jewish southerners; southern blacks sought survival and accommodation. Yet there was a comparability between black and Jew in the act they played for the dominant white Protestant society. Their relationship reflected both the possibility of shared community and the bitter disappointment of missed opportunities.

Blacks generally perceived Jews as whites, but different from Gentiles, and in some cases, even a differenct race. Keen to the ways of discrimination, they saw how some Gentiles treated and talked about Jews. In the early 1900s, when the Richmond YMCA accepted Jews as members but not as lodgers, the black Richmond *Planet* commented, "It may not be too much to say that in some sections of the country the antipathy to Jews in the hotels is almost as marked as it is to Negroes." Blacks often noted approvingly how Jews stayed together and married among themselves. One black writer observed, "Only now and then does a Jew cross the line and marry into another race."[21]

The affinity blacks perceived went beyond mere observation and extended into the same areas that connected Jewish southerners to white Gentiles. Jewish history in general and the Old Testament in particular provided sustenance and proof for the ultimate redemption and success of African Americans. Slaves sang out the lessons of Exodus: "Go Down, Moses / way down, in Egypt land; / tell old Pharaoh, Let My People Go." One of the leaders of Gabriel's revolt in Virginia in 1800 inspired his followers by reminding them of the days "when the Israelites were in servitude to King Pharaoh and they were taken from him by the power of God."[22]

21. Both quotes in Arnold Shankman, *Ambivalent Friends: Afro-Americans View the Immigrant* (Westport, Conn., 1982), 129, 135.

22. Quoted in Joseph P. Weinberg, "Black-Jewish Tensions: Their Genesis," *CCAR Journal*, XXI (Spring, 1974), 32.

The affinity extended after the Civil War. Booker T. Washington found "the most fascinating portion of the Bible the story of the manner in which Moses led the Children of Israel out of the house of bondage, through the wilderness, into the promised land." Black novelist Zora Neale Hurston took Old Testament stories as inspiration for some of her early works, especially *Moses, Man of the Mountain,* a takeoff on the Book of Exodus. Hurston admired the Jews for having "a God who laid about [them] when they needed Him." Most blacks took to the Hebrew Scriptures "as a duck to water," according to NAACP offical and Howard University professor Kelly Miller.[23]

Black affinity for Jews reached into the southern secular world. Jewish merchants and black customers established a close relationship in the Jim Crow era. Most black neighborhoods in the urban South included at least one Jewish-owned store. Theodore Coleman, the son of Miss Daisy's chauffeur, recalled moving frequently within Atlanta's black neighborhoods before World War II, but no matter where "we lived, there seemed to be a Jewish store on the corner."[24]

The history of this relationship extends back to the Civil War era when Jewish peddlers—"rolling store men," as Alice Walker remembers her parents calling them—penetrated the rural South and provided one of the few nonthreatening white contacts for black families.[25] Some peddlers catered exclusively to a black clientele. Sometimes they "graduated" to a small store in the black section of a town, where they provided services most white merchants refused to offer.

Jewish merchants occasionally, and always quietly, extended courtesies to black customers that white businessmen rarely offered. They allowed black customers to try on clothing and referred to them as "Mr." or "Mrs." Alex Haley noted how Jewish store owners in Henning, Tennessee, treated his parents with respect. Southern historian Bell Wiley related that the Jewish owner of a dry-goods store in his small Tennessee hometown "got most of the black trade because he treated Negroes as human beings and was kindly to them, taking time to joke, inquire about their families and otherwise manifest interest in them." Kelly Miller praised the "tutelage" of Jewish merchants who hired black clerks.[26] The clerks often became fluent in Yid-

---

23. Quoted in Shankman, *Ambivalent Friends,* 115; quoted in Andrew Delbanco, "The Mark of Zora," *New Republic,* July 3, 1995, 32; quoted in Shankman, *Ambivalent Friends,* 115.

24. Quoted in Auchmutey, "Daisy," 43.

25. Quoted in Evans, *Lonely Days,* 7.

26. *Ibid.,* 11; quoted in Shankman, *Ambivalent Friends,* 114, 121.

dish, a phenomenon northern and foreign travelers often found amazing. Jewish businesses advertised heavily in the black press. Scarcely a southern black existed prior to 1960, before the chain stores gobbled up free enterprise in the urban South, who had not spent some time in a Jewish-owned store.

Witnessing Jewish business acumen first hand, blacks often cited Jews as positive examples for their own race. Black Louisiana politician P. B. S. Pinchback offered an audience of discouraged Mississippi blacks in 1876 the example of Jewish upward mobility: "Like you they were once slaves and after they were emancipated they met with persecutions. Generation after generation they fought their oppressors, and backed by principles they believed were right they finally emerged victorious. Once despised, they are now leaders of education and princes of the commerical world." [27]

Two decades later, black leader Booker T. Washington picked up the refrain. He often presented the tale of a Jewish emigré who arrived in a small town near Tuskegee in 1890 with "all of his possessions in a single satchel." He built a store, and within four years his business grossed fifty thousand dollars annually. Investing some of his profits in land, he acquired a plantation of several hundred acres by the late 1890s. Washington concluded that blacks should emulate "the saving and economical qualities of the Jews." Ironically, Washington continued to emphasize the type of vocational education that would preclude most blacks from following the Jewish example. Yet the analogy persisted in Southern black culture. In 1926, a black editor in Norfolk, summarized the Jewish example for his readers: "In many ways the Jews show us how to succeed. The Jews have taught the Afro-American people how to organize and stand together; how to make money and how to save and wisely spend it, and how to conquer prejudices, obstacles, by mastering for themselves a place in all of the thought and efforts of our tremendous civilization. . . . How do they do it? They do it by sticking together; by taking a commanding part in the trade and finance of the world and by going into all of the intellectual fields where money and influence are possible to be made." [28]

Although blacks acknowledged that Jewish southerners were different in some positive ways from other southern whites, the dividing lines of race, class, and culture tempered black perceptions. As with southern whites, a tradition of anti-Semitism existed alongside a tradition of philo-Semitism.

27. Quoted in Shankman, *Ambivalent Friends,* 116.
28. Quoted *ibid.,* 118; "The Jew Shows Us How in Many Ways," Norfolk *Journal and Guide,* May 22, 1926.

In some respects, the origins of black anti-Semitism reflected their southern heritage more than their racial background; in others, it related directly to the Jewish response to blacks.

Despite the religious and commerical affinities, blacks grew up with grave doubts about Jews. Black novelist Richard Wright acknowledged that growing up in Arkansas, "To hold an attitude of antagonism or distrust toward Jews was bred in us from childhood; it was not merely racial prejudice, it was a part of our cultural heritage." In 1945, the Nashville-based *National Baptist Voice,* a black newspaper, conceded that "Negroes are filled with Anti-Semitism. In any group of Negroes, if the white people are not around, the mention of the Jew calls forth bitter tirades." [29]

Black hostility toward southern Jews focused on the issues of Judaism and economic exploitation. After 1800, many slaves converted to evangelical Christianity. Although they derived much from the Old Testament for their purposes, they also imbibed the prevailing notion of Jews as Christ killers. Richard Wright's initial distrust of Jews emerged, as he explained, "because we had been taught at home and in Sunday school that Jews were 'Christ killers.'" Although most slave spirituals exalted Old Testament prophets, one included the following lines: "The Jews killed poor Jesus, an' laid him in a tomb. / He 'rose, he 'rose, and 'went to heaven in a cloud." [30]

The familiar relationship between Jewish shopkeepers and black customers often bred contempt, reflecting differences of both class and race. Black leaders, such as Booker T. Washington, who praised Jewish ambition publicly (many of his benefactors were Jewish), worried privately that "we are getting our trade too much centered in the hands of a few Jews." At the same time, black editor T. Thomas Fortune, who grew up in Florida, blamed Jewish merchants for squeezing white planters, who in turn exploited black laborers. In the 1930s, Kelly Miller traced the origins of exploitation to ancient Egypt, where "Jewish servant women borrowed earrings and fingers rings of their Egyptian mistresses [and] set up their husbands in the jewelry business." [31]

29. Richard Wright, *Black Boy* (1937; rpr. New York, 1951), 71; quoted in Leonard Dinnerstein, *Uneasy at Home: Antisemitism and the American Jewish Experience* (New York, 1987), 230–31.

30. Wright, *Black Boy,* 70; quoted in Shankman, *Ambivalent Friends,* 134.

31. Quoted in Leonard Dinnerstein, "The Origins of Black Anti-Semitism," *American Jewish Archives,* XXXVIII (November, 1986), 118; David J. Hellwig, "Black Images of Jews: From Reconstruction to Depression," *Societas,* VIII (Summer, 1978), 218; quoted in Shankman, *Ambivalent Friends,* 122.

Some of these remarks were tinged with the bitterness of betrayal: the feeling that Jews had traded friendship for racial solidarity. As black educator Horace Mann Bond noted in 1965, "Much of the sharpest feeling among Negroes about Jews arises from a feeling that this man has especially let you down; he, of all men, ought to know what it was like; and how it had been." [32]

The dance that Jewish southerners performed to keep their place in southern society precluded a close relationship with blacks. In the triangular relationship between Jew, black, and white Gentile, southern cultural traditions (including religion and race) drew Jewish southerners closer to other whites. The dance required Jewish southerners to maintain a low profile, especially with respect to race. To call attention to themselves meant to call attention to their difference. And to comment on racial matters would reinforce the perceptions of the affinity of blacks and Jews. Eli Evans, who is generally positive about his family's life in the South, admitted that "the Jews in the South have internalized a deep lesson: that the best way to survive was to be quiet about their presence." [33] Silence even extended to not speaking out on anti-Semitism for fear of being linked in the Gentile mind with blacks.

Nowhere was this silence more evident than in the area of race relations. A survey of the Nashville Jewish newspaper between 1939 and 1949 revealed that the paper discussecd racial discrimination just four times, and briefly at that. And when they commented on racial matters, editors often repeated the views of the larger white community. In the process of wishing for a white hope to defeat black heavyweight champion Joe Louis, an editorial asserted, "The color line is one which the colored folk may never hop to cross as a race, but the colored folk have given us some whom we are proud to claim as citizens." [34]

Even when Nashville Jews performed good deeds on behalf of the city's black community, they did not publicize them. During World War II, the Nashville chapter of the National Council of Jewish Women (NCJW) operated a day-care center for black children. Nashville's white Gentile community displayed no similar benevolence. The city's Jewish newspaper made no mention of the day-care center, although several major articles appeared on NCJW participation in funding a nonsectarian children's hospital. The

---

32. Horace Mann Bond, "Negro Attitudes Toward Jews," *Jewish Social Studies,* XXVII (January, 1965), 9.

33. Evans, *Lonely Days,* 30.

34. Nashville *Observer,* May 8, 1942.

latter demonstrated, as one NCJW member asserted, that Jews are "contributing agents to the community in which we live." The NCJW never commented on the day-care center.[35]

During the civil rights era, many Jews remained on the sidelines, even if privately they cheered black protest. In smaller towns in the Deep South, Jews rarely spoke out. As one Meridian, Mississippi, Jew put it in the 1950s, "We have to work quietly, secretly. We have to play ball." Jews were so successful in maintaining their silence that white southerners had little clue about Jewish views on race relations. Although polls revealed Jewish southerners supported civil rights initiatives more than other white southerners, only 15 percent of Gentiles polled in a 1959 survey believed that Jewish southerners favored intergration; a whopping 67 percent replied that they had no idea about Jewish racial views.[36]

Equally as frustrating for blacks, some Jews seemed unconscious of black distress. David Cohn wrote of Greenville in the 1930s that bigots formed only "a tiny minority" of the town. Did Delta blacks feel that way? During the civil rights era, southern Jewish leaders often confronted their northern brethren and either warned them out of town or implored them to remain silent. A Jewish political leader in the Deep South advised northern co-religionists to stay away, assuring them that "there is no race problem here except when it is created from the outside."[37]

This is not to say that Jews failed to respond positively to black civil rights initiatives. Even before the civil rights era, prominent Jews moved to the liberal edge of community sentiment, especially in the larger cities of the South. Early in the century, southern Jews played an important role in the Committee on Interracial Cooperation. Southern chapters of the NCJW supported Jessie Daniel Ames's Association of Southern Women for the Prevention of Lynching. And while Alfred Uhry's grandmother thought that blacks were like children at times, she supported their right for equal, though segregated, education—a rather advanced position in the 1930s. When Jews served on southern school boards in the Jim Crow era, they frequently advocated upgrading black public schools. Occasionally, southern Jews participated in NAACP lawsuits when their interests matched those of local blacks. In the 1920s, for example, the Savannah Jewish community

35. Nashville Council on Jewish Women, "Annual Report, 1942–43" (Jewish Federation Archives, Nashville, Tennessee).

36. Quoted in Rabinowitz, "Nativism, Bigotry and Anti-Semitism"; Hero, *The Southerner and World Affairs*, 496.

37. Cobb, ed., *Cohn*, 197; Hero, *The Southerner and World Affairs*, 479.

supported an NAACP protest against housing discrimination. As the black Savannah *Tribune* noted, Jews were interested in the issue "because of the effect the case will have on similar lawsuits involving Jews."[38] And when the civil rights movement emerged in the 1950s, some Jewish clerics joined their black brethren.

The post–civil rights era in the South has not brought about an appreciable improvement in black–Jewish relations. Although there are numerous examples of cooperation, such as the Atlanta Black-Jewish Coalition and Jewish involvement in Habitat for Humanity, a gulf between Jewish southerners and blacks persists, reflecting both the racial divisions in the larger society and the anomalous place of Jews in the South.

Jews still feel the need to dance the delicate line between assimilation and distinctiveness. The merging of the radical Christian right and Klan elements in the South concern Jewish southerners. The growing influence of the Christian Coalition also generates uneasiness. When Rabbi James Bennett of Charlotte spoke out against school prayer, an angry letter writer to the local newspaper ordered the rabbi to return to his own country, since "America serves God," and the rabbi does not.[39] Rabbi Bennett, incidentally, is from Ft. Worth, Texas. Also in Charlotte, a proposal to move the city's two synagogues to a campus adjacent to the new Jewish Community Center touched off a bitter debate within the Jewish community. The essence of the controversy was whether the grouping would look too much like "clannishness" to the Gentiles and feed a perception that Jews were withdrawing from civic life into their historical ghetto. The plan went forward. Oddly enough, most Gentiles thought the concept was attractive, and today more than one-quarter of the center's membership is non-Jewish. Many of the Jewish members are newcomers from the North; their racial attitudes on the whole are little different from Jewish southerners and, if anything, less liberal.

The point is that Jewish life in the South remains wonderful but conditional, and race relations still reflect that. In *The Mind of the South,* W. J. Cash stated that "the Jew, with his universal refusal to be assimilated, is everywhere the eternal Alien; and in the South, where any difference had always stood out with great vividness, he was especially so." A few years after Cash wrote, David Cohn recalled, "I was born and raised in a good world. It was far more Gentile than Jewish, but I never felt alien there, nor was any attempt made to make me feel alien." When Eli Evans undertook

---

38. Quoted in Shankman, *Ambivalent Friends,* 131.
39. Charlotte *Observer,* October 12, 1994.

research for his book on southern Jews, he discovered that "Jews were not aliens in the promised land, but blood-and-bones part of southern history."[40]

So who is right, Cash the Gentile, or Cohn and Evans, both of whom grew up as Jewish southerners? It may be that all three are correct and reflect the contradictions inherent in contemporary southern culture: Jews as indelibly part of the South, yet apart from it; as sharing a common culture with white Gentiles, yet often reminded of cultural differences; as historically and culturally sympathetic to black equality, yet distanced by the realities of race in the South and the Jewish instinct for self-preservation in a foreign land.

40. Cash, *Mind of the South,* 334; Cobb, ed., *Cohn,* 197; Evans, *Lonely Days,* xxii.

BLACK POLITICAL POWER AND PUBLIC

POLICY IN THE URBAN SOUTH

Yellow Jim was a resourceful slave. Between 1847 and 1853, Yellow Jim earned nearly nineteen hundred dollars for his master, James Rudd. If you asked Rudd what Yellow Jim did in Louisville to receive such a handsome sum, however, his response would be vague. In truth, Rudd probably did not care to know the secret of Yellow Jim's success as long as his slave dutifully remitted a fair return. A terse notation on Yellow Jim in Rudd's ledger indicates that Rudd should have been more involved in the slave's activities: "Dec. 11, 1853. Ranaway." [1]

There were many Yellow Jims in the antebellum urban South—a maddening fact to those who worried about the effect of urban life on slavery. Yellow Jim was able to expand the narrow margins of his life by hiring out his own time, selecting a place to live, frequenting shops that sold liquor, attending church, mingling with whites and fellow blacks, slave and free, and even learning to read and write. His very name bespoke the ambiguous lines of race in the Old South. Yet almost all of his activities were at one time or another illegal, not only in Louisville but also in most other antebellum southern cities.

Yellow Jim's ambiguous status reflected both the tensions within white society on how to regulate urban blacks and the persistence of blacks to test the limits of their bondage. The crucial role of black labor in the antebellum urban South drove a wedge into white society. Slave and free-black males

---

1. Richard C. Wade, *Slavery in the Cities: The South, 1820–1860* (New York, n.d.), 53.

worked in the tobacco factories of Richmond; drove the drays from the wharves of Charleston, Mobile, and New Orleans; paved the roads; shod the horses; and cut the hair of whites in Louisville and Savannah. Black women performed domestic services, including caring for children, laundering, marketing, and housekeeping. Restricting the mobility and choice of labor meant limiting access by employers, which in turn adversely affected economic development. Occasionally, especially during the turbulent 1850s, crackdowns occurred; local authorities increased police patrols and closed shops, churches, and schools. But the value of black labor generally overcame the misgivings of white decision makers, and cities invariably lapsed back into customary patterns.

Such indulgence angered working-class whites in particular: it blurred racial boundaries and threatened their livelihood. Although regulations barred blacks from the professions, they were free to take artisanal trades that competed directly with whites. City councils, concerned about the growing political clout of working-class whites, often responded positively to their antiblack petitions. Enforcement was another matter. There the interests of the slaveholders prevailed. To restrict and remove slaves from the workplace damaged the investment of the slaveholder. As the example of Yellow Jim indicates, slaves could earn respectable sums for their masters. The proliferation of regulation and the weakness of enforcement reflected these opposing interests in white urban society.

The efforts of urban blacks played a role in the distinction between legislation and enforcement. The free-black population, existing precariously between slavery and freedom, had managed to carve a place in urban society. Free blacks had formed churches, mutual-aid societies, and social clubs. They also had maintained close ties with the white elite. Their gentle entreaties to influential white patrons often spared their class from harsh legislation. The fascinating correspondence of James M. Johnson reveals these delicate and crucial relations in Charleston, especially in the years immediately preceding the Civil War, when the city's white workers mounted strong campaigns to expel free blacks. Combined with the paternal bonds that existed between some masters and their urban-based slaves, these relationships implied that blacks had at least some influence among the white power structure.[2]

2. For the annotated version of James M. Johnson's correspondence, see Michael P. Johnson and James L. Roark, eds., *No Chariot Let Down: Charleston's Free People of Color on the Eve of the Civil War* (Chapel Hill, 1984).

RACIAL POLICIES DURING SEGREGATION
AND BEFORE VOTING RIGHTS

The relative protection from adverse policies that urban blacks experienced in the antebellum era vanished after the Civil War. The abolition of slavery removed a major obstacle to white solidarity. The urban South still needed dependable black labor, but protecting investments was no longer a reason to prefer or indulge black workers. Urban leaders forged white solidarity to secure their economic and political dominance in the new era. White supremacy was the carrot offered to whites for surrendering their political autonomy; black rule and race war were the alternatives. Urban policies restricted black geographic and occupational mobility, segregated blacks in public facilities and schools, and excluded them from urban services. Although urban blacks persisted in challenging these conditions, often at great personal peril, their economic and political fortunes suffered serious setbacks through the early decades of the twentieth century.

The flurry of adverse legislation directed at urban blacks during the decades after the Civil War reflected the growing concentration of blacks in southern cities. The percentage of blacks in the urban South declined steadily in the late antebellum period. After the war, however, blacks flooded into southern cities, seeking friends, family, and work. The memoirs of Frederick Douglass and other former slaves make it clear that before the Civil War, slaves considered work in the city a significant upgrade in their status.[3] But slaves, of course, could not make that decision—to leave the farm for the city. People freed from slavery could and did.

When blacks arrived in southern cities after the Civil War, they found black-run institutions to help them with the transition to urban life. Many plantation slaves were already familiar with some aspects of city living, either through relatives or through occasional excursions to sell produce. Also, southern cities were hardly metropolises, so adjustments were not difficult. Blacks from rural areas eagerly joined churches, filled schools, and entered the local economy and political culture.

By the early 1870s, and especially after the depression of 1873, the fortunes of urban blacks began to decline, though not without a struggle. The reassertion of conservative white power across the South was especially noticeable in the cities, where intimidation, violence, and exclusion marked

---

3. See, for example, Frederick Douglass, *My Bondage and My Freedom* (New York, 1855), 318, 328.

race relations for the rest of the nineteenth century, culminating in the lynching spree of the 1890s.

The policies emanating from these changed circumstances are well known. Segregation was a means to redefine race relations after slavery. Although some historians have noted that segregation actually was an improvement over the exclusion urban blacks experienced in the antebellum era, the result of racial separation was exclusion—from jobs, from a decent education, from numerous public facilities, from public services, from politics, and from the courts.[4] The system not only separated but humiliated as well, identifying black facilities as inferior and establishing a complex etiquette that explicitly reinforced that inferiority.

Another consequence of readjusted race relations was the limiting of urban economic opportunities. The definition of "nigger work"—menial tasks relegated to blacks—narrowed. By the early decades of the twentieth century, whites were moving into such occupations as barber, tailor, waiter, dockworker, and construction worker. The urban educational system reinforced a future of menial labor for black boys and girls. The curriculum at inferior black schools stressed vocational subjects, and blacks were discouraged from attending secondary schools. Most cities lacked a black public high school during the first decades of the twentieth century. As the urban South industrialized and mechanized after 1900, whites excluded blacks from the new industries and technologies. A postbellum Yellow Jim would not have had to turn over his earnings to his master, but he would have had fewer employment options.

The removal of blacks from the political arena was another consequence of racial policies. In southern cities, the removal was never total. In the 1940s, roughly one out of five southern blacks was registered to vote, 85 percent of whom lived in cities.[5] In cities such as Mayor Edward H. Crump's Memphis or Mayor William B. Hartsfield's Atlanta, blacks voted in significant numbers, although their votes were captive of white political organizations that occasionally doled out some patronage. The consequences of political impotence were evident to casual visitors to southern cities before the 1950s (and later in some smaller communities). Paved roads typically ended at the borders of black neighborhoods. The neighborhoods themselves were poorly drained, rarely serviced, and fitted with dilapidated hous-

---

4. Howard N. Rabinowitz, *Race Relations in the Urban South, 1865–1890* (New York, 1978).

5. David R. Goldfield, *Black, White, and Southern: Race Relations and Southern Culture, 1940 to the Present* (Baton Rouge, 1990), 47.

ing. Black schools were often makeshift, ramshackle, and overcrowded. If visitors entered a downtown store, a government office, or a bank, they would not see any black faces, save those performing janitorial work. Furthermore, if visitors entered the leading club or attended church, they would not see black members in either place. In the informal world of southern decision making, these institutions were important conduits to power. Blacks—inconsequential players in the public arena—were invisible in the private city as well.

Southern urban blacks were not uncomplaining victims of these racial policies. Building on antebellum traditions, black neighborhoods became communities. Black churches offered more than spiritual sustenance: they provided leadership, fellowship, recreational and educational facilities, and a variety of social service functions. Black culture and history often were bootlegged into black schools. Businesses owned and operated by blacks opened to serve a clientele ignored or insulted by downtown merchants. Life insurance companies and clothiers owned and operated by blacks and black barbers, attorneys, physicians, and restaurateurs expanded the traditional teacher-preacher middle class while providing essential services for the black community. Scarcely a southern city existed without a fashionable black business thoroughfare—Sweet Auburn in Atlanta, for example.

Black neighborhoods were especially successful in shielding children from the harsh and humiliating aspects of a segregated society. Black leaders such as Charleston native Harvey Gantt and Supreme Court Justice Thurgood Marshall, who grew up in segregated Baltimore, recall their sheltered childhood as a time when they were virtually oblivious to the realities of southern race relations.[6]

Blacks also launched protests against their inferior status. They boycotted streetcars early in the century, they joined white workers in labor actions, and they applied for membership in local National Association for the Advancement of Colored People (NAACP) chapters during the 1920s and 1930s. Most of these activities were unsuccessful and fraught with danger. Still, they reflect that race relations in the urban South during the first third of the twentieth century were not set in stone. Victories were small but significant and perhaps included the funding of a black high school, the appointment of a black health official, the expansion of black voter registration, the capitalization of "Negro" by the local newspaper, the use of "Mr." or "Mrs.," and the growing numbers of whites at home and in Wash-

6. *Ibid.,* 92.

ington who were willing to speak out, however timidly, for moderation in race relations.

Inspired by the New Deal and spurred by the opportunities of World War II, southern urban blacks launched major campaigns on two fronts in the two decades after 1945. First, urban blacks sought to expand voting rights. Yellow Jim had some freedom because he had some economic leverage; his postbellum offspring lost much of that leverage. Economic hardship and declining political fortunes increased the vulnerability of urban blacks to adverse economic and social policies. The prospect of challenging these policies looked dim unless southern urban blacks could break white solidarity and one-party rule. Fighting for political rights seemed the most promising strategy from the perspective of the 1940s: without political pressure to open up employment, housing, and education, the economic status of urban blacks would remain low. The U.S. Supreme Court decision in *Smith* v. *Allwright* (1944) to abolish the white primary was an important step in securing political rights. In response, chapters of the Negro Voters' League sprung up in cities across the region to register blacks and to take advantage of the ruling. During the 1940s and early 1950s, black registration in New Orleans, for example, jumped from four hundred to twenty-eight thousand.[7] Political advances inspired other actions.

The attack on segregation became a second front in the strategy of urban blacks to secure their civil, economic, and social rights. With the assistance and leadership of the NAACP, urban blacks filed court cases challenging the constitutionality of segregation, especially in education. They attempted, at least in the upper South (Virginia, Kentucky, North Carolina, and Tennessee) in 1947, to integrate public waiting rooms. More direct action was too dangerous at this time. Urban blacks eventually sought to improve their economic status by eliminating segregation and exclusion in employment and lending practices.

During the 1940s, it seemed as if voting rights would become the major focus of southern urban blacks. The *Smith* v. *Allwright* decision had galvanized urban blacks; a new breed of white political leader emerged in southern cities that was more interested in economic development than in race-baiting (William Berry Hartsfield in Atlanta and DeLesseps S. Morrison in New Orleans were only two of the more prominent examples);[8] and

7. *Smith* v. *Allwright*, 321 U.S. 649 (1944); figures from Arnold R. Hirsch and Joseph Logsdon, "Simply a Matter of Black and White: The Transformation of Race and Politics in Twentieth-Century New Orleans," in *Creole New Orleans: Race and Americanization*, ed. Arnold R. Hirsch and Joseph Logsdon (Baton Rouge, 1992), 293.

postwar migrations had swelled the numbers of blacks in the urban South to the point where they could influence policy. But the civil rights initiatives of Harry S. Truman's administration and the effective use of race- and red-baiting by old guard southern politicians froze the southern political spring and helped divert black efforts elsewhere. The 1954 *Brown* v. *Board of Education* decision, the Montgomery bus boycott, and the electrifying sit-in demonstrations beginning in 1960 further reordered priorities.[9] Still, black leaders recognized that the ballot was essential to changing racial policies in the urban South, even after segregation had fallen. It was not yet clear how the freedom to eat at a lunch counter, sit in the orchestra of a movie theater, or try on a pair of shoes would appreciably improve the situation of rank-and-file blacks. The successful demonstrations leading to desegregated public facilities imparted a sense of mission, identity, and power to southern urban blacks. The psychological gains were real and important. More substantive victories would prove elusive, however, without the right to vote.

Although southern black leaders could agree on little else after 1965, there was a consensus that the ballot would work as a magic elixir on the southern body politic. Martin Luther King predicted on the eve of the Selma demonstrations in 1965, "If Negroes could vote . . . there would be no more oppressive poverty." A year later, Stokely Carmichael was more practical but no less enthusiastic about the potential of voting rights. He reasoned that "if a black man is elected tax assessor, he can collect and channel funds for the building of better roads and schools serving black people—thus advancing the move from political power into the economic arena."[10]

In the quarter century since Martin Luther King and Stokely Carmichael hailed the ballot, the political landscape of the urban South has changed dramatically. Only a handful of southern towns and cities in 1965 had black elected officials. Two decades later, there were 3,500 local black elected officials in the South and 2,100 local black elected officials in the rest of the nation. Although more than 70 percent of these leaders served communities of fewer than five thousand people, black politicians made notable gains as big-city mayors by the mid-1980s, holding office in cities such as Charlotte,

8. See Harold H. Martin, *Willliam Berry Hartsfield: Mayor of Atlanta* (Athens, 1978), and Edward F. Haas, *DeLesseps S. Morrison and the Image of Reform: New Orleans Politics, 1946–1961* (Baton Rouge, 1977).

9. *Brown* v. *Board of Education of Topeka*, 347 U.S. 483 (1954).

10. Both quotes from Goldfield, *Black, White, and Southern*, 193, 206.

Atlanta, New Orleans, Little Rock, and Birmingham.[11] Yellow Jim had affected urban policy through his initiative and his economic value to whites; his progeny now had political leverage. Would beneficial public policies and economic opportunity follow?

BLACK POLITICAL POWER
AND URBAN SERVICES

Poor or absent urban services in black neighborhoods historically have reflected white supremacy and black political impotence in southern cities. Since the Voting Rights Act of 1965, black elected officials have had a significant effect on the provision of services to black neighborhoods. Surveys of communities with black elected officials have indicated that paved streets and recreational facilities were direct consequences of black officeholding.[12] Part of the service improvement reflected changes in federal policies and the ability of black elected officials to take advantage of those changes. The application of these policies not only addressed service shortcomings but also sought to rectify the historic isolation and official neglect of these neighborhoods.

During the 1920s, southern cities institutionalized the segregation of black neighborhoods through zoning and planning policies. As a 1929 Houston city planning commission report noted, "Because of long established racial prejudices, it is best for both races that living areas be segregated."[13] In subsequent years, cities adopted strategies designed to confine blacks to certain areas and eliminate slum housing in districts adjacent to vulnerable white neighborhoods. Federal policies after World War II complemented southern urban strategies.

Federal urban renewal renewal enabled southern urban leaders to accomplish two objectives. First, they demolished unsightly dwellings occupied mainly by blacks near the city center. Second, in place of these structures, cities erected hotels, office buildings, civic centers, or highways. Aside from destroying existing black neighborhoods, such policies created a major housing crisis for blacks. In Atlanta between 1957 and 1967, urban renewal

11. Figures from David R. Goldfield and Blaine A. Brownell, *Urban America: A History* (2nd ed.; Boston, 1990), 431.

12. See especially James W. Button, *Blacks and Social Change: Impact of the Civil Rights Movement in Southern Communities* (Princeton, 1989).

13. Quoted in Robert D. Bullard, "Blacks in Heavenly Houston," in *In Search of the New South: The Black Urban Experience in the 1970s and 1980s,* ed. Robert D. Bullard (Tuscaloosa, 1989), 20.

accomplished the demolition of twenty-one thousand housing units occupied primarily by blacks; during this time, the city constructed only five
thousand public housing units. City officials reserved renewal land for a
stadium, a civic center, and acres of parking lots.[14]

By the late 1960s, federal urban policy retreated from renewal and
stressed conservation. Lyndon B. Johnson's administration designed the
Model Cities program to create self-sufficient neighborhoods and residents.
Atlanta was the first city in the nation to receive a Model Cities grant. The
target neighborhood included a population of forty-five thousand people,
indicating that the program allowed cities to define *neighborhood* loosely. The
city used the funds to provide shuttle-bus service, a day-care program, the
construction of an educational complex, and the resurfacing of streets. In
Tampa, city officials expended nearly twelve million dollars in Model Cities
money between 1970 and 1975, mostly in black neighborhoods. "The tally
of accomplishments was impressive: the renovation of more than two thousand homes; the construction of a multipurpose service center; the paving
of streets; the refurbishing of playgrounds; the construction of a new park
and picnic grounds complex; and the building of a 1,648-unit moderate-
income housing project."[15]

The shift in federal urban policy coincided with the growing power of
black neighborhoods at city hall. Neighborhood politics became a key factor
in upgrading low-income neighborhoods during the 1970s and in the electoral campaigns of Maynard Jackson in Atlanta, Henry L. Marsh III in Richmond, and Clarence Lightner in Raleigh. The neighborhood preservation
movement also figured in the mayoral elections in San Antonio, Houston,
and New Orleans in the late 1970s.[16]

But the legacies of discrimination and federal policies and the limits of
southern urban politics transcended the abilities of black elected officials
and their white allies to make significant service improvements in black
neighborhoods, especially in those areas at the lower end of the economic
scale. The first problem was financial. Black urban neighborhoods were so
badly serviced before the 1960s that to bring streets, housing, parks, police,
fire, and health services to the quality of white areas would break the budgets

14. Robert D. Bullard and E. Kiki Thomas, "Atlanta: Mecca of the Southeast," *ibid.,*
79–80, 84.

15. Goldfield and Brownell, *Urban America,* 366; Robert A. Catlin, "Blacks in Tampa,"
in *In Search of the New South,* ed. Bullard, 151, 154.

16. See Richard M. Bernard and Bradley R. Rice, eds:, *Sunbelt Cities: Politics and Growth
Since World War II* (Austin, 1983).

of most southern cities. Atlanta mayor Ivan Allen, Jr., posed the problem for himself and his successors in the mid-1960s:

For one hundred years, metropolitan and city centers of the Southeast almost totally ignored anywhere from 25 to 40% of the population. . . . There were no building regulations. There was no code enforcement. There was no planning. There was no effort to provide any form of housing . . . garbage was not picked up regularly, the streets were not paved. . . . Today in a rapidly expanding market, as millions more people move into urban centers, we find a great need of running fast in both directions. Not only are we endeavoring to provide extended and better services for all the people who live in the city, but also we are trying to take up the slack of what has been the slums of the deteriorated areas of each city.[17]

Federal programs picked up some of the financial slack, but Congress spread Model Cities funds among one hundred fifty cities, thinning out the program's budget. The demise of Model Cities during the Nixon administration and the substitution of Community Development Block Grants further vitiated service assistance to black neighborhoods. Congress intended the block grant program "principally [to] benefit people of low and moderate income." In practice, most of the money went to assist not the poorest neighborhoods but the marginal areas where local politicians could boast quick results. In Memphis, for example, a local advisory panel designated most of the grants for black neighborhoods, but only those black neighborhoods of moderate income with a relatively high proportion of homeowners.[18] Also, some city administrations used the block grants to fund long-term capital improvements, such as sewers and road throughout the city.

The withdrawal of Ronald W. Reagan's administration from the urban programs was less traumatic in southern cities than elsewhere because the percentage of federal funds rarely exceeded 10 percent of local budgets. Southern cities and states, therefore, were better able to fill the funding gap, as opposed to places such as St. Louis and Detroit, where upward of 25 percent of those cities' budgets depended on federal funding.[19] As the block grant program suggested, however, the problem was less financial than one of setting priorities.

17. Quoted in Goldfield, *Black, White, and Southern,* 192–93.
18. Quoted in Goldfield and Brownell, *Urban America,* 389; Christopher Silver, "The Changing Face of Neighborhoods in Memphis and Richmond, 1940–1985," in *Shades of the Sunbelt: Essays in Ethnicity, Race, and the Urban South,* ed. Randall M. Miller and George E. Pozzetta (Westport, Conn., 1988), 120–21.
19. Figures from Goldfield and Brownell, *Urban America,* 434.

BLACK POLITICAL POWER
AND ECONOMIC OPPORTUNITY

On the issue of economic opportunity for southern urban blacks, the results were similarly mixed. One of the most successful economic policies instituted by southern urban administrations after 1965, and especially in the 1970s and 1980s, has been affirmative action. Under the direction of Richmond's black mayor, Roy West, and his allies on the city council, for example, the city instituted an aggressive affirmative action program that required public contractors to set aside 30 percent of their subcontracts for minority firms. Before 1983, when the city initiated the policy, 0.67 percent of Richmond's contracts went to minority-owned businesses. By 1986, that figure had jumped to nearly 40 percent. Black-run administrations also have expanded black participation in the city bureaucracy. During Maynard Jackson's first term as mayor of Atlanta (1973–77), the percentage of professional and administrative positions in city government held by blacks jumped from 19 percent to 42 percent.[20]

Generally, white economic leaders have gone along with affirmative action policies. Former Atlanta Mayor Andrew Young offered two reasons for this consensus: expanded consumer demand, and insurance against civil disturbances. As he explained in 1985, "We've given out 230 contracts worth $130 million to blacks in the last three years. That circulates to beauty parlors, barber shops, gets young people off the street. That's why we don't have black people jumping up and down . . . like black folks in Jamaica or Miami."[21]

The minority set-aside programs and the presence of blacks in the city bureaucracy also may have opened doors for blacks in the private sector. The performance and visibility of white-collar blacks in public-sector positions set examples and loosened reservations among some private employers. Also, as black populations increased in several southern cities and as their political power grew, white employers found economic advantages in hiring blacks. As one white executive noted, "It is simply good business" to hire blacks. Some communities have taken pride in the visibility of blacks in professional positions. In Jackson, Mississippi, for example, by the mid-1970s, it was routine for whites to see black reporters and announcers on local television stations, black managers in downtown stores, and black bank

20. *Ibid.*, 432–33.
21. Quoted in Goldfield, *Black, White, and Southern,* 229.

employees. One white Jackson official boasted that his city was "the most integrated place in America."[22]

One result of these changes in public- and private-sector employment has been the expansion of the urban black middle class. Leslie Dunbar of the Southern Regional Council wrote in 1980 that the "irreversible achievement of the civil rights movement . . . is that the black middle class has greatly expanded." Political scientists Earl Black and Merle Black estimated that by 1980, nearly 30 percent of southern black workers were employed in middle-class occupations, more than 40 percent of them in metropolitan areas, compared with 4 percent in 1940. The best indirect evidence was the continued in-migration: between 1975 and 1985, more than 850,000 blacks moved south, compared with slightly more than 500,000 who left. These in-migrants tended to be younger and better educated as a group than earlier black in-migrants—nearly two out of three held at least a high-school diploma (compared with a 45 percent rate among blacks already living in the South). Metropolitan areas in the South Atlantic states have been the major recipients of black middle-class migration. Cities such as Atlanta, Charlotte, Richmond, and the Raleigh–Durham–Chapel Hill area, with expanding service economies, have been attractive to white-collar blacks. These interregional movements have resulted in an increase in the percentage of blacks in the South for the first time in the twentieth century—from 53 percent in 1980 to 56 percent in 1988.[23]

Although the black middle class has expanded, there has not been a corresponding decline in black poverty in the urban South. The number of blacks below the poverty line increased during the 1980s, and the income and employment disparities between whites and blacks were as great as ever. In Houston, the average black family earned roughly 60 percent of what their white counterparts earned, and the black unemployment rate was three times that of whites. In Atlanta, the "black mecca," approximately the same disparities prevailed in income and unemployment. In Birmingham, blacks earned just 58 percent of what whites earned and were more than four and a half times as likely as whites to be below the poverty line.[24]

22. Quoted in Button, *Blacks and Social Change,* 196; quoted in Goldfield, *Black, White, and Southern,* 209.

23. Quote and figures *ibid.,* 244; Earl Black and Merle Black, *Politics and Society in the South* (Cambridge, Mass., 1987), 53; "Black Migration Shifts," Washington *Post,* January 10, 1990.

24. Figures from Bullard, "Heavenly Houston," in *In Search of the New South,* ed. Bullard, 24; Bullard and Thomas, "Atlanta," *ibid.,* 89, 93; Ernest Potterfield, "Birmingham: A Magic City," *ibid.,* 135–36.

Employed blacks were concentrated in the most menial occupations, even in public sector work, where white-collar blacks had made significant advances. In Birmingham, for example, 45 percent of the city's black employees worked in maintenance positions, compared with 14 percent of whites; 16 percent of blacks worked in managerial and professional occupations, compared with 30 percent of whites. Job-growth statistics in Atlanta belied Mayor Andrew Young's trickle-down theory. Between 1960 and 1988, whites enjoyed a 90 percent job gain; for blacks, the increase was 5 percent.[25]

Although proponents of the Sun Belt South talked wistfully of avoiding the fate of hard-pressed northern cities, the extent of black poverty in the urban South indicated that southern cities shared unhappy circumstances with their counterparts elsewhere. During the 1980s, the overwhelmingly black downtown residential core of Atlanta was the second-poorest neighborhood in the nation. Despite Sun Belt hyperbole, some southern cities ranked at the bottom of the so-called hardship rating, a measure documenting the degree of unemployment, limited education, crowded housing, and poverty in a particular city. Based on these indices, New Orleans, Miami, and Birmingham ranked below Cleveland or Detroit.[26]

Despite the advance of urban black political power and the growing numbers of black elected officials since 1965, the economic status of the majority of the black urban population has not changed. At least three factors account for this situation. First, the changing nature of the national economy has drastically reduced the demand for remunerative semiskilled occupations. Second, the social and spatial configurations of the modern metropolis lower the visibility of the poor populations. Third, the policy priorities and administrative objectives of modern local government limit redistributionist responses to the problem of the black underclass.

SERVICE-ORIENTED ECONOMY AND URBAN POLICY

Urban blacks had been involved only on the margins of southern industry before 1960. In response to federal legislation, new industrial opportunities in textiles and steel opened to blacks during the 1960s. The irony was that these industries were already in decline and poised to lay off tens of thou-

25. Potterfield, "Birmingham," *ibid.,* 136; Neal Peirce, "Atlanta Booming But Still Deeply Divided," Charlotte *Observer,* July 16, 1988.

26. Robert D. Bullard, "Introduction: Lure of the New South," in *In Search of the New South,* ed. Bullard, 9.

sands of workers over the next two decades. The economy of the South and of the nation was changing to a service orientation. Cities no longer hosted industries but became the location of so-called knowledge functions: higher education; legal, financial, and accounting services; insurance; data processing; government; and corporate administration. These functions generated high-skilled, high-paid positions beyond the reach of most black urban residents.

There was, however, another tier of employment in the service economy. During the 1960s, the majority of service jobs were minimum wage, or scarcely above the minimum wage, with limited futures. These were the jobs flipping hamburgers, cleaning high-rise office buildings and hotels, and washing cars. In addition, many of the low-tier openings were in the burgeoning suburbs of metropolitan areas and, therefore, were inaccessible to inner-city blacks. The middle-class population and economic base were leaving southern cities, as they had left cities elsewhere. Between 1960 and 1975, for example, Atlanta experienced an absolute loss of two thousand jobs because the city's share of metropolitan employment fell from 20 percent to 12 percent. In 1960, central Atlanta contained 90 percent of the metropolitan area's office space. By 1980, that proportion had declined to 42 percent because nearly one hundred industrial parks ringed the city. Blacks were unlikely to move to suburban jurisdictions. There were transportation problems and housing discrimination, with housing prices beyond the reach of most low-income blacks because suburbs zoned residential land to effectively eliminate or reduce the likelihood of low-income or multifamily dwellings. The future composition of the service economy is unlikely to improve the prospects of the black underclass. Better than 80 percent of the service jobs that will be created in the 1990s are in the lower tier.[27]

MULTICENTERED METROPOLIS AND URBAN POLICY

As the disjunction between jobs and residence has implied, the social and spatial configuration of the southern metropolis has militated against the black underclass. Through most of the twentieth century, the metropolitan area has consisted of city and suburb. Since 1970, however, there has been a concentration on the settlement, economic base, and even culture and entertainment of the metropolitan periphery. These out-towns are often parts of what the New York *Times* in 1978 called a "multicentered urban

27. Figures from David R. Goldfield, *Promised Land: The South Since 1945* (Arlington Heights, Ill., 1987), 155–56; Goldfield and Brownell, *Urban America*, 426.

chain" held together by ribbons of highway.[28] They have attained a sufficient residential density to support even major league sports franchises, such as the Texas Rangers in Irving, Texas, between Dallas and Fort Worth. Though most southern metropolitan areas are not as large as the Dallas–Fort Worth metroplex, the sprawling, automobile-dependent metropolises of the 1990s suit the spatial traditions of the South well.

In racial terms, the multicentered metropolis stretches distances between blacks and whites, middle-class and poor. Commuting patterns in southern metropolitan areas are more often cross-suburban than suburb to city. Even commutes to the central city frequently are along elevated freeways separated from the decay below. Hermetically sealed office buildings and underground garages further shield the middle class from urban problems. If the problem cannot be seen, it may not exist.

The class divisions implied by contemporary metropolitan spatial arrangements may, however, be more serious than the racial separation. For the first time in southern history, the urban black middle class is becoming detached from the rest of the black population. Fair housing laws, greater affluence, and the absence of exclusionary traditions in the new out-towns have accelerated middle-class black suburbanization. Blacks in Atlanta's suburbs, for example, increased by 200 percent between 1970 and 1980.[29]

Intellectual isolation has accompanied physical separation among different black social groups. Black Charlotte attorney Mel Watt noted that the attitude of many successful young black urban professionals seems to be, "I have made it and I don't owe anybody from the past or future anything." The "me" generation is color blind. Eddie Williams, a southern black who currently heads the Joint Center for Political Studies in Washington, D.C., urged blacks to "move from an era of moral persuasion with its nonnegotiable demands, to an era of politics, where everything is negotiable."[30]

In the era of white supremacy, all blacks had shared segregation and the demeaning etiquette of southern race relations; the virtual demise of those constraints broke the bond of suffering uniting all blacks, whatever their socioeconomic differences, as well as some of the institutions that bound them to each other, such as black businesses and black schools. Although there had always been divisions within the black community, most could

28. "New Metropolitan Areas," New York *Times,* November 14, 1978.

29. Bullard and Thomas, "Atlanta," in *In Search of the New South,* ed. Bullard, 78. Some of this increase undoubtedly resulted from the inclusion of historically black rural or small-town communities that date from the post–Civil War era.

30. Quotes from Goldfield, *Black, White, and Southern,* 254.

agree on the need to break down the barriers of racial inferiority. Since agreement can occur only on an intellectual rather than an experiential level, both the intellectual and experiential gaps between the two groups have been widening. As black sociologist William Julius Wilson predicted in 1978, "There are clear indications that the economic gap between the black underclass . . . and the higher-income blacks will very likely widen and solidify."[31]

The policy implications of social and spatial stratification are that black underclass issues are less likely to receive high priorities at city hall, regardless of the race of the mayor and city council. Black voters are no longer content with having a black face in city hall; they are restless, as was reflected by the Rev. Hosea Williams' challenge to Maynard Jackson in Atlanta's 1989 mayoral race. Black elected officials, for their part, complain that black voters do not understand the limits of the political process. A black council member in Riviera Beach, Florida, complained recently that "black expectations are high when a black is elected. They want us to change the world in one day, and when we don't do this they brand us as 'Uncle Toms.' " Atlanta's Andrew Young was more philosophical about the pressure: "For ten years we went around yelling 'Freedom Now'—and a lot of people translated that into having a black congressman, meaning we're going to have all of our freedom now, so on Monday morning they come to city hall and say, 'Where is it?' "[32]

POLITICAL CULTURE AND URBAN POLICY

The nature of the southern political process in the 1990s and the changes in urban administration reinforce the other difficulties in framing social policies. The reality of southern urban politics is that although blacks currently may control or have a major influence over electoral politics in most southern cities, whites still control the urban economy. Atlanta political scientist Mack Jones put the matter simply: "The economy is controlled by white interests . . . and black elected officials need the support of these same white elements in order to maintain existing services."[33] During his first term as mayor of Atlanta, Maynard Jackson discovered that confronting the

31. Quoted *ibid.*, 221.

32. Quoted in Button, *Blacks and Social Change,* 229; quoted in Goldfield, *Black, White, and Southern,* 191.

33. Quoted in Bullard and Thomas, "Atlanta," in *In Search of the New South,* ed. Bullard, 94.

white economic establishment severely limited his ability to govern—to build support for affirmative action programs and to target development that would benefit blacks. As federal funds diminished, the role of local banks and other major businesses increased.

Cultivating white economic leaders is necessary for black candidates as well as black elected officials. Blacks in the antebellum urban South often advanced their fortunes by connecting with a prominent white. The modern version of this relationship is the Manhattan coalition. Atlanta's mayor during the 1940s and 1950s, William B. Hartsfield, perfected this alliance of blacks and wealthy whites. Both groups were frightened by the growing numbers of working-class whites who proved susceptible to race-baiting candidates. The white elites were concerned about the city's image—"too busy to hate," as Hartsfield coined it—and blacks worried that their modest gains could be jeopardized by racist officeholders.[34]

As black political power grew after the Voting Rights Act of 1965, the Manhattan coalition spread through most of the urban South. New Orleans' first black mayor, Dutch Morial, won his initial term by combining a sizable black vote with the support of "business-oriented" whites.[35] In the 1980s, Charlotte mayor Harvey Gantt and Birmingham mayor Richard Arrington put together similar coalitions to gain victory.

Well-to-do whites are less important to black candidates for their votes than they are for their campaign financing, political expertise, and access to the media. This should not imply that once in office, black elected officials do the bidding of downtown elites. It does mean that economic development, especially the development of downtown, enjoys a high priority at city hall. Perhaps the best contemporary example is Andrew Young, who was mayor of Atlanta from 1981 to 1989. In July 1988, Atlanta Chamber of Commerce president Gerald Bartels assessed Mayor Young's contribution to the city's economic development. "The mayor is our clean-up hitter," Bartels noted. "He is such an eloquent speaker, and he has an outstanding grasp of worldwide economics." Young took office in 1981, and Bartels acknowledged that "it's been a love affair ever since."[36] Young was particularly effective in luring foreign, especially Asian and Middle Eastern, firms into Atlanta. Between 1983 and 1988, nearly two hundred foreign com-

34. See Virginia H. Hein, "The Image of 'A City Too Busy to Hate': Atlanta in the 1960s," *Phylon* (May, 1972), 205–21.

35. Beverly Hendrix Wright, "New Orleans," in *In Search of the New South,* ed. Bullard, 58.

36. Quoted in "Atlanta: A Tale of Two Cities," Charlotte *Observer,* July 10, 1988.

panies established operations in the city. The mayor also convinced the black community to go along with a regressive sales tax to fund infrastructure.[37]

Implicit in the equation between black political power and white economic power is the notion that politics in the 1990s is often a question of resources. If politics is a question of resources, then black politicians have few of those resources, and their black constituents even fewer. The media, campaign financing, economic leadership, and political campaign consultants and experts (from pollsters to advertising personnel) are dominated by whites. This does not mean they are hostile or indifferent to black interests. It may mean, however, that they are less sensitive to and less aware of the needs of poor black urban residents.

Aside from resources, the increasing competitiveness of the Republican party at the local and state levels furthers policy options. White Democratic candidates must walk an electoral tightrope: their major constituencies are blacks and working-class whites, two groups with little in common. Depending on the size of the black electorate in the state or county, Democratic candidates also must appeal to the crucial and ever-growing middle-class white electorate. That electorate, more often than not, is concentrated in a state's metropolitan areas. Black candidates, running in jurisdictions where the black electorate is less than 60 percent, also must appeal for some white votes and retain white economic support once elected. As state legislatures use 1990 census figures to redistrict, they are creating more majority-black districts. The benefits of increasing the number of blacks in the state legislature, however, may be undermined by further isolating black voters. Democratic leaders will ignore such districts, assuming a victory, and Republicans will concede them to concentrate on winning new majority-white districts. These factors combine to favor policies that ensure low taxes, promote economic development, and provide modest social services. Although other policy priorities such as education and the environment have broken through, even at the expense of raising taxes, these issues often are framed in terms of economic benefits.[38]

Future political trends in the urban South do not augur well for social policy. First, local politics have become increasingly pluralistic with the addition of new ethnic groups such as Asians and Latin Americans. An estimated one hundred thousand Salvadorans currently live in Houston, for example, most of whom are unregistered but who will be eligible to vote

37. See Art Harris, "Atlanta, Georgia: Too Busy to Hate," *Esquire* (June, 1985), 129.
38. For a complete discussion of blacks in southern politics, see Merle Black and Earl Black, *Politics and Society in the South* (Cambridge, Mass., 1987).

within the next five years. In Atlanta, there are sizable blocs of Vietnamese, Koreans, Cambodians, and Laotians whom blacks, Jews, and other groups are seeking out to forge political coalitions. More than seventy-five thousand Hispanics resided in the Atlanta metropolitan area in 1987. As early as the 1970s, the Atlanta Community Relations Commission translated all city documents into Spanish. In recent years, there have been efforts to increase the hiring of Hispanic police officers, and in 1986, Andrew Young pledged to "see that Hispanics get a fair share of the [city] contracts." Young also established the mayor's task force on Hispanics. During the 1970s, the total foreign-born population in the South rose 120 percent, compared with an increase of 46.4 percent nationally.[39] The point is that the much-publicized ethnic cauldron of Miami politics is no longer a regional anomaly. If pluralistic politics in the urban South plays out as it has elsewhere, policies directed to a particular race will unlikely receive much support.

Another adverse future trend for urban social policy is the growing awareness of the need for regional cooperation. The idea of metropolitan government boomed in the 1960s and took root in a few areas of the South such as Miami, Jacksonville, and Nashville. Elsewhere, though, racial and tax issues limited cooperation. Since then, there has been a de facto or creeping metropolitanism, with the establishment of special districts and authorities to deal with issues such as airport management, mosquito control, and pollution. Metropolitan regions recently have discovered the economic advantages of cooperation. The Denver region formed the Metro Denver Network in 1987, a regionwide information system for business recruitment. Currently, Charlotte, Atlanta, and Columbia, South Carolina, are beginning to market themselves in regional terms. Social issues must play a subsidiary role in such efforts, given the growing racial disparities between central city and suburb in the South.[40] Staunch opposition to annexation in suburban Richmond and to the extension of the Metropolitan Atlanta Rapid Transit Authority rail system to suburban Atlanta, along with the general unwillingness of suburban school districts to merge with city schools almost everywhere in the metropolitan South mean that those who

39. Louis Dubose, "Invisible City," *Southern Exposure*, XVI (Winter, 1988), 24–26; figures and quote from Ronald H. Bayor, "Models of Ethnic and Racial Politics in the Urban Sunbelt South," in *Searching for the Sunbelt: Historical Perspectives on a Region,* ed. Raymond A. Mohl (Knoxville, 1990), 109; Elliot R. Barkan, "New Origins, New Homeland, New Region: American Immigration and the Emergence of the Sunbelt, 1955–1985," in *Searching for the Sunbelt,* ed. Mohl, 144.

40. Goldfield and Brownell, *Urban America,* 442–43.

want to achieve metropolitan cooperation will not discuss any issues that will raise the racial concerns of suburban counties and localities.

We are, as political scientist John J. Harrigan has noted, in the "post-reform era" of urban policy.[41] The federal government has pulled back sharply from the massive grant programs of the 1960s and 1970s. Southern state and local governments are more concerned with public-private partnerships, major building projects, and maintaining current tax advantages. Perhaps local government in the South—traditionally not strong, especially compared with county and state governments—is receding in power and effectiveness. The fragmentation of authority among boards, authorities, special districts, citizen groups, city managers, and council members has eroded executive authority. The result is usually that no one government body has exclusive authority over a major problem.

Changes in metropolitan administration are reflected in the transformation of urban administration over the past decade. Mayors and council members are "managers," even when a city manager is present. James Peterson of the Council for Urban Economic Development noted this transition: "The old mayor [divided] up the pie by special-interest groups and [by] going to the state and local government for help. The new mayor is the manager." The management metaphor stresses financial responsibility, reliance on computers, and "work management systems" borrowed from private industry. The result is a streamlined administration, with fewer, better-paid workers, higher technology, and marketing and service innovations.[42]

In keeping with the objective of efficiency, some local governments have begun to privatize their services. If elected black and white officials pay less attention to the most needy neighborhoods, what can one say about private franchises? It is not farfetched to depict a southern city of the twenty-first century where public services are no longer public. Already in some communities, police functions have become privatized. In 1988, neighborhoods in Fort Lauderdale, Florida, began to barricade streets and hire private security guards to check entering motorists. In the meantime, the unfortunate residents of poor neighborhoods, virtually unprotected by public or private security, are the victims of escalating violence.

This is not to say that urban policy has abandoned the black underclass. Middle-class black leaders stress that a broader class agenda is more likely to

41. John J. Harrigan, *Political Change in the Metropolis* (Boston, 1985), 341.
42. All quotes from Neal Peirce, "'New Mayors Slash Staff, Act Like Corporate Boss,'" Washington *Post*, May 4, 1985.

achieve a policy consensus than narrower racial concerns. These leaders are supportive of affirmative action policies and economic development initiatives. Black elected officials argue that such strategies eventually redound to the benefit of low-income blacks. Andrew Young's administration increased minority contracts to 35 percent of the total. These funds, Young explained, "bubble up to feed the hungry, clothe the naked, and heal the sick." However, one of Young's black adversaries in Atlanta, the Rev. Hosea Williams, questioned the mayor's trickle-down theory, that is, "how the mayor [planned] to cure Atlanta's black inner-city problems, second only to those of Newark on the poverty charts."[43]

Young and his colleagues responded by arguing that a prosperous city would more likely be an equitable city. Curtis B. Gans, director of the black-oriented Committee for the Study of the American Electorate, summarized this thinking in 1985: "Blacks . . . must have an economic-class agenda rather than a black agenda." He admitted that "ending racism does not result in significant change for the . . . black underclass." The trick is to devise "programs that speak to the unique problems of the long-term poor" of both races.[44] It is difficult, however, to see how broadening the social policy agenda will ease its acceptance among political leaders of any race or shake the belief that economic development is itself the best social policy. The assumption is that the white middle-class will be more likely to go along with social policy as long as the word "black" is not attached to it. The objection, though, is less to the racial association than to the policy itself.

RECENT POLICY INITIATIVES

Recent policy initiatives have focused on self-help or what was called "ghetto enrichment" during the late 1960s. These initiatives have sought to upgrade not only the physical environment but also families and individuals trapped in these communities. Black middle-class leaders are increasingly willing to discuss aspects of life among the black poor that were taboo before the mid-1980s. Mary Pringle, a black educator from Virginia, has claimed that racism is no longer a valid defense for black poverty. Even if it were, the example of recent immigrants from Southeast Asia indicates that culture—in this case, "their traditional background values, their col-

43. Both quotes from Goldfield, *Black, White, and Southern*, 245, 246.
44. Quoted in William Raspberry, "The Dilemma of Black Politics," Washington *Post,* January 9, 1985.

lective achievement orientation, their patience and diligence"—has de-
flected the effect of racial animosity. Pringle believes that the black poor
need "new myths" that depict them as "destined for success rather than
doomed to failure."[45]

Some believe that one obstacle to the creation of "new myths" is the
dependence of the black underclass on government programs. This notion
not coincidentally follows the erosion of federal urban policy and the growing limitations on social policy options of local government. The alternative
is self-help. Robert L. Woodson, head of the National Center for Neighborhood Enterprise and chair of the Council for a Black Economic Agenda,
has become one of the leading advocates of the self-help approach. He has
urged blacks to quit "waiting for a government Moses to save them. . . . If
black America is to achieve its rightful place in American society, it will not
be by virtue of what white America grants to black Americans but because
of what black Americans do for themselves." Specifically, Woodson has suggested black enterprise for poor black districts; the use of traditional institutions such as churches to purchase and develop land, upgrade housing,
and lease properties; and the formation of tenant groups in public housing
to manage these units, as is already the case in several southern cities. One
resident-manager group in New Orleans boasted fewer than thirty evictions
between 1978 and 1985.[46]

Many of these efforts come under the heading of "empowerment."
When profiling most poor black neighborhoods of the urban South, however, that heading does not come immediately to mind. Many of these
neighborhoods have been victims of urban renewal, discriminatory zoning,
and historically skewed service budgets. It is one thing to make urban social
policy but quite another to "unmake" generations of policies that have had
severe social effects. The people in these neighborhoods are often young,
undereducated, and plagued by problems ranging from poor nutrition to
high crime. The policy problems of these areas are so diverse and overwhelming that they require diverse policy approaches and overwhelming
resources. The same public-private partnership that characterizes economic
development policies needs to be applied to the black underclass. That is
already occurring in some communities in the form of low-interest loans,
fair-share job programs, head-start programs, day-care facilities, nutrition

45. Quoted in William Raspberry, "Why Blacks Need a New Myth," Washington *Post,*
July 19, 1985.
46. Robert L. Woodson, "Self-Help Is the Answer for Poor Blacks," Washington *Post,*
May 12, 1985.

education, and housing repair and construction initiatives. The policy solutions are out there if only the numerous obstacles to implementation can be overcome.

Recall the brief story of Yellow Jim, the slave who apparently defied many of the policy proscriptions of his society. Yellow Jim eventually committed the ultimate defiance by running away. White urban residents in the Old South were unwilling to practice the racial policies they preached. Cities are basically economic engines unless they are artificially propped for governmental or military exigencies. Antebellum urban southerners bowed both to the economic realities of urban life and to the close connections—perhaps an antebellum Manhattan coalition—between white master and black slave.

Currently in the urban South, the black underclass is in some respects more constricted than Yellow Jim. To where can blacks run away? Also, political coalitions and social relations are much more fragmented and ephemeral in the contemporary South than they were in the antebellum era. Economic development policy may be one of the few cohesive instruments left in the political arena. Here is the element of continuity with the earlier era—urban policy still revolves primarily around economic issues. Perhaps it is as black Atlanta politician Michael Lomax asserted in 1988: "We'll see these problems [of the black underclass] addressed when the business community understands the total cost." Then maybe we can answer positively the question posed by Lewis Mumford a half-century ago: "Does a city exist to promote the life of its citizens? Or do the citizens exist in order to increase the size, importance, and the commercial turnover of the city?" [47]

47. Quoted in "Atlanta: A Tale of Two Cities," Charlotte *Observer,* July 10, 1988; quoted in Daniel Schaffer, *Garden Cities for America: The Radburn Experience* (Philadelphia, 1982), 62.

III

CITIES

CITIES IN THE OLD SOUTH

With independence fulfilled, the American people set out to create a viable nation. Viability to the new nation's leaders was synonymous with economic stability and growth. Beginning with Alexander Hamilton's plan for recovery, the pursuit of prosperity became a national policy that filtered down to pervade every hamlet in the country. The nineteenth century became the age of commerce; the age of canals; the age of railroads; and the age of industry. The American cornucopia overflowed with people, produce, and technology. The riches of a new continent lay open for the common man. Energy and enterprise were the keys that unlocked this bounty.

In the forty years between 1820 and 1860, the United States underwent some remarkable changes. By the latter date, the outline of an emerging urban industrial giant was clearly evident. A national economy functioned in place of local and regional economies.[1] Cities were the repositories of the changes. Wealth, technology, produce, people, railroads, canals, and industry concentrated in the metropolis, as if some supernatural centripetal force propelled the American dream into an urban setting. The possibilities transcended reality but not the imagination. It was an era when one dusty street could become a metropolis and when populations bloomed overnight. Urban promotion developed into a fine art and did its best to transform

1. See Douglass C. North, *The Economic Growth of the United States, 1790–1860* (Englewood Cliffs, N.J., 1961); see also Louis B. Schmidt, "Internal Commerce and the Development of the National Economy Before 1860," *Journal of Political Economy,* XLII (December, 1939), 798–822.

dreams into reality. The cities appropriated the dream of prosperity and recognition and pursued it vigorously.

Southern cities sought the promise of American life along with their contemporaries elsewhere. Now, southern cities are beginning to receive the study they deserve.[2] Urban biographies, monographs dealing with various aspects of antebellum southern urban life, and a spate of articles have depicted the urban South as a vibrant, progressive, and influential milieu.[3] Some southern cities during the early national period registered population gains that compared favorably with other cities. Older cities, like New Orleans and Savannah, increased their populations by 45 percent, while relatively new Memphis registered an impressive gain of 155 percent. Fledgling cities like Atlanta and Houston promised great advances in the future urban South.[4] Leonard P. Curry recently developed an index, the Comparative Urban Rate of Increase (CURI), by dividing the rate of increase in the urban population by the rate of increase in the total population. Curry calculated that the urban population in the South increased three and one-half times as fast as the total southern population in the first half of the nineteenth century, as compared with the northern urban growth rate of two and one-half times the entire northern population.[5]

But population statistics reveal only one aspect of urban growth in the Old South, as Curry himself acknowledged. Qualitative changes that improve and rationalize urban life are more important in revealing urban modernity than the number of inhabitants. Nineteenth-century Tokyo possessed more than three million residents but could hardly be called a city in

2. See David L. Smiley, "The Quest for a Central Theme in Southern History," *South Atlantic Quarterly,* LXII (Summer, 1972), 307–25.

3. See, for example, D. Clayton James, *Antebellum Natchez* (Baton Rouge, 1968); David G. McComb, *Houston: The Bayou City* (Austin, 1969); Merl E. Reed, *New Orleans and the Railroads: The Struggle for Commercial Empire* (Baton Rouge, 1966); Kenneth W. Wheeler, *To Wear a City's Crown: The Beginnings of Urban Growth in Texas* (Cambridge, Mass., 1968); Blaine A. Brownell, "Urbanization in the South: A Unique Experience?" *Mississippi Quarterly,* XXVI (Spring, 1973), 105–20; Leonard P. Curry, "Urbanization and Urbanism in the Old South: A Comparative View," *Journal of Southern History,* XL (February, 1974), 43–60; Lyle W. Dorsett and Arthur H. Shaffer, "Was the Antebellum South Antiurban? A Suggestion," *Journal of Southern History,* XXXVII (February, 1972), 93–100. The three articles contain extensive bibliographic references on the literature of the urban South.

4. Statistical references helpful to studies of the urban South include the U.S. Bureau of the Census, *Compendium of the Census* (1850–70 for the antebellum era); "Progress of the Population in the United States," *Hunt's,* XXXII (February, 1855), 191–95; Donald B. and Wynell S. Dodd, *Historical Statistics of the South, 1790–1979* (University, Ala., 1973).

5. Curry, "Urbanization and Urbanism in the Old South," 43–60.

the modern sense—without extensive commercial connections, internal organization, urban services, and civic pride. Besides, population comparisons of the South with the Northeast are unfair, since the Northeast urbanized faster than any other area in the world. A portion of the lower Mississippi Valley was frontier well into the 1830s, postdating urban settlement in the Northeast by two centuries. Thus, population is an index of urban growth that must be employed in conjunction with other measures of development.

In nineteenth-century America, the extent of a city's commercial empire and the quality of life enjoyed by its citizens were the primary measures of urban success. It was a competitive era, and both individuals and cities vied for prosperity and recognition—the fulfillment of the American dream. Internal improvements were the means to commercial empire. "In sleepless and indefatigable competition," the Baltimore *American* declared, "success is best secured by transportation."[6] When New York completed the Erie Canal in 1825, to forge the first major trade link to the West, eastern cities besieged their state governments to aid them in duplicating the feat. Imitation worked well for some, disastrously for others. Philadelphia's rail-canal line to Pittsburgh, for example, was more a caricature than a transportation facility.[7] Although the canal was the first artificial link to the trade of the West, cities looked to the railroad to secure a commercial empire.

Americans endowed the railroad with almost magical powers. The more obvious attributes of railroads—facilitating business relationships by cutting time and risks, raising property values, and stimulating subsidiary business activities—were so widely known by 1845 that few promoters bothered to regale prospective subscribers, passengers, and other patrons with such mundane information. Indeed, people believed that these aspects of the railroad arrived with the first locomotive. What was more wondrous was the manner in which the iron horse pervaded and influenced most facets of life. Railroads could attract populations, promoted "human enjoyment," were military weapons, would "kill abolition in Congress," and could generally "reorient society." Ultimately, the railroad assumed the status of a demigod.

---

6. Baltimore *American* (n.p., n.d.), quoted in Alexandria *Gazette,* May 9, 1859.

7. See Wyatt W. Belcher, *The Economic Rivalry Between St. Louis and Chicago, 1850–1880* (New York, 1947); Julius Rubin, *Canal or Railroad: Imitation and Innovation in Response to the Erie Canal in Philadelphia, Baltimore, and Boston* (Philadelphia, 1961); Charles W. Dabney to Robert L. Dabney, January 31, 1855, in Charles W. Dabney Papers, Southern Historical Collection, University of North Carolina at Chapel Hill; Richmond *Enquirer,* August 28, 1855; B. M. Jones, *Railroads Considered in Regard to Their Effects upon the Value of Land in Increasing Production, Cheapening Transportation, Preventing Emigration and Investments for Capital* (Richmond, 1860).

Senator Charles Sumner of Massachusetts, who frequently discerned divine purpose in the course of daily living, wrote in 1852: "Where railroads are not, civilization cannot be. . . . Under God, the railroad and the school-master are the two chief agents of human improvement." A Presbyterian minister from New York went even further. He saw railroads as "the evo-lution of divine purposes, infinite, eternal—connecting social revolutions with the progress of Christianity and the coming reign of Christ."[8] Small wonder that communities enthusiastically embraced this iron messiah.

Both urban and rural Americans supported the cause of the railroad. In fact, it is difficult to discuss the pursuit of the American urban dream with-out acknowledging the contribution of rural America. Some historians have contended that the plantation was inimical to southern urban development.[9] Without commercial agriculture, though, southern cities would have been dusty outposts in the backwaters of American civilization rather than a part of the national economy. Cooperation and mutuality of interest between city and country built railroads.

Wealthy planters and farmers in both the North and the South invested liberally in railroad stock.[10] C. S. Tarpley, a promoter of New Orleans rail-roads, was a prominent Mississippi planter. Tarpley believed that a railroad connection with New Orleans would transform central Mississippi from an area of plantation monoculture to one where small, diversified farms pre-dominated. Henry Varnum Poor, the nation's leading railroad expert before the Civil War, emphasized the mutual benefits of railroads: "Railroads . . . are necessary to farming communities in creating a value for their products, in opening a market for them. They explain the rapid growth of cities that are the *termini* of a large number of railroads." In a similar vein, Virginia's George Fitzhugh, an ardent supporter of the American urban dream, predicted that with the advent of railroads "around all these Southern cities, the country will become rich . . . [and] there will be increased property values in town and country." Fitzhugh concluded by observing

9. See, for example, Eugene Genovese, *The Political Economy of Slavery* (New York, 1965); Fred Bateman, James Foust, and Thomas Weiss, "The Participation of Planters in Manufacturing in the Antebellum South," *Agricultural History,* XLVIII (April, 1974), 277–97; Alfred H. Conrad *et al.,* "Slavery as an Obstacle to Economic Growth in the United States: A Panel Discussion," *Journal of Economic History,* XXVII (December, 1967), 518–60.

10. See, for example, "Inventory and Appraisement of the Estate of William Massie, 1862" (William Massie Notebooks, Duke University Library); "Annual Meeting of the Stockholders of the Orange and Alexandria Railroad," Alexandria *Gazette,* October 23, 1857; see also Bateman *et al.,* "The Participation of Planters," 277–97.

that "rapid intercommunication is the distinguishing feature of modern progress."[11]

The era of "rapid intercommunication" began in a southern city, when John C. Calhoun and Robert Y. Hayne promoted a railroad from Charleston to Hamburg, South Carolina. The impetus behind the scheme was a desire among Charlestonians to reassert their commercial dominance by making access to Charleston from the upland cotton regions less costly. The South Carolina Railroad, completed in 1833, covered 136 miles and was the first steam-powered railroad in the nation. Charleston, its appetite whetted, next sought rail connections to Cincinnati, the new commercial emporium of the West. In the pursuit of the American urban dream, the commerce of the West was the greatest prize. In 1836, with a charter secured, Hayne asserted, "The South and the West—We have published the banns—if any one knows why these two should not be joined together, let him speak now, or forever after hold his peace." The outlook for Charleston's future was favorable: "The far and fertile West will pour her inexhaustible treasures into our lap." The scheme ran aground when rival cities like Louisville and Lexington objected to becoming way stations for Charleston's benefit. There were similar abortive attempts at railroad building by New Orleans and by Athens, Georgia, in the 1830s.[12] The Panic of 1837 and the long depression that followed dampened southern urban enthusiasm for the railroad.

The late 1840s brought renewed interest in the railroad. The necessity of securing the trade of the West became more urgent for the South with the worsening sectional crisis following the Mexican War. Urban rivalry for the trade of the West, never a friendly competition, would now be carried on within the context of sectional conflict. Southerners in cities and on farms became alarmed at the growing economic and political strength of the North. The increasing economic dependence of the South on the North was especially distressing. In an era when the connection between wealth and power was a national axiom, the sectional crisis took on an economic emphasis. Economic weakness was an invitation to aggression. In 1851, a Portsmouth, Virginia, editor viewed the conflict as "a contest for political power as a means of securing pecuniary and commercial supremacy." The

11. Reed, *New Orleans and the Railroads*, 88–89.

12. Charleston *Courier*, August 31, 1836; Thomas D. Clark, "The Lexington and Ohio Railroad: A Pioneer Venture," *Register of the Kentucky Historical Society* (1933), 9–28; Reed, *New Orleans and the Railroads*, 9; W. K. Wood, "The Georgia Railroad and Banking Company," *Georgia Historical Quarterly*, LVII (Winter, 1973), 544–61.

Virginia senator R. M. T. Hunter agreed: "If we are ever to divide, it will probably be brought on by a war of commercial restriction." Southerners talked of releasing the section from "commercial vassalage."[13] If the South could cast off its economic shackles, political strength and sectional equilibrium must follow.

The trade of the West became the target for southern patriots. J. D. B. De Bow, the Old South's foremost urban booster, outlined the task for the South after the Mexican War: "A contest has been going on between North and South . . . for the wealth and commerce of the great valley of the Mississippi. We must meet our Northern competitors . . . with corresponding weapons." Cities assumed a leading role in the effort for economic independence. As George Fitzhugh stated, "We must build centres of trade, of thought, and fashion at home." The Richmond *Enquirer* volunteered the Old Dominion's cities for the cause and predicted that "building up Virginia's cities will save the South from an indelible brand of degradation."[14] The cities were to be the South's weapons against the power and influence of the North. Just as New York, Boston, and Philadelphia set the pace for their section's economic success, so the South's cities would fill a similar mission.

Railroads took on a new importance against the background of sectional strife. William M. Burwell, a Virginia urban booster and later editor of *De Bow's Review,* wrote in 1852 that railroads "will result in the rapid increase of our cities . . . and the South will be restored to her former position in the Union and render that Union more stable and firm." A writer in the *Southern Literary Messenger* in 1849 reviewed New York's success and concluded that the railroad had secured her position as the nation's commercial center. He recommended a similar course for southern cities. De Bow predicted that with efficacious rail lines, New Orleans and Norfolk could command two-thirds of the nation's trade. Accordingly, New Orleans civic leaders developed a railroad scheme that would reverse prevailing patterns of western trade away from northeastern cities. James Robb, a New Orleans entrepreneur, directed efforts to recapture the trade. Robb's vehicle was the Great Northern Railroad, which would terminate in Nashville, Tennessee.

13. Portsmouth (Va.) *Daily Pilot,* August 17, 1850; speech by Senator R. M. T. Hunter in U.S. Senate, quoted in Richmond *Enquirer,* April 5, 1850; Lynchburg *Virginian,* October 19, 1848; "Baltimore: Her Past and Present," *De Bow's Review,* XXIX (September, 1860), 291–93.

14. "Contests for the Trade of the Mississippi Valley," *De Bow's Review,* III (February, 1847), 98; George Fitzhugh, *Cannibals All! or, Slaves without Masters* (New York, 1857), 59; Richmond *Enquirer,* February 27, 1854.

Norfolk embarked on a plan, also in 1851, to reach Memphis, thus securing for herself the very cotton trade New Orleans hoped to maintain.[15] The similar but conflicting aims of New Orleans and Norfolk underscored the point that rivalry was just as severe within as between the sections. Neither city, however, was able to realize its plans before secession. Only Baltimore, in the southern urban railroad-building effort of the 1850s, successfully reached the West with the completion of the Baltimore and Ohio Railroad in 1853.

The Old South, belying contentions that southerners invested only in land and in slaves, staged a prodigious railroad-building effort in the 1850s. Local interests financed most of the construction. Between 1850 and 1860, southern railroad mileage quadrupled, whereas northern (including western states) mileage only tripled. Virginia was typical of the pattern of southern railroad-building after the Mexican War. In 1847, Virginia possessed six railroads and 270 miles of track, ranking her seventh in the nation in railroad mileage. By 1852, Virginia had doubled her railroads to fourteen and track mileage to 548 miles, though she still ranked seventh nationally. By 1858, the number of railroad companies increased to nineteen and the length of open track to 1,321 miles, placing Virginia third in the country, behind only New York and Pennsylvania.[16]

Railroads were the most effective but not the only means to an urban commercial empire. Southern cities sought to establish direct trade with Europe and other foreign ports. The objectives were to lessen dependence on northern shipping and to attract trade from the interior. Atlantic ports, such as Charleston, Savannah, and to a lesser extent Alexandria and Norfolk, enjoyed a lively trade with foreign ports prior to the Revolution. The removal of British aegis, the upsets of war, and the shift of prosperity in the section to the Gulf states precipitated a long decline in these port cities. New Orleans and Mobile became the chief export centers of the South. The trade on the Atlantic coast went primarily in one direction—north. To construct railroad lines only to see trade flow ultimately to the North would defeat the purpose of rail connections to the West. Direct trade in southern vessels would remedy the imbalance of trade and dependence on

15. William M. Burwell, "Virginia Commercial Convention," *De Bow's Review,* XII (January, 1852), 30; John Y. Mason, "Letter to D. H. London, Esq.," *Southern Literary Messenger,* XVIII (October, 1852), 588–92; "Trade of the Mississippi," 98–108; Reed, *New Orleans and the Railroads;* Norfolk *Southern Argus,* September 29, 1851.

16. U.S. Bureau of the Census, *Compendium of the Eighth Census, 1860: Mortality and Miscellaneous,* IV, 331; "Railroads of the United States," *Hunt's,* XXVIII (January, 1853), 110–15; "Railroads of the United States," *Hunt's,* XLI (August, 1859), 241.

the North. "By showing our determination and ability to conduct our own foreign trade," a Portsmouth editor reasoned in 1850, "we shall soon lessen the existing disparity between the northern and southern sections of the country."[17]

Southerners searched for a qualified import-export center to challenge New York's monopoly of foreign trade. J. D. B. De Bow recommended Norfolk as the most likely Atlantic outlet to Europe. Geographic determinism was prominent in predicting urban greatness in antebellum America, and De Bow applied it to Norfolk. He noted the city's temperate climate, her fine harbor, and her position midway between North and South as positive factors for the development of direct trade. De Bow was not partial to Norfolk, however. When it appeared that Richmond would block any attempts by Norfolk to establish connections with Europe, the editor touted Baltimore, employing the same geographic arguments he had advanced in support of Norfolk: "Baltimore possesses in its locality . . . advantages surpassing those of any city in the world." Southern cities successfully developed direct trade ties with Latin American countries during the 1850s. Savannah established lumber commerce with several Caribbean islands. By the end of the decade, Richmond's exports to South American ports exceeded that of all other United States ports, including New York.[18] But the European connection remained elusive for the Atlantic coast cities.

Although South Atlantic cities were dependent on the coastwise trade because of their inability to develop direct trade, the Gulf coast cities of Mobile and New Orleans possessed extensive commercial contacts abroad. Between 1840 and 1860, Mobile usually sent two-thirds of its cotton receipts abroad. New Orleans—the nation's premier cotton port and a constant rival to New York's supremacy as an export center—shipped, on the average, 83 percent of its cotton receipts to foreign ports. De Bow, reviewing the Crescent City's commercial progress from 1830 to 1860, declared: "No city of the world has ever advanced as a mart of commerce with gigantic and rapid strides as New Orleans." In 1830, New Orleans received $22 million in southern and western produce. Thirty years later, the value of produce received by the port had risen to $185 million. As cotton prosperity

---

17. Portsmouth (Va.) *Daily Pilot,* July 8, 1850.
18. "Foreign Trade of Virginia and the South," *De Bow's Review,* XIII (November, 1852), 493–503; "Baltimore," *ibid.,* 291–93; John A. Eisterhold, "Savannah: Lumber Center of the South Atlantic," *Georgia Historical Quarterly,* LVII (Winter, 1973), 526–43; "Exports of Flour to South America," *Hunt's,* XL (March, 1859), 351.

returned to the Mississippi Valley, New Orleans bloomed again. The decade before the Civil War was indeed the golden age of river commerce.[19]

Manufacturing was a necessary but anomalous part of the American urban dream. Industry at railroad termini ensured a balance of trade for both upward and downward railroad traffic. Direct trade also benefitted from industry in that the raw materials consumed by factories created high prices for farm and mineral products, thus securing a bountiful flow of commerce necessary for direct trade. Finally, industry seemed to generate great wealth—a requisite for urban success. On the other hand, manufacturing was not necessarily synonymous with urbanization. Francis Lowell rejected the pernicious urban environment for a more pastoral setting in establishing his textile mills. Southerners like South Carolina's William Gregg and Alabama's Daniel Pratt followed Lowell's example by eschewing the urban environment for their enterprises.[20] Further, the relationship between industrialization and urbanization was not clear. Even after 1840, the great urban centers of the Northeast operated from a commercial economic base. In the West, Cincinnati by 1835 demonstrated that a city could win economic supremacy in a region without developing industry.[21]

Despite the difficulties attendant upon assessing the role of industry in pursuing the American urban dream, some southern cities believed in the necessity of industry. "A large industrial class," the Norfolk *Southern Argus* claimed in the 1850s, "is the greatest builder-up of a prosperous city." Southerners also looked to manufacturing to diversify their economy. The Panic of 1837 devastated southern agriculture and left the South prostrate. The Southern Commercial Convention became an annual fixture in the Old South after 1837, when delegates met to devise a remedy for low cotton prices. Manufacturing was one of the solutions suggested by the convention. As the South struggled through the depression, investment in manufacturing increased, and both William Gregg and Daniel Pratt inaugurated their rural-based textile mill experiments. When the sectional crisis worsened in the late 1840s, some southerners urged manufacturing as another weapon for southern economic independence. A Mobile journal declared that domestic manufacturing was "the only safe and effectual remedy against Northern

19. Quoted in Schmidt, "Internal Commerce," 802.

20. Clement Eaton, *The Growth of Southern Civilization, 1790–1860* (New York, 1961), 173; Randall Miller, "Daniel Pratt's Industrial Urbanism: The Cotton Mill Town in Antebellum Alabama," *Alabama Historical Quarterly*, XXXIV (Spring, 1972), 5–35.

21. See Richard C. Wade, *The Urban Frontier: The Rise of Western Cities, 1790–1830* (Cambridge, Mass., 1959); Allan R. Pred, "Manufacturing in the American Mercantile City, 1800–1840," *Annals of the American Association of Geographers*, LVI (June, 1966), 307–25.

oppression." A Richmond resident echoed these sentiments in 1851: "No people are independent who are compelled to rely upon others for industry." [22]

Southerners answered the call for the development of industry by establishing agricultural processing industries. Since cotton was a leading southern export, textile mills seemed an appropriate industry for the urban South. Georgia's cities were pioneers in the southern urban textile industry. Between 1828 and 1840, in response to declining agriculture and emigration to the Gulf states, urban Georgia embarked on a program to develop the state as the foremost textile center south of Massachusetts. By 1840, Georgia had nineteen textile factories, and Savannah industrialists issued a proclamation in favor of a protective tariff. Investment in manufacturing increased during the 1840s as prices dropped precipitously. By 1848, there were thirty-two cotton mills in urban Georgia, with more than one-third of the manufactured product finding markets outside the state. By the mid-1850s, De Bow was referring to Georgia as the "Empire State of the South" and applauded planters whose investments helped to build the mills. The return on some of these investments was remarkably high. One mill in Macon earned 17 percent semiannually on its capital. Augusta was the state's foremost textile center, though Columbus became a serious rival in the late 1840s. A new cotton factory erected in the latter city in 1845 caused one enthusiastic local editor to remark: "Columbus will, if not compare advantageously with Lowell, at least have begun the good work in such a manner as to place beyond conjecture the feasibility of the South's manufacturing her own cotton goods." By 1851, citizens had invested nearly 1 million in local textile industries. [23]

In the upper South, tobacco and wheat were the dominant products of the soil, and industries sprang up to process these crops. Flour milling and tobacco manufacturing were most evident in Virginia. Richmond manufactured more tobacco than any other city in the world by 1860 and was among the nation's leading flour-milling centers. Richmond possessed fifty-two tobacco factories by that date, and James Thomas, Jr., its leading tobacconist, had markets throughout the country for his popular chewing brands. Richmond's Gallego flour endured voyages in excess of two months

22. Norfolk *Southern Argus,* September 20, 1851; Herbert Wender, *Southern Commercial Conventions, 1837–1859* (Baltimore, 1930); Mobile *Register,* quoted in Miller, "Daniel Pratt's Industrial Urbanism," 7; Richmond *Enquirer,* December 17, 1850.

23. Richard W. Griffen, "The Origins of the Industrial Revolution in Georgia: Cotton Textiles, 1810–1865," *Georgia Historical Quarterly,* XLII (December, 1958), 355–75.

and was ideally suited for trade with South America and the Orient. In addition to processing industries, the Tredegar and Belle Isle Iron Works gave Richmond an industrial diversity that was unusual in southern cities. In the 1850s, Tredegar entrepreneur Joseph Reid Anderson developed an extensive southern market for railroad locomotives. By the time of the Civil War, Richmond could well lay claim to being the "Lowell of the South."[24]

With the return of cotton prosperity in the 1850s, investments in textile industries tended to decline slightly. Nevertheless, investments in processing industries and heavier manufacturing in the upper South cities allowed the South to maintain industrial investment almost comparable to the North and West during the 1850s. Whereas northern and western investments in manufacturing enterprises increased by 83 percent between 1850 and 1860, southern investments rose 64 percent.[25] The South, therefore, was not antagonistic to manufacturing. Considering the lure of railroad investments, such as increase in industrial capitalization was impressive.

Southern cities learned their lessons well. Railroads and to a lesser extent factories and shipping were essential parts of the blueprint for fulfilling the American urban dream. In the community of cities that characterized the new urban nation of the nineteenth century, imitation was a prevailing aspect of urban growth.[26] De Bow, Fitzhugh, and Burwell educated their readers with tales of northern cities and their formulas of success. While pursuing commercial empire and their northern competitors, southern city dwellers were undergoing changes in their daily lives. These alterations in urban life touched everyone, from the urban elite to the very poor, and every institution from local government to slavery. The changes affected southern life sufficiently to transform towns to modern cities on the threshold of maturity.

Three basic features of southern urban life stood out as central to this transformation: leadership, labor, and local government. During the antebellum era urban leaders in the South emerged as spokesmen for their cities

24. Fisher and Co. to James Thomas, Jr., June 7, 1855, in Beale-Davis Family Papers, Southern Historical Collection, University of North Carolina at Chapel Hill; Richmond *Enquirer,* November 4, 1853; Richmond *Daily Dispatch,* September 22, 1859; see also Kathleen C. Bruce, *Virginia Iron Manufacture in the Slave Era, 1800–1860* (New York, 1931); Joseph C. Robert, *The Tobacco Kingdom: Plantation, Market and Factory in Virginia and North Carolina, 1800–1860* (Durham, N.C., 1938); Thomas S. Berry, "The Rise of Flour Milling in Richmond," *Virginia Magazine of History and Biography,* LXXVIII (October, 1970), 387–408.

25. U.S. Bureau of the Census, *Compendium of the Ninth Census: 1870,* 798–99.

26. See Wade, *The Urban Frontier,* 314–17.

and for their section. J. D. B. De Bow epitomized the trend of southern progressive thought following the Mexican War. His *Review* alternately vilified and cajoled southerners and helped cities to set their sights on their dreams: "Once Baltimore, Richmond, Charleston, Savannah, Mobile, and New Orleans will supply all goods foreign and domestic, how easily we might cut off all dependence on the North." De Bow indefatigably collected statistics on southern industry, trade, and population—never using them to lull the South's cities into the false belief of a contest won but rather to spur city dwellers and the rest of the region to greater enterprise. James Robb, a New Orleans neighbor of De Bow, represented the best of urban leadership emerging from the depression of the 1840s. Robb was the personification of the successful pursuit of the American dream in the antebellum era. He had arrived penniless in New Orleans from Pennsylvania in the 1830s. Within a decade of his arrival, Robb was a prominent banker and a respected member of local government. He was Louisiana's most prominent railroad promoter in the 1850s, and his singular purpose and energy were responsible for the Great Northern Railroad project. Joseph Reid Anderson, born into a yeoman farmer family on the frontier of western Virginia, became one of the South's leading industrialists. By the time he was forty years old, Anderson was operating the Tredegar Iron Works in Richmond, directing a major bank in that city, promoting several railroad and canal schemes, serving on the city council, and traveling throughout the South pressing for improved rail connections among southern cities.[27]

Most southern urban leaders did not cut so wide a swath through the region as did De Bow, Robb, and Anderson. They were, however, a hardworking, concerned elite, no different from urban leaders elsewhere. A survey of leadership in Richmond during the two decades preceding the Civil War reveals the same pattern of elitism demonstrated in studies of northern communities by such scholars as Walter S. Glazer, Clyde Griffin, and Edward Pessen.[28] Richmond's sixty-five leaders, constituting 2 percent of the city's heads of household, were chosen for their visibility—leadership

27. "Commercial, Agricultural, and Intellectual Independence of the South," *De Bow's Review,* XXIX (September, 1860), 467; Reed, *New Orleans and the Railroads,* 81–83; S. Bassett French, "Biographical Sketches" (MS in French Papers, Virginia State Library), 160.

28. See Walter S. Glazer, "Participation and Power: Voluntary Association and the Functional Organization of Cincinnati in 1840," *Historical Methods Newsletter,* V (September, 1972), 151–68; Clyde Griffen, "Occupational Mobility in Nineteenth-Century America," *Journal of Social History,* V (Spring, 1972), 310–30; Edward Pessen, "Who Governed the Nation's Cities in the Era of the Common Man?" *Political Science Quarterly,* LXXXVII (December, 1972), 591–614.

in business associations, social clubs, government, industry, and transportation companies. Eighty-six percent of Richmond's elite in 1850 held proprietary or professional occupations, and 12 percent were small proprietors or shopkeepers (owning less than $1,000 in property); only one leader was classified as a minor civil servant. They were a mature yet vigorous group; forty was the median age. Richmond's elite was wealthy. Three-quarters of them owned real estate, the median being $14,897. Family patterns implied stability and security. Nearly two-thirds of the leaders lived in households that ranged in size from five to nine individuals; 80 percent were married; families included, on the average, three or four children, ranging from fourteen years for the average eldest child to three years for the average youngest child. More than one-half of the leaders lodged at least one boarder under their respective roofs. Slaveholding was widespread. More than three-quarters of the elites owned slaves, though more than one-half of the slaveholders owned less than six slaves. The leaders were white, male, and native. The persistence of the elite was relatively high compared with the rest of Richmond's population. Eighty-six percent of the leaders lived in Richmond either ten years prior to 1850, ten years after 1850, or through the entire twenty-year period. Less than 40 percent of the population citywide were persisters. These figures agree with analyses of elites in Cincinnati, Poughkeepsie, and Philadelphia, which depicted early nineteenth-century urban leadership as wealthy, established, and native.[29]

Elite studies have discovered that civic leaders formed an interlocking directorate permeating every aspect of city life that counted in guiding their city toward prosperity and recognition. Richmond leaders exhibited the pattern of common leadership as well. Forty percent of Richmond's elite served in the city government; one-fourth were prominent stockholders in railroad or canal companies; and one-third participated in charity organizations. Control of the local press was perhaps the most important aspect of the common leadership. The press was the major medium for advertising, information, and city boosterism. The editor could achieve national prominence like Thomas Ritchie of Richmond, and Horace Greeley and William Cullen Bryant of New York. Prominent southern urban journals such as the Richmond *Enquirer,* the Charleston *Mercury,* and the New Orleans *Bee*

29. Data obtained from the following sources: U.S. Bureau of the Census, Seventh Census of Virginia, 1850: Free Inhabitants, 11, Slave Schedule, 4; *Eighth Census of Virginia, 1860: Free Inhabitants,* 12, Slave Schedule, 4; William L. Montague, *Richmond Directory and Business Advertiser for 1852* (Baltimore, 1852); James Butter, *Butter's Richmond Directory, 1855* (Richmond, 1855); French, "Biographical Sketches"; Richmond *Daily Dispatch, 1852–61, passim.*

matched any northern urban press in style, content, and influence. The press was a vital tool for civic leadership in pursuit of the American urban dream. The Norfolk *Southern Argus* stated an axiom of the day when it observed: "The mighty influence of this silent teacher [the press], pouring its lessons every day into the minds of men, it is impossible to estimate. Not all other influences combined can compare with or stand against it." Or as George Fitzhugh put it, "The meanest newspaper in the country is worth all the libraries in Christendom."[30]

The urban press was the cheerleader for urban growth. Its editors were themselves community leaders. James A. Cowardin, editor of the Richmond *Daily Dispatch*—one of the first of the popular penny presses—was a member of the Richmond Board of Trade, vice president of the Virginia Mechanics' Institute, president of a brokerage firm, and a representative from Richmond to the Virginia House of Delegates. The *Dispatch* and other urban journals urged their citizens to the offensive in pursuit of prosperity and recognition: "We hold it to be a self-evident truth," the *Dispatch* declared in a familiar paraphrase, "that no community ever became great, that did not do something great themselves. Individuals may have greatness thrust upon them, communities never do." The New Orleans *Bee* warned its readers that the Crescent City could "bid adieu to much of their western trade unless they adopt more resolute measures than any now in progress."[31]

The urban press also defended cities from spurious allegations by rivals concerning health, market capabilities, and enterprise. Urban rivalry was an important theme of nineteenth-century city development. Cities jockeyed for advantage, and no detail was too small to be overlooked. Though cities constantly borrowed ideas from one another, it was more in the spirit of bitter rivalry than friendly competition. Rivalry was typically more intense within sections. The conflicts between Louisville and Lexington, New Orleans and Mobile, Savannah and Charleston, and Richmond and Norfolk were more acrimonious than contests across sectional lines. The urban press was the sentry—the city's image maker and preserver. Though "Galveston is the New York of the South" and "Augusta is the Lowell of the South" were farfetched assertions, they were typical declarations of urban pride indulged in by the press.[32]

30. Norfolk *Southern Argus*, December 29, 1853; Fitzhugh, *Cannibals All!*, 145–46.

31. Richmond *Daily Dispatch*, September 23, 1860; Montague, *Richmond Directory*, 102; Richmond *Daily Dispatch*, April 19, 1860; New Orleans *Bee*, quoted in Reed, *New Orleans and the Railroads*, 22.

32. Gail Borden, quoted in Wheeler, *To Wear a City's Crown*, 70; quoted in Griffen, "Origins of the Industrial Revolution in Georgia," 365.

Richmond leadership conformed as well to the associational proclivities of urban elites everywhere. As Tocqueville observed, "These people [Americans] associate as easily as they breathe."[33] Voluntary associations were important to the process of urbanization. As a city grew, these associations rationalized growth and enabled leaders to control the development of their city with greater facility.[34] The Board of Trade was probably the earliest voluntary association formed by urban leaders, emphasizing the mercantile cast of the early nineteenth-century urban elite. In New Orleans it was the Chamber of Commerce, in Natchez the Mechanical Society, and in Richmond the Board of Trade. Whatever the name, the function in all cities was similar: to crystallize and channel business sentiment in a more orderly fashion. The board defined urban needs, lobbied for urban interests before local and state lawmakers, and served as a clearinghouse for information by establishing reading rooms and libraries.

Since commerce was "the goddess of Christianity" and the key to fulfillment of the urban dream, the mercantile associations directed their efforts toward rationalizing the increasing flow of commerce to serve their customers better. Warehouse and market house facilities were important in attracting and retaining commerce. De Bow believed that one of New York's greatest commercial attributes was its commodious wharf and storage facilities, which kept produce dry and intact. He suggested that New Orleans install colonnades over its wharves, but the enterprise was too expensive to implement. The Richmond Board of Trade, directed by Horace L. Kent, a dry goods merchant, and R. B. Haxall, proprietor of one of the nation's largest flour mills, successfully persuaded the city council to appropriate three thousand dollars to refurbish market stalls in order "to better accommodate buyers and sellers." The board also attempted to improve coordination between railroad arrivals and city conveyances so that goods would not rot on railroad platforms or wharves.[35]

Just as the members of the Board of Trade expressed anxiety over appropriate accommodations for their customers' produce, they were also concerned about comfortable facilities for the customers themselves. Southern

33. Quoted in Jonathan Lurie, "Private Associations, Internal Regulation and Progressivism: The Chicago Board of Trade, 1880–1923, as a Case Study," *American Journal of Legal History,* XVI (July, 1972), 215.

34. See *ibid.,* 215–38; Wade, *The Urban Frontier,* 185; Wheeler, *To Wear a City's Crown,* 72; Richard D. Brown, "The Emergence of Urban Society in Rural Massachusetts, 1760–1820," *Journal of American History,* LXI (June, 1974), 29–51.

35. "Trade of the Mississippi," 291–93; Richmond *Daily Dispatch,* June 15, 1855, September 23, 1853.

cities soon outgrew the shabby elegance of their old hotels. Savannah boasted of the Screven House but simultaneously complained about the difficulty visitors faced when staying in the city. New Orleans possessed some of the most opulent hotels in the nation and probably alone among southern cities had sufficient accommodations for the crush of fall and spring trade. Richmond's Exchange Hotel, remodeled in the late 1840s to accommodate the city's renascent prosperity, was the most impressive lodge in the state. Visitors commented on its well-appointed rooms, fine fare, and courteous service. Its French chandeliers and English broadlooms rivaled, according to contemporaries, New York's famous Astor House. Richmond's Board of Trade, however, was unhappy with the city's other hotel facilities. In 1857, the members chartered a hotel company and raised two hundred thousand dollars for the new edifice, "so that our customers have the best accommodations that can be afforded."[36]

Voluntary associations were not exclusively concerned with placing customers and their goods in the most commodious surroundings. The horizon of southern urban leaders stretched far beyond nearby farm communities to encompass an urbanizing nation. They were competing against other cities, and they had to adapt their prosperity to the exigencies of a national economy. Commodity exchanges developed in nineteenth-century cities for the purpose of regulating the buying and selling of a particular crop. Exchanges were tools employed by civic leaders to rationalize economic growth. The evolution of Richmond's Tobacco Exchange demonstrates how national market mechanisms began affecting southern cities in the 1850s.

The Panic of 1857 closed Richmond's tobacco factories and created widespread unemployment. The delirium in Richmond's tobacco community resulted from the default of New York tobacco houses on their obligations to Virginia tobacco manufacturers. Richmond alone lost $1 million literally overnight.[37] The crisis embarrassingly revealed the degree of Richmond's dependence on New York as well as the deficiencies with which city leaders carried on the tobacco trade.

Richmond tobacconists called a convention, which assembled in that city in December, 1857, to rectify the situation. The one hundred manu-

36. "The Cities of Georgia: Savannah," *De Bow's Review,* XXVIII (January, 1860), 20–28; Richard Irby, "Recollection of Men, Places, and Events, 1845–1900" (MS in Richard Irby Papers, Alderman Library, University of Virginia); Richmond *Daily Dispatch,* March 18, 1857.

37. Richmond *Enquirer,* May 26, 1858.

facturers who attended adopted resolutions designed both to rationalize the tobacco trade within Virginia and to establish new ground rules in dealing with New York factors. The credit system received the greatest attention of the manufacturers. Urban merchants sold their tobacco on long-term credit providing for the collection of debt in eight to twelve months. New York merchants and factors, on the other hand, extended only short-term credit—usually four months. This meant that New York factors could call up debts before Virginia tobacconists could call in theirs, thus placing a great strain on the financial resources of the manufacturer. Also, when hard-pressed New York factors purchased manufactured tobacco on long-term credit, they would immediately dump the tobacco on the market at a price below cost, depressing the market for the manufacturers. Some of these factors went bankrupt periodically, leaving Virginia manufacturers with worthless longterm notes. The manufacturers resolved, therefore, to limit their credits on the sale of tobacco to four months, beginning July 1, 1858.

The establishment in May, 1858, of the Tobacco Exchange in Richmond was another procedure for rationalizing the tobacco trade. Tobacco merchants rather than manufacturers composed the exchange. In addition to enforcing the resolution passed by the manufacturers, the exchange provided that all buying and selling of tobacco was to be done only with the association. This agreement eliminated auction sales at various warehouses throughout Richmond. By creating a monopoly of sales, tobacco buyers and merchants could set uniform prices and regulate other procedures of the trade. With commission merchants dealing directly with planters, greater profits and regularity would result. Farmers, of course, protested the exchange. "Corporations have no souls," stormed one farmer, "and this 'Exchange Association' is governed only by the dictates of its own interests." Another farmer condemned "*coercive* measures entered into by a *combination*."[38] But for Richmond's tobacco merchants and manufacturers, the reforms induced by "combination" were essential to survival in a competitive national economy. Southern cities could never hope to confront the North on a basis of equality if they failed to establish a more equal economic relationship with northern cities.

Leaders devised another means besides association to rationalize urban growth—the city directory. City directories not only facilitated the process of locating businessmen but also provided an opportunity to organize the city's population between the covers of one readily accessible book. It is true that not all or even most of a city's residents found their way into the

38. *Ibid.*, May 26, 1858, June 11, 1858.

directory, but comprehensiveness was not the goal. The directory was a businessman's guide to other businessmen. In addition to names and addresses, city directories often proudly displayed the social and commercial organizations of the city as well as a list of hotels and newspapers—items that a visitor would find useful. City directories had proved helpful in northern cities like Boston and New York in the 1830s and 1840s, as these centers became international trade marts. Southern cities soon followed the northern example and published directories as well, though New Orleans' inhabitants had had the benefit of a register since the French period. The appearance of directories seemed to relate directly to urban maturation. Richmond published a directory in 1819, but it was a very modest effort. Another directory appeared in 1845, but not until 1852 did its publication become a biennial event.[39]

By 1860, city boosters in the South had articulated their cities' needs in the new urban age and had defined their cities' goals in the section and in the nation. They were ubiquitous in government, business, and society. They were cosmopolitan men, well aware of what was occurring in other cities and what should occur in theirs. As much as the railroads, urban leaders helped to dissipate the insularity of city life. The city and its residents became more wordly in their outlook. Richard D. Brown, discussing the role of associations in organizing and expanding community interests, observed that "townspeople were now members of many communities—their own organizations as well as the state and the nation."[40] Communication and interaction among themselves and with city dwellers elsewhere characterized the urbanizing process. Leaders met and conversed constantly— in hotel lobbies, in countinghouses, on loading platforms, in parlors, and on the wharves. They talked of repealing usury laws, increasing capital in circulation, and eliminating tax burdens on merchants. These leaders set the tone for their city and created its image. In doing so, they made their urban milieu distinctive from the countryside and more similar to cities elsewhere. In a section rampant with ironies, southern cities had stronger economic ties and were more similar to northern cities on the eve of civil war than at any other time. It was, after all, a brothers' war.

39. See Peter R. Knights, *The Plain People of Boston, 1830–1860: A Study in City Growth* (New York, 1971), 7; Montague, introduction to *Richmond Directory.*

40. Brown, "The Emergence of Urban Society," 50; see also Carl Abbott, "Civic Pride in Chicago, 1844–1860," *Journal of the Illinois State Historical Society,* LXIII (Winter, 1970), 421; J. Christopher Schnell and Patrick E. McLear, "Why the Cities Grew: A Historiographical Essay on Western Urban Growth, 1850–1880," *Bulletin of the Missouri Historical Society,* XXVII (April, 1972), 162–77.

Slavery was a major factor in precipitating the brothers' war and also in facilitating urban growth. The superstructure of the American urban dream—railroads, factories, and shipping—required a prodigious labor force. Labor in the urban South invariably meant slave labor. It was true that railroads and factories employed other systems of labor. Immigrants, though never a force in southern cities as they were in the North, performed a variety of tasks in the growing southern city. The Irish found work on railroad gangs and as day laborers on the numerous construction jobs offered by a growing city. Germans made an impact on the labor force in San Antonio, Baltimore, and Richmond. German domestics were beginning to replace slaves in upper South cities by the end of the antebellum era. Immigrants constituted more than 40 percent of the total population of New Orleans in 1860. German and Irish immigrants in New Orleans generally performed tasks that were deemed too dangerous for slaves, like deck and boiler work. Immigrants also worked as stevedores, screwmen, and teamsters. By the time of the Civil War, a distinct labor consciousness was developing among the immigrant work force of New Orleans. The Screwmen's Benevolent Association, which included a large proportion of Irish members, struck steamboat companies successfully for higher wages in 1853.[41]

Immigrant labor proved too intractable for southerners used to a more malleable labor force. Although the inviolability of southern womanhood is one of the givens of Old South historiography, urban southerners did not hesitate to employ women in factory occupations. Travelers reported women workers in the textile plants of Athens and Columbus, Georgia. In James Thomas, Jr.'s Richmond tobacco factory, women prepared chewing tobacco for the presses. One Richmond manufacturer even erected a dormitory for women employees similar to the accommodations for young women in Lowell, Massachusetts. The Mount Vernon Cotton Factory in Alexandria employed 150 "industrious females," with wages ranging from twelve dollars to seventeen dollars a month—the latter figure just slightly below the national average (which included male labor). The Alexandria *Gazette* claimed that the production per hand at the textile mill surpassed

---

41. The manuscript census schedules for 1850 and 1860 provide information on the occupation and property holdings of immigrants; see also Earl F. Niehaus, *The Irish of New Orleans* (Baton Rouge, 1965); Wheeler, *To Wear a City's Crown*; M. Ray Della, Jr., "An Analysis of Baltimore's Population in the 1850s," *Maryland Historical Magazine*, LXVIII (Spring, 1973), 259–63; George P. Marks III, "The New Orleans Screwman's Benevolent Association," *Labor History*, XIV (Spring, 1973), 259–63.

that of Lowell. In Norfolk, merchants employed women in their counting rooms, to the satisfaction of all. The Norfolk *Southern Argus* was so impressed with the efficacy of women in industry that it suggested widespread hiring of unemployed women. Not only would this alleviate a labor shortage experienced by the city in the 1850s, but it would also ease one of the city's ills—prostitution.[42] The Civil War intervened before an empirical study could confirm the *Argus's* logic.

Although southerners were willing to accept and even welcome women into the work force, there were limitations to their employ. For heavier tasks, such as work on railroads, in city streets, mines, and factories, other labor forces were necessary. Free blacks were a growing if somewhat distrusted labor supply in southern cities. The free-black population of the urban South increased during the antebellum period, despite harassment from anxious city officials in the 1840s and 1850s. The tasks they performed were basically menial, but they were necessary to a growing urban society. Free blacks were an anomaly in southern society—not quite free but not enslaved. The lot of the free black was unfortunate in northern cities as well. A Philadelphia judge noted in an 1837 case that the black in that city was "free, but not a freeman."[43] Blacks were often the target of rioting whites, as in Philadelphia and Washington, D.C., during the 1830s. Their civil rights gradually dwindled with each passing year. Although Cincinnati's infamous expulsion decree of 1829 found no imitators elsewhere, free blacks were no longer accepted on juries, their voting rights were curtailed, and segregation began to define social relations between the races in northern cities. Free blacks in southern cities fared about as poorly as their northern urban brethren. Both sections could point to exceptional blacks, but they were truly exceptional. Most free blacks toiled as laborers or in service occupations, such as domestic, barber, washer, or cook.[44]

42. Griffen, "Origins of the Industrial Revolution," 355–75; "White Girls in Tobacco Factories," *Hunt's*, XL (April, 1859), 522–23; Alexandria *Gazette*, May 6, 1852; March 2, 1854; *Norfolk Southern Argus*, March 17, 1854.

43. Quoted in W. E. B. Du Bois, *The Philadelphia Negro: A Social Study* (New York, 1899), 370.

44. See Ira Berlin, *Slaves Without Masters: The Free Negro in the Antebellum South* (New York, 1974); David M. Katzman, *Before the Ghetto: Black Detroit in the Nineteenth Century* (Urbana, 1973); Leon F. Litwack, *North of Slavery: The Negroes in the Free States, 1790–1860* (Chicago, 1961); see also Donnie D. Bellamy, "Free Blacks in Antebellum Missouri, 1820–1860," *Missouri Historical Review*, LXVII (January, 1973), 198–225; Della, "Analysis of Baltimore's Population," 20–35; Dorothy Provine, "The Economic Position of Free Blacks in the District of Columbia," *Journal of Negro History*, LXII (January, 1973), 61–72.

Southern cities enacted laws similar to the Black Codes of the New South to restrict free black mobility. Anxiety over social intercourse between free blacks and slaves prompted these ordinances. The laws also ensured the stability of an important labor force. In Virginia cities, selective enforcement of restrictions against free blacks suggests that view. When agitation for free black removal increased in the 1850s, a Richmond editor pleaded, "They are not a bad class; their labor is needed." Predictably, Richmond authorities rigorously enforced the law providing for forced labor for misdemeanor violations. The chain gang evolved from the zealous application of the forced labor law. By 1860, the gang was a common sight in Richmond streets, repairing pavement, building bridges, and maintaining the wharf.[45]

On the other hand, employers of free blacks openly violated laws requiring them positively to ascertain the status of their help—slave or free. The urban press supported the lawbreakers, contending that compliance would discourage the employment of an important labor source. The Norfolk *Southern Argus* warned that "full enforcement of such a law will act seriously detrimental to the thriving prospects of our city."[46] Businessmen came to view the free black less as a social pariah and more as an economic asset. Testimonials from urban employers depicted the free black as quite the opposite of the shiftless individual that his detractors pictured him: "They [free blacks] are more docile, less expensive, and less prone to riot than Irish laborers."[47] Figures are unavailable on the extent of free black employment in Old South cities. With an expanding economy, increased demands for labor, and more free blacks in the labor pool, it seems safe to conclude that their use and value as a labor force was growing.

Slavery was the most malleable of all urban labor systems. Since slaves vastly outnumbered free blacks in every southern city except Baltimore, cities relied heavily on slave labor for tasks ranging from streetcleaning to blacksmithing to that of factory foreman. Historians have disagreed on the impact of the urban environment on the slaves. Some have viewed urban slavery as a step toward freedom, others as a darker, harsher form of the "peculiar institution."[48] All scholars agree, however, that slavery in the cities

45. Richmond *Daily Dispatch,* January 26, 1853; Governor's Message to the General Assembly, December 13, 1859 (Virginia House of Delegates, 1859–60), docs. 1, 44.

46. Norfolk *Southern Argus,* July 25, 1853; see also Alexandria *Gazette,* February 15, 1853; Richmond *Daily Dispatch,* November 25, 1859.

47. Virginia Board of Public Works, *Thirty-Ninth Annual Report* (Richmond, 1855), cxx.

48. See Robert S. Starobin, *Industrial Slavery in the Old South* (New York, 1969); Richard C. Wade, *Slavery in the Cities: The South, 1820–1860* (New York, 1964); Charles B. Dew,

was different in some fundamental manner from the more traditional agricultural slavery. Perhaps the most unique version of slave labor in southern
cities was the slave-hiring system.

Slave hiring had existed since the colonial period on farms and in towns.
When slave prices began skyrocketing in the late 1840s, slave buying, especially in the upper South, became prohibitive for many prospective urban
employers. Urban merchants and manufacturers found it more economical
to hire their work force. As British traveler Robert Russell observed, "Were
they [the hired slaves] to be bought it would require too much capital to
carry on business." [49] Slave hiring was a temporary relationship more suited
to factory work and seasonal construction tasks than was slave ownership.
Parties could frame the hiring bonds from one day to one year. Slave hiring
became widespread in tobacco factories following the Mexican War. During
the 1850s, Virginia tobacco manufacturers hired 164 percent more blacks
than in the previous decade. The iron industry also participated extensively
in slave hiring. Tredegar Iron Works shifted to employing rather than purchasing its work force in the 1850s. Newspaper advertisements for hired
slaves represented a catalog of urban employment: waitress, cook, washer,
cotton factory operative, smith, drayman, and wharf personnel. Employers
ranged from struggling young businessmen without property to railroad
presidents. Free blacks hired slaves as well. Slave hiring thus adapted well to
both situation and employer. [50]

Slave hiring was another example of a fruitful urban-rural coalition.
Farmers, sometimes in small groups, supplied urban slave-hiring needs. Urban agents appeared by the late 1840s, when slave hiring became institutionalized as an urban labor system. Commission merchants sometimes
doubled as hiring agents. In addition to dealing in corn, tobacco, and wheat
for their clients, they would also seek appropriate situations for their customers' slaves. By 1860, 52 percent of the slaves hired in Richmond were

---

"Disciplining Slave Ironworkers in the Antebellum South: Coercion, Conciliation, and Ac-
commodation,"*American Historical Review,* LXXIX (April, 1974), 393–418; Clement Eaton,
"Slave-Hiring in the Upper South: A Step Toward Freedom," *Mississippi Valley Historical
Review,* XLVI (March, 1960), 663–78.

49. Robert Russell, *North America: Its Agriculture and Climate* (Edinburgh, 1857), 152.

50. Robert, *The Tobacco Kingdom, passim;* for advertisements of owners and agents with
tobaccco factory hands for hire, see Richmond *Daily Dispatch,* January 4, 1853, January 3,
1855; for advertisements of coal mines seeking to hire slave labor, see Richmond *Daily
Dispatch,* January 1, 1853, January 1, 1854; "Forge Wages to Negro a/c," in *Tredegar Journals,*
1850, 1852, Virginia State Library; see also Eighth Census of Virginia, 1860: Slave
Schedule, IV.

hired through an agency. The arrangement was mutually profitable to agent and farmer. The agent received his 2.5 percent commission and sought the highest rate of hire for his client.[51]

The position of the urban slave in the hiring relationship was ambiguous. In the absence of the traditional master-slave relationship, some employers cruelly mistreated the slaves; others allowed their hirelings wide latitude in choice of housing, pace of work, and leisure time. A few of the more talented slaves hired their own time, but this was not usual in the slave-hiring system. Attempts to secure legislation fixing the responsibility of the employer generally failed. Slave hiring was a lucrative urban business, and participants in the system, though they might complain from time to time, were wary about tampering with a profitable enterprise. The average rate of hire for a prime unskilled male increased from $85 to $175 per year during the fifteen years prior to secession in urban Virginia. Skilled laborers commanded $225 or more. The inflated prices prompted some enterprising individuals to purchase slaves for the express purpose of hiring them out.[52]

The prevalence of the slave-hiring system in Virginia cities demonstrated that the urban environment and the institution of slavery were not antagonistic to each other. Slave hiring, in fact, underscored the flexibility and versatility of both slavery and the slave. Southerners who knew the structure of cities and the mechanisms of slavery understood that the city and slavery were well suited for each other. George Fitzhugh, Virginia's leading defender of slavery, urged the extensive employment of slave labor in cities. De Bow believed that southern cities could build railroads more cheaply than cities elsewhere because of the profitability of slave labor. Regardless of age or sex, slave labor proved a versatile labor source in southern cities. De Bow commented, for example, that women slaves made excellent ditch-diggers. In 1860, more than seventy thousand slaves were living in the South's eight largest cities, and their numbers were increasing in Mobile, Savannah, and Richmond. In cities that lost a portion of their slave population, the reasons for the decline lay not in the decreasing vitality of the

51. Eighth Census of Virginia, 1860: Slave Schedule, I, 322, 326, 327, 328; R. Lewis to Dr. A. G. Grinnan, December 29, 1860, in Grinnan Family Papers, Alderman Library, University of Virginia; N. B. Hill to Mr. Atkinson, February 7, 1855, in James Southgate Papers, Duke University Library); Eighth Census of Virginia, 1860: Slave Schedule, IV.

52. Alexandria *Gazette,* February 29, 1856; Richmond *Daily Dispatch,* April 15, 1859; "Hiring Negroes," *Southern Planter,* XII (December, 1852), 376–77; Norfolk *Southern Argus,* April 27, 1857; A. A. Campbell, "Capital and Enterprise: The Bases of Agricultural Progress," *Southern Planter,* XX (January, 1860), 36–39; Edmund Ruffin, "The Effects of High Prices of Slaves," *Southern Planter,* XIX (August, 1859), 472–77.

institution but rather in the increased demands for unskilled labor from the agricultural sector, which resulted in a smaller but more select urban slave force attuned to the urban economy. Slavery, far from being an albatross to urban progress, grew more valuable to city dwellers as secession approached. If, as a Wheeling journal observed, the survival of slavery was a matter of "dollars and cents," then slavery in southern cities was in robust health.[53]

The emergence of a leadership class and the ready adaptability of slavery to the exigencies of modern urban life were two important developments in the pursuit of the American urban dream by southern cities. The final and perhaps the most dramatic change affecting daily life in the southern city was the increasing role of local government in urban affairs.

The evolution of local government from a cipher to an active participant in community life was a consequence of urban growth and maturation in nineteenth-century America. As southern cities grew from frontier outposts and dusty market towns, the limitations of the small group of elites that defined community interests became apparent, even to the leaders themselves. Basic urban services such as fire, police, water, lighting, and disease prevention were necessary if a city were to carry on with the business of growth and prosperity. Few visitors and customers would be attracted to a city that was a firetrap, crime-ridden, or unhealthy. Moreover, the pressures of competition made the provision of such services prerequisites for modern urban life.

The structure of urban government in the Old South was familiar to city dwellers everywhere. The city council—a single body in some cities, a bicameral legislature in others—was the primary governing institution of the city. In the 1820s and 1830s, the council typically appointed the mayor, who generally rubberstamped council decisions and presided over the city court. During the last two decades before the Civil War, in a democratic wave that washed over urban America, the office of mayor became elective and the quasi-judicial functions of the office gradually disappeared. The urban legislature, however, still maintained the balance of power up to secession. The council was a carefully guarded club where civic leaders could direct the progress of their community.[54]

53. George Fitzhugh, *Sociology for the South,* (New York, 1854), 87; J. D. B. De Bow, "Address to Railroad Convention," *De Bow's Review,* XII (September, 1852), 557–59, and XVIII (April, 1855), 350–51; Wheeling *Daily Intelligencer,* May 28, 1858; Claudia D. Goldin, "Urbanization and Slavery: The Issue of Compatibility," in *New Urban History,* ed. Leo F. Schnore (Princeton, 1975), 231–46.

54. See Charles N. Glaab and A. Theodore Brown, *A History of Urban America* (New York, 1967), Chap. 7.

City charters changed as well during the antebellum period. Local officials flooded state legislatures with requests either to grant routine amendments to existing city charters or to approve entirely new charters. Dividing the city into wards was a major distinction of urban status that accompanied new charters. In 1860, for example, Nashville and Louisville had eight wards, Wheeling had six wards, Petersburg had four wards, and Richmond had three wards. Ward division had little to do with population. It was, rather, the city fathers' conception of how their city should be partitioned to provide more efficient government. By 1851, all southern cities provided for universal white adult male suffrage. Thousands of new voters entered the urban political process. Although their impact on decision making and the composition of government was considerably less than their numbers warranted, the expanded electorate generated a need for a rational organization of the city. Citywide constituencies generally disappeared, and wards became the basic political units. City administrators also discovered that the ward system allowed for a more effective distribution of urban services and patronage. It was another method used by urban boosters to rationalize their growing cities.[55]

The city charter detailed the limits of local government power. Changes in this instrument reflected the changing needs of a maturing city. The most significant alteration—incorporation as a city—engendered greater home rule, especially in the area of taxation and debt ceiling. In the railroad-building era of the 1840s and 1850s, respective state legislatures allowed cities like New Orleans, Louisville, Mobile, and Richmond to subscribe to railroads.[56] Since most southern railroads were financed locally, such charter provisions were essential to urban prosperity. The ability to levy taxes ensured that the growing number of services overseen by city government could be funded.

Standing committees were another feature of expanding urban government. City officials could no longer afford to deal with problems on an ad hoc basis. A permanent bureaucracy was necessary to grapple with the troublesome aspects of daily urban life. The standing committees in southern urban government approximated those of northern cities and indicated

55. See Eaton, *Southern Civilization,* 249; Brown, "The Emergence of Urban Society," 29–51; Curry, "Urbanization and Urbanism in the Old South," 43–60.

56. See John Little, *History of Richmond* (Richmond, 1933), 292; James, *Antebellum Natchez,* 79–82; Reed, *New Orleans and the Railroads,* 82; Wade, *Urban Frontier,* 270; see also Robert A. McCaughey, "From Town to City: Boston in the 1820s," *Political Science Quarterly,* LXXXVIII (June, 1973), 191–213.

local government's concern with almost every aspect of urban life. Alexandria, for example, possessed eight standing committees in 1860: finance and salaries, streets, lighting, real estate, public schools, claims, the poor, and fire. In the same year, Natchez had a similar committee arrangement, including two additions: health and safety. Fifteen years earlier, there had been half as many committees in Natchez city government.[57]

City officials proliferated with the growth of urban government. In 1856, Wheeling voters received a ballot with twenty-six offices, from mayor to measurer of grain, and at least twice as many candidates. Since most cities held annual elections, the electoral process threw cities into periodic political agitations that distracted from business pursuits. With the multiplicity of offices and candidates and with major issues generally absent, emotion and personality sometimes dominated the proceedings. Baltimore's election-day riots during the Know Nothing ascendancy in the 1850s, Louisville's "Bloody Monday" in 1855, and similar though less violent disturbances in New Orleans and Norfolk emphasized that nativism was a southern phenomenon, too.[58]

The expanding personnel of city government resulted from the increasing need for urban services. The provision of urban services was generally a mixed enterprise in nineteenth-century America—a partnership between government and citizen. This was an optimum arrangement because city funds were limited, and the private sector possessed expertise and a small amount of capital. Combined, government and citizen provided the full range of services, not always equally distributed but sufficient to improve the quality of urban life.

Disease prevention was probably the first government venture into urban services. Disease was a scourge of nineteenth-century cities, even more so in the South. Killing frosts arrived later than in the North and kept authorities vigilant for the slightest indication of the presence of disease. Because the etiology of diseases was unknown, escape was the only "cure" for epidemic outbreaks. Urban governments and their citizens therefore directed their efforts at prevention. The devastating cholera epidemic of 1832 illustrates the mechanisms of disease prevention relatively early in the antebellum period.

In 1826, the Charleston Board of Health, a government-appointed body that served in a part-time capacity, organized the Committee of Medical

57. Alexandria *Gazette,* March 18, 1860; James, *Antebellum Natchez,* 79–82; see also Wade, *Urban Frontier,* 273.

58. Wheeling *Daily Intelligencer,* April 28, 1856; see W. D. Overdyke, *The Know Nothing Party in the South* (Baton Rouge, 1950).

Police, headed by a prominent Charleston physician. Its primary charge was to study epidemic diseases. When cholera first appeared in New York in mid-1832, the committee established a rigorous quarantine around the port of Charleston, much to the dismay of local businessmen. Since directives of the Board of Health and its committee had the force of law, the quarantine held and Charleston escaped unscathed. Unfortunately, four years later a ship brought the disease directly to Charleston without warning. Prevention now impossible, the city government issued a series of regulations intended to control the disease and empowered the Board of Health to enforce them. The city council expanded the board and ordered the inspection of all outhouses, the drainage of stagnant water, the erection of hospitals, and the imposition of a quarantine. Officials successfully confined the disease to the poorer sections of the city.[59] The measures approved by city government demonstrated that city leaders were aware of some link between filth and disease.

Cleanliness was indeed the primary preventive measure instituted by urban government. "Of all preventive means yet discovered," a Norfolk journal averred, "cleanliness is by far the most important." The Baltimore Health Act of 1832 was a model of public health legislation and more effective than the feeble and disorganized attempts of New York City to deal with health problems. The act required the superintendent of streets, a council-appointed official, to physically inspect cellars, privies, and yards. The New York measure, passed several months earlier, required only an "inquiry" into conditions in those places. Further, the model measure provided for the whitewashing of cellars and the liming of homes at public expense if residents were too poor to pay.[60] As a result, cholera was relatively mild in Baltimore in 1832.

Savannah probably had the most unique solution to eliminating filth and "bad vapors." Between 1817 and 1820, the city placed large tracts of land surrounding the city—mostly low wetlands with fetid pools—in dry culture. The city council appointed a Dry Culture Committee to ensure that proper drainage and irrigation maintained the land in a dry rather than wet state. The city government paid planters forty dollars an acre to grow, within a mile radius of Savannah, only crops that required dry culture. The government financed this plan in typical mixed enterprise fashion. It floated a

59. Charles E. Rosenberg, *The Cholera Years* (Chicago, 1962), 13–37; Joseph I. Waring, "Asiatic Cholera in South Carolina," *Bulletin of the History of Medicine,* XL (September–October, 1966), 462.

60. Norfolk *Southern Argus,* December 16, 1848; Rosenberg, *The Cholera Years,* 27–37.

bond issue for two-thirds of the two hundred thousand dollars required to implement dry culture, and private citizens supplied the remainder. The "sanative cordon" of dry culture land around the city was Savannah's major defense against yellow fever.[61]

Most southern cities did not go to such elaborate lengths as Savannah to purify their environment. Local governments concentrated on streetcleaning—a neverending task in the days before there were proper sewage facilities. Some cities solved the problem of filthy streets by allowing animals to scavenge. The animals, however, sometimes proved more dangerous to residents, especially children, than their usefulness as scavengers warranted. The Richmond *Enquirer* recommended, in 1854, a time-honored if not very neighborly method of removing offal from the streets by collecting and dumping it into the nearby James River. The city council agreed and ordered the superintendent of police, an elected official, to implement the suggestion. Alexandria's city council undertook a careful study of refuse disposal in other cities. The study recommended and the council implemented a plan to station garbage carts in strategic locations so that citizens would use the carts instead of the streets for refuse disposal. The council report noted that "in the cities of Philadelphia and Baltimore, this arrangement has been in operation for a series of years and fully accomplished the desired end."[62] This was another example of the community of cities.

Street drainage was another problem, especially in cities prone to yellow fever, like Norfolk and New Orleans. "It is of vast importance to the trade and prosperity of Norfolk," the *Argus* warned, "to say nothing of the lives of the people, that the standing pools in our streets should be removed by the appropriate committee of the councils instantly." Baltimore undertook streetcleaning operations for a time, but in the 1850s contracted for a private firm to handle such chores. Both filth and mortality rates increased.[63] Although the expense was great, proper streetcleaning, preferably under the auspices of the city government, proved profitable in the long run, since it made the streets more attractive for visitors and customers and perhaps even prevented or mitigated a devastating epidemic.

Despite efforts of urban government to provide a modicum of cleanliness for its citizens, the fight was a losing one. Local government lacked the

61. Savannah *Daily Morning News,* April 28, 1851; James J. Waring, *The Epidemic of Savannah* (Savannah, 1879), 16–17.

62. *Richmond Enquirer,* June 8, 1854; Alexandria *Gazette,* June 23, 1854.

63. Norfolk *Southern Argus,* January 16, 1856; *Report of the Baltimore Board of Health* (Baltimore, 1860).

necessary manpower to scour a city. Before Alexandria enacted its garbage cart law, garbage collection was carried out by one scavenger. Further, although the relationship between filth and disease was well known to board of health officials, the majority of citizens probably appreciated this bit of intuitive medicine only slightly. They had, after all, seen loved ones carried off when streets were clean as well as when they were dirty. Finally, because of limited personnel and funds, streetcleaning and garbage-collection efforts, were selectively applied. Two citizens of Alexandria complained irately, "No garbage cart in the South End of the City. The inhabitants of that quarter pour all their slop and kitchen offal into the streets." Another citizen, identifying himself as "Health," scoffed, "What a humbug is the 'Garbage Cart' law! In some parts of the city, the garbage cart never goes—never has gone." Invariably, the business district received priority in any streetcleaning scheme. The areas that went without such services were usually the poorer, nontaxpaying districts which, ironically, were most vulnerable to disease.

Southern cities were not alone in neglecting poorer residents in disease prevention operations. In 1856, the Boston *Herald* took the local government to task for its callous disregard of the health needs of the poor: "The filthiest localities which need most of the care of the city authorities are, in general, most neglected. . . . If a nuisance should be created on the upper-crust of the town, it would receive the attention of the powers that govern our municipality much more promptly." [64]

The dominance of businessmen in urban affairs not only led to a scanting of health measures but also hampered government efforts once epidemics were underway. Disease was bad business. A healthful image was essential to a city's prosperity. No farmer wanted to trade cotton or tobacco for yellow fever or cholera. In pursuit of their dream, America's cities realized the potential of disease for wrecking their hopes in the competition for trade. Early in the century, a New York journal placed the specter of epidemic in its proper catastrophic perspective: "Nothing but pestilence on the one hand, or such untoward political events as destroy our national power can prevent our becoming the first city on the western continent." The mere rumor of a cholera outbreak in Richmond in 1849 sent the entire legislature fleeing northward. In 1855, the proximity of Richmond to fever-ridden Norfolk resulted in calls for the permanent removal of the capital to "some more healthy clime." [65] The urban press, consequently, spent a good

---

64. Alexandria *Gazette,* April 7, 1856, June 10, 1856; Boston *Herald,* May 13, 1856.
65. Quoted in Samuel Mills Hopkins, *Letters Concerning the General Health* (New York, 1805), 2; Alexandria *Gazette,* June 8, 1849; Richmond *Enquirer,* October 2, 1855.

deal of time both creating a healthy image and dispelling any rumors of epidemic, even if the allegations were true.

Rival city newspapers, the civic leaders' image makers and preservers, hurled allegations at each other concerning health conditions. In August, 1858, the Augusta *Dispatch* charged that the Charleston *Courier* had deliberately suppressed yellow fever statistics, and the *Dispatch* considered this suppression a "penal offense." At the same time, a Norfolk paper reported that "people are fleeing [from Charleston] in every direction." Charleston sources repudiated both stories but several months later published the following comment: "The *Courier* decided it was not necessary to report the epidemic cases, but it is now safe for any American . . . to visit in Charleston." Amid charges from rival cities that cholera was victimizing Savannah, a local journal made the following declaration: "Savannah is free from all epidemics or malignant diseases; our general health is good as usual." Two weeks later, however, the same newspaper admitted: "We have had a sickly season, but we have had no epidemic, and few deaths among our native southern population." Withholding disease information might have protected business assets, but it was a disservice, even a tragedy, to other residents and travelers. For one thing, unsuspecting visitors could contract the disease. Second, since the press was virtually the city's only medium, citizens themselves could be caught in the web of epidemic. Finally, the Board of Health could not initiate control mechanisms until the disease was far advanced. When yellow fever struck Norfolk in early June, 1855, Norfolk journals suppressed the information until July 30. Later investigation suggested that the frightful toll of the disease might have been lessened by prompt action of Norfolk authorities.[66]

The fear of economic disaster prompted urban leaders to suppress facts detrimental to their city's image. In 1850, a group of southern physicians estimated that the cost of disease and death in New Orleans alone totaled $45 million annually in business and in trade.[67] It took Norfolk five years to recover the population and business lost by the tragic yellow fever epidemic of 1855. The psychological damage was probably as great as the economic and human casualties. During the Norfolk epidemic, all major Virginia cities, as well as Baltimore and New York, issued interdicts against

66. Charleston *Courier,* August 26, 1858, November 11, 1858; Savannah *Daily Morning News,* September 22, 1852, November, 6, 1852; Committee of Physicians, *Report on the Origins of the Yellow Fever in Norfolk During the Summer of 1855* (Richmond, 1857).

67. Richard H. Shryock, *Medicine in America* (Baltimore, 1966), 50; see also John Duffy, *Sword of Pestilence: The New Orleans Yellow Fever Epidemic of 1853* (Baton Rouge, 1966).

trade from Norfolk. Wharves, streets, and business establishments became deserted. The charitable Howard Association hastily transformed Norfolk's major hotel into a hospital—which in most cases proved to be a mere way station en route to the grave. Among those who perished were Mayor Hunter Woodis and more than half of the city's ministers and physicians. The disease left countless orphans. One man, a clergyman, recorded the passing of his wife, daughter, and sister-in-law within six days. By late summer, such tragedy was commonplace. In two adjoining houses, thirty-four of thirty-six residents died. During the first week in September, at the height of the pestilence, there were at least eighty deaths a day. Within a short time, the supply of coffins in the city was exhausted. Ships that had once brought produce to the docks began to bring in hundreds of coffins— and still there were too few. At times, survivors buried loved ones in blankets, and sometimes they placed them in common graves of forty or more victims. A resident fortunate to escape the scourge wrote sadly to a friend, "My heart sickens when I think of it. The place where my most sacred interests are located, but a short time ago, full of joy and gladness is now the scene of sorrow and distress. . . . Poor Norfolk, when will it survive the shock!"[68]

The yellow fever epidemic shattered the prosperity of Norfolk. Time seemed to date from before or after the "summer of pestilence." Monuments to heroes of the plague, prayers of thanksgiving, and health statistics reminded citizens of their collective tragedy. The editors of the Norfolk *Southern Argus*, upon resuming publication, wrote of a "plague spirit." In 1859, the paper admitted that the "advancement" of Norfolk was "slow, too slow." The plague had "melted away the population like snow" and had shaken the self-confidence of the city.[69]

City government, with its committees, boards of health, and special officials armed with regulations on everything from garbage collection to privy inspection was fighting a superior enemy. Nevertheless, public health was an early attempt of southern urban governments to control their city. It was a precedent for activity in other spheres of urban life. Public health, for example, demonstrated the financial versatility of city governments. General funds from the city treasury sometimes supported the health bureaucracy, but cities also employed the devices of special bond issues and taxes to secure necessary funds. Nor were southern urban governments

68. David R. Goldfield, "Disease and Urban Image: Yellow Fever in Norfolk, 1855," *Virginia Cavalcade,* XXIII (Autumn, 1973), 34–41.
    69. *Ibid.*

entirely oblivious to the needs of the poor during an epidemic. Charleston, for example, divided the city into health districts in the 1850s and appointed physicians to service each district. The ordinance further required physicians to attend to the sick in the almshouse, pesthouse, workhouse, and orphanage.[70] In an era before the germ theory of disease and in a period when doses of calomel and vigorous bleeding were accepted treatments for cholera, southern urban governments employed the tools and the knowledge available to them.

Disease was the most devastating aspect of life in the maturing city, but crime was an equally ubiquitous if less destructive problem confronting urban government. From 1830 to the Civil War, when riots were virtually an annual phenomenon in northern cities,[71] southern cities were less prone to massive disturbances. The existence of slavery and the greater homogeneity of the southern urban population probably mitigated potential violence. During the Know Nothing campaigns in the mid-1850s, there were several serious outbreaks of mass violence, but these were exceptions to the general trend. For a region that has a reputation for being militant and prone to violent confrontation, the Old South (at least in its cities) was no more violent—probably less so—than northern counterparts. Violence in southern cities generally appeared in poorer districts, instigated by drink, sex, or both. Drunkenness was common, especially in frontier towns like Houston, but it seems more appropriate to categorize it as an affliction than as a crime.[72] The two most common crimes reported by the press in southern cities were arson and burglary. Since these actions were crimes against property, business leaders reacted vociferously, and their governments entered the crime-prevention field. The crime rate in cities was probably higher than reported because, like disease, crime was bad business. As a Wheeling paper reasoned, "It is not agreeable to the feelings of any person who cherishes city pride, to have it go forth that crime exists in their midst."[73] Thus when complaints reached a public forum, the situation was serious.

Citizen unhappiness over law and order centered on the inadequacy of police protection. A Norfolk resident linked his city's rising crime rate to an impotent police force and appended the following picture of anarchy:

70. Robert Lebby, *Digest of Acts of the Assembly of South Carolina and Ordinances of the City of Charleston Relative to the Health Department from 1763 to 1867* (Charleston, 1870).

71. See David Grimsted, "Rioting in the Jacksonian Setting," *American Historical Review*, LXXVII (April, 1972), 77; John C. Schneider, "Community and Order in Philadelphia, 1834–1844," *Maryland Historian*, V (Spring, 1974), 15–26.

72. See Wheeler, *To Wear a City's Crown*, 54.

73. Wheeling *Daily Intelligencer*, February 25, 1860.

"Vice and crime are walking rampant through our streets. Our dwellings are fired by the heartless incendiary, and the privacy of our chambers invaded with impunity by the midnight burglar." Southern cities, like northern cities until the end of the antebellum period, lacked a professional police force or even any organization deserving the term "force." Though some cities like Louisville and Lexington possessed an adequate number of salaried police, even the alleged fear of slave rebellion in southern cities did not motivate local governments to establish proper police service. Even if a southern city supported a police organization, its presence offered little security to the citizenry. New Orleans police were probably the most profligate crew in the country, except for New York's finest. The police protecting Charlestonians were more of a menace to public quietude than the criminals they reputedly sought. When the police were not perpetrating crimes themselves, they usually could be found either sleeping on duty or imbibing at the local grog shop. A Norfolk businessman charged that "in the past few weeks there have been a wave of burglaries. Nothing has been done to detect the perpetrators." After a particularly rampant series of robberies and assaults, another exasperated Norfolk resident asked, "Have we any police?"[74]

In some cities, the answer to that query was an anguished "no"; so business leaders organized their own force. In June, 1854, in response to a growing wave of burglaries, Alexandria civic leaders established a private night watch in the city's business district. When the cold winter months arrived, the private force proved unable to sustain its initial enthusiasm, and "propertyholders" reported an increase in crime. In March, 1855, the councils of Alexandria appointed a force of twelve night watchmen and named a superintendent. Following the usual urban pattern, the watchmen were less than zealous in their duty. To remedy this situation, the councilmen extended greater control over the watch by requiring the superintendent to issue a monthly report on the number of nights, with specific dates, that individual watchmen were on duty. There were no further complaints from the business community prior to secession. Alexandria remained without a day police until after the Civil War.[75]

The record of southern urban government on fire protection reveals a pattern similar to police services: early attempts at voluntary action, financial

74. Norfolk *Southern Argus,* June 18, 1850; Eaton, *Southern Civilization,* 251; George C. Rogers, Jr., *Charleston in the Age of the Pinckneys* (Norman, Okla., 1969), 167; Norfolk *Southern Argus,* January 9, 1856, July 21, 1857.

75. Alexandria *Gazette,* June 8, 1854, December 5, 1854, March 29, 1855, March 11, 1858.

and performance shortcomings, and the gradual assumption by local government of fire regulations and fire fighting. Between 1830 and 1860, most southern urban governments passed ordinances prohibiting the construction of wooden buildings in the downtown area. The Fireproof Building in Charleston, built in 1826, was the first structure in America to be deliberately planned and constructed to resist fire.[76] Businessmen favored such ordinances because of the obvious destructive capabilities of a conflagration. Further, merchants found it virtually impossible to purchase fire insurance without such ordinances. Firefighting was almost as rudimentary as disease control; once a fire began, given just a little wind, it would easily spread to adjacent stores and residences. As with other services, fire protection as a public service was a response to the demands of an increasingly prosperous business community.

The fire-protection system in southern cities initially consisted of private, nonprofessional companies or, more appropriately, clubs that competed more against themselves than against fires. Sometimes the free flow of liquor and the heat of competition, if not of the fire, provoked a general melee, though none as serious as the disturbance in Cincinnati in 1853 that prompted the formation of the nation's first public fire department. Efficiency seemed to drop as the number of volunteer companies increased. In the late 1850s, Charleston possessed twenty volunteer companies, but the city's fire protection was notoriously poor. In some cases, volunteer companies merged into one association to pool resources, manpower, and equipment. The advantages in proficiency and in economic terms were numerous. The Richmond Fire Association, which included seven companies by 1850, offered fire insurance, for example. It is hoped that this arrangement inspired members to greater diligence in firefighting, though there is no evidence that fire was less of a disaster in Richmond after 1850. The New Orleans Firemen's Charitable Association, formed in 1855, fought fires on a franchise basis, receiving a contract of seventy thousand dollars from the city fathers, but with equally mediocre results.[77]

By the 1850s, urban growth and the national urban competition engaged in by southern cities resulted in sufficient intolerance of fire-protection laxity to warrant government action. Some cities were already furnishing companies with equipment and engine houses. Mobile's well-regulated volunteer fire department of eight companies received a new hook and ladder

76. Williams O. Stevens, *Charleston* (New York, 1940).
77. See Glaab and Brown, *A History of Urban America,* 97; Eaton, *Southern Civilization,* 257.

in 1860. Alexandria in 1857 purchased a lot for one of its voluntary companies to erect a new firehouse. In 1858, the Wheeling city council donated three hundred dollars worth of hose to one volunteer group, a stone wall around the engine house of another company recently and embarrassingly destroyed by fire, and sixty dollars for miscellaneous equipment for a third company. This civic activity ensued from a disastrous fire that destroyed the wagon factory of a prominent Wheeling citizen. The fire companies had arrived on the scene in due course, but their archaic equipment proved unequal to the task. Richmond abandoned its volunteer system in 1858 in the interests of efficiency and inaugurated a public paid department.[78]

Fire protection improved with increased involvement of city government. Some cities even purchased steam engines to aid firefighting companies. Firefighting was spotty, however, and, as with wealth and police services, was geared toward the protection of the business district. Six or seven volunteer fire companies converging on the home of a poor resident on the city's periphery was an unusual if not improbable sight in northern or southern cities in the nineteenth century. Fire protection was inadequate regardless of section. A review of the New York City Fire Department in 1856 admitted that the department possessed the best engines in the country but accused the members of "rowdyism" and "inefficiency."[79] The move toward public fire departments was a beginning toward fire protection for the entire community. After the Civil War, with increased financial outlay, southern cities built on the precedents established in the antebellum era.

The water system in southern cities reflected the inadequacy of fire protection. In New Orleans, it was unsafe to drink the water until the twentieth century. There were a few southern cities, however, where it was possible to quench one's thirst without seriously endangering one's health. De Bow cited Savannah's municipal waterworks, replete with lead pipes, as providing a salubrious liquid refreshment. Natchez possessed a similar system dating to 1819. The Natchez Water Company was a private enterprise. Nashville also developed a waterworks relatively early (1833) that was municipally owned. A steam engine pumped water from the Cumberland River to a reservoir and thence to dwellings via cast-iron pipes. Richmond organized a similar system at the same time, employing six pumps to raise water from

78. "Mobile: Its Past and Present," *De Bow's Review,* XXVIII (March, 1860), 305; Alexandria *Gazette,* April 10, 1857; Wheeling *Daily Intelligencer,* November 13, 1858, January 5, 1859; "Commercial and Industrial Cities of the United States: Richmond, Virginia," *Hunt's,* XL (January, 1859), 61–62.

79. "Fires in Cities: London and New York," *Hunt's,* XXXV (July, 1856), 300–301.

the James River to a reservoir with an 11-million-gallon capacity. Iron pipes distributed the water to the rest of the city. The project cost Richmond $625,000—a good reason why not too many other southern cities were willing to risk constructing a municipal waterworks.[80]

Other urban services, such as street lighting and street repair, were more decorative than vital to southern communities. These services, though, are essential artifacts of modern urban life. Southern cities involved in and aware of advances of competing cities across the nation sought these attributes of modernity. Street repair demanded the city council's time and the city's money more than any other urban service.[81] This was not surprising, since streets in the urban nation resembled steeplechase courses rather than pedestrian and wheeled thoroughfares. The complaint of the Boston *Courier* in 1849 depicted a typical condition: "The sidewalks are in terrible condition and it is at great risk of life and limb that pedestrians can venture across our thoroughfares." Frederick Law Olmsted, during his travels across the Old South, repeatedly referred to the rutted quagmires that passed for streets in southern cities. A farmer visiting Alexandria after several years absence appreciated the improvement in the city's major business avenue and recalled that in the past, "I expected nothing else, than the wagon would be smashed all to pieces, and the old woman too." Paved and graded streets were thus helpful to the city's interests. As an Alexandria paper noted, "There are few things which operate against a city more than bad streets, and especially when they are the principal ones."[82]

The role of local government in street repair was the familiar one of cooperation with the private sector. Individuals petitioned the appropriate council committee for street repair or paving. If the council members acceded to the request, the appropriate city official—usually the superintendent of streets or the superintendent of police—proceeded to pave the street. The city charged private property owners for this service, so that paving, like other city services, was nonexistent in the poorer districts of the city. In paving its major thoroughfare—King Street, Alexandria levied a special tax on property holders fronting the street at a rate of $1.25 to $1.30 per

80. "Savannah," *De Bow's Review,* XXVIII (January, 1860), 20–28; James, *Antebellum Natchez,* 84; Eaton, *Southern Civilization,* 254; "Richmond," 61–62; see also Nelson M. Blake, *Water for the Cities: A History of the Urban Water Supply Problem in the United States* (Syracuse, 1956).

81. See Wade, *Urban Frontier,* 276, 282–85.

82. Boston *Courier,* January 8, 1849; Frederick Law Olmsted, *A Journey Through the Seaboard Slave States* (New York, 1856), 132; Alexandria *Gazette,* April 18, 1858, January 26, 1858.

front foot, depending on value, and issued eight thousand dollars worth of corporate bonds. The total cost of the project was thirteen thousand dollars.[83] For such major projects, cities expected abutting property owners to pay for only a portion of the paving cost.

Street lighting was another service that appealed to civic leaders. It, too, represented an attempt to rationalize urban life. Gas lighting was a sign of modernity, and it impressed visitors: "The mere fact that a town is lit with gas [intoned the Lynchburg *Virginian*] is an assurance to a stranger that there is an intelligent[,] enterprising and thrifty people, that understands its interests, appreciates the blessings of a well-organized government and is not forgetful of the comforts of home. It is a passport to public confidence and respect, a card to be admitted into the family of well-regulated cities." It appeared as if Lynchburg were transferring the miraculous attributes of the railroad to the gas light. In 1851, Lynchburg councilmen organized the Lynchburg Gas Light Company.[84]

The extent of government involvement in lighting service varied from city to city. When Baltimore became the first American city to provide gas lighting for its streets in 1816, it was a public utility. Funding came directly from council appropriations, and administrators of the gasworks received commissions from the city council. The city connected gas outlets upon the request and prepayment of individuals desiring the service. As with other urban services, street lighting was available only to the more affluent businesses and residences in the city. The city erected and maintained lighting fixtures in the street at public expense. The lamps, however, did not extend beyond the business core. In 1835, New Orleans lit the city with gas light by awarding a franchise to the New Orleans Gas Lighting and Banking Company, headed by theater entrepreneur James H. Caldwell. Caldwell later received a gas lighting franchise from Mobile.[85]

Street lighting and paving made the southern city more attractive. The emphasis upon materialism in the mid-nineteenth century city was not so pervasive as to induce officials to ignore the more aesthetic aspects of urban life. Indeed, aesthetics and business could be mutually reinforcing. Progress and growth often meant the disappearance of open spaces. Further, population growth and the increased pace of life meant that city dwellers appreciated and needed moments of recreation. The pastoral ideal still possessed a strong attraction, and such writers as Henry David Thoreau and Ralph

83. Alexandria *Gazette,* March 8, 1859.
84. Lynchburg *Virginian,* April 21, 1851.
85. Eaton, *Southern Civilization,* 257–58.

Waldo Emerson enshrined this ideal in their poetic prose. Descriptions of cities, especially those written by natives, emphasized the rural aspects of urban life, as if describing these aspects would preserve their verdant loveliness in perpetuity. Usually, these descriptions took the broadest possible perspective, thereby eliminating some of the more noisome aspects of modern life. Thus, from a building roof, a Houston editor observed this view of his city in 1858: "From the feet of the beholder, the city stretches away from a mile in three directions, while in the fourth, the green prairie, dotted here and there with white houses, and covered with the beauties of spring is bounded by the timber of Bray's bayou. The young shade trees in our streets and gardens, scarcely large enough yet to attract attention from the ground, here show to a better advantage, and give the town the appearance of a forest city, the house-tops everywhere peeping out from green bowers and luxuriant colors." In 1853, Cleveland looked like this to one observer: "On an elevated plain above the Cuyahoga, commanding a fine view of the lake and rivers, planted with groves of forest trees, interspersed with fine squares, Cleveland [is] a very desirable place for residences."[86]

The city beautiful movement as an organized national phenomenon flowered in the late nineteenth century. The antebellum decades, however, saw some cities across the nation concerned about the aesthetic qualities of their environment. Before Frederick Law Olmsted and Calvert Vaux inspired cities to imitate Central Park in the 1850s, the most common open-space facilities for urban families were cemeteries. Greenwood Cemetery in Brooklyn had its southern counterpart in Greenwood Cemetery in New Orleans. Cave Hill Cemetery in Louisville was a popular park for quiet meditation and rambles through its winding pathways and "natural" pools. Probably few urban cemeteries in the nation surpassed the beauty of Richmond's Hollywood Cemetery, designed in the 1850s, on a hill commanding a view of the lush James River valley and the city of Richmond.[87] Such areas, however, could not long withstand the increasing crush of weekend crowds without losing the solemnity for which the city initially designed the park.

Although southern cities did not come forth with grand plans similar to Central Park, they set a realistic, if modest, estimate of their citizens' rec-

86. Quoted in McComb, *Houston,* 17; quoted in Lyle W. Dorsett, "The Early American City," in *Forums in History,* ed. Harold Woodman (St. Louis, 1973), 2.

87. John W. Reps, *The Making of Urban America: A History of City Planning in the United States* (Princeton, 1965), 325–47; Curry, "Urbanization and Urbanism in the Old South," 43–60.

reational needs. Savannah city officials designed parks and squares with such efficiency during the 1840s that by 1850, it was the only city in the country with open spaces sufficient for the needs of its population. Olmsted himself designed parks in Baltimore, Knoxville, and Louisville following the Civil War, applying the methods of romantic planning that he had perfected in his Central Park design. In 1854, the Alexandria common council, impressed by "the importance to the City of Public Parks, and urged by similar action in almost all the cities of the Union," resolved to initiate a search for suitable park grounds. A year later, its mission accomplished, the council rejoiced that, as in other cities, "all classes of citizens may enjoy a pleasant walk and breathe fresh air without cost." A Norfolk newspaper registered concern that the city was behind the times in failing to prepare adequate park space and concluded its discussion on an ecological note: "In Norfolk we have sadly neglected to promote those public improvements which take the shape of verdant interspaces in the midst of population. . . . The City would be wise to purchase appropriate areas like New York's Central Park or Boston's Common. A few years hence will see our places of recreation closed up by masses of brick and mortar."[88]

Since parks development, unlike most other urban services, was entirely a public chore, some southern cities were unable to appropriate sufficient funds to design and maintain a park. There were, however, other methods of romantic planning to alleviate the strains of modern urban life. Trees, for example, were a source of enjoyment and relaxation, and were healthful besides. The demise of a venerable oak for a railroad depot or a new market house usually evoked some pangs of regret, even from city boosters. In the fall of 1849, the Norfolk *Southern Argus,* under the heading "Progress of Civilization," recorded the passing of two weathered but sturdy sycamore trees: "Yesterday the axe penetrated those ancient trees—they were doomed to be cut down because they obstructed the way where the railroad is to pass." Accordingly, southern cities sought to plant new trees to give some comfort to their residents from the summer heat, and to provide an aesthetic and healthful aspect to the city's quality of life. "Strangers and visitors to our town," the Alexandria *Gazette* observed, "notice the improved appearance of many of our streets in consequence of the beautiful shade trees that have, in recent years, been planted along the sidewalks. Both for health and ornament these trees are worth double the cost of planting and rearing them." Natchez underwrote a tree nursery from the beginning of the nine-

88. "Savannah," 20–28; Reps, *The Making of Urban America,* 331–39; Alexandria *Gazette,* January 22, 1854, August 7, 1855; Norfolk *Southern Argus,* December 4, 1852.

teenth century. In addition, the city prompted residents to plant and to cultivate chinaberry trees in order to "contribute as well to the health as to the beauty of the city." Savannah enhanced what ordinarily would have been a monotonous gridiron street plan by lining its long streets with trees. On the widest streets the city also planted trees down the middle of the thoroughfare. Travelers visiting Savannah during the torrid summer months appreciated these leafy oases.[89]

The attempts of southern urban governments to beautify their city for reasons of health, image, and comfort demonstrated that even beauty can be placed in a business context to work for the prosperity of the city. Poor relief, on the other hand, could not readily be justified in terms of dollars and cents. The attention of southern cities to the condition of their indigenous poor reveals a record that compares well with northern counterparts— which is to say that it was paternalistic, haphazard, and limited. Urban growth compounded the problem of poor relief by increasing the number of urban poor at a time when local government funds went toward more glamorous—and what many considered more necessary—urban services, such as utilities, crime and disease control, and street repair. Further, poverty ranked about the same as disease in aiding a city's image, with the added point that rampant poverty had little effect on business. Finally, many citizens believed poverty to be synonymous with immorality, so public assistance would be contradictory. It was not surprising, therefore, that relief for the poor received a low priority from urban governments across the nation.[90]

Private voluntary associations dominated poor relief in nineteenth-century cities, with local government becoming an increasingly important financial source. Mobile, for example, possessed a Protestant orphan asylum and a Catholic orphan asylum. The Female Benevolent Society was the major relief organization in Mobile. It owned and operated a row of twelve brick houses called the Widow's Row in order "to rescue 'the lone ones' from the pangs of poverty and desolation." The city's contribution to the poor was a charity hospital. Considering the medical treatment available to even the most wealthy citizens, the hospital probably functioned more as an almshouse than as a medical facility. In 1848, several civic leaders in

89. Norfolk *Southern Argus,* November 14, 1849; Alexandria *Gazette,* May 21, 1853, quoted in James, *Antebellum Natchez,* 83; "Savannah," 20–28.

90. See Robert H. Bremner, *From the Depths: The Discovery of Poverty in the United States* (New York, 1956); Raymond A. Mohl, "Poverty, Pauperism, and Social Order in the Preindustrial American City, 1780–1840," *Social Science Quarterly,* LII (March, 1972), 934–48.

Norfolk formed the Norfolk Association for the Improvement of the Condition of the Poor, modeled after an organization of the same name in New York. The founders possessed the prevailing paternalistic attitudes toward poverty and relief. They approached poor relief in much the same manner as they dealt with marketing procedures. Organized aid to the poverty-stricken was another means of rationalizing the city and bringing it in line with the national urban community. "It has been tried in other cities and has worked well," noted one Norfolk Association member. A spokesman for the association praised the inauguration of "a systematic plan for the judicious distribution of alms to the poor of our city." The group divided the city into districts, and its members visited the homes of the poor. In this manner "artful mendicants" could be ferreted out and dropped from the relief rolls: "*Sound discrimination* then, is the first principle of this Association. It will give to none who will not exhibit evidence of improvement from the aid afforded." Whatever its biases, the association provided the poor of Norfolk with the city's first year-round assistance program.[91]

The almshouse was the major contribution of local government to poor relief in southern cities. This was a venerable institution established early in the nineteenth century and before 1800, in the case of Charleston. The Overseers of the Poor, a body similar to the Board of Health, administered the almshouse. Living conditions there were primitive. In 1824, Robert Greenhow, president of the Overseers of the Poor in Richmond, observed that the poorhouse was the last resort of the poverty-stricken, with most preferring even begging in the streets. Occupancy was low, rarely exceeding seventy indigents. The almshouse in Richmond, like the one in New York, also provided outdoor relief to more than two hundred families. Most donations by the city consisted of wood, clothing, and some food, and were welcome supplements to hard-pressed private charity. By 1860, Richmond allotted more to the poor per capita than New York City. In Alexandria, the almshouse operated by the Overseers of the Poor recorded only eighteen residents during the winter of 1854; all but four were immigrants. An Alexandria ordinance required that the Overseers collect kitchen offal for use and "benefit" of the almshouse.[92]

Poor relief in southern cities was generally seasonal. The almshouse was a year-round service, but outdoor relief and the ladies' and religious groups

91. "Mobile," 305; Norfolk *Southern Argus,* November 27, 1848; December 6, 1848.

92. "The Almshouse Experience," in *Poverty, U.S.A.: The Historical Record* (New York, 1971), 1101–1104; "Richmond," 61–62; Alexandria *Gazette,* August 3, 1855, August 21, 1855.

operated only during the winter months. Money for the poor, though, occupied an increasingly greater proportion of city expenditures. In Alexandria, the budget for the Overseers of the Poor represented 2 percent of the city's expenditures in 1859, whereas a decade earlier the proportion was less than one-half of 1 percent.[93] Social welfare was not the strong suit of southern urban government; in this regard it followed too well the path laid out by northern cities.

Southerners viewed education with the same suspicion as they viewed poverty. Education was, of course, potentially dangerous as an instigator of slave unrest. Also, southerners tended to associate public education with social welfare—as an adjunct to poor relief. But southern higher education was more than adequate, with such fine institutions as the University of Virginia, and Transylvania University in Lexington. As with poverty, though, southern cities recognized that general illiteracy could not be tolerated in a modern urban society. If the future of the South lay in its youth, then the concentration of population in the cities afforded singular opportunities for establishing educational facilities.

In some southern cities, public education was an established tradition. The depression following the War of 1812 and the introduction of the steamboat on the Ohio River had apparently sealed Lexington's doom. Civic leaders attempted to recover prosperity by transforming Lexington into the "Athens of the West." In 1833, Lexington established its first public school. Twenty years later, Lexington public schools, now numbering four, were educating 93 percent of the city's white school-age children. In Natchez, the Natchez Institute, formed in 1845, monopolized nearly one-half of the city's budget. When sectional animosity heightened, public education received more vocal support because southerners looked upon it as security for the future. Henry A. Wise, the irascible soon-to-be governor of Virginia, chose the topic of public schools for a July 4 oration in 1850: "The *ends* of our Republic are Liberty, Equality, and Fraternity, and they depend on *Popular Education*. . . . The people universally must be trained alike in schools of one common education." The Richmond *Enquirer* was equally emphatic: "The *Public Good* demands that every white boy should be educated." Echoed George Fitzhugh, "Free schools should at once be established; educate the people, no matter what it may cost."[94]

93. Overseers of the Poor, *Annual Report, 1859,* quoted in Alexandria *Gazette,* December 15, 1859.

94. Wade, *Urban Frontier,* 185; Eaton, *Southern Civilization,* 258; James, *Antebellum Natchez,* 221; quoted in Richmond *Enquirer,* September 10, 1850, February 6, 1857; Fitzhugh, *Sociology,* 144–48.

The evolution of a free school system in Norfolk followed a pattern set by cities in the North. In January, 1849, the state legislature amended the Norfolk city charter, granting the councils the power to establish free schools. It was not until the spring of 1855 that councilmen authorized the levying of a capitation tax of two dollars for every white male over twenty-one in order to establish a public school system. Yellow fever interrupted the free school effort, and it was not until January, 1856, that the bicameral city legislature established the bureaucracy to administer the new system. The councilmen divided the city into four districts and provided for the popular election of a school commissioner for each district to compose the Board of Education. The four commissioners would then elect one of their members to the office of superintendent. Each commissioner would oversee one school in his district. Any white male child between the ages of six and twenty-one was eligible to attend. Following site selection, some construction, and staffing, the system of four schools opened in September, 1858. The citizens of Norfolk responded with such enthusiasm that the rooms set aside for the schools were soon overcrowded, and a long waiting list developed.[95]

Although free schools educated a future generation of urban Virginians, there was a large mass of adults who never benefited from formal education. To meet this need, southern cities ran lyceums and opened libraries. Lecture series drew crowds. James Silk Buckingham, a British traveler, reported that in Mobile, five hundred people listened to one of his lectures on the Middle East. Civic leaders, in conjunction with a small but helpful subsidy from the city government, engaged in their proclivity for organization by establishing mercantile library associations to provide informal adult education. The Baltimore Mercantile Library Association, organized by leading merchants in 1839, possessed six thousand volumes by the mid-1840s—the largest such establishment in the urban South. The Association included five hundred members, generating an annual revenue of $2,205. The Kentucky Mechanic's Institute opened in Louisville in 1853 and served about one thousand readers in its library by 1860. Richmond's Mechanic's Institute operated a night school for working adult males that concentrated on mechanical arts.[96]

95. Norfolk *Southern Argus,* January 29, 1849, May 12, 1855, January 31, 1856, June 15, 1857, October 13, 1857.

96. Eaton, *Southern Civilization,* 259; "Baltimore Mercantile Library Association," *Hunt's,* XVIII (March, 1848), 230–31; Eaton, *Southern Civilization,* 259–60; Richmond *Enquirer,* January 7, 1859.

Libraries in antebellum cities were not public in the modern sense but usually existed on donations from local elites. City government did not usually venture into adult education, although occasionally city councils like Richmond's might donate a site for a Mechanic's Institute fair or establish a library fund of two hundred dollars per annum.[97] Public financial resources were, of course, finite. Each city, North and South, set priorities for its services, and in this age of urban enterprise, services that improved the immediate prospects for business prosperity were most likely to receive the greatest attention from city leaders, who were themselves part of the mercantile elite. Thus, adult education could not compete successfully for the public dollar with street repair and lighting, fire and police protection, public health, and the city beautiful.

As the list of urban services grew and the local government participation in these services increased accordingly, the expense of rationalizing urban growth became more burdensome. For one thing, the need for urban services in the 1840s and 1850s came when city governments had plunged heavily into financing railroads. The business community, which also directed the course of local government spending, believed that expenditures for railroads would eventually benefit the entire community. The logic was sound, but more immediately, debts generated more debts until city officials were floating in a sea of red ink. In Wheeling, for example, city government expended $385,000 in 1853, with $261,000 of this sum going toward railroad stock subscription. Of the $2 million debt hanging over Richmond in 1857, $1,266,000 resulted from internal improvement expenditures.[98] The dilemma of urban governments was how to reconcile soaring debt with increased demands for urban services.

Urban services were expensive. Natchez, where railroad subscription was relatively minor, resorted to bond issues to maintain educational, lighting, and street facilities. The salaries of city officials rose as their role in urban life increased. The mayor of Natchez had an annual salary of six hundred dollars in 1847; in 1859, it was one thousand dollars. The bulk of antebellum Houston's public expenditures went toward supporting urban services, specifically street repair, salaries, and the city hospital. Education, fire and police protection, health and market control, and poor relief completed the impressive range of urban services provided by Houston—a city barely removed from the frontier.[99]

97. Richmond *Daily Dispatch,* July 28, 1857.

98. Wheeling *Daily Intelligencer,* January 20, 1854; Richmond *Daily Dispatch,* March 27, 1857.

99. McComb, *Houston,* 71–72; James, *Antebellum Natchez,* 87–91.

A comparison between the expenditures of Richmond in 1839 and in 1858 reveals the growth of public urban services. In the former year, the city spent $40,000 for interest on the debt; $20,000 for salaries; $9,000 for police protection; $5,000 for fire protection; $5,000 for poor relief; $4,000 for street repair; and $2,000 for public schools and the orphan asylum; total expenditures: $85,000. In the 1858 budget, loans accounted for $71,000 (primarily for railroad stock subscription); interest for $125,000; waterworks for $45,000; gasworks for $75,000; street repair for $40,000; James River improvements for $3,500; the market house for $2,500; the cemeteries for $3,000; fire protection for $10,000; poor relief for $11,000; salaries for city officials (including police) for $40,000; total expenditures: $826,000. Such services as water, gas lighting, cemeteries, and the market house and river improvements had not appeared in the previous budget. Some services declined as a percentage of the budget, such as poor relief and fire protection, demonstrating the presence of not only competing services but also of the increasingly burdensome debt incurred by Richmond's city government. The role and fiscal power of urban government gained considerably during the two decades.[100]

City officials, confronted with the prospect of an empty treasury and a variety of urban services, concluded, not surprisingly, that their fellow citizens must share the burdens as well as the comforts of modern urban life. State governments granted cities the power of local taxation as a provision in their charters. City government, usually composed of merchants, treated that group generously when framing revenue bills. In Galveston in 1839, merchants paid a tax of $25 for the privilege of doing business, whereas competing peddlers and auctioneers received an assessment of $50 and $100, respectively. A capitation tax of $2 on all white males and $1 on all slaves between ten and fifty years of age was a major revenue source for Galveston in addition to the license fees. License fees, in addition to being a revenue source for the city, were also a form of business regulation. Thus, bars had to pay a license tax of $100—a prohibitive sum in that era—that eliminated the small, sleazy hideaways for vice that plagued some communities. Natchez, on the other hand, received the largest portion of its revenues from the property tax, which reached $0.25 per $100 valuation in the late antebellum period; license fees were a second major source of revenue. Mobile demonstrated the importance of property tax to a city government. In 1841, for example, receipts totaled $114,976.02. The property tax accounted for 65 percent of that figure, with license fees second at 13 percent.

100. "Richmond," 61–62.

Charleston was one of the first cities in the country to levy an income tax. In 1816, the city taxed income received from trades and professions, except for teachers who, the council concluded, were too poor to pay the tax anyway. Charleston received most of its revenue, though, from the property tax, with citizens supporting the relatively high rate of $1.50 per $100 valuation.[101]

Cities continuously searched for new sources of revenue, because property taxes were unpopular with civic leaders. Alexandria officials voted to lower the real estate tax in 1855 from $1.10 per $100 valuation to $0.90 while increasing the capitation tax on white male inhabitants from $1 to $1.50 and the tax rate on cows from $0.25 per $100 valuation to $0.50. The most significant differences in the new revenue bill were the additions: omnibuses—$15; boarding houses—$10; biscuit bakers—$20; loaf bread bakers—$10; horse dealers—$25; express agents—$25; and savings banks—$10. What with other license fees, there was scarcely an activity in Alexandria that escaped taxation and thus regulation. Citizens were naturally upset at the tax increases and at the preferential treatment of the business community. A taxpayer in Alexandria could not see the logic of repairing the city's major business thoroughfare while finances were so precarious. The list of taxable items that appeared on the revenue bill led "Grey Hairs" to reminisce that he could "remember when I took up the morning's paper before we sat down to breakfast, what Corporation taxes I should have to pay, in 5 minutes by the clock. To-day I undertook the annual duty, and before I got through, was peremptorily stopped and asked if I intended to keep the children and servants from their accustomed meal for *an hour* longer than usual." [102]

Richard C. Wade commented that complaints over city extravagance were a tribute to the new urban statesmanship, but citizens clearly did not appreciate the fiscal course of their leaders. A common reaction, both North and South, was to boot the spendthrifts out of office.[103] Replacements may have cut salaries and held the line on taxes and services, but it was inevitable in a growing metropolis that citizens would not stand for a regression in their more comfortable way of life. Although cities applied some services in a manner calculated to benefit one segment of the community, and although fiscal impecunity dogged some urban administrations, the southern city was a better city to live in by the end of the antebellum period.

101. Wheeler, *To Wear a City's Crown,* 73; James, *Antebellum Natchez,* 87–91; *Code of Ordinances* (Mobile, 1859); Charleston *Courier,* February 26, 1816, February 29, 1816.

102. Alexandria *Gazette,* April 12, 1855, May 22, 1855, June 14, 1856.

103. Wade, *Urban Frontier,* 280.

The southern city was a part of the modern urban nation. The American city came of age in the mid-nineteenth century, and if it was an ungainly giant beset with the usual pains of rapid growth, it was the locus of the nation's economic and political power. It was a time when cities as well as individuals dreamed the American dream. Southern cities reached out with iron arms to capture the commerce of a bountiful west; their railroad depots and wharves groaned from the weight of crates, hogsheads, barrels, and bales; their citizens enjoyed the conviviality of the club, the exchange, the countinghouse, and the park, as the old intimate way of life blended gracefully into the new; their visitors enjoyed elegant hotels, paved and lighted streets, commodious market houses, and informative columns at breakfast. Their civic leaders boosted their cities' prospects to anyone who would listen, and if the present was exciting with promise, the future was even more tantalizing. True, some urban streets made visitors choke from the dust or sink in the mud; disease struck without warning, often violently; taxes were high; and some services did not reach much of the population. There was poverty, and blacks—slave or free—lived in a perpetual state of uncertainty. This was not, however, a uniquely southern urban situation; it was the urban condition. Civic leaders in the urban South coped with growth with the available tools. They left problems and remnants of the primitive past to future generations, who are still trying to alleviate the negative aspects of urban life.

The growth of southern cities in terms of identity and prosperity, impressive by itself, receded in magnitude in comparison with urban development on a national scale. In fact, the very success of southern cities in achieving maturity sealed their ultimate failure. While southern cities were building railroads and extending their commerce beyond the region, northern cities were drawing them into an inextricable web of commercial relationships. Southern cities were victimized not by their own lethargy, slavery, or planter hegemony, but rather by national economic forces that were beyond their control by 1850. In a region where ironies grew like cotton in black soil, it was the South's irony that urban growth resulted in greater dependence on northern cities rather than in the hoped-for economic freedom.

By the end of the Mexican War, a national economy had developed, with its center in New York. The Empire City had accumulated the financial and commercial expertise necessary to carry on large-scale trade enterprises—what the business historian Thomas C. Cochran termed the "Business Revolution." An early entry into the transatlantic trade following the War of 1812 and effective trade links to the West enabled New York to cultivate efficient business practices and arrangements that dispatched agents, ships, and railroad cars throughout the world. Commerce gravitated to the city, manufacturers sought its market and distributive network, specialization increased, and trade expanded.[104]

Antebellum import and export statistics indicate the centralization of trade at New York (see Tables 1 through 4). The city's share of exports increased from one-fifth of the nation's total export value during the years immediately after the War of 1812 to better than one-third following the Mexican War. Boston and Philadelphia declined as export centers as the Empire City rose. Boston accounted for nearly 10 percent of the nation's exports in 1815 but for only slightly more than 4 percent by 1860. In 1853, a Boston merchant complained bitterly about "the removal of commerce from Boston to New York."[105] Philadelphia's share of export value declined from almost 8 percent in 1850 to slightly above 1 percent in 1860.

Southern port cities actually fared better than New York's northern rivals. New Orleans, which challenged New York's export leadership in the 1830s, slumped slightly to 26.8 percent by 1860. Except for Mobile, southern ports experienced the same deterioration in their export trade as the northern ports. Cotton prosperity during the 1850s and the development of Mobile as an export center enabled the South to claim sectional supremacy in the export trade. The import trade, however, reflected a more serious picture of the southern urban economy.

Northern cities received the bulk of the import trade throughout the antebellum period. New York, however, monopolized an increasing share of the trade—a reflection of its financial and commercial apparatus, nearly doubling its value of imports between 1821 and 1860. Except for New Orleans, which registered only a slight gain (4.8 percent to 6.1 percent), all major ports suffered a decline in their import trade. Northern and southern ports fared just as poorly.

The coastwise trade was another indication of economic centralization as well as of southern urban dependence. Boston, for example, received

104. On the centralization of the national economy at New York, see Allan R. Pred, *Urban Growth and the Circulation of Information: The United States System of Cities, 1790–1840* (Cambridge, Mass., 1973); Thomas C. Cochran, "The Business Revolution," *American Historical Review,* LXXIX (December, 1974), 1449–66; Peter G. Goheen, "Industrialization and the Growth of Cities in Nineteenth-Century America," *American Studies,* XIV (Spring, 1973), 49–65; see James A. Ward, "A New Look at Antebellum Southern Railroad Development," *Journal of Southern History,* XXXIX (August, 1973), 409–20.

105. "The Removal of Commerce from Boston to New York," *Hunt's,* XXX (April, 1854), 391.

TABLE 1
SHARE OF TOTAL VALUE OF EXPORTS OF PRINCIPAL PORTS, 1815–1860*
(MILLIONS OF DOLLARS)

Year	Total Value	New York		Other Northern Ports (Boston, Philadelphia)		Southern Ports (Savannah, Richmd.-Norf., New Orleans, Baltimore, Charleston, Mobile)	
1815	$52	$10	19.2%	$9	17.3%	$26	50.0%
1820	69	13	18.8%	16	23.2%	31	44.9%
1825	99	35	35.4%	22	22.2%	35	35.4%
1830	73	19	26.0%	11	15.1%	33	45.2%
1835	121	30	24.8%	13	10.7%	71	58.7%
1840	132	34	25.8%	16	12.1%	71	53.8%
1845	114	36	31.6%	13	11.4%	56	49.1%
1850	151	52	34.4%	14	9.3%	75	49.7%
1855	275	113	41.1%	34	12.4%	102	37.1%
1860	400	145	36.2%	22	5.5%	198	49.5%

*Percentages are state totals; but each port selected monopolized its state's import-export trade. The percentages do not add up to 100 percent because several minor ports were omitted.

Source for all tables: Secretary of the Treasury, Reports on Commerce and Navigation, annual reports, 1815–60.

40,000 tons of rice from south Atlantic ports in 1848; six years later, the figure was 110,000 tons. Savannah, through a vigorous railroad-building program in the late 1840s, became the South's third leading cotton port by 1860. By that date, sixteen steamships were operating regularly out of the harbor, compared with only one in 1848. All vessels went coastwise to northern ports—nine of them to New York. Southern railroads and shipping lanes, developed after the Mexican War, became funnels to northern cities. As one southern entrepreneur noted, "We are mere way stations to Philadelphia, New York, and Boston."[106] The prevailing pattern of trade focused on the Northeast, especially on New York. Railroads, canals, and the business revolution won the West and conquered the South. New Orleans, the bellwether of southern commercial prosperity, remained an independent bastion, but she, too, was succumbing to the attractions of a national economy centered in New York.

The flush times enjoyed by New Orleans in the 1850s concealed a serious weakness in the city's trade network. The centralization of commerce in

106. "Export Trade of Charleston, South Carolina," Hunt's, XXXI (November, 1855), 604–605; Savannah Evening Express, March 31, 1860; Virginia Board of Public Works, Annual Report (Richmond, 1858), 68–69.

TABLE 2

SHARE OF TOTAL VALUE OF EXPORTS OF INDIVIDUAL PORTS, 1815–1860

(MILLIONS OF DOLLARS)

Year	Boston		Philadelphia		New Orleans		Baltimore		Charleston		Mobile*		Savannah		Richmd.-Norf.	
1815	$5	9.6%	$4	7.7%	$5	9.6%	$5	9.6%	$6	11.5%	—	—	$4	7.7%	$6	11.5%
1835	10	8.3%	3	2.5%	36	29.8%	3	2.5%	11	9.1%	7	5.8%	8	6.6%	6	5.0%
1840	10	7.6%	6	4.5%	34	25.8%	5	3.8%	10	7.6%	12	9.1%	6	4.5%	4	3.0%
1860	17	4.3%	5	1.3%	107	26.8%	9	2.3%	21	5.3%	38	9.5%	18	4.5%	5	1.3%

*No trade data available for Mobile in 1815.

TABLE 3

SHARE OF TOTAL VALUE OF IMPORTS OF PRINCIPAL PORTS, 1821–1860*

(MILLIONS OF DOLLARS)

Year	Total Value	New York		Other Northern Ports		Southern Ports	
1821	$62	$23	37.1%	$22	35.5%	$11	17.7%
1825	96	49	51.0%	30	31.3%	9	9.4%
1830	70	35	50.0%	18	25.7%	12	17.1%
1835	149	88	59.1%	31	20.8%	23	15.4%
1840	107	60	56.1%	24	22.4%	16	15.0%
1845	117	70	59.9%	30	25.6%	11	9.4%
1850	178	111	62.4%	42	23.6%	17	9.6%
1855	261	164	62.9%	60	23.0%	20	7.7%
1860	362	248	68.5%	55	15.2%	33	9.1%

*Import data not available prior to 1821.

New York and New Orleans's tardy entry into railroad building were eroding the Crescent City's hinterland. Although cotton receipts increased 160
percent in the 1850s, receipts of western products remained stationary despite a jump in western crop yields. More revealing was the fact that in
1820, western produce accounted for 58 percent of the total receipts at the
port of New Orleans; by 1860, the figure was 23 percent. The national
economy, linked by railroad lines from Atlantic ports, permanently diverted
trade from the Mississippi River and New Orleans. In 1860, the superintendent of the United States Census declared, "As an outlet to the ocean
for the grain trade of the west, the Mississippi River has almost ceased to
be depended upon by merchants." De Bow agreed, and added with sadness
that the mouth of the Mississippi "practically and commercially is more at
New York and Boston than at New Orleans."[107]

The pattern of urbanization followed the pattern of trade, as New York
outlasted and outbid pretenders to its economic preeminence. All roads,
even for southerners, seemed to lead to the Empire City. As one southerner
wrote home from a New York crowded with southern merchants in 1860,
"Southern people, despite of everything said and done, buy where *they think*
they can get the best assortment, and purchase at the *cheapest* rates."[108]
Southern urban merchants increased their contacts with northern cities as
secession approached and borrowed ideas on urban services, from the collection of garbage to the installation of street lighting. The urbanization of

107. Quoted in Wender, *Southern Commercial Conventions,* 3; quoted in Schmidt, "Internal Commerce," 803; see also North, *Economic Growth of the United States.*
108. Letter from "Linsey-Woolsey" to Alexandria *Gazette,* March 6, 1860.

TABLE 4

SHARE OF TOTAL VALUE OF IMPORTS OF INDIVIDUAL CITIES, 1821–1860
(MILLIONS OF DOLLARS)

Year	Boston		Philadelphia		New Orleans		Baltimore		Charleston		Mobile*		Savannah		Richmd.-Norf.	
1821	$14	22.6%	$8	12.9%	$3	4.8%	$4	6.5%	$3	4.8%	—	—	$1	1.6%	—	—
1835	19	12.8%	12	8.1%	17	11.4%	5	3.4%	1	0.7%	—	—	—	—	—	—
1840	16	15.0%	8	7.5%	10	9.3%	4	3.7%	2	1.9%	—	—	—	—	—	—
1860	41	11.3%	14	3.9%	22	6.1%	9	2.5%	1	0.3%	—	—	—	—	—	—

*Less than 0.1 percent share of the total import trade.

the mid-nineteenth century produced a national urban network that complemented the national economy and transcended sectional feeling. Edmund Ruffin paraded in homespun, but profit-minded civic boosters formed packet companies to secure the latest fashions from New York.

Thus, as the sectional crisis threatened to tear the nation apart, commerce was drawing the cities of both sections closer together. George Fitzhugh, one of the most prominent spokesmen for southern economic independence, believed that these new commercial ties generated by a national economy would save the Union: "Heretofore, domestic weakness and danger from foreign foe has combined the States in sustaining the Union. Hereafter, the great advantages of friendly and mutual intercourse, trade and exchanges, may continue to produce a like result."[109] Others thought differently. In all southern cities, regardless of geographical location, secession divided the population. Cosmopolitan seaports such as New Orleans and Baltimore especially contained vigorous Unionist sentiment, whereas in Charleston, secessionists prevailed. Natchez, deep in the Mississippi delta but with strong economic ties to the North, voted for Unionist delegates by almost a four-to-one margin. In general, the majority of opinion in both northern and southern cities wished the crisis to go away.[110] The ongoing crisis after November, 1860, was bad for business, since it disrupted the free flow of commerce between North and South—a trade that had grown more intimate since the Mexican War. It was a commercial age, and commercial considerations not only weighed heavily in the minds of urban delegates but also at times played a dominant role in the secession conventions.

Southern cities were caught between the two sections—economic ties pulled in both directions. At the Virginia convention, urban delegates and their rural colleagues expressed this dual pressure. "The question before us," a delegate from Lynchburg observed, "is not Union or disunion, but which will we join—North or South." The hinterland towns picked up the refrain: "Will Virginia join the Northern or the Southern Union—that is the True Issue."[111] The answer depended to a large extent on how Virginians viewed their commercial future. The delegates placed even slavery in this context.

109. Fitzhugh, *Cannibals All!*, 248.

110. See Ollinger Crenshaw, "Urban and Rural Voting in the Election of 1860," in *Historiography and Urbanization: Essays in American History in Honor of W. Stull Holt,* ed. Eric F. Goldman (Baltimore, 1941), 55–60.

111. *Proceedings of the Virginia State Convention,* quoted in Richmond *Enquirer,* February 22, 1861, February 28, 1861; see also William W. Freeling, "The Editorial Revolution—Virginia and the Coming of the Civil War: A Review," *Civil War History,* XVIII (April, 1972), 64–72.

Two decades of bitter competition with northern and southern urban rivals caused Virginians to weigh the answer to their question carefully.

Some Virginians regarded union with the cotton South with open hostility. Some urban businessmen had been complaining that the demand for slaves in the Deep South was threatening Virginia's urban economy as slave labor became scarce and expensive in her cities. On the other hand, those who profited from the domestic slave trade similarly viewed Deep South intentions with suspicion. Baltimoreans feared the potential havoc of a renewed transatlantic slave trade. The possibility of the reopening of the trade was a major reason that Fitzhugh opposed secession. The renewed slave trade could result in a severe loss to Virginia's economy. Alexandria and Richmond were two centers of the domestic slave trade, a business that generated $4.5 million annually—more than the entire state's tobacco receipts.[112] The loss of that revenue could affect growth in both cities. It was not outrageous to argue, therefore, that union with the North would be the best protection for the institution of slavery.[113]

Others saw a southern confederacy as hostile to Virginia commercial interests in general. Virginia's cities dutifully sent delegates to the various southern commercial conventions but unanimously pronounced them "abortions" or "useless." The conventions were typically forums for fire-eaters rather than for commercial enterprise. Even when the delegates dropped their radical rhetoric and settled down to more fruitful discussion, Deep South rail lines and developing New Orleans or Mobile, rather than Norfolk or Richmond, seemed to dominate debate. Manufacturers feared the cotton South's obsession with free trade would ruin their struggling industries, even though below Virginia sentiment for a tariff was growing. George W. Brent, delegate and Alexandria merchant, advanced a more cogent argument with respect to manufacturing. He argued that political considerations would force the southern confederacy into intimate economic

112. See Fitzhugh, *Sociology,* 211; James F. W. Johnston, *Notes on North America: Agricultural, Economical, and Social* (2 vols.; Boston, 1851), II, 356. In his calculations Johnston, a British traveler, used the extremely conservative estimate of three hundred dollars for a prime field hand. Thus, he probably understated the actual figure.

113. Speech of George W. Brent of Alexandria, in *Proceedings,* quoted in Alexandria *Gazette,* March 18, 1861; see speech of Samuel McD. Moore of Rockbridge County, in *Proceedings,* quoted in Richmond *Enquirer,* February 26, 1861; speech of Thomas M. Branch of Petersburg, in *Proceedings,* quoted in Richmond *Enquirer,* March 19, 1861; see also Norfolk *Southern Argus,* December 11, 1860; William C. Rives, *Letter from the Hon. William C. Rives to a Friend on the Important Question of the Day* (Richmond, 1860).

relations with Great Britain and France. As a result, both the manufacturing and eventually the commerce of Virginia's cities would suffer gravely.[114]

Other urban Virginians assumed with equal fervor that union with the southern confederacy would ensure their security and prosperity. Tredegar's Joseph Reid Anderson, whose products enjoyed an extensive southern market, believed that his ironworks would enjoy a virtual monopoly in an independent South. The Richmond *Enquirer* agreed with Anderson, arguing that with the North, "Virginia declines, shrivels up and finds no markets for her manufactured goods." Urban secessionists placed a different perspective on the Unionists' contentions that close economic ties with the North precluded secession. Under the heading "Unnecessary Tolls and Tribute the Southern States Pay to the North," the Montgomery *Advertiser* related the annual cost of the South's economic dependence on the North: customs disbursed in the North—$40,000,000; profits from manufacture of southern raw materials—$30,000,000; profits from imports destined for southern market centers—$17,000,000; profits from export of southern goods—$40,000,000; profits from southern travelers—$60,000,000; profits of teachers and others in the South sent North—$5,000,000; profits of agents and brokers, and commissions—$10,000,000; capital drawn from the South—$30,000,000; total—$231,000,000. The *Advertiser* concluded: "The establishment of a new Government might cost something; but nothing in comparison to the stream of wealth that would flow to the commercial, manufacturing, and mechanical interest, by withholding this annual tribute and working ourselves."[115]

With these figures evidently fermenting in his mind, a writer in *De Bow's Review* predicted that Richmond would become "the greatest city of the Southern Union." Virginia's Burwell forecast a flourishing direct trade from Norfolk, with transportation lines bringing cotton through Memphis. The Charleston *Mercury* envisioned its city as the New York of the South, and added: "There are no people in the Southern States who will gain so certainly by a dissolution of the Union as the merchants of our cities. . . . Those who have ears to hear, let them hear what a calculation of dollars and cents

114. Alexandria *Gazette,* August 31, 1852; Norfolk *Southern Argus,* April 18, 1854; Richmond *Enquirer,* May 25, 1858; Wheeling *Daily Intelligencer,* May 13, 1858; Jere W. Roberson, "The South and the Pacific Railroad, 1845–1855," *Western Historical Quarterly,* V (April, 1974), 163–86; speech of George W. Brent, in *Proceedings,* quoted in Alexandria *Gazette,* March 18, 1861.

115. "Cities of the South: Richmond," *De Bow's Review,* XXVIII (February, 1860), 187–201; Richmond *Enquirer,* March 23, 1861; Montgomery *Advertiser,* quoted in Christiansburg (Va.) *New Star,* November 24, 1860.

teaches."[116] For a city—for any southern city for that matter—that had spent millions to capture the trade of the West to compete on an equal basis with northern cities, this was heady stuff.

Urban advocates of the southern confederacy argued further that the federal government under Republican control would throw its weight behind the commercial aspirations of northern cities, to the neglect of the South. Distrust of Washington was not exclusively a southern phenomenon. Northern cities resented the obstacles states' rights southerners placed in the path of federal aid to harbor improvements. As Republican strength grew in the 1850s, though, southern wariness of the national government changed to anxiety. The southern trade imbalance, the specter of a high tariff in a section that manufactured relatively little, and the strident economic nationalism of Republican leaders indicated that a solid factual foundation underlay these fears. If, as the Charleston *Mercury* observed, "Charleston, Mobile, and Savannah [were] suburbs of New York, Philadelphia, and Boston" *before* a Republican president occupied the White House, what could southern cities and the South generally hope for after Lincoln's election? Moreover, some Virginians believed that Washington, even prior to the existence of the Republican Party, had come under the influence of northern business and financial interests. In 1851, the *Enquirer* noted testily that while northern cities received federal aid, Richmond was unable to obtain even a pittance from Congress for the James River Harbor. A year later, a Norfolk merchant blamed his city's difficulty in obtaining direct trade with Europe on "the centralizing action of the Federal Government in favor of New York."[117] Now that the Republicans controlled the executive branch of the government, northern ports would inevitably receive even greater preference. The pattern that had been developing during the 1850s portended ill for southern urban interests.

The Republican Party platform specified that the federal government would play an active and guiding role in the new national economy. Urban leaders feared a loss of federal contracts, such as for mail carrying and the

116. "Cities of the South," 187; William M. Burwell, "The Commercial Future of the South: Theory of Trade Lines, or, Commercial Magnetism Applied to a Direct Intercourse Between the City of Memphis and the Market Cities of Europe," *De Bow's Review,* XXX (February, 1861), 129–56; Charleston *Mercury,* quoted in New York *Herald,* November 4, 1860.

117. Buffalo *Republic, ca.* 1856, quoted in Bayrd Still, *Urban America: A History with Documents* (Boston, 1974), 114–15; Charleston *Mercury,* quoted in New York *Herald,* November 4, 1860; Norfolk *Southern Argus,* March 16, 1858; Richmond *Enquirer,* July 25, 1851; Norfolk *Southern Argus,* February 12, 1852.

navy, under a Republican president. When the Republicans ran their first presidential race in 1856, the *Enquirer* estimated a loss of "50 or 60 million in the granting of numerous lucrative contracts," if the voters elected Fremont. Industry would also be a target for a Republican executive. An Alexandria merchant predicted that "the federal government will fetter Southern industry and pay bounties to Northern industry." Substantial federal aid and a northern route for the transcontinental railroad would accompany a Republican administration, thus effectively destroying southern dreams for a commercial empire in the Far West. Southerners were concerned that the Republicans would tip the balance of economic power irrevocably toward the North.[118]

The question of secession for Virginia's cities and for other southern cities as well was not one of "preserving its own way of life" but rather of where best to secure the fruits of the American urban dream of commercial empire. Slavery was an important element in the secession debate because it was an integral part of the urban economy. Slaveholding per se was irrelevant to secession. The votes of Virginia's urban delegates on secession reflected their perception of the American urban dream. There were two secession votes: one defeated on April 4, and one passed on April 17, after Lincoln's call for troops made secession a fait accompli. In the April 4 voting, the twelve urban delegates divided their vote with four ayes, six nays, and two absent. On April 17, there were seven ayes and five nays. Wheeling rarely dealt with southern markets, and 90 percent of Norfolk's trade was with northern ports. On the April 4 vote, one Norfolk delegate was absent and one voted against secession. On the April 17 vote, the two delegates split. Wheeling's two delegates never cast a ballot for secession. Lynchburg, the Old Dominion's major interior market, had the least direct commercial relations with the North. The city was also the eastern terminus of the Virginia and Tennessee Railroad, a line extending to Memphis. Its two delegates voted aye on both occasions. Unionist sentiment prevailed in Alexandria, though not so strongly as in Norfolk or Wheeling. Alexandria's delegate George W. Brent, an outspoken critic of the cotton confederacy's economic policies, cast ballots against both secession ordinances. Petersburg's Thomas Branch personally opposed secession, but pressure from constituents who hoped for a flourishing cotton trade via the Virginia and Tennessee Railroad induced him to vote for secession on both occasions. Richmond possessed the widest market of all Virginia cities, and its equally

118. Richmond *Enquirer,* October 7, 1856; Alexandria *Gazette,* December 15, 1859; Richmond *Enquirer,* January 28, 1859.

close connections with southern and northern market centers divided the city and its four delegates. On the first ballot, Richmond's delegates voted three to one against secession and on the second, three to one for secession. The result implied that market orientation, that is, where best to pursue the urban dream, might have influenced secession sentiment, as the rhetoric suggests. Other variables such as slaveholding, geographic location (Tidewater versus trans-Allegheny, for example), property holding, age, and political party do not seem to form as distinctive a pattern as market orientation.[119] A detailed correlation analysis of urban votes in all secession conventions would reveal the validity of this hypothesis.

Southern cities encountered a variety of fates in the Civil War, from a business-as-usual atmosphere prevailing throughout most of the war in New Orleans, to the chaos and confusion in Richmond, to the stark destruction in Atlanta. Their resurrection after the war was by no means immediate, but in the process of rehabilitation, southern cities became enshrined in the pantheon of the New South—a creed developed primarily by urban southerners. The foundation for this new urban hope, though, lay solidly within the Old South. W. J. Cash first expounded the theory of the continuity of southern history. The urban South's pursuit of the American urban dream not only remained viable through the Civil War but also emerged with a new dignity and place in southern society. The railroads, the street lights, and above all, the urban consciousness, were there in 1865, as southern cities renewed their quest for what was to become in the ensuing decades an impossible dream.

119. Virginia State Library, *Journals and Papers of the Virginia State Convention of 1861* (3 vols.; Richmond, 1966), I, 31–32 (appendix); William H. Gaines, Jr., *Biographical Register of Members: Virginia State Convention of 1861* (Richmond, 1969).

THE URBAN SOUTH IN WORLD WAR II

It is 1940. The scene from the typical southern urban place has changed only in particulars over the previous half century. Life still revolves around the courthouse square. Perhaps a Confederate memorial graces the area, or a floral planting donated by the women's club. Automobiles outnumber the wagons now, but visitors and residents continue to go about their usual business of shopping, gawking, or being gawked at. The barber shop displays a portrait of President Roosevelt, and the proprietor dispenses free and abundant political advice. Outside, the quadrille of race proceeds, with both partners knowing who is to lead and who is to follow, the black man stepping off the curb to make way for the two white women who pretend not to notice. Children run in and out of the crowd, and women stop and talk to each other. Times are better. A tractor, a new car, and maybe a refrigerator if you lived in town and took electricity. The local newspaper brings stories of fighting in strange-sounding places that still seem unconnected to life here. Talk turns from the war to the church barbecue or the local election. Life moves along and you move with it, but not very earnestly.

It is 1945. The courthouse square still looks the same. Fewer new cars—you could not buy them during the war. There are also fewer young people about; the war has carried them off to exotic places, and maybe the town is too plain and confining now. Or they may have gone off to the city to work and liked the money and become accustomed to city life. The dance of racial etiquette persists around the square, but the blacks are fewer and older. They have even less reason to return. Roosevelt's picture is gone from the barber shop. But President Truman's portrait has not taken its place. Times are better. There is new construction; maybe some industry moving in; a raw subdivision emerging out of red-clay fields off the bypass. In town, a chain grocery store has moved in, much to the delight of housewives who shop in pants and sandals on warm spring days. Editorials in the local daily still discuss strange-sounding foreign places, though citizens pay more attention these days when they aren't gazing at the array of ads touting everything from washing machines to vacations at Myrtle Beach.

The world has come to this urban place. It has come with new inventions, new homes, new shops, and maybe some new ideas. But the world also takes away. Youngsters, black and white, went off to war and saw the world—or at least other places—close up and decided to test their imaginations and talents in a larger arena. They grew accustomed to regular paychecks, new movies every two weeks, and steak and eggs for breakfast.

If World War II did anything to the South, it shook up the population like wild dice and sprinkled greenbacks over the region like paper rain. This was no random movement, though. Cities attracted both the money and the people, and the consequences for the South over the next half century were enormous. But the war did not invent the urban South; it accelerated changes already occurring there. In turn, because the southern city changed and became more central to southern economy and culture, the South changed as well.

As early as the 1890s, the urban South had become both the staging area and terminus for the region's migrating rural population. The Great Migration of the early twentieth century did not so much lead from southern farm to northern factory as from southern farm to southern city and then, perhaps, to the North. This migratory stream ended with the Depression, but southerners continued to move about the region, as the Agricultural Adjustment Act (AAA) unintentionally forced thousands of tenants and sharecroppers off the land, adding to the misery of the Depression-era South. The region's plight became a national cause in 1938, when President Roosevelt released the *Report on Economic Conditions in the South,* a searing portrait of deficiency that labeled the South the nation's "Number One economic problem."

As the Roosevelt administration geared up the war economy in 1939 and 1940, the South's economic shortcomings weighed heavily in federal decisions to locate training facilities and place defense contracts in the South. Also, the president's personal attachment to the region, as evidenced by his frequent trips to Warm Springs, Georgia, and the heartbreaking scenes of poverty he saw from his train window, played an important role in directing federal funds to the South. Finally, for strategic reasons, the dispersion of war plants and bases was encouraged.

These factors had a major impact on economic development in the urban South during the war. More than two-thirds of the nation's domestic army and navy bases were located in or around southern cities. Recruits pumped money into the urban economy at such a rate that one northern soldier complained that the draft was a "Southern trick, put over by Southern merchants to hold the big trade they get from the training camps." Shipyards and aircraft plants mushroomed in tidal flats and red-clay fields. The Gulf Coast from New Orleans to Pascagoula to Mobile became one long ship-building operation. Inland cities such as Dallas–Fort Worth, with its B-24 Liberator plant, and Marietta, Georgia, where workers assembled the first B-29 Superfortresses in December, 1943, foretold a new era of high-tech, high-wage industry for the urban South. Supporting industries, such as steel, oil and natural gas, and synthetic rubber, also received major infusions of federal funds during the war.

The new or expanded southern industries required large labor forces and contributed to a vast reshuffling of the South's population. The shock was equally great for those who came to the city and for those who already lived in the urban South. With the possible exception of post–Civil War Bir-mingham, the South had never experienced instant urbanization. The ma-jority of its urban places held under ten thousand residents. Even though the urban South grew steadily through the first third of the twentieth cen-tury, by 1920 the region had only seven of the nation's fifty largest cities. By 1940, the number had climbed to fourteen, but only one out of eight southerners lived in cities with more than one hundred thousand residents that year, compared with one out of three Americans.

The war changed both the pattern of southern settlement and the nature of southern urbanization. During the 1940s, the region's farm population decreased by 20 percent, whereas the urban population grew 36 percent. Between 1940 and 1943, at the height of the southern urban war buildup, 43 of the South's 49 metropolitan areas reported population increases, com-pared with 25 of 74 metropolitan areas in the North. Some cities experi-enced a population explosion. From 1940 to 1944, Mobile experienced the highest growth rate in the nation, with its population increasing by 65 percent. The population of the Norfolk–Hampton Roads area jumped 45 percent, and Charleston County, South Carolina, experienced a 38 percent increase.

The urban South was changing its basic function, from serving as a mar-ket for the surrounding countryside to serving as a magnet for economic opportunity. Moving to the nearest large city became as inevitable as the summer rain, as Harry Crews wrote in his autobiography. Among his neighbors in rural southern Georgia, "Jacksonville came up in conversations like the weather. Farmers' laconic voices always spoke of Jacksonville in the same helpless and fatalistic way. *Everybody* had to go." As Crews implies, migrants did not view this journey to prosperity with unmitigated glee. When they arrived in such places as the Springfield district of Jacksonville, they encountered marginal living conditions, prejudice, and alien work environments. Crews's neighbors worked in the King Edward cigar factory at grueling, tedious jobs and went home to neighborhoods permeated with "the odor of combustion." Crowds jammed the streets and overflowed apartment buildings. There was no room to grow a vegetable garden or to keep an animal. This was no longer the friendly Jacksonville market town but a new and starkly urban surrounding.

Newcomers often felt lost, not in a geographic sense but in a psychological one; they experienced a sense of dislocation, as if they had moved from earth to Mars, with little preparation to adjust to the different atmosphere or pace of life. The towns they knew as youths had suddenly become unrecognizable cities. Pascagoula, Mississippi, a quiet fishing village of six thousand residents in 1940, boomed to twenty-five thousand residents four years later. Migrants poured into trailer camps and tents and floundered in their confrontation with urban life, especially the women, to whom fell the responsibility of shopping and contacting school and medical service personnel. John Dos Passos reported that these innocents were "lost" in the grocery stores: "They do not know what to buy, cannot make up their minds quickly in the crowd, and get jostled around by the others." The federal government worried that disoriented families would hurt productivity in urban defense plants. Perhaps an urban immersion program or counseling of some sort would ease the transition. As one federal report on the situation in Huntsville, Alabama, explained, "The family which worked at odd jobs, tilling a few acres in a haphazard manner, and augmenting earnings through scouring the woods for sassafras roots, picking dallas grass seed, trapping coons and skunks, snaring fish in baskets . . . could not be dumped into another community with the expectation that the resourcefulness of the family would enable it to get by."

But southern cities were in no position to offer crash courses in urban living. For one thing, they had little experience, having served mostly as adjuncts to the countryside. More important, the Depression had sapped the energy and means of whatever public welfare apparatus existed. Private sources could not be expected to fill the gap. Infrastructure such as water and sewer facilities, roads, and electric utilities remained bare bones in many communities. Southern cities, like the South in general, believed in low taxes and minimum service levels. The confrontation with World War II proved jolting.

The Washington *Post* sent reporter Agnes Meyer on a tour of the South in 1943 to determine the impact of the war on the region's cities. The urban South had become a national phenomenon of sorts by this time, as feature articles appeared in several major publications touting the unprecedented economic development in the region. Meyer traveled south to see how the nation's former economic basket case was taking its newfound prosperity. *A Journey Through Chaos,* the title of her collected observations and of her trip, summarized her findings, and at every stop a newfound horror seemed to await her.

In Beaumont, Texas, city fathers could no longer cope with garbage removal and basic sanitation. The garbage dump that had served the sleepy city for decades now expanded faster than the adjacent Pennsylvania Shipyards. The stench was so overwhelming that "the people of Beaumont are nauseated and nearly choked by the unwholesome fumes." Executives of the shipyard could scarcely work in their offices for the thickness of the flies that streamed through unscreened windows. Spraying dispersed the flies temporarily but left an odor that rivaled the aroma from the dump.

Mobile offered the most shocking scene of wartime glut. Southerners knew Mobile as an overgrown fishing village with Spanish moss–shrouded trees and a yearly Mardi Gras celebration that rivaled the New Orleans version in enthusiasm, if not in scale. But an air base, an army supply depot, an Alcoa plant, and two massive shipyards changed the city dramatically. Well before Agnes Meyer's visit, Mobile had become a national synonym for urban collapse. Writer John Dos Passos reported early in 1943 that the city looked "trampled and battered. . . . Sidewalks are crowded. Gutters are stacked with litter. . . . Garbage cans are overflowing. . . . Cues wait outside of movies and lunchrooms." Residents kept taps open all day to catch trickles of water; teen-aged gangs roamed the streets looting stores and overwhelming Mobile's nineteen-member police force; and blacks and whites jostled each other in crowded streetcars and sidewalks, heightening racial tension until a full-scale race riot erupted later that year.

Agnes Meyer's report to her Washington *Post* readers in 1944 confirmed Dos Passos' observations. She was especially concerned about the impact of the war in Mobile on family life. Meyer noted the sharp rise in juvenile delinquency, which she attributed in part to teenaged boys and girls moving alone to the city from the country and living in dormitories with no guidance. But wayward behavior also afflicted middle-class youngsters. Meyer explained that with fathers off to war and mothers working in defense plants, inadequate daycare facilities could not absorb the large numbers of unsupervised children. Even if middle-class mothers stayed home, they had to assume cooking and household chores, since their black maids and cooks had left for better-paying war work. Such mothers, according to Meyer, "neglect their children as much as those who have jobs."

Mobile's worst problem, Meyer reported, was "the sex-delinquency of very young girls." The city's police chief told her of eleven-year-old girls involved in prostitution rings. Illegitimacy rates soared, and "many of these young mothers," Meyer reported, "do not know more than the first name of the baby's father." Absolving sailors and defense workers from the rampant promiscuity, Meyer noted that the girls were frequently "the aggressors," pursuing men and openly purchasing contraceptives.

Meyer proposed a sweeping social welfare program for Mobile that focused on child-care services, family welfare personnel, and on upgrading an inadequate public school system. Of course, the city could not afford any of these services. Mobile's Roman Catholic bishop, equally troubled by the city's libidinous youth, urged mothers not to work—a futile suggestion in the midst of a war. Some relief occurred in 1944, when the federal government, under the Committee for Congested Production Areas, assumed control over basic city services. The committee also operated in Norfolk, Charleston, Pascagoula, Beaumont, and Knoxville.

Meyer's report and the comments of other observers blamed much of the urban South's wartime problems on the rural migrants themselves. Meyer referred to them as "very primitive, ignorant people from the backwoods." But the migrants and the families they left behind had different perspectives on the urban South. They viewed urban life as less a trial than an opportunity. They were accustomed to inadequate housing, poor services, and unsanitary conditions in the rural South. That they met these conditions in the urban South did not detract from the fact that they were earning regular cash wages. For rural migrants, Dos Passos observed, "Everything's new and wonderful. They can make more spot cash in a month than they see before in half a year." Electricity, running water (even if it was not running very much), and a trailer were "dazzling luxuries to a woman who's lived all her life in a cabin with half-inch chinks between the splintered boards of the floor."

These urban newcomers were not likely to return to the farms after the war. Once crowding eased and services returned to even prewar levels, the disparity between urban and rural life—at least the rural lives led by many of the migrants—was too great. And if they did return to the farm or small town, their expectations rose considerably. As one federal official in a rural

Arkansas county noted, young people from cropper families "won't go back to that sort of family unless [they] have tractor machinery & chances to get ahead more than croppers do." So the farms and small towns of the South lost many of their young people for good.

Their new urban homes improved. The war had provided "shock therapy" for civic leaders. Although southern urban boosters had been seeking outside investment since the nineteenth century, the war generated too much of a good thing. The war demonstrated both the need for an active local government and the benefits of federal funding. Pushed by returning G.I.'s and war workers, civic leaders no longer looked upon government as a negative entity. The federal government, a traditional nemesis of southern leaders, now seemed more benign, especially as southern congressmen and senators accumulated power in Washington. Evidence of federal generosity surrounded civic boosters. Defense plants not only provided jobs but also brought in new technologies and infrastructures, such as roads, water and sewer systems, and airports. Facilities that northern cities had paid for dearly came to southern cities relatively cheaply. So successful were southern urban leaders in keeping up the flow of federal funds after the war that William Faulkner remarked in 1956, "Our economy is no longer agricultural, our economy is the Federal Government."

But civic leaders did not strive merely to become wards of the state. They recognized that local government must provide the services so embarrassingly absent or deficient during the war. A new wave of urban administrations came to power in the South during the last years of the war and the first years of peace. William B. Hartsfield had taken control of Atlanta in 1937, but it was not until World War II that he forged a business-government coalition to expand the airport, renovate the downtown, and attract major investors to the city. In Norfolk, a group called the "People's Ticket" ousted the local machine, won power, and established the Norfolk Port Authority as the city's major economic development agency. The city's new leaders also formed the Norfolk Redevelopment and Housing Authority to secure federal grants and loans for badly needed housing. Even in corruption-ridden New Orleans, business leaders succeeded in installing a returning veteran, de Lesseps Morrison, as mayor in January, 1946. Morrison established a housing authority and renovated the city's crumbling sewer and water systems. *Time* magazine noted the changes taking place in New Orleans and declared that Morrison "symbolized as well as anyone or anything the postwar energy of the nation's cities."

Planning—which for southern cities was a rudimentary exercise prior to the war—became a prerequisite for a modern, dynamic, postwar urban

South. Most southern cities began plotting their urban-planning strategies during the war. Atlanta's business leaders commissioned a study on intra-metropolitan transportation needs in 1944. The resulting Lochner report became the blueprint for road and interstate expansion for the next generation. Charleston, in a semislumber since the Civil War, shook off the cobwebs and secured a twenty-four-thousand-dollar grant from the Rockefeller Foundation in 1942 "to further its work in city planning" for the central business district. The city's mayor declared that postwar planning was "second only to the actual war effort itself." Some cities, such as Richmond, had already seen the danger signs of downtown erosion and suburban flight. Richmond civic leaders commissioned planner Harlan Bartholomew to devise a comprehensive plan for the city. Although Bartholomew had been advising cities since the 1920s, his 1946 Richmond plan was one of the first in the nation to recognize the need for central-city revitalization and renewal.

All the while, civic leaders skirted a time bomb in their midst—race. Like their booster predecessors, the new leadership did not seek to disturb the prevailing racial customs of the urban South. Some leaders, among them Atlanta's Hartsfield, incorporated blacks into their political coalition, but beyond that, they hoped race issues would remain out of sight. The war's impact on the urban South, however, changed race relations to the point where the status quo—if such a thing ever existed—would be impossible to maintain. Much as rural migrants and returning G.I.'s expected more, African Americans in the urban South looked forward to a new era in race relations.

Early in the war, it became clear that, however vigorously southern whites fought racism abroad, they had no intention of relinquishing white supremacy at home. Cities became sensitive testing grounds between differing conceptions of race relations. As rural blacks and whites flooded the urban South seeking the same jobs and competing for housing, and meeting each other at close range in the street and on public conveyances, they joined black and white urbanites who had increasingly contested racial boundaries during the 1930s. The National Association for the Advancement of Colored People (NAACP) initiated membership drives throughout the urban South in the thirties, as well as litigation challenging segregation in higher education and exclusion in the political process. As the contradiction between war aims abroad and inequalities at home sharpened during the war, the racial contest in the urban South was joined.

Wartime employment became the first and most bitter racial battleground in southern cities. The urban South's workforce had been segregated since the Civil War. Certain jobs, designated "nigger work," were reserved for black men and women. The definition of "nigger work" narrowed during the early twentieth century and especially in the thirties, when New Deal legislation pushed wages higher and attracted whites to previously black-only work. But African Americans hoped that manpower requirements would ease labor market restrictions. They were wrong, at least in the urban South.

The United States Employment Service (USES) was responsible for matching defense jobs with workers. Most USES personnel in southern cities were local residents with ties to the ruling Democratic party. They had little desire to upset racial hiring customs or to cut into the domestic service and laundry job market to fill defense plant quotas. Southern USES officers typically hired white women rather than black men or women when shortages occurred in defense industries. When Bell Aircraft near Atlanta informed USES in 1942 that the company planned to employ forty thousand people, government officials estimated that white women would constitute 75 percent of the work force, with white men filling the remaining slots. The plan froze out more than thirteen thousand potential black workers in the Atlanta area from a major defense employer. At the time, black unemployment in Atlanta was 43 percent, compared with 5 percent for whites.

Other government agencies scarcely compiled better records than USES. The U.S. Customs Service in New Orleans employed two hundred workers, only ten of whom were black. They rejected four blacks as "unsuitable" for guard work, even though one of the applicants had a college degree and eight years' teaching experience in local public schools. In Atlanta, the Civil Service Commission hid job listings from blacks, permitting only whites to see the openings. And in Jacksonville, the agency scheduled civil-service examinations in a building that prohibited blacks.

Even when black applicants secured work through USES, they rarely received employment outside traditional jobs reserved for blacks. In October, 1942, and again in January, 1943, Ella Dotson, a black woman in Memphis, wrote to President Roosevelt that she could not secure defense work through USES: "They could give me white lady day work in their homes . . . which they have always gave me . . . but that is not defence work to help my country." Black welders completing a training institute course in Memphis passed their arc-welding tests qualifying them for work in defense plants. But USES placed them as porters, busboys, and truck drivers.

Federal agencies were not the only culprits in perpetuating job discrimination in the urban South. All-white unions worked out closed-shop agreements with southern shipbuilders that not only barred blacks from employment but also squeezed out those few blacks already working in skilled positions at the yards. Black workers in some urban industries succeeded in organizing unions with the Congress of Industrial Organizations (CIO), as in Winston-Salem's tobacco factories, for example, but many of these unions vanished after the war. White workers strenuously objected to working with blacks at defense installations. When the Fair Employment Practices Committee (FEPC) finally convinced the Alabama Dry Dock and Shipping Company in Mobile in 1943 to hire seven skilled black workers for a workforce of more than two thousand employees, their employment touched off two days of rioting. Little wonder that thousands of blacks responded to job discrimination by streaming north to Detroit, Chicago, Philadelphia, and New York, never to return to their southern homeland.

Southern urban blacks achieved more success with respect to political rights. The landmark U.S. Supreme Court ruling in *Smith* v. *Allwright* (1944) outlawed whites-only primaries and inspired black voter-registration drives across the urban South. By 1946, there were three times as many black voters registered in the South as in 1940. More than 80 percent of those new registrants resided in southern cities. Two immediate results of the new black political power were additional black civil-service workers in Hartsfield's Atlanta and the election in Winston-Salem of Kenneth Williams to the Board of Aldermen. Williams was the first black city official elected against a white opponent in the twentieth-century South.

While southern urban blacks pushed against the barriers of political white supremacy they also challenged public segregation. Public conveyances became particular targets, because attempts to separate the races on increasingly crowded vehicles led to humiliation, jostling, and occasionally violence. In Birmingham, for example, a bus driver shot a black passenger six times. The difficulty of enforcing racial separation on public transportation and the potential for violence led Virginius Dabney of the Richmond *Times-Dispatch* to issue a bold call for an end to segregation on the city's streetcars. Dabney's editorial, however, aroused strong opposition throughout the South, and he quickly dropped the idea. It would take another decade before segregation on public conveyances ended in most southern cities.

More successful were challenges by black public school teachers in several southern cities to equalize pay. Following a successful federal lawsuit by black teachers in Tampa, Florida, teachers in Charleston, Columbia, Newport News, Little Rock, and Birmingham won pay equalization cases.

Southern urban blacks also sought to take advantage of wartime patriotism and idealism to develop a comprehensive strategy to attack segregation. In June, 1943, a group of black and white southerners gathered in Richmond to outline postwar strategies to improve regional race relations. The result was a new interracial organization, the Southern Regional Council, headed by University of North Carolina sociologist Howard W. Odum.

Southern whites met increasingly assertive blacks in the region's cities during the war, on the streetcar, at the county courthouse, and on the job. Never in the history of the South were so many blacks and whites thrown together in such close quarters at such an uncertain time. The mixture proved volatile. The riot in Mobile was merely one instance of racial violence that flared in the urban South during World War II. There were six civilian riots, twenty military riots, and more than seventy lynchings during the war years. *Fortune* magazine reported that whites in several Deep South cities enforced segregation more strictly during the war than before. The magazine quoted one Birmingham judge as calling for a "League to Maintain White Supremacy," and noted that several of the city's residents were forming a "home guard" against blacks. Even white liberals such as Virginius Dabney retreated. He warned in an editorial that "if an attempt is made forcibly to abolish segregation throughout the South, violence and bloodshed will result." Dabney's comment provoked the NAACP's Walter White to remark, "The highest casualty rate of the war seems to be that of southern white liberals." The pattern of white resistance and liberal flight familiar to observers of the 1950s civil rights movement was already evident during World War II.

Despite white resistance, southern urban blacks experienced some solid gains during the war. Their modest incursions into the political process, unionization, and government employment provided a base from which to launch further assaults against white supremacy after the war. The surging national economy provided more work options for blacks than ever before. Although many left the South to exercise those options up North, many remained. Black women, receiving checks from relatives in the service or in war industries, and securing some industrial jobs, left the arduous and low-paying work of domestic and laundry service. Their defection was so widespread that some whites suggested a conspiracy was afoot: that black women had formed a secret society—"Eleanor Clubs," named after the First Lady and dedicated to "putting a white woman in every kitchen by 1943." No such organization existed, of course, but the rumors reflected fears of white southerners that traditional racial occupational categories might not last out the war.

Finally, blacks discovered that southern cities were convenient venues of protest. Here, black institutions such as newspapers, churches, and social and political groups organized protests and provided the important safety in numbers. Federal policy, mechanization, and discrimination had closed out options for southern blacks on the farm. The future for southern blacks lay in the cities, and by the end of the 1940s, for the first time in southern history, the black urban population of the South exceeded the black rural population.

What should we take as our symbol for the changes that occurred in the urban South and its people during World War II: the garbage littering the streets of Mobile, the sleek bombers rolling out of hangars near Atlanta, the fast roads connecting plants in Dallas, black citizens demonstrating for voting rights in Birmingham, rural migrants squeezing into trailer parks in Pascagoula, or white women shouldering steel beams in a Nashville defense installation? The snapshots tell too little and too much. After the war, some places such as Pascagoula and Beaumont reverted to their previous insignificance, perhaps a bit more squalid than before. The cities that were well placed before the war—Atlanta, Charlotte, Nashville—retained many of their activities and population after the war. Those cities that were struggling before the war—Mobile, Richmond, and Beaumont—continued their struggle against decay, blight, and white flight after the war. Urban blacks stepped up their tradition of protest during the war, but it would be another two decades before federal legislation outlawed job discrimination and secured voting rights. Some white middle-class women stepped out of traditional roles during the war, only to be criticized for it. After the war, they returned to the home. The growth rate of southern white women in the workforce during the 1940s was the lowest in the nation, despite the rapid urbanization that historically has signified higher participation rates by women.

World War II, in other words, did not create a new urban economy or culture in the South. The war was less a watershed for southern cities than an accelerant for future change. The shape of the Sun Belt was visible in the wartime industries of Atlanta and Dallas, the new highways, and the new urban administrations. Money coming into the South fueled consumer demand, and suddenly the urban South became attractive to northern corporations expanding their distribution networks and establishing branches in the region. The outlines of the civil rights movement were evident in the fugue of black protest and white resistance, and in the minds of thousands of black and white northerners who ventured south for basic training and came away wondering how such race relations could exist in America. And as the shift of power and influence in the South became inevitable during the war, the small town and the farm receded quietly, adopting the newfangled chain stores, California-style houses, and television while holding on to racial and social values increasingly at odds with the rest of the South.

The urban South led the region into a brave new era. And it was not altogether certain that in leaving behind the past, at least the landscape of the past, the South was moving up in the world. For the changes in the economy and the new demands of its people meant that sooner or later, the South would have to confront its history, a process that would prove discomforting. Could the region continue to support the aristocratic ideal, the Lost Cause, and white supremacy while it pursued the profit that now at last was within its grasp? Could the South redeem its sons and daughters lost, or more properly exiled, to another part of America, as well as the sons and daughters who sent them there in the first place?

What happened in the urban South during World War II inevitably held momentous consequences for the region. Southern history, as Robert Penn Warren wrote in his first postwar novel, *All the King's Men* (1946), is like an "enormous spider's web," which, when touched, even if inadvertently, carries vibrations to its "remotest perimeter." Southern cities would now become the engine, for better or for worse, that would drive the South to its destiny, to understanding its past, and to shaping its future.

EDUCATION, EQUITY, AND QUALITY OF LIFE

IN THE SUN BELT SOUTH

Some decades before the Civil War, Thomas Sutpen came down from the hills of western Virginia to establish a landed empire on the Mississippi frontier. Working alongside his slaves, Sutpen hewed a prosperous plantation out of swamps and hardwood forests. Eventually, both Sutpen and his domain disintegrated, victims of avarice and a race pride that denied kin and love. As Sutpen's fate unfolds in William Faulkner's *Absalom Absalom!* (1936), it becomes a biblical parable: God presented the southerner with a kingdom rich and beautiful; but the southerner yielded to temptation, to the lure of profits generated from the callous exploitation of the land and the false pride of white supremacy.

When Faulkner published the book in 1936, race pride and environmental exploitation still cursed the South. And like Sutpen, the South's Faustian deal for power in exchange for the denigration of its human and natural resources led to disaster. A majority of the region's residents lived and worked under the burdens of a ruinous agricultural system and a biracial society that impoverished the minds and souls of southerners, whites, and blacks alike.

In the decades after 1940, southerners began to expiate their sins, albeit with considerable federal intercession. The land and labor systems that undergirded monocrop agriculture crumbled. The South segued gracefully from a commercial-agricultural economy to a postindustrial society, without so much as a by-your-leave to the industrial revolution. The omission meant that the physical and human debris littering the cities of the Northeast and

Midwest would not obstruct new forms of economic development in the metropolitan South. And the service-oriented economy was kinder on the environment than was the industrial economy. Indeed, the cities themselves were not so much cities as extended suburbs—low density and squeaky clean. As with the economy, the new southern city seemed to have jumped a century, moving from village to suburb, confounding urban scholars more used to Chicago, Boston, or New York than to the medium-sized, sprawling entities that marked the southern landscape.

Finally, southerners have attained a measure of racial accommodation. If whites have not been totally successful in expiating the sin of race pride, at least white supremacy is no longer the controlling factor of southern life. The net inmigration of blacks beginning in the late 1960s is testimony both to the altered racial climate and the new economic opportunities. The accommodation unleashed a new energy and an optimism in the region and attracted renewed attention from outside investors eager to do business in a place where relative racial harmony existed alongside traditional southern attributes of lifestyle, climate, labor, and taxes.

One of the more remarkable aspects of these economic and racial transformations has been the retention of southern traditions that enhance and make distinct the region's quality of life. As sociologist John Shelton Reed, among others, has demonstrated, southerners in the 1980s still evince a strong sense of past and place, deeply held religious beliefs, and concern about good manners. Coupled with differences in food, music, speech, and climate, the South persists as a distinctive region despite its integration into the national (and international) economy. In fact, these aspects of southern lifestyle have enhanced the region's economic position as national lifestyle preferences have changed since the 1960s. Pace of life, leisure, esthetics, space, and roots have become more important to Americans, especially since these attributes have diminished in many parts of the country.

But these traditions are not impermeable. The South has undergone three stages of economic development since 1940. The first period, extending from 1940 to 1965, was the era of transition, when the South shed its historic dependence on agriculture for more urban-oriented activities, ranging from high-tech to finance, administration, and education. The second era, lasting from 1965 to 1980, was a time of consolidation, when the metropolitan economy completed the transition to a postindustrial base and began to generate related subsidiary activities, especially those derived from local entrepreneurial energy and the branching of major corporations located elsewhere. It was also an era when blacks began to participate meaningfully in regional life, reducing the wastefulness of a segregated society and broadening the potential talent base within the region. This period coincided with the rise of the Sun Belt, an artificial, media-inspired region (including much of the South) that allegedly drained the nation's economic, demographic, and political lifeblood and faced a promising future.

Since 1980, we have entered an era of competition. The Northeast and parts of the Midwest have extricated themselves from the economic doldrums, retooled, and come out fighting for economic development. The limitless economic horizon seems more restricted for the South today. In 1985, the states with the largest employment gains were California, New York, and Ohio. By the year 2000, the Ford Foundation has predicted that more than one-half of all new jobs will be concentrated in thirty metropolitan areas—most outside the South—with Los Angeles and Boston leading the way.

Three interrelated issues hold the potential for either enhancing or limiting the South's effectiveness in this new national competition: education, equity, and quality of life. We are entering an era of new partnership concerning economic development. The withdrawal of the federal government from numerous pump-priming programs requires creative relationships at the state and local levels. The most productive of these is the university-business-government consortium, an arrangement that helped to produce the Research Triangle Park in North Carolina and the NASA complex in Houston. It is a partnership that has proved crucial in the resurrection of the ailing Northeast and of such Midwestern centers as Chicago and Minneapolis. There are several top-flight universities in the South, but not enough. Resources are spread too thin over biracial systems, and some legislature engage in pork-barrel education, resulting in the proliferation of community colleges, technical schools, and redundant programs.

The problem extends far below the university level, of course, to public school systems that produce students ill-suited to participate either as citizens or workers in the technological and informational activities that characterize the nation's new economic life. When no southern state meets the national average for teachers' salaries, and when one out of three adult southerners lacks a high school degree, the South becomes less attractive to post-industrial economic investors. As former Tennessee governor Lamar Alexander noted, "If 90 percent of the people have a high school education in Minneapolis and 67 percent do in Tennessee, we're not going to be able to keep up, much less catch up."

Several southern states have passed comprehensive educational packages, some including tax increases to fund necessary improvements. The battle will be a long and difficult one because of the South's lengthy tradition of low taxes and the relative absence of a culture of education. In an overwhelmingly rural region, work—not education—was the prized commodity, and for at least two segments of the population—blacks and women—formal education was futile if not dangerous. Moreover, there is a strong anti-intellectual tradition in the region, what journalist W. J. Cash termed "the savage ideal": a demanding fealty to racial and political orthodoxy that restricted free thought and speech and cast suspicion on intellectuals in general. Though variety has replaced orthodoxy for the most part, the periodic outbursts of pressures to conform to particular values and the overemphasis on athletics indicate that an educational culture—a love of learning and inquiry—remains an unfulfilled regional objective. State-directed educational campaigns on this issue, as well as the growing influence of newcomers from other parts of the country, will, it can be hoped, moderate those attitudes.

The second issue crucial to economic development is equity—geographic equity and social equity. Wide disparities exist between southern states—Louisiana and Florida, for example—and within states, between urban and rural areas. Unemployment in the rural South is 37 percent higher than in the urban South. The postindustrial economy will merely exacerbate this gap, since the metropolitan South possesses the requisite transportation and communications networks, educational facilities, cultural activities, and health facilities to attract and maintain a modern economic base. Once the repository of cheap labor and land, low taxes, and a pliant elite that proved attractive to labor-intensive industries, the rural South is searching for a future. And the small town, the characteristic southern urban place, is bleeding. Rural enterprise zones, incentives to generate local investments, and road-building programs are potential policies designed to ameliorate rural distress. But if rural-urban disparities widen, the social and financial burdens on the states and the cities could impinge upon economic development.

The postindustrial economy has also produced a bifurcated metropolitan labor market, where low-skilled or unskilled workers are separated from potential jobs on the metropolitan periphery. The types of service jobs available for this group offer a minimum wage with little hope for advancement. The shape of the southern metropolis further inhibits an assault on this problem, since vast distances sharply separate metropolitan populations from one another. Poverty is not thought to exist or is not considered a problem because it is unseen by the white collar army that advances and retreats from home and workplace in hermetic safety, with many no longer needing to venture into the city at all, either for work or for shopping.

The third issue related to the South's future economic development is the fate of the quality-of-life attributes, especially attachment to past and place. Southerners have evinced a strong sense of history. In earlier eras, this backward gaze became fixed and so clouded by myth that history became another obstacle to dealing with the harsh realities that characterized regional life for nearly a century after the Civil War. In another sense, however, history has served as a valuable means of connection to ancestors and events that provide a sense of continuity and rootedness in the ephemeral and mobile postindustrial society. Southerners are not above conversing with long-dead forebears or anthropomorphizing buildings, trees, or pickup trucks. The rapid growth after World War II, however, has jeopardized and even destroyed some of the South's built heritage, especially in the cities.

Even though the region has been a pioneer in the historic preservation movement, the booster ethic—an exaggerated fixation with growth born of the South's long economic inferiority to the rest of the country—has bulldozed a significant portion of the region's built environment and worse, erected structures that bear scant architectural relationship to the region's past. The homogenization of downtown, residential, and shopping mall design cuts southerners off from their past and offers no clues for newcomers about what this place is about, about its heritage and meaning. The inattention to history is also bad business, for history is something that the South can offer in the new competitive era of economic development. Specifically, cities and towns have taken and can take the following steps to renew their past:

1. establish design review panels to ensure that new structures relate in some way to a community's history or to regional themes in general;
2. encourage communities to use such techniques as infill and adaptive re-use in order to preserve the physical scale of residential and commercial districts;
3. draft local legislation to protect historic structures and use preservation techniques, such as historic district zoning, to ensure the character of a particular area as well as the protection of individual structures;
4. develop downtown, either through constructing a marketplace, a cultural center, or a commercial row, to provide a direct link to a community's origins. Downtown would also be the location for a history museum depicting a community's past through material culture, photographs, and documents.

Intimately connected with the sense of past as a quality-of-life issue is the sense of place. From music to literature, from avocation to vocation, southerners have demonstrated their attachment to the land. As the Sutpen saga implies, intimacy has often bred profligacy. Yet even as the South has urbanized, southerners have sought to moderate that urban environment through plantings, landscaping, and a low-density spatial profile, continuing a tradition dating at least as far back as James Oglethorpe's 1733 plan for Savannah. "Beauty is our money crop," a character in a Flannery O'Connor short story boasted of his town, and the numerous azalea and dogwood festivals, the spring home tours, and the beautification boards support the connection between economy and esthetics. The danger is that administrators and planners may consider beauty expendable, an elitist concern of those who have the time and money to contemplate such things. This is untrue, as Charleston, South Carolina, has discovered in its design and setting of public housing recently, adapting the graceful single detached house to multifamily needs, at the same time reinforcing the sense of past. Further, newcomers often remark on the relative beauty of southern cities and towns, enhanced by the long growing season and the attempt to modify the harsh summer climate with trees and bushes placed at strategic and frequent intervals. The southern city is a middle landscape combining rural elements with urban features, and urban policy should reinforce this concept.

The South has been fortunate to experience its most significant growth in an era of raised environmental consciousness. Though paper mills in the Savannah area, chemical factories in the Richmond region, land development in marshlands and along the coast, and the petrochemical industries in Louisiana and Texas have threatened areas of the natural South, state environmental legislation in the 1970s and early 1980s has reduced the opportunities for future defacement. In addition, public awareness is such that political support for polluting industries has declined. The difficulty, however, is that such industries are usually attracted to rural areas or small communities, and the temptation will be great as the urban-rural gap widens to accept the environmental costs in favor of immediate economic benefits. In addition, as the national competition for economic base accelerates, there could be less pressure on new economic activities located in metropolitan areas to plan their complexes with environmental sensitivity or to maintain the historic character of buildings or parklands in the path of development.

Whatever the benefits of such temptations in the short run, they are, like Thomas Sutpen's exploitation, false economies in the long run. As we are confronted with the demise of the Sun Belt and the rise of the Brain Belt, the quality of amenities—especially education, culture, and environment—become central factors in locational decisions by both individuals and firms. That Massachusetts and Ohio have emerged among the national leaders in economic development indicates that tax incentives, low tax base, nonunion labor, and cheap land costs are no longer the surefire attractions they once were. Rather, the advantages possessed by areas within both states include education, culture, history, and attention to reversing the environmental depredations of an earlier era.

Though southern states continue to lag in educational and cultural amenities, most have programs in place to upgrade these areas. The region's great advantages in the competitive Brain Belt era are its rich history and its relatively unspoiled environment. These attributes should be nurtured and promoted as among the South's major economic attractions. And the types of individuals and firms attracted by the anchors of past and place are likely to contribute significantly to reducing the threats of educational inadequacy and inequitable distribution of resources.

The three major issues influencing future economic development in the region are, then, closely connected. Without a significant educational base, it is likely that the South will lose its favored position in the national economy over the next several decades. This, in turn, will make it more difficult to redress locational and social inequities, and will increase burdens on local and state governments. And, finally, as has been the case historically, these burdens will threaten the distinctive southern quality of life, particularly impinging on past and place. The turning away from regional heritage will complete the vicious cycle by further reducing the competitiveness of the South within the national economy. What is required, therefore, is an integrated approach to economic development that takes particular notice of the changing economic role of the South and the attributes necessary to maintain and enhance the region's status.

THE CITY AS SOUTHERN HISTORY

Not long ago, I took a walk down Monument Avenue in Richmond. The avenue is a broad, tree-lined memorial to a pantheon of Confederate heroes. Foremost among the sculpted poses is the equestrian statue of General Robert E. Lee. The imposing statue rises seven stories above the street. As I maneuvered myself to get the best angle for a photograph, I recalled the stories of how the citizens of Richmond, nearly a century earlier, had carried sections of the statue from the railroad depot all the way out to what was then a cornfield, beyond the city limits. They were like medieval burghers carrying the stones that would become part of a new cathedral. They were pilgrims of the faith espousing a creed long dead but not buried, erecting an icon to the only dream that had mattered so they could keep on dreaming.

While I was snapping some photographs, a well-dressed elderly gentleman approached me and commented matter of factly, "Quite a man, isn't he?" The question startled me a bit because I had never thought of the general in the present tense. Thinking about it later, I understood that the question was not surprising, because time in the South seems to run together. As William Faulkner summarized the phenomenon, "Yesterday, today, and tomorrow are Is: Indivisible: One." [1]

LOOKING BACKWARD IN A FORWARD TIME

Although the Civil War provided the greatest impetus for timelessness, southerners maintained a loose definition of the present before then. Fred-

---

1. William Faulkner, *Intruder in the Dust* (New York, 1948), 194.

erick Law Olmsted, farmer, landscape architect, and journalist, visited Richmond during the 1860s and came away convinced that the city was moving
forward and backward at the same time: "[Richmond] is plainly the metropolis . . . of a people who have been dragged along in the grand march
of the rest of the world, but who have had, for a long time and yet have, a
disposition within themselves only to step backward."[2] And here was a city
which, at that time, was among the nation's foremost industrial centers, a
thriving port, and the terminus of two major rail lines.

There is no record that Olmsted stopped at Richmond's Hollywood
Cemetery during his brief visit to the city. Had he done so, he might have
happened on a ceremony that would have only confirmed his initial impression. The city was staging an elaborate celebration for the reinterment
of ex-president James Monroe's remains. Monroe had died in New York
City in 1830 and was buried there. New Yorkers graciously offered the
bones to Richmond and assisted in their transfer to Hollywood. In the
meantime, another group of Richmonders, led by women, was developing
plans to purchase the decaying Mount Vernon estate of George Washington.
Today, both of these events would likely make good cover stories for
Southern Living. But at the time, there was something queer about such
nostalgic indulgence. It was a time of manifest destiny, of the steam engine,
of improvement societies of every stripe. Holding onto the past reflected
an ambivalence about the future, and the mid-nineteenth century was not
a time of ambivalence.

Richmonders held legitimate concerns about the future, however. The
age of Jackson had given free rein to greed, and although some southerners
may have publicly disavowed the profit motive, most eagerly participated in
the developing national economy. Southern cities became focal points for
the scramble after commerce and industry. And most did quite well, especially during the prosperous 1850s. But it was a losing proposition for several
reasons. First, railroads, credit facilities, distribution networks, information
flows, and marketing connections favored northeastern cities, particularly
New York. Second, a sectional political party emerged—the Republican
party—that promoted, among other things, a vigorous program of economic nationalism. The new party favored a northern route for a transcontinental railroad, a high tariff to protect primarily northern industry, a
homestead act designed to limit southern access to the West, and the use of

2. Frederick Law Olmsted, *A Journey in the Back Country* (New York, 1860),
279–80.

the federal treasury and patronage to subsidize river and harbor improvements.[3]

CITIES OF THE COUNTRYSIDE

There was a third obstacle to southern economic and urban development that few southerners acknowledged openly because it questioned the basic institutions of their society. Urbanization is a process that depends on the interaction of the city and the surrounding countryside. Eventually, connections with other cities, other regions, and other countries enhance the process, but initially, it is the city-hinterland connection that provides the foundation for all future development.[4]

Southern cities were ill served by their hinterlands. Cotton and tobacco were the two major staple crops of the South. Neither crop required significant marketing, storage, or processing that would generate urban growth and in turn other economic activities that would induce further growth. Soil and climate dictated that mixed farming, with grains the dominant crop, characterize the agricultural Northeast. As cities grew in size, hinterland towns began to take on specialized functions, even manufacturing for the expanding urban demand. Reciprocal trade increased, profits mounted, and investments in diverse economic activities and internal improvements followed.[5]

The southern countryside had none of these advantages. Cotton and tobacco cultivation required huge tracts of land because of the rapid soil

3. For a discussion on the relationship between sectionalism and urban development in antebellum Virginia, see David R. Goldfield, *Urban Growth in the Age of Sectionalism: Virginia, 1847–1861* (Baton Rouge, 1977). See also Allan R. Pred, *Urban Growth and City-Systems in the United States, 1840–1860* (Cambridge, Mass., 1980), on the South's weakening position within the national economy.

4. The crucial nature of city-hinterland relations in the process of urbanization is best explicated by Diane Lindstrom, *Economic Development in the Philadelphia Region, 1810–1850* (New York, 1978). See also Roberta Balstad Miller, *City and Hinterland: A Case Study of Urban Growth and Regional Development* (Westport, Conn., 1979).

5. The literature on the relationship between crop type and patterns of urbanization is extensive. Three of the more recent and more helpful works are Carville Earle and Ronald Hoffman, "The Foundation of the Modern Economy: Agriculture and the Costs of Labor in the U.S. and England, 1800–1860," *American Historical Review,* LXXXV (December, 1980), 1055–94; Thomas M. Doerflinger, *A Vigorous Spirit of Enterprise: Merchants and Economic Development in Revolutionary Philadelphia* (Chapel Hill, 1986); and Frederick F. Siegel, *The Roots of Southern Distinctiveness: Tobacco and Society in Danville, Virginia, 1780–1865* (Chapel Hill, 1987).

erosion. Travelers often commented on the wasted aspect of a rural South pockmarked by deep gullies, barren old fields, and fallow land held for a future that would come too quickly. So when southern cities built railroads, they ran through mostly empty countryside rather than connecting with prosperous towns and cities. Charlestonians built the longest railroad in the world in the 1830s, and nothing happened. As one disappointed investor explained, it was a railroad "which ran into uninhabited wilderness in the absurd and chimerical expectation that [it] would create commerce and build New Yorks in a day."[6]

Beyond the wasted tracts of South Carolina lay the fertile fields of the Black Belt, of Alabama and Mississippi, of land but once removed from the wilderness where wealthy pioneers and their slave armies created a cotton empire. The profits from cotton trickled into the cities of the South in the form of railroad subscriptions, hotels and market houses, and industrial enterprises. But it was not enough. The planters were not ideologically adverse to manufacturing or to occasional investments in such activities. Like most investors, they preferred the sure things—land and slaves—where returns were steady and tested. Controlling capital and labor, planters controlled the southern economy. And the cities experienced chronic shortages of both workers and investment capital.[7]

The shortcomings of antebellum southern urbanization would not have been easily apparent to the casual observer. Just pick up a newspaper, and the columns would be crowded with development schemes, current price lists, the latest news from the northeastern commercial centers, and advertisements for a variety of enterprises. The editor's rhetoric would be snappy and upbeat, sometimes too much so for a visitor accustomed to more sophisticated journalism. Alexander MacKay, a Scottish sojourner in Richmond in 1846, offered this perspective on editorial puffery:

Richmond . . . is a small, but certainly a very pretty town, if its people would only content themselves with having it so. It is a weakness of theirs to be constantly making the largest possible drafts upon the admiration of the visitor, by extorting

---

6. Quoted in William H. Pease and Jane H. Pease, *The Web of Progress: Private Values and Public Styles in Boston and Charleston, 1828–1843* (New York, 1985), 219.

7. Considerable debate exists on whether or not southern planters invested in land and slaves because they perceived such investments as providing the highest rates of return or whether noneconomic factors motivated them. Gavin Wright, *The Political Economy of the Cotton South: Households, Markets, and Wealth in the Nineteenth Century* (New York, 1978), Chap. 3, pp. 43–88, supports the view presented in this chapter, whereas Eugene Genovese argues the opposite case in several works, most notably *The Political Economy of Slavery: Studies in the Economy and Society of the Slave South* (New York, 1965).

his assent to the fidelity of comparisons which would be amongst the very last to suggest themselves to his own mind. He is reminded, for instance, that the prospect which it commands is very like the view obtained from the battlements of Windsor Castle. . . . He is also given to understand that it occupies more hills than imperial Rome ever sat upon, and if the number of hills on which the capital rested was an essential element of Roman greatness, this is one way of proving Richmond superior to Rome.[8]

Such extravagance was undoubtedly jarring to the Scotsman but quite common in antebellum America. Equally surprising to European visitors was the diversity of people in southern cities. Blacks and whites mingled on the streets, in residential areas, and in the raucous taverns down by the wharves. Whether the blacks were slave or free, it was impossible to tell. Such was the nature of the urban milieu that distinctions of caste became less distinct. Slaves often hired out their own time, found their own lodgings, and participated in black institutions, especially the church. Urban work also held out the possibility of freedom. Although few slaves were able to purchase their freedom, the occasional examples were well enough known in the black community to establish the cities of the Old South as places of opportunity, however limited.[9]

There were opportunities as well for European immigrants. Although immigrants did not flood southern cities as they did the major urban centers of the North, their presence was evident, especially in the workforce. The further south one traveled, the greater the proportion of immigrants in the free workforce. They constituted a majority of the free labor in several southern cities, including more than 60 percent in Mobile. Except for the Irish, immigrants were concentrated in skilled labor positions, with slaves and free blacks primarily occupying unskilled jobs. Apparently, slavery did not inhibit the migration of foreign-born labor; to the contrary, immigrants tended to depress the occupational status of blacks, slave and free.[10]

The nativism that peaked in the mid-1850s was generally mild in the South. Roman Catholics and Jews not only practiced their religions without

8. Alexander MacKay, "The People of Richmond Are a Peculiar People," in *A Richmond Reader, 1744–1983*, ed. Maurice Duke and Daniel P. Jordan (Chapel Hill, 1983), 87.

9. Richard Wade argued the incompatibility of slavery and cities in *Slavery in the Cities: The South, 1820–1860* (New York, 1964), but most of the more recent work has challenged that view. See especially Claudia Dale Goldin, *Urban Slavery in the American South, 1820–1860: A Quantitative History* (Chicago, 1975).

10. Ira Berlin and Herbert G. Gutman, "Natives and Immigrants, Free Men and Slaves: Urban Workingmen in the Antebellum American South," *American Historical Review*, LXXXIX (December, 1983), 1175–1200.

interference but also rose to positions of public prominence. Gustavus Myers, one of Richmond's leading Jewish citizens, was elected to the state
legislature and the city council, helped to found the Virginia Historical
Society, and supported numerous economic development projects, including a publishing house and a railroad. William Thalhimer, Myers' coreli-
gionist, opened the South's first department store in Richmond in 1852.
In fact, assimilation may have been too easy for some immigrants. A common complaint of the older generation was that their children were losing
their cultural heritage.[11]

Although relatively little is known about immigrant life in the Old South,
it seems apparent that the attention focused on the color line—and segregation, however informal, emerged in the cities of the Old South—de-
flected attention from distinctive groups of whites. Because most of the
immigrants provided important work and entrepreneurial skills, their presence was an advantage to cities struggling to keep up with the growing
national economy.

Alas, that struggle fell short. Southern cities were unable to shake their
role as agricultural marketing way stations. Their residents followed the
seasonal cycles of farming. Life coursed through the streets of southern cities
from October to April. But once the warm weather set in and the crops
began their long growing seasons, urban residents left. The episodic nature
of rural time may have suited farm life, but it left cities bereft of year-round
leadership and direction. A visitor to Mobile in 1840 summarized the effects
of these migrations: "Mobile might be made a delightful place in Winter
and a pleasant one in Summer, but unfortunately like too many of the
Southern Towns & Cities but little attention is paid to it by the authorities. . . . So many of the inhabitants leave there in the Summers, that their
erratic life forbids them making improvements or paying much attention to
these little conveniences & comforts without which any life & especially a
city one is unpleasant."[12]

The inconsistent quality of services, especially streets, reflected the seasonal nature of urban life, as did the general inattention to such common
public responsibilities in northern cities as education and poor relief. Intellectual life was limited (especially after 1840 when the sectional debate
restricted the list of appropriate topics for public discussion), and social life

11. Myron Berman, *Richmond's Jewry: Shabbat in Shockoe, 1769–1976* (Charlottesville,
1979).

12. Quoted in Harriet E. Amos, *Cotton City: Urban Development in Antebellum Mobile*
(University, Ala., 1985), 78.

was carried on in private clubs and associations. The common denominator in discourse was cotton or tobacco, and the health of these crops determined the success or failure of the city. A visitor to Mobile in 1858 expressed this propensity as follows: "Mobile—a pleasant cotton city of some thirty thousand inhabitants—where people live in cotton houses and ride in cotton carriages. They buy cotton, sell cotton, think cotton, eat cotton, drink cotton and dream cotton. They marry cotton wives, and unto them are born cotton children."[13] Simply put, antebellum southern cities were adjuncts to the countryside.

Identities were derived from roles in marketing a crop. There were considerable profits in these roles, but northeastern mercantile houses, bankers, and shippers secured an increasing share. In spatial terms, no sharp edges delineated the country from the city. Many urban residents kept farm animals and planted garden crops through the 1850s, and the larger plantations assumed industrial and marketing functions normally reserved for cities. Most streets were unpaved, and services were haphazard. Visitors often commented on the natural beauty of southern cities, even more striking amid the slovenly appearance of streets and alleys. But beneath it all there was a sadness, of falling behind in an age of progress, of being different in a national culture of conformity, and of trying to reconcile a heritage of greatness with an indifferent present.

The sadness would deepen and spread with the Civil War. Southern cities, like southerners, would cope with defeat in different ways. Some would bury it quickly with an obligatory offering to the Old South; others would linger at the grave, deny the present, and embrace a vision of their history that bore little resemblance to that past. All would remain connected to agriculture, for better or for worse. And all would experience the strain of existence in a society that demanded the separation and exclusion of races from each other.

STARS AND SCARS IN THE PIEDMONT CRESCENT

Atlanta dusted off the ashes and went quickly to work, establishing itself as the paragon of what came to be called the "New South." Henry W. Grady, a stocky, boyish-looking newspaperman, became the city's prophet for the new creed. "As I think of it, a vision of surpassing beauty unfolds to my eyes," he exclaimed in typical fashion. "I see a South the home of 50 millions of people; her cities vast hives of industry; her countrysides the treasures

13. Quoted *ibid.*, xxi.

from which their resources are drawn; her streams vocal with whirring spindles . . . sunshine everywhere and all the time, and night falling on her gently as wings of the unseen dove." [14]

For northerners equally eager to forget the past and invest in the future, Grady's words were comforting indeed. Although relatively little northern capital flowed into southern cities, agents, bank notes, and railroads did. And, just as important for Grady and his colleagues, the North was content to adopt an attitude of political laissez-faire so that the Atlantas of the South could get on with the business of business.

Atlanta also became the symbol for a major shift in the pattern of southern urbanization. The Georgia capital was an offspring of the railroad, and its strategic location astride a middle land known as the Southern Piedmont ensured its prominence in carrying the wealth of the South into the coffers of the North. Atlanta became a regional capital as the Piedmont developed after 1870 along the route of the Southern Railway and dozens of small branch lines. By 1880, ten towns came into existence along the rail corridor from Charlotte to Atlanta. Sleepy courthouse and market towns such as Greenville and Spartanburg, South Carolina, came alive with the railroad. [15]

As the railroad crossed the Piedmont, so did industry. It had long been the dream of Old South entrepreneurs to develop an indigenous textile industry. But not until the 1880s did the right combination of transportation (the railroad), capital (from the growing urban merchant class), expertise (from northern-trained engineers and technicians), and a labor surplus (released by an agricultural depression) occur to encourage industrial enterprise. Like dark flecks in a landscape of white grits, mill villages became a new and distinctive type of urban settlement across the rural South. [16]

Mill owners typically erected their new towns in unincorporated rural areas, often adjacent to larger existing towns. The village included worker

14. Quoted in Lawrence H. Larsen, *The Rise of the Urban South* (Lexington, Ky., 1985), 15. The definitive work on Atlanta's recovery is James M. Russell, *Atlanta, 1847–1890: City Building in the Old South and New* (Baton Rouge, 1988).

15. David Carlton, *Mill and Town in South Carolina, 1880–1920* (Baton Rouge, 1982), 21–24. Carlton's book is the most important work to date on the socioeconomic implications of urbanization in a portion of the Piedmont. Although there have been studies on a few individual cities of the Piedmont, such as Atlanta, and on peripheral places, such as Richmond and Birmingham, there has not yet been a comprehensive analysis of the Piedmont as an urban region.

16. There is a considerable literature on mill villages and workers. One of the most important contributions to this literature in recent years is Jacquelyn Dowd Hall *et al., Like a Family: The Making of a Southern Cotton Mill World* (Chapel Hill, 1987).

housing, leased from the mill owner, churches whose ministers served at the pleasure of the owner, social facilities, and schools that provided enough education for younger operatives to master the techniques of textile production but not enough to open their minds to the possibilities of a life away from the mill. Judging, however, by the large outmigration from the South, the high turnover rates, and the periodic attempts at labor organizing, job dissatisfaction ran high.

The spatial configurations of the mill village reflected the lines of authority in much the same way as the big house and slave quarters denoted particular work and living arrangements on the antebellum plantation. The three-story brick factory with an ornate facade and "stair tower, corbelled cornice, quoined stucco corners, and heavily stuccoed window labels" stood in contrast to the simple vernacular clapboard structures that constituted the workers' housing. The modest homes often had garden patches, even pens for farm animals. A church, a company store, and a small schoolhouse completed the physical landscape of the mill village. The foremen or supervisors typically resided in the largest of the frame houses at the head or top of the street, specifying a status within the operative community.[17]

The mill village, like the antebellum town or city, was close to the countryside. The boundaries between village and countryside were permeable. Workers moved in and out of the village from their farms. The so-called public work offered by the mills was, for many, the only way to maintain an unprofitable farming life. Mill workers were often commuters, especially after 1910, when automobile use spread across the rural South. They traveled not only from farm to village but also between villages up and down the Piedmont. Journalist Arthur W. Page noted in 1907 that the Piedmont was "one long mill village." Kinship, shared work experiences, and popular culture wove these villages together.[18]

Although the mill villages themselves were not major urban centers, their appearance generated urban specialization in the Piedmont region. Until the 1920s, most of the capital and entrepreneurial expertise for Piedmont industry came from surrounding areas. Places such as Greensboro and Charlotte, North Carolina, and Greenville, South Carolina, became financial and administrative centers for the textile industry. These cities boasted affluent neighborhoods where the textile barons and their banking colleagues re-

17. Jacqueline Dowd Hall *et al.*, "Cotton Mill People: Work, Community, and Protest in the Textile South, 1880–1940," *American Historical Review*, XCI (April, 1986), 255.
    18. *Ibid.*, 261.

sided. One-quarter of South Carolina's spindles were controlled by sixteen mill presidents who lived within a single ward in Greenville.[19]

The growing urban specialization reflected a growing social separation between mill and town, more specifically between mill workers and town residents. Mill operatives were "lint heads," and town dwellers alternately feared and despised them. Town parents warned their children against mingling with mill offspring; the children attended separate schools; and merchants set aside special shopping days for mill workers, as they did for blacks. Social gaps had always existed between white southerners, of course. But in a rural society, such differences were not constantly and readily apparent. In an urban setting, distinctions were likely to be more evident.

The stigma of mill villages and the workers' culture that evolved in them lent a particular identity to mill operatives. A similar self-consciousness emerged among middle-class residents of the town. Although historians disagree over whether these were new men or merely old landed elites in new environments, it is clear that their attitudes favoring economic development were similar to their antebellum urban predecessors. The major differences, however, were that their numbers were greater after 1880; their role in the postbellum economy was more crucial—they supplied goods and credit to planters; and they and their wives possessed the spiritual, financial, and organizational means to effect a wide range of reforms in southern society.

THE URBAN SOUTH IN THE AGE OF REFORM

The urban middle class was not, of course, confined to the southern Piedmont. Railroads, marketing arrangements, migration, and modest efforts at industrial enterprise spawned towns throughout the South, particularly after 1880. Between 1880 and 1910, the number of urban places in the South nearly quadrupled from 103 to 398. The former figure represented 11 percent of the nation's urban places, compared with 17 percent for the latter figure. The urban population grew from 280,000 in 1870 to nearly two million by 1910. Only 8.7 percent of the South's population resided in urban places in 1880; thirty years later, that proportion jumped to 20 percent.[20]

This period—1880 to 1910—coincided with the rise of organized urban reform efforts, which often grew out of church groups. Middle-class women

19. Carlton, *Mill and Town in South Carolina*, 106.
20. Don H. Doyle, *New Men, New Cities, New South: Atlanta, Nashville, Charleston, Mobile, 1860–1910* (Chapel Hill, 1989).

were especially prominent in these activities, which focused on child labor, education, and city beautification. It is uncertain whether the movement represented a particularly novel innovation for southern women or whether the concern about children in the factory and in the school, and the interest in providing an esthetic urban environment, were extensions of the traditional domestic role for southern women, a role that southern men were glad to concede. Their public statements frequently drew the connection between domesticity and reform. In 1896, for example, the newly formed Atlanta Woman's Club announced that its work would "prove to the world that women could mean even more in their homes by participating in the civic, philanthropic and legislative interests of their growing city and in standing side by side with the development of the times they could aid in the progress of a great city."[21] It is not clear whether this public statement was a carefully crafted effort to defuse potential male opposition or whether it was a heartfelt statement of ideology. It is clear, however, that once women attempted to transform some of these issues—particularly child labor, lynching, and city planning—into public policies, male civic leaders often intervened to short-circuit their efforts.

Civic leaders developed their own reform agenda, which often diverged from the reform objectives of women. Good government was a major target of urban reformers. The idea was to provide efficient, business-oriented administration, but this idea had been extant since the antebellum era. The new feature was the desire to shield public officials as much as possible from the vagaries of partisan electoral politics. Cities would be managed, not governed. The South pioneered two major administrative innovations in the early 1900s: the commission form of government (first established in Galveston in 1900, in the wake of a devastating hurricane) and the city manager system, inaugurated in Staunton, Virginia, in 1910. In the commission system, each commissioner was responsible for specific administrative tasks, such as waste disposal, street repair, and police and fire services. The city manager was an appointed official whose role was to administer the city and its services on a day-to-day basis. The council and mayor would make the policies, but the manager would carry them out, presumably in an efficient and nonpartisan manner.

21. *Ibid.,* 323. On the role of southern women in urban reform during the late nineteenth and early twentieth centuries, see also James L. Leloudis II, "School Reform in the New South: The Woman's Association for the Betterment of Public School Houses in North Carolina, 1902–1919," *Journal of American History,* LXIX (March, 1983), 886–909; Darlene R. Roth, "Feminine Marks on the Landscape: An Atlanta Inventory," *Journal of American Culture* (Winter, 1980), 673–85.

Urban southerners were not unique in their desire for efficient local government; a major thrust of progressive urban reform was changing the structure of city politics. But in the context of the South, where recent constitutional revisions eliminated much of the black vote and placed potential restrictions on the white electorate, the move to reduce public participation in government took on other implications. The development of cities, industrialization, the increase in class divisions, and the growth of the urban black population created anxieties. Codified segregation was one response to these urban changes; governmental reforms, from the commission system to disfranchisement, were other responses. In the meantime, business leaders could harness local government to work for economic development objectives without threatening social relationships.

Within the prevailing racial and social frameworks, urban progressivism accomplished some important objectives. Expenditures for educating blacks and whites increased significantly during the first two decades of the twentieth century. City planning to order the chaotic and often unhealthful urban environment became an integral part of urban administration. And major construction projects, including the paving of streets, the laying of sewer and water lines, and the erection of public buildings, added to the health and efficiency of southern cities. Urban leaders also became a more cosmopolitan group.

Southern cities invested in public utilities and adopted the technologies to support them. The urban South also benefited from the growth of federal defense expenditures during and after the Spanish American War. Civic leaders adapted national innovations in teaching methods and curriculum as well. And most urban residents tapped into the latest trends that arrived over the telegraph wires, via the railroad, and through countless advertisements in national magazines and in the ubiquitous Sears catalog.[22]

DANCING AS FAST AS THEY COULD

The contact with the outside world led to some perceptual changes as well. Some small towns with big ambitions demonstrated their seriousness by

22. The literature on southern progressivism is extensive, and there are disagreements concerning the origins of progressives and the true extent of their reforms. The most balanced perspective is Dewey W. Grantham, *Southern Progressivism: The Reconciliation of Progress and Tradition* (Knoxville, 1983). His article, "Review Essay: The Contours of Southern Progressivism," *American Historical Review,* III (December, 1981), 1035–59, provides a fine historiographical analysis. For a dissent from Grantham's even-handed treatment, see J. Morgan Kousser, "Progressivism—For Middle-Class Whites Only: North Carolina Education, 1880–1910," *Journal of Southern History,* XLVI (May, 1980), 169–94.

changing names. Harmony Grove, Georgia, became Commerce, and Big Lick became Roanoke, Virginia. Impressed by the value of national advertising, civic leaders launched promotional schemes to enhance their city's image. The exposition became a common enterprise in the larger cities, building on a theme and showing off new buildings (such as the Parthenon in Nashville's centennial exposition of 1897), or new technology such as Atlanta's 1909 fair featuring the automobile, or even new Negroes (Booker T. Washington presented his famous "Atlanta Compromise" speech as part of the festivities connected with the 1895 cotton exposition in that city).

The hyperbole that had emerged in the cities of the Old South became an art form in the decades after 1900, the major difference being that latter-day civic leaders acted on their rhetoric, often with silly results. The skyscrapers erected in the early 1900s by the civic leaders of Greensboro and Charlotte were notable less for their architectural merit than for the fact that, as Charlotte journalist W. J. Cash noted, these cities had as much need for such structures "as a hog has for a morning coat." Atlanta's leaders, concerned that the 1930 census would not support their boasts of dramatic population gains, took in pieces of surrounding counties as "autonomous boroughs." Census-takers were not taken in, however. Atlantans compounded their antics by filing an unsuccessful lawsuit against the U.S. Census Bureau.[23]

Occasionally, the promotions paid off. Atlanta's successful technology exposition of 1909 led to automobile distributorships. A booster organization known as "Forward Atlanta," organized in 1925, initiated a million-dollar national advertising campaign. Between 1926 and 1929, the city received more than $34.5 million in new investments. In Nashville, the appropriately named Joel O. Cheek founded the Nashville Coffee and Manufacturing Company and, beginning in 1892, experimented with blending various high-quality coffee beans. The results were successful, but the blend was expensive. In order to promote his upscale product, Cheek persuaded the elegant Maxwell House Hotel in Nashville to serve his coffee, and he used the hotel's name on his label. In 1907, President Teddy Roosevelt visited Nashville and stayed at the Maxwell House. Cheek served the coffee to the president, and as he drained his cup, Roosevelt declared that the coffee was "good to the last drop," thus coining a national advertising slogan.[24]

---

23. W. J. Cash, *The Mind of the South* (New York, 1941), 219; Roger Biles, "The Urban South in the Great Depression" (MS in author's possession), 21.

24. On the New South promotional efforts of Nashville and Atlanta, see Don H. Doyle,

The growth ethic espoused by the leaders of the New South's new cities (many of these cities, such as Atlanta, Greenville, and Charlotte, were not major urban centers in the antebellum era, and Birmingham did not exist prior to 1870) had several benefits quite apart from its sometimes dubious value as an economic development tool. First, growth prompted few dissenters. In a society increasingly troubled by racial and class distinctions, by problems attendant upon urban growth, ranging from crime to service delivery, and by issues that ignited fierce if often irrelevant debate, such as prohibition and evolution, the ability to generate a consensus on anything was a major attribute. Second, although the gap between rhetoric and accomplishment was great, the achievements of southern cities in the half century after Reconstruction were sufficient to stimulate a considerable degree of pride. Here were places that had overcome the burdens of poverty and defeat, even of destruction. They were taking their position in the national pantheon of cities. They were drawing outside investments, visitors, and tourists. If the South was finally an integral part of the nation again, the southern city was perhaps the greatest symbol of that integration.

But even in the prosperous places, there was a crassness that implied inferiority. The boisterous boosterism and the frenzied construction were less examples of progress than witnesses to an aimless desire to be something else. The results were ugliness and emptiness. Witness Rock Hill, South Carolina, one of the instant communities of the growing Piedmont region, at the turn of the century: "Rock Hill has no pleasure grounds, few gardens for flowers, no pretty public park with gushing fountains and shaded walks. There seems to be a dearth in the social atmosphere of sentiment and song, and lack of poetic shadings in the constituted nature of things. The town seems to have been built, not in a day, but hurriedly, and for business." [25]

Perhaps even sadder were those places, once lovely, that had succumbed to the fever of what leaders called progress. Thomas Wolfe offered a thinly veiled critique of Asheville's destruction in the 1920s in *You Can't Go Home Again:*

A spirit of drunken waste and wild destructiveness was everywhere apparent. The fairest places in the town were being mutilated at untold cost. In the center of town

---

Nashville in the New South, 1880–1930 (Knoxville, 1985), 43, and Howard L. Preston, *Automobile Age Atlanta: The Making of a Southern Metropolis, 1900–1935* (Athens, 1979), 21–29. The classic work on the southern urban growth ethic of the early twentieth century is Blaine A. Brownell, *The Urban Ethos in the South, 1920–1930* (Baton Rouge, 1975).

25. Quoted in Carlton, *Mill and Town in South Carolina,* 28.

there had been a beautiful green hill, opulent with rich lawns and lordly trees, with beds of flowers and banks of honeysuckle, and on top of it there had been an immense, rambling, old wooden hotel. From its windows one could look out upon the panorama of mountain ranges in the smoky distance. It had been one of the pleasantest places in the town, but now it was gone. An army of men and shovels had advanced upon this beautiful green hill and had leveled it down to an ugly flat of clay, and had paved it with a desolate horror of white concrete, and had built stores and garages and office buildings and parking spaces—all raw and new and were now putting up a new hotel beneath the very spot where the old one had stood. It was to be a structure of sixteen stories of steel and concrete and pressed brick. It was being stamped out of the same mold, as if by some gigantic biscuit-cutter of hotels, that had produced a thousand others like it all over the country.[26]

Some cities sought to obliterate the present, not the past. They could not or would not forget; they did not follow the Yankee way. Whether in shock or in mourning, these southern cities withdrew from the economic competition, seeking solace in a vision of the past that, however false, was comforting and secure. There was Richmond, the once-great Confederate capital, now stumbling, its commerce eroded by the railroad and by large ships that could not navigate the James River. Richmond became a shrine. In historic Hollywood Cemetery, citizens unveiled a statue of General J. E. B. Stuart with the inscription, "Dead, yet Alive—Mortal, yet Immortal."[27]

Shortly after the war, Charleston settled into a comfortable negligence, allowing its beauty to seep through the ruins but showing little else to a hostile world. John T. Trowbridge, a northern correspondent, surveyed the desolation in 1865: "Broad semi-circular flights of marble steps, leading up to once proud doorways, now conduct you over cracked and calcined slabs to the level of high foundations swept of everything but the crushed fragments of superstructures, with here and there a broken pillar, a windowless wall." Still, Trowbridge admitted, Charleston's "ruins are the most picturesque of any I saw in the South." A decade later, the melancholy scene had scarcely changed, although the beauty was more difficult to discern. One foreign visitor found people constantly talking about life "before the war." All around her were "the battered walls, and broken pillars of churches standing in desolate dignity . . . and the stagnation reigning over a city once

---

26. Thomas Wolfe, *You Can't Go Home Again* (New York, 1934), 111–12.

27. Quoted in Mary H. Mitchell, *Hollywood Cemetery: The History of a Southern Shrine* (Richmond, 1985), 71. For a detailed discussion on the postwar decline of Richmond, see Michael B. Chesson, *Richmond After the War, 1865–1890* (Richmond, 1981).

so beautiful, wealthy, and full of vitality, could not but strike the stranger with a sense of desolation, and even of awe." [28]

The New South of Henry W. Grady was a stranger to Charleston, and strangers were likely to be ignored in that city of ancestry and tradition. An editorial in the Charleston *News and Courier* in 1898 declared: "There is no 'New South' in the sense of a departure from and a protest against an old South. The New South is a phantom. Its prophets are fakirs and fanatics." History was what mattered. An anecdote of the time went, "Inquiring of a young stranger, it is asked in Boston 'How much does he know?'; in New York, 'How much is he worth?'; in Charleston, 'Who was his grandfather?' " As one chronicler of the city's past noted, "It was almost bad form to be rich." Charleston did not court commerce or outside investment; it cultivated history. When a prominent resident built a home in the decades after the war, he did not follow the design fashions of New York or Chicago. Rather, according to artist Willis John Abbot, who visited the city in 1896, "He builds it in all architectural essentials exactly like the house which the oldest banker . . . built some 150 years ago." [29]

It is hardly surprising, then, that the formal beginning of the historic preservation movement in the United States occurred in Charleston in 1910, with the formation of the Charleston Art Commission, dedicated to preserving the "city historic." A decade later, a small group of elite Charlestonians organized the Society for the Preservation of Negro Spirituals. DuBose Heyward, one of the organizers, explained that this was "not a gesture of patronizing superiority, but a natural and harmonious collaboration wrought in affection and with a deep sense of reverence." In other cities, Heyward continued disapprovingly, blacks "will be taken from our fields, fired with ambition, and fed to the machines." But in Charleston, "where isolation and time have retarded the process," old relationships and cultures would be maintained. [30]

Charleston also held fast to its antebellum spatial arrangements. Whereas other New South cities such as Atlanta, Nashville, and Charlotte experienced an increasing social and racial residential segregation, Charleston did not. The former sprouted streetcar suburbs by the early 1900s, some elegant like Druid Hills in Atlanta, and some for the rising middle class, like Dil-

28. John T. Trowbridge, *The Desolate South, 1865–1866,* ed. Gordon Carroll (New York, 1956), 274–75; quoted in Doyle, *New Men, New Cities, New South,* 82–83.
29. *Ibid.,* 159, 336–37, 332.
30. *Ibid.,* 329, 446–47.

worth in Charlotte (Frederick Law Olmsted, Jr., planned both communities), but Charleston's elite remained steadfastly a downtown group, with their black servants casually interspersed among them.[31]

Charleston was not alone in its pursuit of the past, although its dedication was perhaps singular. All over the urban South, in cities large and small after 1880, city dwellers immortalized war heroes and common soldiers with statues, parades, conventions, and memorials. Part of this outpouring of reverence resulted from the natural evolution of the grieving process. The period of pain and humiliation had passed, but it was important to hand down the memory to the next generation. There was also the growing realization, almost as painful as the memory itself, that recovery was not a simple matter of will. The South was a very poor region. Although the cluster of bumptious Piedmont towns and cities spoke to a new South, most southern cities shared the misery of the countryside, especially those places located along the coast away from major rail connections. A few New York *Tribune* reporters who toured the South in 1879 found Mobile "dilapidated and hopeless"; Norfolk "asleep by her magnificent harbor"; and life in Wilmington and Savannah "at a standstill."[32]

But the New South failed not necessarily because of what it did not do, but for what it did. In many respects, the prosperous cities of the New South inherited the worst of both worlds, of the Old and the New South. They eschewed the progress that could come with investments in human capital, embracing instead aggrandizement and monumentality while at the same time casting off the sense of *noblesse oblige* and grace that marked the old order and retaining its bitter race and class distinctions.

Still, life for most urban southerners in the half century after Reconstruction moved slowly, if at all. The small town, the county courthouse town, and the one-gin-general-store-railroad-depot town—more than the larger city—characterized the urban South. The town square was usually the focus of activity, crowded with horses and wagons and automobiles. Blacks and whites and children and grown-ups mingled about, gossiping,

31. The rise of the urban middle class and the new technology of the electric trolley combined to create a suburban movement by the late nineteenth century. Although not of great proportions compared with the major urban centers of the North, the movement was significant enough to attract the nation's most prominent suburban planners. See Catherine W. Bishir, ed., *Early Twentieth Century Suburbs in North Carolina* (Raleigh, 1985), and Dana F. White and Victor A. Kramer, eds., *Olmsted South: Old South Critic/New South Planner* (Westport, Conn., 1979).

32. Quoted in Larsen, *Rise of the Urban South,* 11.

ogling, whittling, and shopping. This was not the New South or the Old South, merely the South, "familiar and familial," as one historian put it. It was the South of soft talk on long porches, of twilight suppers, of screen doors closing, of the wake-up scent of collards, and of stillness. Were these places passing—"drowned," as Thomas Wolfe asserted, "beneath the brutal flood-time, the fierce stupefaction of that roaring surge and mechanic life which had succeeded it?"[33] Or were they holding fast, neither buried by the past nor lured by the promises of a false future?

ON THE MOVE: DEPRESSION AND WAR

Holding fast would be difficult after 1930. First depression and then war transformed southern cities and towns because they transformed the South. It was not the purpose of the New Deal to alter the South's social and political traditions, but its policies set the stage for changes in succeeding decades. The Agricultural Adjustment Act solved the problem of declining staple prices and overproduction, but it also resulted in the displacement of thousands of sharecroppers and tenants. They moved to Memphis, Little Rock, Jackson, and Birmingham. They moved up North. Southern cities soon found their limited resources strained, and only federal bailouts from such agencies as the Federal Emergency Relief Administration, the Public Works Administration, and the Works Progress Administration (WPA) stemmed a potential social disaster. Federal officials were shocked by the apparent indifference of local government to the basic needs of its citizens. One official called Houston "parasitic" for its refusal to take on some responsibility for relief; others expressed dismay when Memphis cotton brokers protested the presence of WPA projects in the city because they drained needed labor from the cotton fields. Racial discrimination was rife in dispensing relief. In Atlanta, blacks received $19.29 per month, compared with $32.66 for whites. Southern cities were merely following an old southern custom of absorbing change while maintaining the status quo.[34]

33. Robert C. McMath, "Community, Region, and Hegemony in the Nineteenth-Century South," in *Toward a New South? Studies in Post-Civil War Southern Communities*, ed. Orville Vernon Burton and Robert C. McMath (Westport, Conn., 1982), 284; Thomas Wolfe, *Of Time and the River* (New York, 1935), 898.

34. See Roger Biles, *Memphis in the Great Depression* (Knoxville, 1986), and Douglas L. Smith, *The New Deal in the Urban South* (Baton Rouge, 1988). For the regional context of urban change during the 1930s, see James C. Cobb and Michael V. Namorato, eds., *The New Deal and the South* (Jackson, 1984).

Southern cities managed to obtain sewer and water systems, public buildings, roads, power plants, and public housing. But this was only a prelude to the boom that occurred during World War II. Two things happened to the urban South during the war. First, following a policy of defense dispersal, as well as the persuasion of powerful congressional committee heads and the attractions of a moderate climate, the federal government awarded more than $8 billion in defense contracts and related work to southern cities. For the first time in decades, and possibly ever, southerners had money to spend; consumer demand, which had been a negligible factor outside the major cities, soared despite wartime shortages. A reporter for *Fortune* magazine interviewed an erstwhile sharecropper, now a defense worker in Panama City, Florida, whose newfound affluence created an unanticipated dilemma: "Hit's got me right bothered how I'm a-goin to spend it all."[35]

The second impact of war on southern cities was the crush of population. The South's farm population declined by 20 percent between 1940 and 1945, whereas southern cities gained nearly 30 percent, exceeding the national rate of increase. Between 1940 and 1943, Mobile was the fastest-growing city in the nation, with a 61 percent population increase; Norfolk was right behind with a 57 percent jump. Smaller communities experienced proportionally greater increases, such as Pascagoula, Mississippi, which was a small town of four thousand residents in 1940 and a small city of thirty thousand four years later. The poor service and fiscal tradition of the urban South meant that many cities were unprepared for the population onslaught. Mobile collapsed under the pressure, and the federal government had to assume many essential services.[36]

The flow of money and people carried over in the decade following the war. Defense contracts diminished, but with the emergence of the Cold War and the continued power of southern Democrats in Washington, defense plants and shipyards hummed profitably away. And the cities continued to attract newcomers. The southern countryside emptied and poured its

35. "The Deep South Looks Up," *Fortune*, XXVIII (July, 1943), 100.

36. Quoted in David R. Goldfield, *Promised Land: The South Since 1945* (Arlington Heights, Ill., 1987), 8. See also David R. Goldfield, *Cotton Fields and Skyscrapers: Southern City and Region, 1607–1980* (Baton Rouge, 1982), 182–84. The urban South during World War II is a major historiographical frontier. So far, we have had only indirect evidence of the war's importance: Morton Sosna's essay, "More Important Than the Civil War? The Social Impact of World War II on the South," in *Perspectives on the American South*, ed. James C. Cobb and Charles R. Wilson (New York, 1987), IV, 145–58; and Pete Daniel, *Breaking the Land: The Transformation of Cotton, Tobacco, and Rice Culture Since 1880* (Urbana, 1985), which provides a thorough account of the exodus from the rural South.

ambitions into the cities. During the 1950s, most of the croppers and tenants who had worked the cotton fields of South Carolina—150,000 of them— were gone to such cities as Columbia, Spartanburg, and Greenville. And most of the cotton was gone as well. In 1950, South Carolina still produced more than seven hundred thousand bales; by 1960, cotton cultivation had virtually disappeared as the white fields receded before a green wave of pasture, soybeans, and corn.[37]

COMING OF AGE: CITIES AND CIVIL RIGHTS

Of greater portent for the future of the urban South was that a growing proportion of these newcomers were blacks. Within the confines of the South's biracial society, cities were havens for blacks. In the antebellum era, cities offered slaves a limited mobility and the possibility, however remote, of eventual freedom. And free blacks could learn, if not practice, occupational skills and accumulate modest amounts of property. During the last months of the Civil War and for half a decade after the conflict, blacks flocked to southern cities. They came to seek family, jobs, and above all, freedom. They associated slavery with agriculture, not with urban life. A black Baptist minister recalled the scene in Richmond after the war, where the black population had doubled since 1860 to thirty thousand. "The colored people from all parts of the state," he said, "was crowding in at the capital, running, leaping, and praising God that freedom had come at last. It seems to me that I can hear their songs now [1893] as they run through the air: 'Slavery chain done broke at last; slavery chain done broke at last— I's goin' to praise God till I die.'"[38]

The conditions that confronted the freedmen soon tempered their enthusiasm. They discovered that only menial, low-paying occupations were available, regardless of skill level. Where blacks and whites toiled at similar work, black wages were lower. As cities expanded and distinctive residential areas emerged, blacks invariably occupied the most unhealthy, least desirable locations, devoid of city services and prone to vice and crime. Their daily lives provided constant reminders not only of their distinction but also of their inferiority. The segregated streetcars, the segregated schools, the forbidden parks, hotels, and restaurants, and a narrow future became fixtures of urban life for blacks in the South. Historians have noted that in some

---

37. Goldfield, *Cotton Fields and Skyscrapers,* 142–43.
38. Quoted in Peter J. Rachleff, *Black Labor in the South: Richmond, Virginia, 1865–1890* (Philadelphia, 1984).

ways, the decades after the Civil War represented an advance for blacks. They moved from exclusion to segregation. But the distinction may be more semantic than real. Segregation *was* exclusion. It meant exclusion from a competitive education, regardless of the presence of schools; it meant exclusion from meaningful participation in the political process and in economic development; and it meant exclusion from the dignity and self-worth that accompanies the free and equal intercourse between citizens.[39]

But exclusion held open a few possibilities, and urban blacks made the most of them. They built communities, however fragile and subject to the whims of law and to violence and economic upheaval. The black church was the centerpiece of black urban life in the South. Much more than a religious institution, it served as a welfare collective, as an educational center (most southern cities refused to build black schools), and as a leadership-training facility. Although not entirely independent of the white community, the black church was a bulwark of black culture and identity. Segregation also meant the development of black businesses to serve black customers and black real estate to satisfy the property-holding and residential demands of a growing black middle class. By 1900, distinctive black communities with some degree of affluence were emerging across the urban South. Their names—"Slippery Log Bottoms" and "Queen Bee Bottoms" in Memphis; "Beaver Slide" in Atlanta; "Elm Thicket" in Dallas; and "Tuxedo Junction" in Birmingham—reflected both a geographical poverty and a richness of life. The main business street of the black district indicated the growth of black enterprise since the Civil War. "Sweet Auburn" (Auburn Avenue) in Atlanta and East Hargett Street in Raleigh were among the more famous black middle-class shopping districts in the South. On East Hargett, by 1915, there was an office building for professionals, barber shops, beauty parlors, a hotel, a bank, and numerous retail stores. East Hargett was also a social center, as one habitué recalled: "Anyone who wanted to pass the time away and just generally 'shoot the breeze' made his way [there]."[40]

---

39. The definitive work on urban life for southern blacks during the generation after the Civil War is Howard N. Rabinowitz, *Race Relations in the Urban South, 1865–1890* (New York, 1978). Rabinowitz develops the exclusion-to-segregation model in the book, challenging C. Vann Woodward's argument, put forth in *The Strange Career of Jim Crow* (New York, 1955), that segregation occurred relatively late in the nineteenth century.

40. Quoted in Thomas C. Parramore, *Express Lanes and Country Roads: The Way We Lived in North Carolina, 1920–1970* (Chapel Hill, 1983). Although blacks became increasingly urban during the first half of the twentieth century, we know more about their antebellum counterparts. There are a few exceptions, such as Lester C. Lamon, *Black Tennesseans, 1900–1930* (Knoxville, 1977), and George C. Wright, *Life Behind a Veil: Blacks in Louisville, Kentucky, 1865–1930* (Baton Rouge, 1985).

These communities provided the foundation in terms of leadership, financial support, and inspiration for the mass protests that were to occur in the 1950s and 1960s. The civil rights movement was primarily an urban phenomenon. The leaders were urban middle-class blacks—ministers, attorneys, and college students—who used the built-in organizational networks of churches, schools, and political groups, and who chose urban venues—parks, lunch counters, courthouses, and the streets—to forge a movement. In an era of visual media, cities provided the opportunity for the massing of large numbers of people in discrete areas to maximize the impact of a demonstration. Protests in rural areas, even the Mississippi Freedom Summer of 1964, rarely moved national public opinion or Congress. The key locales of the civil rights movement were not the farms of the Mississippi Delta but the cities and towns of the South—Little Rock, Albany, Birmingham, Selma, and Montgomery. The scenes that lingered in the public mind were the screaming mob at Central High in Little Rock, Bull Connor's dogs and hoses in Birmingham, and Sheriff Jim Clark's posse poised by the Edmund Pettus Bridge in Selma.[41]

The civil rights movement marked an important coming of age for southern cities. The successes of the crusade were directly related to the urbanization of black southerners and to the urban institutions they patronized. In 1940, roughly one out of three blacks in the South lived in the region's cities. By 1960, better than one out of two blacks had an urban address. A critical mass existed to wage massive, organized protests. In addition, the changing political climate in the urban South promoted civil rights accommodations. After World War II, a new generation of urban political leaders emerged. Although they were just as dedicated to economic development as their predecessors, they were also aware that racial moderation and increased service levels were essential to sustained development. Although southern businessmen were hardly in the forefront of the civil rights movement, their eventual support was important in gathering a community consensus for racial change. They had concluded that racial turmoil was bad for business and that racial harmony was profitable. Atlanta, for example, received much favorable national publicity after its peaceful desegregation of schools and public accommodations in 1961. Atlanta was "a city too busy to hate."[42]

41. For a discussion on the relationship between urbanization and the civil rights movement in the South, see David R. Goldfield, *Black, White, and Southern: Race Relations and Southern Culture, 1940 to the Present* (Baton Rouge, 1990).

42. For a discussion on how southern businessmen handled desegregation in the urban

By the mid-1960s, the urban South was not only riding a crest of racial accommodation while the rest of the nation was in the process of exploding in a series of long, hot summers, but it was also in the process of outdistancing northern rivals in terms of economic development. Although the term *Sun Belt* was coined only in 1969 and not employed very much until a series of New York *Times* articles in 1976, the urban South was clearly an economic phenomenon before the general public knew about it. The phenomenon resulted from a remarkable juxtaposition of circumstances.[43]

CITIES IN THE SUN

Racial accommodation was one important element of an improved urban economy, of course. The improvement in race relations enabled black southerners to become more active participants in the political and economic life of cities. The rise of the black middle class, especially since the mid-1970s, and the growing numbers of black elected officials contributed to the image of a chastened and prosperous South, an image that often translated into economic development. A second factor involved national trends that favored the urban South. As the economy moved from an industrial to a service base, northeastern and midwestern cities declined. Southern cities that had little in the way of industrial infrastructure were well positioned to take advantage of the change. Unlike the situation in the nineteenth and early twentieth centuries, the economy no longer centered almost exclusively on New York. Washington was now a power in its own right, the federal reserve system regionalized finance to some degree, and technological innovations in transportation and communications no longer required high degrees of resource concentration. The urban South offered cheaper land, cheaper labor, lower taxes, fewer racial problems, and perhaps most important, growing demand. Although relatively few firms picked up lock, stock, and briefcase, the South became a favorite location for branch plants. The ability of the urban South to attract high-class industry was underscored by the success of Research Triangle Park, straddling an urban region comprising Raleigh, Durham, and Chapel Hill in North Carolina.

South, see Elizabeth Jacoway and David R. Colburn, eds., *Southern Businessmen and Desegregation* (Baton Rouge, 1982). Generally, business leaders in cities that were growing and had good prospects for future economic development were more inclined to agree to a racial accommodation in the early 1960s.

43. On the origins of the Sun Belt concept and its application to the South, see Carl Abbott, "New West, New South, New Region: The Discovery of the Sunbelt," in *Searching for the Sunbelt,* ed. Raymond A. Mohl (Knoxville, 1990).

A third factor in the urban economic renaissance was the changing life-style patterns of Americans. People were retiring earlier. They were also concerned about an elusive concept called "quality of life." Long commuting trips, air and water pollution, crime, crowding, the breakdown of services, the decline of public school systems, high taxes and property costs, and the disappearance of open spaces characterized the lives of many northerners. To them, the urban South offered many of the advantages of urban living with few of the drawbacks. In the 1960s, for the first time in more than a century, more people moved into the South than moved away. Historically, the southerner had been the major export of the South; not so any longer. In 1950, about one out of twelve southern residents was born in the North; by 1980, that figure had climbed dramatically, and one out of five southerners had Yankee roots. Ratios were even higher—better than one out of four—in the states of the peripheral South—Virginia, North Carolina, Florida, Texas, Arkansas, and Tennessee. Perhaps even more significant, a growing number of these migrants were black. In the 1970s, for the first time since the end of the slave trade, more blacks moved into the South than left.

By the early 1970s, a cycle of development had been established. As more jobs were created in the urban South, more people came. In turn, these new residents increased the demand for consumer goods and for services, which generated more employment, which attracted more people. As with any other major event in southern history, the economic revival spread unevenly across the South, indicating the persisting diversity of the region and its cities. In the antebellum era, the seaports were the favored urban centers, to be replaced by interior cities, especially in the Piedmont crescent in the New South era. After World War II, the pattern changed again. Economic development is no longer confined to a specific geographic region; a more dispersed pattern prevails, not only in the region as a whole but also within metropolitan areas and within cities.[44]

44. Although there is no comprehensive treatment of southern urban economic development since World War II and especially since 1965, several helpful works provide historical context for that development. See, for example, Richard M. Bernard and Bradley R. Rice, eds., *Sunbelt Cities: Politics and Growth Since World War II* (Austin, 1983); Bernard L. Weinstein and Robert E. Firestine, *Regional Growth and Decline in the United States: The Rise of the Sunbelt and the Decline of the Northeast* (New York, 1978). For a debunking view of the Sun Belt phenomenon, see George B. Tindall, "The Sunbelt Snow Job," *Houston Review,* IX (Spring, 1979), 3–13. James C. Cobb's two books, *The Selling of the South: The Southern Crusade for Industrial Development, 1936–1980* (Baton Rouge, 1982), and *Industrialization and Southern Society, 1877–1984* (Lexington, 1984), contend that some traditional characteristics, such as exploitation of land and labor, persist alongside Sun Belt hyperbole.

In the early 1970s, a persistent question that emerged whenever more than two urban southerners met was, How can we avoid northern mistakes in a southern setting? It was the wrong question for at least three reasons. First, the problems of the urban North—eroding tax bases, white flight, racial tensions, rising social service costs, deteriorating housing stock and infrastructure—resulted less from conscious local decision making than from national demographic and economic trends and from federal policy initiatives with good intentions but bad results. Second, whatever contribution northern cities had made to their own decline, by the early 1970s, southern cities were well on their way to imitating them. The question was less one of avoidance than of minimizing the damage. Third, even if local officials were to follow the northern policy course, the results would be different because of demographic, economic, geographic, and cultural distinctions in the urban South.

FRINGE BENEFITS AND CENTRAL COSTS

Southern cities discovered in the 1970s that the Sun Belt contained numerous shadows. The same national trends that had worked against northern cities began to appear in the South. A historical combination of cheap and available land on the urban periphery, a broad middle-class affluence, and the cultural preference for single-family homes had made suburban residence attractive to families since the nineteenth century. Pent-up demand from more than a decade of depression and war, as well as federal subsidies in the form of tax breaks and mortgage guarantees, fueled a major exodus from cities in the decades after World War II. The 1970 census confirmed what most observers had already surmised: we were a suburban nation. Southern cities, growing more slowly than their northern counterparts, did not experience a significant land rush until the late 1950s. Even then, liberal annexation policies masked the decline of central cities. Atlanta, for example, declined in population at a faster rate than both Newark and Detroit between 1970 and 1975. New Orleans and Norfolk lost population faster than New York and Detroit. The growth of the Sun Belt was primarily a growth of the urban periphery, of the metropolitan area as a whole, but not of the central city. During the 1960s, Atlanta's population increased by 1.9 percent, whereas its metropolitan area grew at a rate of 36.7 percent. More ominous, 80 percent of new jobs in metropolitan Atlanta between 1975 and 1984 were located in the suburbs.[45]

45. Goldfield, *Cotton Fields and Skyscrapers,* 193.

A walk through some of the major southern urban downtowns in the 1970s confirmed the statistics. A Memphis resident described his downtown perspective in 1978: "You can stand on Main Street now and see to where the city limits were fifty years ago and it's all vacant land." Retail establishments were closing and moving to the suburban shopping malls. Downtown Memphis accounted for only 5 percent of the metropolitan area's retail sales.[46]

Some cities saw the trend early and began to plan for it, assisted by federal urban renewal policies that encouraged the destruction of dilapidated residential properties and the construction of tax-rich office highrises, expensive condominiums, and hotel and entertainment complexes. As a result of the promotional guile of architect-developer John Portman, Atlanta became a national leader in downtown revitalization. Rocket-style elevators, spinning rooftop restaurants, atrium lobbies, and cocktail lounges in lagoons returned some excitement to central Atlanta, but it was an environment more for conventioneers and tourists than for residents. In the evenings, downtown turned into a ghost town, with dark and looming office towers and an ominous sea of empty parking lots. While the downtown glittered, elsewhere in the city the public school system deteriorated and neighborhoods choked on traffic congestion and neglect.[47]

URBAN REVIVAL: BACK TO THE FUTURE

By the mid-1970s, new and more effective urban revival strategies emerged. Pressures from minority groups recently energized by the 1965 Voting Rights Act, and from neighborhood organizations angered that downtown development projects and service commitments in annexed areas meant neglect and decline for their areas, transformed the priorities and the personnel in local government. Changes from at-large to district representation enhanced the possibilities for black candidates who, once in office, let more city contracts to minority firms and hired blacks for administrative positions. Atlanta was a prototype of the new emphasis in local government as a coalition of blacks and neighborhood groups elected Maynard Jackson as the city's first black mayor in 1973.

One strategy adopted by the new governments was to lessen the focus on downtown and concentrate on what southerners are best at—remem-

46. Roger Biles, "Epitaph for Downtown: The Failure of City Planning in Post–World War II Memphis," *Tennessee Historical Quarterly,* XLIV (Fall, 1985), 267–84.

47. For a discussion of Portman's work and its consequences, see Goldfield, *Cotton Fields and Skyscrapers,* 156–57.

bering. Charleston made a career of it, and New Orleans, Savannah, and Richmond soon followed. These were cities that had either no taste for Yankee-style boosterism or had the ill fortune to be on the backwater of American economic development in the century after Appomattox. One circumstance may have generated the other. In any case, after the orgy of obliteration, history emerged by the 1970s as a major tool to revitalize southern cities. Aside from the growth of neighborhood coalitions and black voters, the approaching bicentennial and the churning up of the southern past by the civil rights movement also contributed to a renewed sense of the past. The sense manifested itself in preserving inner-city neighborhoods, such as Ansley Park and Inman Park in Atlanta, and Dilworth and Myers Park in Charlotte. Civic leaders also sought to preserve or even re-create traditional city centers, such as Beale Street in Memphis and Pack Square in Asheville, whose destruction Thomas Wolfe chronicled in the 1920s.

And just as the Civil War produced an outpouring of shrines and holy places in southern cities, so the civil rights movement began to penetrate the historic sense of civic leaders. Tours of historic Selma proceed along the route of the famous voting rights march of 1965, terminating at the newly restored Edmund Pettus Bridge. Birmingham is restoring the jail cell in which Martin Luther King, Jr., wrote his famous letter in April, 1963. A metal street marker stands down the block from where the first sit-ins occurred in Greensboro, North Carolina, in February, 1960. Museums such as the Valentine in Richmond and the state museum in Jackson, Mississippi, devote generous space to the story of the black struggle for freedom. And reenactments abound. The sit-ins, the Selma-Montgomery march, and the Birmingham demonstrations have been the Confederate veterans' parades of the late twentieth century. Although these commemorations and restorations undoubtedly make white people feel good about themselves, symbols and shrines are important in the South, a region that for decades had only symbols and shrines to which to cling.[48]

It was natural that southern cities should become the region's memory. Smaller places, especially in rural areas, were losing the strength to carry on, and the new fringe communities had few traditions on which to draw other than wanderlust. But the central cities continue to play an important role in the multicentered metropolis because the banking, insurance, and government apparatuses that have grown with the metropolitan South have a strong stake in maintaining the vitality of the center. A young girl from

48. On neighborhood revitalization and the urban uses of history, see Goldfield, *Promised Land,* 208–11.

Greenwood, Mississippi, no longer dreams of her before-school shopping trip to Memphis, but there is still an excitement about downtowns in the South—the grand old hotels, such as the Peabody in Memphis and the new-old Tutwiler in Birmingham, the museums, the symphonies—and, yes, even the retail shopping. Taking a page from the suburban shopping mall, cities such as Norfolk, Savannah, and New Orleans have returned to their watery heritage and developed specialty shops and restaurants along neglected waterfronts. Although some of the history is ersatz, it at least reminds visitors and residents alike that this is a place, a place with its own roots, its own story, and its own connection to the South. It is a way to pass on traditions to the children.

While southern urban policymakers have been bringing the past to present tense, they have maintained a steady pace of megaprojects—coliseums, hotel-entertainment complexes, and convention centers. The difference from earlier iterations is that these projects are part of a broader and more balanced strategy. Economic development remains a major priority at city hall. And in southern city halls, governing without the support of downtown banking and commercial interests is difficult. Andrew Young, who succeeded Maynard Jackson in Atlanta, was especially adept at courting the traditional economic elite in that city and in traveling far and wide to deliver the message of what one journalist called "Andynomics." Business leaders discovered the considerable goodwill that a black mayor can generate on the investment front.[49]

The role of a southern urban political leader is considerably more complex than when he (and it was always *he*) could call up the chairman of Coca-Cola or meet the bank directors for lunch at the City Club. In some respects, his role is more similar to that of urban leaders in other parts of the country in that he must practice consensus and coalition politics. For one thing, southern cities are more diverse than at any time since the antebellum era. In addition to assorted Yankees, the urban South is hosting considerable numbers of immigrants. The Hispanic presence and influence in Texas and southern Florida cities is well known, but there are, for example, fifty thousand Hispanics in the Atlanta metropolitan area. There is also a like number of Koreans, Chinese, Indians, Laotians, and Vietnamese. Every major southern city now includes these groups—just look at the supermarket shelves and the restaurants for confirmation.[50]

49. On the effective use of "Andynomics" in Atlanta, see Art Harris, "Atlanta, Georgia: Too Busy to Hate," *Esquire* (June, 1985), 129–33.

50. Historians have only recently begun to analyze and describe the increasingly plu-

Southern urban leaders also face different national and economic realities from their predecessors. Economic competition is global. Very few mayors of major southern cities have not been abroad touting the attributes of their city to foreign investors. In addition, it is no longer morning in the so-called Sun Belt. The reported demise of northeastern and midwestern cities was premature. Cities in New York and Ohio in particular have revived to offer stiff competition to southern upstarts. Cheap land and cheap labor are no longer the main and only attractions. In the postindustrial economy and with the late-twentieth-century American lifestyle, an educated work force, a high-quality school system, and cultural and recreational amenities have become important considerations for firms seeking to move to or establish branches in new areas. Education and service amenities have traditionally not been the strong suits of southern urban governments. Local officials have had to build new coalitions of consensus, including business, universities, and citizens' groups to both upgrade the business climate and devise new development strategies.[51]

Urban Regions

Urban leaders have also had to take their coalition-building expertise beyond the city line. Although southern cities have managed to reverse or at least halt the erosion of their influence within the metropolitan area, the periphery continues to outpace the central city across the South, and they are facing some problems that require regional cooperation. In particular, the migration of northerners fueled the outward drive. It was more a suburb-to-suburb migration than a city-to-city movement. It stood to reason that newcomers would want to reconstruct the positive aspects of their old environment as much as possible—single-family homes, easy access to multipurpose shopping malls, and good school systems. These and other services drove up the tax rates and drastically changed the landscape of rural

ralistic populations of the urban South; see Raymond A. Mohl, "Miami: New Immigrant City," Ronald H. Bayor, "Race, Ethnicity, and Intergroup Relations in the Sunbelt South: Patterns of Change," and Elliott Barkan, "New Origins, New Homelands: Immigration into Selected Sunbelt Cities Since 1965," in *Searching for the Sunbelt,* ed. Mohl; and Randall M. Miller and George E. Pozzetta, eds., *Shades of the Sunbelt* (Westport, Conn., 1988).

51. For a discussion of this competition and its relation to questions of equity and quality of life, see David R. Goldfield, "Economic Development in the South: Education, Equity, and the Quality of Life," in *Education, Environment and Culture: The Quality of Life in the South,* ed. Commission on the Future of the South (Research Triangle Park, N.C., 1986), 13–17.

areas and small towns in the path of metropolitan development. Because southern cities had grown up in the age of the automobile, suburban development went wherever the automobile could go, and that meant hither and yon in areas that had not seen so many people since General Sherman's tour more than a century ago. And some viewed the newcomers as little better than the earlier northern visitors, with the added disadvantage that the twentieth-century invaders were staying.

Gwinnett County, Georgia, was a quiet, sparsely settled farming area in the 1960s. Lawrenceville, the county seat, is thirty-two miles northeast of Atlanta. By 1985, Gwinnett held the distinction of being the fastest-growing county in the country. The county's population grew 38 percent between 1980 and 1984, to a total of 230,000 residents. In another decade, the county should approach the half-million mark. In the meantime, county officials must build new sewage treatment facilities, as the old one is beyond capacity. Traffic is a nightmare in the southern part of the county, and as yet, Gwinnett does not have a land-use plan.[52]

Rural areas all over the South are being thrust into the suburban age with little preparation. The results can be especially jarring to long-time residents, now challenged for political office, burdened with higher taxes, and confronted by a declining quality of life. Counties in the middle of transition offer an interesting juxtaposition of separate lifestyles. Journalist Mary Hood recounted a 1987 visit to her home in Cherokee County, Georgia. Although it is even further away from Atlanta than Gwinnett, the metropolitan area has spread into Cherokee. Hood relates that the county has become three places, each defined by a Wal-Mart discount store. In the traditional portion of the county, where residents still drink well water and pay cash, the Wal-Mart has clerks named Delma, Edna, or Bud, Jr., and the shoppers are mostly from nuclear families. The radio is tuned to the local country station, and the booths at the snack bar are the major media centers. Nine miles to the southeast, there is a four-lane highway, shopping plazas, and water towers. The ball fields, speedway, and churches of the old community persist, but the Wal-Mart in this part of the county does not contain a snack bar, and few people loiter. As Hood notes, "These are busy people, involved in PTA and soccer and tennis camp. They shop in their crisp Realtor's blazer, nurse's or policeman's uniform; everyone has somewhere

52. William E. Schmidt, "Georgia County Knows Beauties, Burdens of Fast Growth," New York *Times,* June 4, 1985.

else to be, and soon." The radio is tuned to 96-ROCK, and the customers' names are Brandon, Angie, Kim, Scott, and Dawn.[53]

Driving (always driving) toward the interstate, apartments and homes have replaced the horse barns and oak trees. "The road names and mall stores," Hood writes, "make no claim on native loyalties and sympathy." At this Wal-Mart, "We are all newcomers, all strangers, and I shop in the same anxiety and alienation as everyone else. . . . I shop here in that anonymity attained more often in large cities." The clerks "are chic, worldly." Yet despite the very real physical and lifestyle changes she witnessed in traveling across her county, Hood concludes that the important things have not been lost: "The purest things, and the everlasting springs, run deep."[54]

Living in three different time zones—past, present, and future—is nothing special for southerners. They have been doing it for a long time, even if a good deal of it is unconscious. As with the gentleman I met in Richmond, there is nothing incongruous about referring to long-dead people, long-past eras, and long-gone places in the present tense. Southerners, as the most mobile Americans, have learned that there is no country but the heart, and they have often worn that heart on their sleeve, carrying it through major upheavals. And the beat goes on. Even in the established cities, and even apart from the conscious efforts to compress time zones, it is still not difficult to find the easy mingling of past and place. Jim Cobb has found "cracklin's and caviar" within two blocks in Atlanta.[55] And even above the hum of the air conditioner, which, not so incidentally, has made much of the urban South possible, conversation for conversation's sake and the courtesies of casual social intercourse in shops, restaurants, and other public places persist.

But the terms on which southern culture persists clearly depend on the metropolitan frame of mind, as more of the countryside becomes part of the southern urban daily orbit. For urban leaders, it is not simply reaching out to suburbs within an easy commute of downtown, it is reaching farther and farther out to what are becoming new cities in new regions. The major urban development of the 1980s was the growth of urban regions. The metropolis has advanced far enough for its outgoing areas to grow together. Interstate highways have been major facilitators for regional urban growth.

53. Mary Hood, "Of Water and Wal-Mart: The Demographics of Progress in a Georgia Community," *Southern Magazine,* II (January, 1987), 22.

54. *Ibid.,* 23.

55. James C. Cobb, "Cracklin's and Caviar: The Enigma of Sunbelt Georgia," *Georgia Historical Quarterly* (Spring, 1984), 19.

The I-85 corridor from Raleigh to Atlanta is host to a growing diversity of manufacturing and retail enterprises. Excellent trucking and air access, the participation of high-quality higher education institutions, and active promotional activities undertaken on behalf of urban regions, rather than merely towns and cities, have enabled the Textile Belt to more than recover lost employment. Winston-Salem, for example, has gained three times more jobs than it lost since 1983. These positions came from small businesses, service industries, health care, and higher education. Spartanburg caught the drift of a declining textile industry a decade ago and went after foreign investment—a relatively new feature in the southern metropolitan economy. Today, Spartanburg has more investment from abroad—$1 billion—than any other American city of its size. The stretch of I-85 that runs past the city is called "the Autobahn," in recognition of the number of German and Swiss firms in the area.[56]

There is a growing concentration within these urban regions, especially on their peripheries, that reflects a new urban form emerging nationwide. These are the "out-towns," the new concentrations of high-rise office buildings, shopping malls, hotels, and residential neighborhoods that are quite different from the traditional suburban bedroom communities of the post-World War II era. Developers promote them more as villages than as suburbs. Las Colinas, west of Dallas, is a model of the out-town. Corporate giants, including Xerox, DuPont, and AT&T, have offices there; there are strict architectural controls, generous park space, canals, a 125-acre lake, a shopping mall, and residences. Its daytime population is roughly forty thousand, and its attractions rival downtown Dallas. Few of the out-towns are as structured as Las Colinas. Most evolved out of a major regional shopping mall, such as River Chase outside of Birmingham, the Cumberland-Galleria complex on the outer edge of the Atlanta metropolitan area, and a massive Edward De Bartolo project outside of Miami. What they offer, according to urban consultant Christopher Leinberger, are places where "people can work, live, shop and play in close proximity, thereby enjoying many advantages of urban density but avoiding its high costs and problems."[57] These communities are the urban South of the twenty-first century. They are the

56. "Winston-Salem Moves to Temper A.T.&T.'s Blow," Charlotte *Observer,* January 24, 1988; David Treadwell, "Gloom to Boom: Spartanburg Saw Textiles' Future Early," Los Angeles *Times,* November 10, 1985.

57. Quoted in Neal Peirce, "Can Urban Villages Become Real People Places?" Washington *Post,* August 17, 1985. See also Peter O. Muller, "The Suburbanization of the Sunbelt City: Metropolitan Restructuring in the South and West" (paper presented at Conference on the Sunbelt, Miami, November, 1985).

new downtowns, and they conform to the relatively low-density residential traditions of southern urban history.

Both the leaders of these new towns and the central cities are seeing themselves less as rivals than as partners in service provision and economic development. Regional airports, waste treatment facilities, and technical training programs are some of the cooperative efforts underway. Regional coalitions have been successful in putting together economic development programs, recognizing that increasing competition from other parts of the country requires the pooling of resources and expertise. Intraregional competition was fierce and nasty in the Atlanta metropolitan area until the formation of the Metropolitan Atlanta Council for Economic Development (MACFED). The council is a cooperative effort of the chambers of commerce in Atlanta and the surrounding suburban and semisuburban counties of Clayton, Cobb, DeKalb, Douglas, and Gwinnett.[58]

There is a danger, of course, in the constant contemplation of growth—how to get it, how to manage it, and how to profit from it. Although southern urban governments are more inclusive and have greater social and historical awareness than they have ever had, economic development has the greatest political rewards. It is the most easily visible success of an urban administration and business community. Less visible, both in terms of urban policy and media attention, are the imbalances in the metropolitan economy and areas beyond. Although they are easy to ignore, these imbalances are difficult to address. But they are as much a part of the urban present and future as the regional shopping malls and the downtown office towers. More seriously, these imbalances can threaten the economic and social vitality of the South's metropolitan regions.

THE LAST PICTURE SHOW

As southern metropolitan areas sprawled outward and as central cities began to recover from the problems of withdrawal, the towns and small cities of the South, especially those away from growth areas, were also undergoing changes. The 1970s and early 1980s were difficult years for the Piedmont textile region. Foreign competition and mechanization struck hard. Because most textile communities were one-industry towns, the closing of the mill meant the closing of the town. The Riegel Textile Corporation created

---

58. Bradley R. Rice, "Searching for the Sunbelt: An Update," in *Searching for the Sunbelt,* ed. Mohl. Although MACFED dissolved, cooperation on economic development persists in the Atlanta region.

Ware Shoals, South Carolina, on the banks of the Saluda River in 1906. The company shut down its plant at the end of 1984, throwing nine hundred people out of work. Young people have moved to find work elsewhere, and 60 percent of the population is retired. Riegel provided 60 percent of the tax base and 20 percent of the school budget. Mayor Hugh Frederick tried to put a brave face on the situation: "Riegel built the town. They built all the homes around the mill. They provided the water, electricity and the company store. It looks bad, but we've got a lot of assets. . . . We're pretty gritty people." [59]

In other Piedmont communities, death did not come so suddenly, but a long decline has set in. Vacant storefronts dot downtown Chester, South Carolina. In Whitmire, South Carolina, as the textile giant J. P. Stevens cut its work force, a department store, a drugstore, and a clothing store have left the downtown. Beauty shops and churches remain, and young people leave. For some of these towns, their new centers have become the highways or the interstate, where shopping malls have sprouted like chickweed. It is here that the K-Marts and Wal-Marts flourish. [60]

The small towns face a difficult prospect. Many, like Woodville, Mississippi, list welfare as their major industry. Their populations are dependent, highly skewed toward the elderly, and offer little attraction for outside investment and little inspiration for indigenous entrepreneurship. They once may have hosted prosperous industries, but they now are competing against Third World nations, a competition they will obviously lose despite a long history of mortgaging their people and their land for dubious short-term gains. These are the towns that would love the problem of a traffic jam and overtaxed infrastructure, but all they are likely to see are roads leading in one direction and structures rotting from disuse. These are the places of high dropout rates, high infant mortality, and high unemployment—37 percent higher than in larger cities. The development coalitions of government, business, and education are considerably beyond the resources and capabilities of these communities. Historically, the fate of the countryside has been inextricably linked to the fate of the city in the South. The depopulation of the rural and small-town South will create burdens on metropolitan areas—the likely destination of rural migrants.

59. "Mill's Closing Cuts to the Heart, Soul of a SC Town," Charlotte *Observer,* November 4, 1984.

60. "Shopping 'Bah, Humbug!' in Small Towns," Charlotte *Observer,* December 20, 1987.

METROPOLITAN IMBALANCES

Although urban-rural distinctions are relatively obvious, there are considerable imbalances both within cities and within metropolitan regions. The service and high-tech economy has created a two-tiered work force of high-skilled, well-educated, white-collar personnel and poorly educated, low-skilled workers who have little hope of upward mobility in salary and responsibility. In addition, the majority of low-skill-level jobs are opening on the metropolitan periphery, where few of the lower-income people live. The inadequacy of public transit in the metropolitan South exacerbates disjunction between work and residence for the poor.

The two-tiered metropolitan economy also raises issues of equity. Given the traditions of southern local government and the expectations of many of its constituents, there is little likelihood that higher taxes and increased social services will emerge as urban policies. Black political leaders, such as Atlanta's Andrew Young and Birmingham's Richard Arrington, shuttled some city contracts to minority firms, but on the whole they adopted the entrepreneurial priorities of their white predecessors. An added difficulty is that environmental concerns have emerged as powerful issues in urban politics. As metropolitan areas spread across the southern landscape, they bring air and water pollution, the destruction of farmland, and the obliteration of historic structures. Growth management has replaced economic development as the key policy phrase in many southern cities, and states such as Florida and North Carolina are supporting such efforts with statewide growth controls. But will it be more difficult to address equity issues in an economy held in check?

There are also persisting imbalances between central city and out-towns. Suburban and out-town communities are overwhelmingly white, as are their school districts and their occupational networks. There is little sentiment to change this situation, and the unwillingness of Atlanta's suburbs to participate in the extension of the city's subway system suggests that race is still an important factor dividing the metropolitan South. The division is especially evident in the separate city and county school systems in most metropolitan areas. City systems are becoming overwhelmingly black, whereas suburban districts are predominantly white. The deliberate resegregation of some public schools in Norfolk and Little Rock is designed to curb white flight. Although metropolitan cooperation has become part of a regional strategy in recent years, such efforts are typically confined to economic development and services. Housing and schools remain off the agenda.

THE PROMISE OF THE URBAN SOUTH

As urban southerners attempt to deal with these imbalances, they have several strengths upon which to draw. First, they have the benefit of scale. Although the South contains roughly the same number of metropolitan areas as other regions, there are very few large ones. The largest southern metropolitan area is Dallas, but it ranks ninth nationally, with Houston, Miami, and Atlanta the only other southern metropolitan areas in the nation's top twenty-five. Smaller scale should mean easier management. It also means that the historical connection with the land is never very far from the doorstep of the metropolitan southerner. In fact, the Southeast interior region (bounded by Nashville in the west and Birmingham and Atlanta in the south, and extending up the Piedmont to the Virginia border), one of the nation's six urban regions designated by the Urban Land Institute, is the least city-dominated, with only 29 percent of its population in central cities. Of the six regions, it has the lowest number of people per square mile—about two hundred. Although growth has overwhelmed some of the smaller places within this region, others have been able to maintain their semirural character. These are, as termed by demographer J. C. Doherty, "countrified cities"—spread-out, low-density communities.[61]

Another positive feature of southern urbanization is the tradition of volunteerism. Private agencies, especially churches, have taken up many activities ordinarily associated with government. Reform movements in the South, from the antebellum era through the civil rights movement, have typically originated in churches, black and white. New organizations are emerging from the churches across the urban South to address housing, job training, and counseling needs. In 1980, for example, a church-based organization, Strategies to Elevate People (STEP) formed in Dallas. STEP mobilized five hundred volunteers from its member churches which, by the rules of the organization, included both black and white congregations, and renovated a black housing project in Dallas. In addition, STEP established a college assistance fund for children from low-income families. By 1987, STEP ministries had appeared in Fort Worth, Richmond, Norfolk, Nashville, and Charlotte. Other STEP services have included pairing adults with

61. On the low-density character of southern metropolitan development and its costs and benefits, see "Development Threatens Farmers," Charlotte *Observer,* May 31, 1987. See also Robert G. Healy, *Competition for Land in the American South: Agriculture, Human Settlement, and the Environment* (Washington, D.C., 1985), Chap. 5. On "countrified cities," see "Census Statistics Don't Reflect Rural Growth," Charlotte *Observer,* May 31, 1987.

low-income elementary school children and operating joint programs with local community colleges to provide adult education. STEP churches have succeeded in leveraging business assistance in the form of supplies, funds, and additional voluntary help. The religious institutions of the urban South represent a moral reservoir that can serve both the region's traditions and its future.[62]

Perhaps the strongest tradition the urban South has in its favor is southern history. Unlike the rest of the country, history in the South has not been a straight-line progression upward. There have been major detours. Only recently, and thanks primarily to southern blacks, has the South shown a willingness to accept its past—not just the good parts, or the parts enshrouded in myth—but all of it. The willingness is especially noticeable in the urban South, among the black middle class, at city hall, and especially in the new shrines and symbols that have become part of the urban iconography as much as the glass skyscrapers and the salad bars. Americans have generally been uncomfortable with the past. Memories are excruciatingly short. Perhaps metropolitan southerners, whom sociologist John Shelton Reed identifies as the new gatekeepers for southern culture, can teach a lesson or two in this regard—that the past, present, and future are all part of the same seamless fabric, and that time zones are not only irrelevant, but they are also barriers to a better understanding of self, of others, and of the environment.[63]

The Madison County, Alabama, tourism board sends out a promotional package entitled "Instant Huntsville." The package contains five plastic capsules. Drop the capsules in a bowl of warm water and suddenly bobbing to the surface are an astronaut, an antebellum mansion, a space shuttle, a southern belle, and the state of Alabama. The promotion covers all time zones and appeals to a wide variety of tastes. It also underscores how much the urban South has become, simply, the South. This does not necessarily mean that we are apt to see gun racks in the backs of BMWs or frog-leg nuggets, but we may. These are no less ironic than the fact that the police chief of Charleston, South Carolina, is black and Jewish or that a black woman is mayor of Little Rock. This is the South of the 1990s, and this is the urban South.[64]

62. "A Giant STEP," Charlotte *Observer,* May 10, 1987.

63. John Shelton Reed, *Southerners: the Social Psychology of Sectionalism* (Chapel Hill, 1983).

64. Journalist Linton Weeks discusses these "ironies" in "The Real South," *Southern Magazine* (May, 1987), 8.

The identity between city and region is not surprising given a historical perspective. Although a minor element in the Old South civilization in terms of population and culture, the antebellum southern city was the focal point for a region's dreams of economic parity. The city's failure was the South's failure. After the Civil War, urbanization required a reorientation of race relations. If "segregation" and "South" became synonymous, then the southern city made it so. It was here also, in diverse ways, that the New South creed battled with scarred traditions, resulting in few victors and many losers. No longer merely an adjunct to the countryside, the urban South was now a partner, sometimes a dominant one. That Scarlett O'Hara moved to Atlanta after the war and established a business was of more than symbolic import.

In depression and world war, the urban South became the repository of regional hope again. People left the countryside, and money flowed from Washington. And the city became a battleground again, for the bodies of blacks and the souls of whites. This time, the winners outnumbered the also-rans. Finally, the urban South, for all its remaining difficulties, is now not only poised to lead the region but also has the opportunity to set an example for the rest of the nation in race relations, in economic development, in the value of traditions, and maybe even in equity. It is a heady role. But the strengths of the city today are the strengths of the region, and both city and South are connected more intimately than ever before. As Judge Reuben Anderson noted in a 1980 Southern Growth Policies Board report, "The future of the South cannot be separated from the future of Southern cities." [65]

65. Commission on the Future of the South, ed., *The Future of the South* (Research Triangle Park, N.C., 1981), 22.

Index